Rethinking American Literature

Rethinking American Literature

Edited by

Lil Brannon
University at Albany, SUNY

Brenda M. Greene
Medgar Evers College, CUNY

National Council of Teachers of English
1111 W. Kenyon Road, Urbana, Illinois 61801-1096

Grateful acknowledgment is made for permission to reprint the following material: "Not Born on the Fourth of July: Cultural Differences and American Studies," by Gregory S. Jay, originally published in *After Political Correctness: The Humanities and Society in the 1990s,* edited by Christopher Newfield and Ronald Strickland. Copyright © 1995 by Westview Press. Reprinted by permission of Westview Press. The excerpt on 57 from "*Cihuatlyotl,* Woman Alone," originally published in *Borderlands/La Frontera: The New Mestiza.* San Francisco: Spinsters/Aunt Lute. Copyright © 1987 by Gloria Anzaldúa; reprinted by permission of the author. The excerpt on 59 from "La Prieta," originally published in *This Bridge Called My Back: Writings by Radical Women of Color.* Eds. Cherrie Moraga and Gloria Anzaldúa. New York: Kitchen Table: Women of Color Press. Copyright © 1983 by Gloria Anzaldúa; reprinted by permission of the author. "'Not in the Least American': Nineteenth-Century Literary Regionalism as unAmerican Literature" by Judith Fetterley appeared in a slightly different version in *College English* 56 (1994): 877–95.

Manuscript Editor: Jamie Hutchinson

Production Editors: Jamie Hutchinson, Kurt Austin

Interior Design: Tom Kovacs for TGK Design

Cover Photographs and Design: Evelyn C. Shapiro

NCTE Stock Number: 41196-3050

It is the policy of NCTE in its journals and other publications to provide a forum for the open discussion of ideas concerning the content and the teaching of English and the language arts. Publicity accorded to any particular point of view does not imply endorsement by the Executive Committee, the Board of Directors, or the membership at large, except in announcements of policy, where such endorsement is clearly specified.

Library of Congress Cataloging-in-Publication Data
Rethinking American literature / edited by Lil Brannon, Brenda M. Greene.
      p.   cm.
    Includes bibliographical references and index.
    ISBN 0-8141-4119-6 (pbk.)
    1. American literature—Study and teaching (Higher) 2. American literature—History and criticism—Theory, etc. 3. American literature—Minority authors—Study and teaching (Higher) 4. Cultural conflict—United States. 5. Canon (Literature) I. Brannon, Lil. II. Greene, Brenda M., 1950– . III. National Council of Teachers of English.
PS42.R47 1997
810'.9—dc21   97-15044
                                                       CIP

Contents

Introduction

Lil Brannon
University at Albany, SUNY

Brenda M. Greene
Medgar Evers College, CUNY

This volume, the fourth in a series, brings together the conversations of the profession that were explored during the 1993 and 1994 Summer Institutes for Teachers of Literature, sponsored by the College Section Steering Committee of the National Council of Teachers of English. The voices represented here come from not only those who participated during the Institutes but extend to the larger conversation that has erupted over the ways American literature has been traditionally practiced. The volume reflects the debate: the theoretical reorientations that cause teachers of literature to question their ideas of "American," of "literature," and of who they are as teachers and what they do in the classroom. Also explored here are the questions of organizing the "American literature" curriculum, of deciding what to teach, and of finding one's way through the political, theoretical, and practical implications of efforts to rethink what one does. This volume continues the tradition of the Summer Institutes of bringing theory and practice together, of presenting not a unified argument but the flavor of the interestingly complicated debate that is sure to have profound impact on the future of the profession. Often the professional debate is highly theoretical and difficult to enter into; at other times, the debate is taken up in heated faculty meetings or in the quiet of faculty offices where one might be struggling alone to make sense of why a student responded to a story in the way that she did. We have tried to capture the richness of all of this theorizing, of this making sense, so that no matter what one's site of teaching is—the community college classroom or the research university—one can find a way into the conversation and determine what texts and issues are important to bring into the classrooms.

The larger aim of this volume is to question to what end teachers of literature seek to establish an American literary canon and to question the processes of the past whereby the knowledge of what constitutes American literature has been produced. The essays explore the historical, sociological, political, and practical implications of questioning our understanding of "American" by exploring the potentialities or the actual consequences of bringing to the classroom literatures that cross cultural boundaries within and outside of the United States. By examining this "new" American literature both from a global and critical perspective and from a local, shifting, and more tentative critical space, this volume offers alternative, and at times competing, strategies for re-seeing, discussing, and teaching traditional and emerging texts in the literature of the Americas.

We have organized the collection so that one might enter the conversation and begin the questioning from different sites. The first section, "Reshaping American Literature," offers theoretical arguments for recovering and examining writers, texts, and traditions not previously included in the field (for example, the slave narrative, nineteenth-century women regionalists, the oral and written literatures of Native Americans, and contemporary women of color). Jay, Fetterley, and Keating assume readers who are thoroughly immersed in current theoretical arguments as they work to complicate traditional understandings of history that have led to their rethinking of the relationship among the literary, the political, and the economic. These essays offer an important framing for the entire volume, but they do not have to be tackled first. What they offer are ways of rethinking American literature—of thinking about how "identity" is part of "ideology."

Gregory Jay's and Judith Fetterley's keynote addresses, as well as an essay by AnaLouise Keating, address the question, "What constitutes American literature and on what basis do we decide?" Gregory Jay opens the volume with an exploration of the United States' multicultural history and the struggle over representation. Within the tradition of radical reform in American literary and cultural studies that Jay sets forth, he argues that the teaching of literature must be to educate a democratic citizenry which "obligates us to engage in complex and difficult acts of identification and imagination . . . [and to] affirm that which we have not experienced." Judith Fetterley examines how "American" in the context of American literature has always been a political category which has excluded particular writers whose stories lie outside the dominant tradition and whose stories challenge the values within canonical works. She argues for these "unAmerican" texts by offering a counterpoint to American realism, literary regionalism, and by exploring the contributions of writers who work within this frame. AnaLouise Keating concludes this section by challenging the dominant view of multiculturalism, the coexistence of a variety of distinct literary and cultural traditions, which she argues is based on a politics of location which "essentializes textuality by equating it with biological 'roots'." Her essay explores the implications of establishing a transcultural dialogue which neither erases nor reifies the many differences among the various texts that we read.

Such rethinking, of course, takes on particular significance in a context of changing student, faculty, and national demographics, for whom we imagine as "American" and what we understand as "literature" will have major implications for how we conceptualize the connection between teaching American literature and preparing a citizenry for the twenty-first century. Section II, "Crossing Cultural Boundaries," gives practitioners a way into the debates by offering firsthand struggles in understanding American writers in a global sense—Caribbean, Asian American, Latino, African American, South American, Central American, Canadian—those writers who participate both inside and outside of the dominant "American" culture and thereby bring different lenses through which they write. The challenge to teachers of literature is exemplified in this section. Here, the reader witnesses the struggle to "make sense" of these new literatures and to make the literature speak to students. Whether or not one agrees with the paradigms that are articulated here, the debate over whether one needs to develop new frameworks for understanding this literature or to build on existing, traditional ones must be engaged so that differences can be acknowledged and negotiated. This section, we hope, is a contribution to this critical dialogue that attempts to address the complexities of identity politics and its implications for teaching.

Elizabeth Nunez begins the section with the keynote address she gave to the Summer Institute, "A Fusion of Cultures: The Complexities of the Caribbean Character in Literature." In this essay she offers a theory for understanding the "paradoxical" character of Caribbean literature and offers a close reading of several Caribbean novels, including *Crick Crack Monkey,* to make her point. Brenda Greene continues this reading of new literatures by theorizing the position of female writers of color as dually constructed both within and outside our understandings of America. She argues, with reference to several novels by women of color, that these writers have developed characters who can cross cultural boundaries and make visible "sites of resistance," those places where reflective activity can bring about transformative action. Joyce Harte follows with an exploration of how a teacher, herself educated within a British colonialist tradition, can rethink the teaching of literature for students in an urban community college by drawing on the theoretical and pedagogical frameworks of reader-response theory, cultural criticism, and feminist theory so that students can enter into conversation with texts written by women and writers of color. She is followed by Robert O'Brien Hokanson, who offers a careful reading of Silko's *Ceremony,* in which he demonstrates how students can understand through their encounter with this novel the dynamism of "multiculturalism." Mary Louise Buley-Meissner demonstrates how her students in both China and America have come to value Asian American literature through an exploration of its artistry, rhetoricity, and history. We end the section with Judith Beth Cohen's delicate exploration of coming to know Willa Cather's *Death Comes for the*

Archbishop—its surface beauty and its problematic political rendering of the
"real." She speaks of her own learning and its relation to her students' learning—an enactment of teaching that is willing to explore its very assumptions
and blind spots.

The final section, "Negotiating Differences," offers ways of developing the
curriculum for this new study of American literature and of thinking through
the problems that arise in teaching. This section offers practitioner/theorists a
way into the volume by exploring the issues of pedagogy: determining what to
teach, organizing the material, developing new ways of reading, and making
the debates in the field visible and productive.

We begin the section with Pat Bizzell's keynote address at the 1994 Institute, "Negotiating Difference: Teaching Multicultural Literature." Basing her
argument on Mary Louise Pratt's "Contact Zone," Bizzell offers a way of selecting and grouping multicultural readings and of integrating literary and rhetorical approaches in the teaching of multicultural literature. Marjorie Pryse
follows with an essay, the material of which was covered during the workshop
she gave at the 1993 Institute. She offers various models for organizing introductory courses in American literature. Frances Foster offers her keynote address next, an exploration of ways of reading African American literature that
demonstrates its complexity and its importance in the teaching of American
literature. John Alberti, then, explores the issues of race and ethnicity as rhetorical rather than "absolute" constructs, "as context-specific discursive practices." He addresses the issue of whether or not white teachers can and should
teach "other" people's literatures by problematizing the category of race in the
act of teaching Frederick Douglass. Louise Z. Smith draws on reception theory
to give us a way into texts which may seem remote or distant to our students. In
so doing, she also gives us a way, as teachers, to examine texts unfamiliar to us.
Using Joan Didion as a focus, Smith creates the exciting possibilities that reception theory offers teachers. We end the volume with essays by Jim Laughlin
and Joseph Trimmer. Laughlin discusses how he engaged students in "teaching
the conflicts" to and for themselves by having them engage in an exploration of
popular culture that had parallels to disputes in the academic work they would
be taking up later in the semester. Trimmer offers a narrative reflection on the
complexities of teaching multicultural literature. He ends by understanding that
teaching and learning about multicultural literature is in large part a process, "a
new method of inquiry that encouraged students to mount their own expeditions through the history and literature of other cultures."

This volume would not have been possible without the support of NCTE's
College Section Steering Committee and the membership of the College Section who made the Summer Institute possible. We also are indebted to Kimberly
Dunn and Tami Britton of the Center for Excellence in Teaching and Learning
at the University at Albany, SUNY, who helped prepare this manuscript. We

thank Leon and Cy, who gave us intellectual and personal support and endured the long telephone conversations as we put this volume together. Our collaboration has been an exciting one. Though we have worked together in many capacities over the last ten years, the product of this collaboration, we hope, will intellectually stimulate and sustain others as our work together has certainly sustained and challenged us.

I Reshaping American Literature

1 Not Born on the Fourth of July: Cultural Differences and American Studies

Gregory S. Jay
University of Wisconsin–Milwaukee

The PC World

The scenario has become familiar. After a long history of apparent uniformity and consensus, a nation suddenly collapses. Political institutions and ideologies that had once been its supposed foundations are blown down like a house of cards. Beneath the appearance of a monolithic history and singular future there abruptly bursts forth the reality of irreconcilable differences. Citizens increasingly see themselves primarily as members of particular regional, racial, ethnic, religious, economic, or sexual groups rather than as individuals with a common society, culture, or system of beliefs. A shrinking economic pie polarizes citizens into competing interest groups. Political correctness (PC) and identity politics become pervasive practices and accusations. Where once the identification of the individual person with the universal national spirit was seen as an equalizing force that promised the eventual participation of all in directing the country's fate, this universalism now is roundly condemned as a ruse that obscures the subordination of disempowered groups exploited by an entrenched elite. The political culture descends into exchanges of condemnation, recrimination, and even gunfire; the fracturing of any sense of commonality leads to an appalling cynicism and lack of compassion. Argument centers on proving who has been the most victimized and who the most reprehensible. The classic question of politics—"What is the common good?"—is replaced by the question, "What's in it for me and my friends?"

Citizens of the United States may take this scenario to describe the former Soviet Union or Yugoslavia; yet, with qualifications, this scenario mirrors the social and political dissensus characteristic of the United States as the twentieth century gives way to a postcolonial (PC), postmodern, multicultural future. Since global patterns link the cultural crises around the world, the forces driving cultural change in the United States ought to be interpreted partly from an international perspective. The struggle for representation knows no borders. Many nations are trying to find a way to balance the claims of individuality, ethnic or racial solidarity, democracy, economic development, and nationalism. The principles of self-determination and freedom abstractly embodied in theories of democracy clash with the desires of particular groups to create social systems predicated on their own traditional beliefs. Perhaps most significant, the globalization of the labor force and the mobility of international commodity capitalism create economic competition that often exploits the resources of patriotic nationalism and of racial, ethnic, and gender bigotry. Films such as the 1996 blockbuster *Independence Day,* marketed for months before its premiere over the Fourth of July holiday, continue to play to the American anxiety about national catastrophe and "aliens," even as the good-guy forces assembled to combat the new "them" now reflect the commodified image of multiculturalism.

Postcolonialism often leaves former dependent states in splintered ruins, while the once imperial powers themselves suffer internal breakdowns complicated by an influx of postcolonial refugees. At the level of political ideology, any recourse to the rhetoric or policies of universalism, humanism, and common culture is often denounced from the start, a victim of its own record of hypocrisy and bad faith. Yet the economic integration of the globe's regions continues, defying the tide of tribalism as multinational corporations transgress political borders. Likewise the technology of communication, from the PC (personal computer) and fax machines to the "information highway" of the World Wide Web, does not respect the lines drawn by factions on a map. The exchange of images and consumer goods bridges peoples to create commonalities in the practices of their everyday lives. My PC can connect me to the world, though of course my ownership of one says something particular about my privileged place in the universe.

Across the globe, one question repeats itself: Is the elemental unit of political theory and culture to be the individual or the group? A series of corollary questions follows: How do we respond to the fact that the creation of any national identity always involves the exclusion of certain citizens, whether through the subtle omission of their beliefs from dominant institutions or through the violence of outright genocide? Is democratic freedom possible for individuals who are seen more as members of groups than as individuals? Can a person resist such oppression (or privilege) individually, or only through changing the way the group is represented? To turn from questions of theory to conditions of history: Can the nation-state be a viable political or cultural entity now that the technology of industrial production, transportation, and communication makes global mobility so pervasive? Can the power of multinational corporations be resisted without strong nation-states predicated on affirmation of common cultural values and social goals? Are categories such as race or ethnicity any longer viable as fundamental components of cultural identity now that science and cultural theory have discredited them and people increasingly marry and reproduce across such lines? Or have our crises been the product of wrongly thinking that we could transcend such categories in appeals to universal principles, whether those of Marxism or Western humanism?

In trying to frame the current cultural discord in the United States today, then, I think it useful to remember that the struggles for representation here are not unique. Yet they do have a very specific and unusual history that ought to be revisited if we are to avoid treating the present crisis as a kind of Fall from an Eden of communal harmony. I believe the divisions in American culture today can only be understood historically, and understood first of all as a symptom of the nation's recurrent historical amnesia. As a nation we do not like to remember the past. Freedom from the past, after all, has been our national myth, and that innocence has often been a key to our achievements. We tell ourselves that we received our unique identity in a moment of revolutionary forgetting, when we declared ourselves independent of an old world. We think a new world can be made because we have shed the old world and renamed ourselves. At some time or other, every American has been Jay Gatsby. Unfortunately, we have gone on fabricating stories about ourselves through repeated acts of amnesia, forgetting our own divisive history in the process of creating our common future. How else could a nation of immigrants, expropriated peoples, and former slaves wake up one morning to a debate over the meaning of multiculturalism?

What so many insurgent groups in the United States today have in common—from African and Native Americans to women, the working class, recent Asian immigrants, and gays and lesbians—is their insistence that we all have an ethical and political responsibility to remember our history differently. That is why the debates over school and university curricula are so important and so symptomatic. The history of oppression in America is tied to the oppressive way history has been represented and taught, in the mass media and popular culture as well as in the schools. Revisionists, moreover, go beyond debating ideas to focus attention on the material institutions that produce cultural identities, and so the agitation of political activists has surprisingly joined forces with the skepticism of poststructuralist academics eager to deconstruct the ideologies of Representational Man.

If politics is in some degree essentially about the distribution of power, and if knowledge about the powerless tends to be biased or simply left out, then redressing the imbalance will be seen by some as a "political" rather than an "academic" matter. But teachers cannot help the fact that they inherit schools, textbooks, and ideas that reflect the biases of the past. Surely it is the responsibility of teachers to correct those biases as best they can. These educational biases are in part caused by the way political power has been distributed in the United States. Through discriminatory application of categories such as race, ethnicity, class, sexual orientation, and gender, people whose perceived identity does not conform to the politically correct line in the past have been excluded from power. This political motive behind traditional educational biases means that those who seek to tell the story differently will inevitably be accused of "politicizing" the curriculum when in fact they are simply trying to point out the effect that politics has already had on what we study and what we value.

We should not have been surprised, then, when the exaggerated story of political correctness gained such rapid and powerful ascendancy in the public sphere. The same biases that dominated higher education also shaped the personnel and policies of broadcasters, magazines, think tanks, and government officials. Even "Marxists" and other "left" intellectuals joined the ranks criticizing feminists, multiculturalists, and literary theorists, for these newer academic movements challenged the cultural politics of the Old Left as well. Thus, from all sides we heard about how a conspiracy of tenured radicals, leftover 1960s activists, feminists, and minority scholars has succeeded in taking over U.S. colleges, imposing upon them a uniform ideological program of lowbrow totalitarianism that rejects Western civilization in favor of Afrocentrism, deconstructive nihilism, Hollywood films, Harlequin romances, and MTV. We are routinely told that the agents of political correctness have brought politics into the ivory tower, indoctrinating their students and tolerating no opinions that do not match their own. This ludicrous exaggeration of the power of groups that are still very much on the margins reflects the degree of fear on the part of the establishment that these groups and their concerns may actually now be winning some influence.

Such attempts to blame progressive intellectuals for imposing a standard of political correctness on our campuses perversely misrepresent the truth of history, which is that educational institutions have always been partly in the service of dominant social and political institutions. After all, most colleges are owned and run by churches, corporate boards, or governmental bodies. Where were today's born-again champions of democracy, freedom of thought, and evaluation by merit during all the years when women were denied admission to many of the nation's top colleges and universities? Where were they during all the years when Jews, blacks, and others were similarly discriminated against? Why were *Atlantic, Time, Newsweek,* the *New York Times,* and the rest of the media relatively silent during the decades when curriculum and teaching practices amounted to a "thought police" on behalf of white Anglo-Saxon males? Who cried out *then* about "political correctness" on campus? The only new McCarthyism in town, sad to say, is still the old one, though now it is busy discovering feminists, black studies scholars, and poststructuralists under every bed.

Although I do not mean to suggest that literary study should become a branch of political science, we ought not complacently imagine that culture and politics have no ties that bind. Contrary to some accusations, it was not the irrelevance of work done by activist academics and critical theorists that precipitated the crisis at the universities. Rather, it was the increasingly irrelevant character

of higher education that prompted the move toward multiculturalism. The viru-
lent campaign of the anti-PC crowd testifies to exactly how relevant the reforms
are, how precisely they have hit the target, and how far the powers-that-be will
go in protecting their privileges. Just take a look at the success with which the
Reagan and Bush administrations reversed the gains made by women and minorities since the 1960s and you can imagine what conservatives have in mind
for education. Defunding and "privatization" have already gone far in destroying the autonomy of schools. Perhaps the Clinton Administration will stall or
reverse these policies, though its opponents have a powerful ideological and
financial machine ready to attack (and, at least at this moment, a majority in
Congress). As for free speech, it was the justices of the Supreme Court of the
United States who ruled that doctors at clinics receiving federal funds could not
even mention abortion to their patients. *They* are the real thought police, and
they remind us of the Court that decided, in the Dred Scott case, that blacks had
no rights that a white man need respect. Fortunately the Supreme Court does
not yet have jurisdiction over our course syllabi; if they do extend their political
control from the womb to the classroom, there are many opinions we in the
universities may be forbidden to express.

The politics of PC in American culture, then, unfolds as part of a contradictory global transformation that has local effects. Whereas the internal history of
American higher education explains some of the present controversy, that history in turn belongs to a larger history that shapes it and that today overdetermines
the campus as a site of racial, economic, political, and social unrest. In the next
section I want to review that larger history, specifically of certain contradictions
in American cultural history, in an effort to better situate present debates over
the politics of cultural identity.

Whose Declaration of Independence?

One can dismantle the various interpretive paradigms that were used in the past
to fabricate the illusion of a singular "American" literature, as many critics over
the last few years have done. Turning from theory to history, one can also show
that the diversity of written texts produced in the colonies and the United States
always amounted to a multicultural dialogue rather than adding up to a single or
univocal voice of the national spirit. In the words of Paul Lauter, general editor
of the *Heath Anthology of American Literature,* "From its start, the New World
community was multi-racial and multi-cultural. . . . The New World, comprised
of defined spheres of influence over territories claimed and counterclaimed by
European sovereign powers, early offered signs of the necessary mingling of
red, white, and black that remain as both a defining and a contested national
vision" (18). The United States became a postcolonial nation on that famous

Fourth of July and went on to become a rarity—a former colony that would itself become an imperial colonial power. This lack of a homogeneous or pure racial, ethnic, or cultural origin meant that the United States would have to struggle to produce a common national culture, even if this meant violently repressing the differences within its borders. What I want to explore in the following pages, then, is how this struggle for representation unfolded around a key document—the Declaration of Independence—whose meaning was constantly contested and revised.

Since the Revolution of 1776, literary journalists, critics, and artists have repeatedly called for a uniquely "American" literature. All about them, however, that uniqueness was already taking the form of a polyvocal, even multilingual, writing that would continually resist formulation into a homogeneous canon. But, as Paul Lauter has concisely demonstrated, literary critics at the colleges and universities largely succeeded during the period from 1920 to 1970 in drastically narrowing the canon of authors and works and in creating textbooks, curriculums, departments, professional organizations, and interpretive studies based on that canon (*Canons and Contexts* 22–97). Throughout this era, from the early essays of Van Wyck Brooks through the decisive works of Vernon Louis Parrington, F. O. Matthiessen, Richard Chase, and Lionel Trilling (who, like Nathaniel Hawthorne, really was born on the Fourth of July), definitions of the American literary canon hinged on the critic's search for a usable past and were motivated by the desire to construct a set of authorizing cultural documents to give foundation to specific notions of a democratic culture (see Reising, Shumway).

In retrospect we can see how limited those notions were, especially as they tended to depend on an ideology of American individualism that emptied the human being of his or her material, historical features—such as race, class, gender, and sexuality. The tendency to focus on common human traits and conditions is of course understandable when one considers the historic diversity of wave after wave of immigrants who, to this day, continue to alter the physical and cultural face of the United States, as postcolonial immigration also brings a crisis of cultural identity and social power to such traditionally homogeneous nation-states as England, France, and Germany, though one should not minimize the cultural diversity that always characterized these geographical regions to some extent (consider the history of the Jewish people in Europe for a lesson in the long-standing relationship of racism to the construction of nation-states). Born during the height of the European Enlightenment, the United States was founded on philosophical doctrines that emphasized the universal rather than the particular. This philosophy produced a legal system of justice predicated on the ethos of an abstract human subjectivity equally shared by all rational creatures. The ringing phrases of Thomas Jefferson's language in the Declaration of Independence forever linked the establishment of the nation to that humanistic idealism. [1]

"We hold these truths to be self-evident, that all men are created equal, that they are endowed by their Creator with certain unalienable Rights, that among these are Life, Liberty, and the pursuit of Happiness." The *subject* of the Declaration of Independence—grammatically and politically—is the rhetorical "we," produced in discourse and on paper before it appears in reality. This "we" creates the theatrical illusion of a preexistent body politic, a univocal subject who originates and speaks the revolutionary utterance. But as Jacques Derrida points out in his commentary on the Declaration, this utterance is what rhetoricians call a "performative" speech-act: it performs an action as well as declaring a set of facts. "One cannot decide . . . whether independence is stated or produced by this utterance" since "this people does not exist, *before* this declaration, not *as such*. If it gives birth to itself, as free and independent subject, as possible signer, this can hold only in the act of the signature. The signature invents the signer" (10). Who signs, asks Derrida, and with what so called proper name, the declarative act which founds an institution or a nation? The "we" of the American people is born during this performance. We become our own subjects, subject no longer to the King but to the higher "Laws of Nature and of Nature's God." While it can be argued that, in a cultural sense, an Anglo-Saxon American nation had already developed by 1776, Jefferson's "we" refers less to an historical population than to a proposed political position (one, not incidentally, that many Americans at the time opposed). As Jay Fliegelman points out in *Declaring Independence: Jefferson, Natural Language, and the Culture of Performance,* the Declaration represents the Revolution as both an unavoidable necessity *and* a free act of will. The language of the Declaration exhibits an uneasy dialectic between mechanical determinism and individual agency characteristic of the period. The Declaration speaks predominantly in the passive voice of what is "necessary for one people" to do after such "patient sufferance" of the willful actions against them of the King. By making their invention of their own rebellious subjectivity sound like a necessity imposed upon them, the colonists mitigate their guilt and obscure the artificial character of the union they declare.

In this "UNANIMOUS DECLARATION" we hear of "one people," of "the Right of the People" and "their duty" to—among other things—commit treason. Although the agency of human action narrated by the Declaration anthropomorphizes the body politic, imagining it as a collective of different persons, this subject nonetheless speaks with one voice, as if it were a particular individual with rights and duties. Was this universalizing presumption ethical, especially considering how many particular people had no voice in this utterance? "Jefferson's statement of equality" in the sense of being equally made by God with moral faculties, writes Fliegelman, "was far from a racial call for social equality" (197). The Declaration postulated an abstractly equal and universal human subjectivity despite the historical exclusion from it of Indians, the enslaved, women, and those men who did not own property. The words of the Declaration have continued to haunt the moral and political life of America, and subsequent generations have both embraced and repudiated them. At the origin of the United States, then, we find an ethically troubling contradiction between enabling fictions of universalism and stubborn realities of particularity and exclusion. What the next two centuries would bring was not simply a history of hypocrisy, however, but a series of appropriating subversions as those who were left out of the original declaration used its own utopian terms both to challenge and to expand the practices of American democracy.

The original draft of Jefferson's Declaration contained a long, hypocritical, and self-serving condemnation of the King's encouragement of the international slave trade, and of the Crown's policy of offering manumission to slaves who rebelled against their rebellious masters. But even Jefferson and his colleagues quickly recognized the folly of citing the King's offer of freedom for the enslaved as an example of the tyranny they opposed; the passage was dropped, though a veiled reference to the Crown's instigation of "domestic insurrections" was inserted (see Wills, *Inventing America,* chap. 5; Fliegelman 189–200). When the Constitution of the United States was eventually negotiated, it counted enslaved Africans as two-thirds of a person for the purpose of determining the representation of districts and states in the Congress. These enslaved Africans, of course, had no vote themselves; nor did women and most unpropertied men, for that matter. The Declaration and the Constitution presented Americanness as a revolutionary identity or ethos for all, but the reality and power of citizenship were in practice restricted.

Even before 1776, the blacks enslaved in Massachusetts were using the language of the Enlightenment, protesting that "we have in common with all other men a naturel [sic] right to our freedoms." In a subsequent petition of January 1777, enslaved Africans in Massachusetts were already appropriating the Declaration of Independence and Jefferson's phrases as they made two claims that would characterize abolitionist (and later women's rights) literature: (1) that African Americans were entitled to equal status as human beings, and (2) that the oppression of African Americans vividly resembled the oppression suffered by the colonies at the hands of King George. These petitioners claimed to "have in common with all other men a Natural and Unaliable Right to that freedom which the Grat parent of the Unavers hath Bestowed equalley on all menkind and which they have Never forfeited by any Compact or agreement whatever"; they further expressed "their Astonishment that It have Never Bin Considered that Every Principle from which America has Acted in the Cours of their unhappy Difficultes with Great Briton Pleads Stronger than A thousand arguments in favours of your petitioners" seeking freedom from slavery (Aptheker 8, 10).

Black and white abolitionists throughout the early 1800s continued to throw the slave owner Jefferson's words back in the face of the political establishment and to make that one sentence ("We hold these truths to be self-evident, that all men are created equal") the most often and ironically quoted text in abolitionist literature. David Walker's 1829 *Appeal to the Coloured Citizens of the World,* perhaps the most fiery antislavery pamphlet before the speeches of Frederick Douglass, pointedly singled out Jefferson for analytical ridicule. Walker responded at length to the assertion of the racial inferiority of blacks in Jefferson's *Notes on the State of Virginia.* He also quoted the first two paragraphs of the Declaration verbatim and asked: "Compare your own language . . . with your cruelties and murders inflicted by your cruel and unmerciful fathers and yourselves on our fathers and on us . . . . I ask you candidly, was your sufferings under Great Britain, one hundredth part as cruel and tyrannical as you have rendered ours under you?" (75). When in 1853 William Wells Brown wrote the first novel by an African American, he called it *Clotel, or The President's Daughter.* Brown based his story on the rumors that Jefferson had fathered two mulatto slave daughters who were subsequently sold south. The epigraph on Brown's title page was, of course, Jefferson's by then notorious sentence about equality from the Declaration of Independence.

This tradition of antislavery responses to the Declaration perhaps reached its climax in Frederick Douglass's spectacular oration "What to the Slave Is the Fourth of July?" An escaped slave and abolitionist leader, Douglass pointedly delivered his speech on the *5th* of July, 1852:

> What to the American slave is your Fourth of July? I answer, a day that reveals to him more than all other days of the year, the gross injustice and cruelty to which he is the constant victim. To him your celebration is a sham; your boasted liberty an unholy license; your national greatness, swelling vanity; your sounds of rejoicing are empty and heartless; your denunciation of tyrants, brass-fronted impudence; your shouts of liberty and equality, hollow mockery; your prayers and hymns, your sermons and thanksgivings, with all your religious parade and solemnity, are to him mere bombast, fraud, deception, impiety, and hypocrisy a thin veil to cover up crimes which would disgrace a nation of savages. There is not a nation of the earth guilty of practices more shocking and bloody than are the people of these United States. (Aptheker 334)[2]

Sadly, some in the United States today would probably dismiss Douglass's speech as merely the hot air of political correctness, but his words can be an antidote to that very historical amnesia that plagues debates about American identity. The apostles proclaiming the univocal, superior virtues of "Western Civilization" seem to forget the role of slavery and the voices of people like Douglass in the history of that civilization.

In analyzing racism in the United States, however, it would be well to remember its economic motive, for this determines its role in building the civilization. Like most discourses of bigotry, this one results in profits for one group at the expense of another. More specifically, the rhetoric of "Negro inferiority" helped justify a system that kept wages for labor at an artificially low—even nonexistent—level. Slavery presents the extreme example of bigotry, for here the subject is not simply represented as a deficient or perverse individual: this subject is not a subject but *property*. As the Boston Tea Party suggests, the Declaration of Independence declared the independence of (some) men to own property. Moreover, it dramatized the dependence of their rights as citizens on their freedom to acquire, sell, and possess property. Insurrectional classes (the enslaved, women, immigrants, etc.) will be subjected to discrimination to the degree that it profitably regulates their relation to (or as) property. For such classes, declaring independence of the Master means taking back their own bodies as property and claiming the political power that comes with the freedom to control property. The original language behind the Declaration, after all, had listed "life, liberty, and property" as the citizen's trinity. The cultural and political history of the United States was and continues to be conditioned by this codependency of freedom and property, with the attendant complicating relation of freedom to wage labor.

Critical economists have argued with some persuasiveness that the enormous and rapid growth of wealth in the United States economy resulted mainly from the successive exploitation of low-wage labor, performed by indentured servants, the enslaved, women, and a wave of different immigrant populations. At the close of the twentieth century, multinational corporations now find this labor abroad, often for pennies a day. Workers in the U.S. find themselves competing with the populations the West once controlled through imperialism; domestically, cultural separatism increases as discrimination works to bar certain groups from gaining access to the increasingly small pool of higher-paid labor. Although the American ethos states that prosperity for all is available through hard work, work is not available for all Americans. To the degree that capitalism's structural necessity for an underclass comes to overlap with groupings by cultural identity, economic strife may take the symbolic form of ideological warfare, from debates over racial and female inferiority to the more recent uproar about multiculturalism and feminism.

It was no accident that Frederick Douglass gave his speech in response to an invitation from the Rochester Ladies' Anti-Slavery Society. For decades the causes of women's rights and antislavery had been closely linked, as women played a key role in advancing the work of abolitionism in the North. Indeed, the association of the condition of women with that of the enslaved goes back at least to 1776. In a famous exchange of letters during the months prior to the signing of the Declaration, Abigail and John Adams gave rare witness in writing to a debate that doubtless raged in many households. "I long to hear that you have declared an independancy," wrote Abigail, "—and by the way in the new Code of Laws which I suppose it will be necessary for you to make I desire you would Remember the Ladies." Observing to her husband that "your Sex are

Naturally Tyrannical," she asked for specific laws to protect women from the "cruelty and indignity" suffered under the "unlimited power" of husbands: "If perticuliar care and attention is not paid to the Laidies we are determined to foment a Rebelion, and will not hold ourselves bound by any Laws in which we have no voice, or Representation" (Lauter, *Heath*, 876).

John Adams responded, "As to your extraordinary Code of Laws, I cannot but laugh." Exploiting the witty tone of Abigail's letter to his own ends, he noted that the revolutionaries had been accused of fomenting a general anarchy and a disruption of traditional social hierarchies: the Tories claimed that children, apprentices, students, Indians, and Negroes all grew "insolent to their Masters." "But your letter," John continued, "was the first Intimation that another Tribe more numerous and powerfull than all the rest were grown discontented." He went on to say, "We know better than to repeal our Masculine systems," and he repeated the myth that men were the victims of what he called the "Despotism of the Peticoat." He (perhaps) jokingly accused King George's government of instigating rebellion among the women as it did among "Tories, Landjobbers, Trimmers, Bigots, Canadians, Indians, Negros, Hanoverians, Hessians, Russians, Irish Roman Catholicks, Scotch Renegadoes" (Lauter, *Heath*, 877). By this argument, the same made by Jefferson in the Declaration's struck passage on slavery, the Founding Fathers meant to declare their independence from women as well as from the King. Their construction of the American political ethos carefully separated a masculine claim to inalienable (property) rights from claims made by the groups whose clamoring for representation they thought ought to be squelched. John Adams's sarcastic linking of women's claims to those of Negroes, Indians, and other oppressed groups would, of course, return as a serious political argument in the hands of feminists and abolitionists in the nineteenth century and remains a logical connection for many cultural analysts to this day. Confirming John Adams's fear, polemicists from the American Indian tribes were also adept at invoking the white man's Revolution and Declaration for their own purposes. In his 1834 *Indian Nullification of the Unconstitutional Laws of Massachusetts Relative to the Marshpee Tribe*, William Apess (himself a Pequot) denounced the expropriation of Marshpee lands and resources by invoking the comparative memory of 1776: "I will ask him [the white man] how, if he values his own liberty, he would or could rest quiet under such laws. I ask the Inhabitants of New England generally how their fathers bore laws, much less oppressive, when imposed upon them by a foreign government" (O'Connell, *On Our Own Ground* 211).

By the late 1820s, women were increasingly apt to compare their situation to that of the enslaved, all the more so when women's attempts to speak in public and exercise political power were met with contempt, ridicule, and violence. One of the first of these women, Angelina Grimké, herself the daughter of a slave owner, wrote Catharine Beecher in 1837 that "the investigation of the rights of the slave has led me to a better understanding of my own." Employing the rhetoric of sentiment, domesticity, and Christianity, Grimké established equality on the basis of morality: "Human beings have *rights,* because they are *moral* beings: the rights of *all* men grow out of their moral nature; and as all men have the same moral nature, they have essentially the same rights. . . . My doctrine, then, is that whatever it is morally right for man to do, it is morally right for woman to do" (Lauter, *Heath,* 1866). This radical feminist assertion of the ethos of a common moral nature aims to stop the particular discrimination against the character of women and blacks; her moral egalitarianism would theoretically prevent the use of character as a justification for subordination by race or gender. In 1845 Margaret Fuller underscored how America's declaration of national independence was "blurred by the servility of individuals," and she too drew the by-then standard analogy between women and the enslaved: "As the friend of the negro assumes that one man cannot by right hold another in bondage, so should the friend of Woman assume that Man cannot by right lay even well-meant restrictions on Woman" (Chevigny 243, 248).

As Barbara Bardes and Suzanne Gossett point out in *Declarations of Independence: Women and Political Power in Nineteenth-Century American Fiction,* women's rights activists and women novelists in the nineteenth century often took up Jefferson's rhetoric for their own subversive purposes. The participants in the historic 1848 Women's Rights Convention in Seneca Falls (which Frederick Douglass attended) left this account of preparing their manifesto, which they would call the Declaration of Sentiments:

> And the humiliating fact may as well now be recorded that before taking the initiative step, those ladies resigned themselves to a faithful perusal of various masculine productions. The reports of Peace, Temperance, and Anti-Slavery conventions were examined, but all alike seemed too tame and pacific for the inauguration of a rebellion such as the world had never before seen. . . . After much delay, one of the circle [Elizabeth Cady Stanton] took up the Declaration of 1776, and read it aloud with much spirit and emphasis, and it was at once decided to adopt the historic document, with some slight changes such as substituting "all men" for "King George." (Buhle and Buhle 92)

In substituting "all men" for "King George," the women turned the strategy of universalization to their own ends—the same strategy that had left them out of the original Declaration when the men's reference to "men" obscured their exclusion of women. To these rebellious ladies, all men were King George. This feminist strategy recast the figure of the oppressor from the particular tyrant King George to the universal tyranny of men over women. And in *their* Declaration, the women boldly rewrote Jefferson's most famous line, thus: "We hold these truths to be self-evident: that all men and women are created equal." By rewriting, with a significant difference, the words of the founding document of the nation's political and cultural identity, the women of Seneca Falls gave voice to something repressed at the nation's origin, even something whose repression was constitutive of that origin. Their Declaration became an uncanny return of the repressed, producing a mocking echo within the univocal expression of American truth, replacing his-tory with her-story. The women's version stated: "The history of mankind is a history of repeated injuries and usurpations on the part of man toward woman, having in direct object the establishment of an absolute tyranny over her" (Buhle and Buhle 94). The women of Seneca Falls exposed the masculine ethos of the Founding Fathers even as they invoked the value of liberty (not least of all in the liberties they took with Jefferson's text).

By the 1850s, an ironic reference to the Declaration of Independence was standard in the rhetoric of the women's rights movement. Sara Parton, who under the pen name of Fanny Fern became perhaps the most famous woman journalist of her day, delighted in satirizing the injustices of patriarchal tyranny—be they in the bedroom and parlor or the houses of prostitution and publishing. In a column of 30 July 1859 for the *New York Ledger,* Parton wrote as if in conscious imitation of Douglass as she took up the theme of women's relation to the promises of the Founding Fathers. Characteristic of her style, the column features the first-person voice of an American woman who speaks up:

> "FOURTH OF JULY." Well—I don't feel patriotic. Perhaps I might if they would stop that deafening racket. Washington was very well, if he *couldn't* spell, and I'm glad we are all free; but as a woman—I shouldn't know it, didn't some orator tell me. Can I go out of an evening without a hat at my side? Can I go out with one on my head without danger of a station-house? Can I clap my hands at some public speaker when I am nearly bursting with delight? Can I signify the contrary when my hair stands on end with vexation? Can I stand up in the cars "like a gentleman" without being immediately invited "to sit down"? . . . Can I go to see anything *pleasant,* like an execution or a dissection? . . . Can I be a Senator, that I may hurry up that millennial International Copyright Law? Can I *even* be President? Bah—you know I can't. *"Free!"* Humph! (Fern 315)

Fanny Fern didn't feel patriotic because, in many detailed ways, she did not live in the land of the free. The nation created by the Declaration treats her like a criminal and a child, denying her the most mundane as well as sublime rights. With characteristic wit, Fern makes it amply clear that her freedom is sharply restricted by gender: she cannot go "out of an evening without a hat" (that is, without a male escort), and she cannot go out wearing a man's hat without fear of arrest. The proper sex roles are literally policed, though Fern has fun pointing out what a superficial costume gender difference may be, if it comes down to what hats we wear. By playing with that well-recognized pun, however, Fern also prompts readers to reconsider seriously the ways we dress up our differences, who controls the show, and the punishments inflicted when the disempowered try to assert their freedom. Freedom of dress and freedom of address—of speech, of bodily movement, of social location—walk hand in hand. Dress how she might, and attend however many Fourth of July addresses as she can bear, Fern's address will never be 1600 Pennsylvania Avenue. The only space of free address Fern can carve out is on the page, where her irreverent authority of experience is worn stylishly. Such cultural literacy as Fern commands serves her well in judging the Founding Fathers: "Washington was very well, if he *couldn't* spell."

In her commentary on this column, Lauren Berlant argues that "to Fern, citizenship is not an abstract condition or privilege: it is a relay to protection and legitimation under the law and in the public sphere, which includes the world of the arts and the more banal experience of the body in the marketplace," including "the absurdity of the degree to which society regulates juridically what women wear and what they say" (442). In contrast to the Enlightenment notion of a universal political citizen with equal rights, Fern portrays the specific ways that society and the law address women and their bodies, disciplining their freedom with an oppressive protective custody. Implicitly, as some feminist legal scholars argue today, women's freedom cannot result from the simple application to them of a doctrine of rights developed on the model of a masculine citizen but must instead be crafted to address the specifics of women's condition in a patriarchal society. Whereas "freedom" remains a universal abstract token of women's desire, the realization of freedom (or of its absence) takes place only in particulars—in the wearing or not wearing of certain hats, in the public display of emotion, in preferring to stand on an omnibus, in watching an execution or dissection, in getting paid for one's work, in being president. In a democracy, part of our ethical responsibility (by which I mean our responsibility to others) involves asking what freedom will look like for particular citizens, not simply for the citizen in the abstract. (See also Fern's piece titled "A Little Bunker Hill," in which she comments about the often-heard demand for rights, "I hope no female sister will be such a novice as to suppose it refers to any but *masculine* rights" [243].)

For white women in antebellum America, it was property rights, not the vote, that dominated the agenda as these women considered the particulars of their lack of freedom. Under the legal doctrine of coverture, women lost their property rights under marriage, even their rights to their children. Upper- and middle-class women found this an increasingly restrictive and shameful state of affairs, as did lower-class women who were beginning to receive wages for labor (such as shoebindery and needlework) that had once been remunerated through barter. The late 1840s saw the first legislative acts guaranteeing property rights for married women. At the same time, women in the manufacturing industries continued to complain about the artificially low wages paid them under the ethos of domestic ideology which defined women first as wives and mothers: women were paid only those wages calculated to compensate the family for time taken from domestic chores. Men were paid under the "head of household" rubric, and so domestic ideology blocked any notion of equal pay for equal work. Women could not be independent of the patriarchal home without a wage, but if they left the home for outside work they found themselves paid as if they were wives or mothers or daughters. True citizenship for women would mean the right to hold property equally and the achievement of a just wage. Any "political" rights granted in the absence of these reforms was of little worth and deceptive, for it would throw a cloak of respectable universal citizenship over the particular reality of women's inequality in a patriarchal society. The claim of women to the universal principles of freedom and equality, however, provided a rhetorical and utopian lever by which to move men off the pedestal of privilege they had erected for themselves.

What the antislavery and women's rights literature demonstrates is that every attempt to rectify a past injustice involves some appeal to universality. As one might expect, these claims usually produce more rather than less social and cultural discord along with any actual progress they achieve in the treatment of individuals. When women and African Americans appropriate Jefferson's voice, they decenter the national rhetoric by speaking it through an unauthorized body.[3] This tactical appropriation of language and ideas seems to express the extension of universality to the formerly excluded subject, but the ironic embodiment this entails seems to underscore the limits of pluralism. Americans previously excluded by prejudice or exploitation cannot lay claim to equal rights in the abstract without eventually upsetting the practical distribution of social power and cultural authority. Equal rights cannot be achieved painlessly by rhetorical or legislative fiat; injustice has meant that some persons have had their bodies, wealth, and rights taken from them, and undoing this injustice means depriving a once-dominant group of the privileges and resources it has taken for granted as its own rights. This redistribution of wealth and power can also be formulated in moral terms as a general ethos of justice to which one submits regardless of one's own particular self-interest.

Promissory Notes of a Dream Deferred

The Enlightenment rhetoric of universality portrays a relatively harmonious society, but that peace obscures the interdependence of rights and powers. The resistance of men and slave owners to the women's rights and abolitionist reformers, like the resistance in the United States today to affirmative action, Indian treaty rights, or gays and lesbians in the military, stems from a realistic understanding that the application of universal principles results in particular change. Since the original postulation of an abstract universal human subject ("We the people") had actually been predicated on an unequal distribution of social power among particular cultural groups (by race, class, gender, etc.), the response of those oppressed must necessarily be double-edged. On the one hand, they must claim membership in the very universal category of humanity from which they have been excluded, and entitlement to the rights that go with it; on the other hand, they must insist on affirming the value of the particular social group to which they feel tied and whose fate has largely determined their destiny as individuals. Somewhat paradoxically, we understand universal rights by recognizing the historical, concrete, and contingent lives led by individuals in real social classes. The contradictions inherent in classical liberal political theory, then, still inform today's struggles for representation, shaping the debate between the advocates of "identity politics" and their opponents (whether liberal humanists upholding Enlightenment individualism or poststructuralists opposed to essentialism).

In the heat of these disputes, it is vital to remember that no group can be formed without postulating some quality, experience, or factor *universal* to members of the group; likewise, any universality that does not have a basis in, and a respect for, the particular qualities and experiences of human lives as actually lived is worthless and may well be an unintended ally when dominant groups force their will on a society. Ultimately, cultural identity is not something inherent in an individual but a meaning that persons give themselves or others as a result of social determinations and subjective choices. Cultural identity is an ethos, a way of life. It follows that an ethics of social change requires altering the systematic, material, and impersonal forces that condition and account for the lives of individuals. At the same time, it also requires respecting the freedom of individuals to determine the character of their lives and to create meaningful accounts of them.

The rigidity of the sides in the dispute over identity politics might be eased if the antagonists concentrated more on its material basis, on how notions of cultural assimilation and the "melting pot" lose their credibility when times are tough. Since the 1960s the United States has experienced a steady decline in the number of entry-level manufacturing jobs that require few skills and offer good wages and a chance for some upward mobility. To this diminution of the manufacturing base one should add the cutbacks in government jobs programs begun under Ronald Reagan and continued by the Congress and subsequent administrations. These kinds of jobs were a vital channel for the assimilation of every immigrant group before today, including the large numbers of African Americans who moved North into industrialized cities after the 1890s. The growing underclass has become more difficult to assimilate into the economy, whatever the social or ethnic group of the individual. As a result, racism, anti-Semitism, xenophobia, violence against women, and overt acts of bigotry are on the rise nationwide. The depravity of our politics feeds at the trough of material despair.

The economic crisis has precipitated a cultural crisis of scapegoating, separatism, selfishness, cynicism, and rank exploitation of anxieties and fears. Social and immigrant groups that cannot look forward to assimilation turn more readily to insisting on the preservation of what cultural identity they do have, since no route toward a common identity or common culture appears open. In an era of scarcity, competition for jobs, housing, college admissions, and other necessities takes the shape of group conflicts as individuals band together to strengthen their hand in the struggle for a piece of the shrinking pie. Scarcity also makes it vastly more difficult to redistribute wealth in order to right past injustices, such as the denial of equal opportunity to women and minorities.

Individuals belonging to social groups that have been the regular victims of bigotry and discrimination fight even harder to get some small increase for themselves, and step up the ferocity of their denunciation of the group that has benefited from their exploitation or oppression. Whites often respond to this challenge to their dominance in the same way in which they respond to the general decline of economic opportunities: they look for a scapegoat and portray themselves as the true victims, fortifying the walls of prejudice and selfishness rather than building bridges of common cause and compassion. On the one hand, women and minorities see the discrimination against them as groups more clearly than ever, and so tend to respond as alienated communities of interest that have no common bonds. On the other hand, middle- and lower-income whites, especially men, react to the reduction in their own economic opportunities by irrationally blaming feminism and affirmative action programs, as if these were responsible for the disappearance of entry-level manufacturing jobs, government employment, and retail expansion. Thus, one should greet the current tendency to portray white men as the unfairly victimized targets of left-wing hate groups by pointing out (as does Michael Lind) the long history of white supremacist attitudes informing U.S. public policy and economic life as well as the continuing position of predominance most white men have in American society (unfortunately, Lind thinks it necessary to balance this account with a hyperbolic jeremiad against affirmative action). If reforms in society and education and government result in targeting the privileges white men have had for so long, it is done not out of a personal hatred of them for their gender or their race but out of historical recognition and moral evaluation of the unjust distribution of social power and knowledge.

At colleges and universities a similar story unfolds. The momentum of the Civil Rights and women's movements of the 1960s created a variety of institutions and ideas, mostly on the periphery of academe, to remedy past intellectual injustices through collective action. Autonomous (though usually precarious and underfunded) programs in Women's Studies, Black or African American Studies, and similar innovations brought identity politics into campus administration and curriculum. Throughout the Reagan and Bush years, however, the moneys and political support for these programs dried up, along with financial aid for the poor and victims of discrimination. Twenty-five years after the Civil Rights Act of 1964, black enrollment in higher education actually began to decline despite affirmative action programs. The fall into poverty of northern black industrial communities that lost their share of the wealth produced by urban manufacture (now exported to the Third World) had a devastating impact on the ability of blacks to attend college. By 1990, after a decade of expanding requirements, tuition increases, and cuts in financial aid, white students too began to feel the economic pinch, and massive numbers of white college students took part-time jobs to pay their way through school. Again, many whites irrationally blamed affirmative action programs for the decline in college opportunities and course offerings rather than pointing the finger at the government officials who stole from the poor and middle-class and gave to the rich. Young Americans of college age now stare hungrily at one another, seeing not friends or compatriots in a common culture but instead eyeing each other as competitors in a grim struggle for money and power.

In debates on multiculturalism and the diversity of educational offerings, one sometimes encounters objections to the constant reiteration of "race, class, and gender" as seemingly the only categories requiring revised representation. Why, critics ask, should we restrict ourselves to this holy trinity? What about all the other, theoretically infinite, kinds of differences that separate people, such as region and religion? Why not affirmative action to ensure representation of evangelical Christians or Irish Americans or short people (the "vertically challenged," as some wags put it)? The answer lies, I think, in the connection between our knowledge about social groups and the relative power they have in a given culture. In the context of the United States, a strong argument has been made that acts of bigotry and discrimination against people on the basis of their race, class, and gender (including sexual orientation) are at their highest point in our history. These groups—people of color, women, the poor, gays and lesbians—are on the whole less socially powerful and more easily targeted than other groups. Although abstract ideas about justice and equality might suggest the arbitrariness of privileging race, class, and gender, *historical* understanding of U.S. society shows the dominant role these categories have played. The fact that everyone can claim to be a victim of some prejudice does not mean that all have been *equally harmed* or that *degrees of oppression* are insignificant. Although it is important to discourage exercises wherein people argue over who has been most oppressed, these disputes seem preferable to the relative silence about bigotry and discrimination that preceded them.

The lack of power of specific social groups has been reflected in the way they have been represented in educational materials and institutions (if at all), and this misrepresentation (or lack of representation) in turn reproduces their social disempowerment. So the reiteration of "race, class, and gender" does not follow from some wrong-headed assertion that non-whites, the working class, and women are the only categories of victimization, or that only these marginalized groups have cultural riches that require study and appreciation. Rather, the argument I am pursuing asserts that throughout America's history the traditions of cultural groups other than these have had relatively more access to representation; thus, such relatively well-represented groups do not require exceptional efforts to gain their place in the national culture. In this way one can understand why questions of educational purpose and scholarship cannot be easily disentangled from political questions, especially when an education often provides the most ready access to better-paid jobs and social power.

Cultural and economic assimilation in the United States has historically been relatively easy for those of European descent, more difficult for those of Hispanic descent, and virtually impossible for those of African descent. American Indians, of course, were removed beyond the pale and subjected to attempted genocide. Assimilation of Asian Americans remains problematic even as they wield great economic power in states such as California and Hawaii. Racial prejudice, then, the ancient human habit of making one's own personal identity dependent on the illusion of superiority over someone else, continues to be decisive in American life and public policy. The last four decades of the twentieth century show a demographic swing toward growth in those very sectors of the population that have been traditionally the most recalcitrant toward assimilation, since assimilation meant either accepting the superiority of Anglo-Saxon culture or melting into the pot of white European pluralism. This has contributed to the ever-stronger tendency to see the nation as a conglomerate of distinct social and cultural groups rather than as a social contract among highly individual and independent persons.

Indeed, many now question whether assimilation should be a goal at all, since it usually means the assimilation of less empowered groups to the cultural values and institutionalized powers of dominant groups. Cities such as Los Angeles, New York, and Chicago are increasingly made up of racially and ethnically distinct neighborhoods, composing together a kind of multicultural metropolis. (A recent article on demographics in California was called "Los Angeles: Capital of the Third World," a title that suggests the white fear of hordes of racial others descending on America in some remake of 1950s horror classics of xenophobia about "Them.") As the cultural critic Todd Gitlin sees it, there has been an almost complete reversal of the political landscape with respect to the old debate between universalism and particularism. Whereas in the eighteenth century, liberal progressives of the Enlightenment swore allegiance to an equal and common humanity transcending material particulars, today leftist reformers insist that political change must start with, and always respect, the

unbridgeable differences between heterogeneous peoples. At this rate we will
soon have difficulty finding anyone who was born on the Fourth of July, who
thinks of himself or herself as "simply an American."

Obviously academic scholars can only indirectly affect the fundamental economic factors that are accelerating the breakdown of cultural consensus in the
United States. But educators can work vigorously to change the policies and
material practices of their own institutions; after all, professors should not protest injustice in faraway places while ignoring its persistence in their own back-
yards. Across the nation, the pressure on universities to make budgetary ends
meet threatens to roll back innovative programs in area studies and to limit the
hiring of younger scholars and nontraditional voices. Administrators may also
be tempted to exploit further the services of poorly paid teaching assistants or
part-time instructors who receive no benefits and are not protected by unions.

Still, most academics will continue, in their professional lives, to respond to
the "culture wars" through the battle of books and ideas, whether in public
forums or classroom syllabi or in the pages of journals and magazines. Here
there are many strategies, many tasks. As intellectuals or cultural historians, we
can object to the language of novelty commonly used about the "disuniting of
America." It can be pointed out that the consensus about the American dream
was never very comprehensive in the first place, and that acceptance of it was
often not a matter of choice. We can also look positively at the multicultural and
multinational demographics of the American population as something to be
proud of and something requiring a new vision of the nation's history and purpose. Reversions to nationalistic patriotism, whether in the political sphere or
in formulas for cultural history, should be strenuously resisted. Intellectuals
have a responsibility to remind the public at large of how such patriotism has
historically been used as a weapon of violence against many of our own citizens and as an excuse for telling lies about our past.

At the same time, it remains indispensable to mark the limitations of identity
politics and cultural separatism, since these repeat at the local level the same
blindness that nationalism perpetuates at the state level. Criticisms of identity
politics, though, should regularly remind the audience that the equation of "race"
with "nation" is a dominant feature of modern European and Western thought,
and that the invention of "whiteness" by Europeans and their American descendants is the key factor in the development of the contemporary problem of identity politics. Rather than taking sides in disputes between fixed positions in the
debates over identity politics, we should be encouraging encounters that focus
on how the ways we represent our differences affect the ways we value one
another and the access each of us has to social and economic opportunities. We
may want to challenge the centrality of "identity" itself in arguments about
culture, for example, by considering the difference between "having" an identity and living by an ethos. At the colleges and universities, cultural difference

cannot help but be a central focus of the agenda, though it should not become the pretext for naive pluralism or heated celebrations of ethnic traditions. Here the poststructuralist critique of identity proves politically useful; the uncritical assertion of the value of one's personal or cultural identity is not ultimately a sufficient response to those who have, on the basis of their own identity politics, repressed and denied one's identity. When we talk about rescuing those "differences within" that are whitewashed by totalizing identity, that goes for the differences within the self as well as within the community or state.

An experience of the relativity of cultural values can lead to an ethical moment of self-criticism. I call this moment ethical in part because in it I submit myself to the judgment of a principle larger than my own self-interest. I hold my cultural identity and its practices to the standard of justice, and ask how my mode of being affects the lives of others. Slavery and patriarchy were, after all, popular because they served the self-interest of a ruling class. What justifies struggles against that ruling class? Merely the desire of other classes, too, for power? Power to do what? For whom? To what end? These are questions, again, of "the good," and they cannot be reduced solely to questions of power. In a pure clash of forces for power, there is no reason to prefer either side. Rather, a real political philosophy requires that I be able to argue that one arrangement of power is harmful, unjust, and immoral. If so, even those who benefit from injustice can (in theory) be persuaded or constrained to give it up.

In raising the question of the good, I mean to suggest that cultural criticism, to be worth the effort, should have an affirmative dimension. Certainly such affirmation may take complex, even ironic forms, as my discussion of the subversive affirmations of the Declaration of Independence has demonstrated. Ralph Ellison continues this tradition in the "Epilogue" to *Invisible Man,* where his narrator gives this final gloss to his grandfather's deathbed injunction to "overcome 'em [whites] with yeses, undermine 'em with grins, agree 'em to death and destruction" (16):

> Could he have meant—hell, he *must* have meant the principle, that we were to affirm the principle on which the country was built and not the men, or at least not the men who did the violence. . . . Did he mean to affirm the principle, which they themselves had dreamed into being out of the chaos and darkness of the feudal past, and which they had violated and compromised to the point of absurdity even in their own corrupt minds? Or did he mean that we had to take the responsibility for all of it, for the men as well as the principle. . . ? Was it that we of all, we, most of all, had to affirm the principle, the plan in whose name we had been brutalized and sacrificed . . . ? (574)

Ellison's affirmation of the white master's "plan in whose name we had been brutalized and sacrificed" is bound to strike many today as naive if not self-destructive. But is Ellison's idealism—his affirmation of principles despite particular individual failures to live up to them—really so ineffectual a course, or so lacking in theoretical strength or practical justification? There has been, I think, too little admission by the left today (at least on campus) that its principles remain indebted to the tradition of the Declaration of Independence, especially as appropriated and extended by successive generations since Abigail Adams and David Walker. Uneasiness about being seen as oppressively "patriotic" or "nationalist" in the wake of the 1960s and the Vietnam War explains some of this hesitance, as does the influence of Marxism on academics, among whom it helped foster an atmosphere hostile to liberalism and suspicious of hypocritical pieties about equal rights, justice, and democracy. Writers who unabashedly espoused belief in American possibilities suffered harsh attack, as was the case with Ralph Ellison. Recalling Ellison at the current moment presents an interesting opportunity to reflect on conflicting intellectual, artistic, and political commitments, as Jerry Watts notes in his recent study of Ellison in *Heroism and the Black Intellectual.* Many of Ellison's views might be dubbed "politically incorrect," and he has indeed been taken to task by the Left and by proponents of the Black Aesthetic and Black Nationalism ever since the publication in 1952 of *Invisible Man.* The criticisms have merit, but one hopes that the days of having to choose between Ellison and Wright (or between Martin Luther King and Malcolm X) are past.

What makes Ellison newly fascinating is his stance as a hybrid character. While grounding his fiction and essays in the black experience—in blues and folklore—Ellison freely adapted techniques and themes from white writers he praised, including Malraux, Joyce, Hemingway, and Eliot. He saw "American" culture, especially in music and literature, as having always been shaped by the contributions of African Americans, so that to speak of American culture as distinct from black culture (or vice versa) made little sense. This position did not endear Ellison to many in the black community, who, even if they acknowledged the truth of his position, could nonetheless rightly argue that African Americans and their art had been regularly discriminated against and violated, to the point where it made no sense not to speak of a difference between white and black cultural experience. And whatever cultural achievements the black community could boast in no way mitigated the extremes of poverty and violence to which it was subjected. Nonetheless, Ellison seems clearly the forerunner of Toni Morrison, who in *Playing in the Dark* demonstrates extensively how white literature is haunted by an Africanist presence.

Ellison's gamble on the tactics of integration and subversive appropriation was a dangerous one, and is obviously still controversial no matter who takes it up. Yet in the current swing away from essentialism and identity politics, Ellison's decision to say "yes" to multiple and contradictory versions of America might offer fresh lessons. The Ellison controversy recalls other such debates over the question "Who is an authentically black (or Jewish or Indian or feminist) writer?"

Ellison's move away from Marxism and social determinism toward an existentialism of the blues emphasized the real power of choice, or agency, in a way that resonates in the aftermath of the determinism of structuralism and debates over the impact of the "welfare state." Watts cautions, however, that "in his public statements Ellison will sometimes offer a perfunctory mention of the dire plight of many blacks before he proceeds into a celebration of black American creative endurance and American possibility. . . . Ellison utilizes hegemonic American democratic rhetoric as well as the resilient hopeful outlooks of many black Americans to divert his attention from the most debilitating aspects of black existence in America" (108). Ellison's championing of the blues and folklore can come to seem like other paeans to popular culture, that is, as an account that overestimates the "resistance" power of popular culture and mistakes the artistic expression of oppression for the practical undoing of its material and political causes.

Ellison's "yes" to American democracy never translated into political action, as his critics in the 1960s were quick to point out. The freedom imagined in *Invisible Man* becomes so universal a principle of enlightenment (recall the room of bulbs and the subversive appropriation of the power grid) that it fails to stay connected to the particulars of the black experience in America. When the Civil Rights movement sought to take to the streets with that "yes" as a weapon of political action, it continued to invoke Jefferson's words. Martin Luther King takes up the theme of the Declaration during his "I Have a Dream" speech at the 1963 March on Washington, combining the oratorical authority of Douglass's cry against injustice with Ellison's idealistic affirmation.[4]

Speaking from the steps of the Lincoln Memorial, King begins by recalling the "Gettysburg Address":

> Five score years ago, a great American, in whose symbolic shadow we stand today, signed the Emancipation Proclamation. This momentous decree came as a great beacon light of hope to millions of Negro slaves who had been seared in the flames of withering injustice. It came as a joyous daybreak to end the long night of their captivity. But one hundred years later, the Negro still is not free; one hundred years later, the life of the Negro is still sadly crippled by the manacles of segregation and the chains of discrimination; one hundred years later, the Negro lives on a lonely island of poverty in the midst of a vast ocean of material prosperity; one hundred years later, the Negro is still languished in the corners of American society and finds himself in exile in his own land.

So much reminds us of Douglass: the cadence, the imagery, the syntactic parallelisms, the evocation of the sermon and the jeremiad. Strategically, though, what interests us is King's implicit comparison of his speech to Lincoln's "Gettysburg Address," perhaps the most famous instance of American democratic rhetoric. King understands that the Civil Rights movement is a continuation of the Civil War by other means. Lincoln had followed (reluctantly) the abolitionist tradition of applying the Declaration and its rights to an unintended beneficiary: the enslaved Africans of America (see Wills, *Lincoln*). The "Gettysburg Address" expresses that extension by first quoting Jefferson's lines: *"Fourscore and seven years ago our fathers brought forth upon this continent, a new nation, conceived in liberty, and dedicated to the proposition that all men are created equal."* (I quote from the first draft, known as the Nicolay version.) Unless we read the "Gettysburg Address" within this context, as one more invocation of Jefferson in a line stretching back through Douglass and William Wells Brown and David Walker, we may miss how pointedly it in fact refers to the liberation of African Americans. In citing Lincoln, or in appropriating him subversively, King reclaims the "Gettysburg Address" for the purposes of the Civil Rights movement, even as he goes on to iterate the undone work of reconstruction.

In once more citing Jefferson, however, King does not restrict his language to the rhetoric of democracy. Instead, his often biblical imagery suddenly takes a very material turn, as he reminds his audience that the "riches of freedom" are counted in money as well as votes:

> When the architects of our republic wrote the magnificent words of the Constitution and the Declaration of Independence, they were signing a promissory note to which every American was to fall heir. This note was a promise that all men, yes, black men as well as white men, would be guaranteed the unalienable rights of life, liberty, and the pursuit of happiness. It is obvious today that America has defaulted on this promissory note in so far as her citizens of color are concerned. Instead of honoring this sacred obligation, America has given the Negro people a bad check; a check which has come back marked "insufficient funds."

King circumvents the intentionalist reading of the Declaration and the Constitution (documents which certainly did not intend to extend the freedoms of citizenship to people of color) by reconstruing them as "promissory notes," or writings of a utopian cast. This recasting puts the founding fathers and their heirs under an obligation which, however morally and politically right, does not strictly follow from the original documents. But from Abigail Adams to Abraham Lincoln to King, this has become standard procedure in uses of the Declaration. More interesting in King's rhetorical troping of the Declaration and Constitution as "promissory notes" is his implication that they constitute economic as well as political obligations. While accounts of the Civil Rights movement sometimes divide its emphases into first a legal and then an economic phase, King's speech shows that black Americans always saw the link between the two, as the boycott in Birmingham earlier that year demonstrated.

The most quoted passage of King's speech is that now-titular paragraph in which he tells us that "I still have a dream. It is a dream deeply rooted in the

American dream. I have a dream that one day this nation will rise up and live out the true meaning of its creed. 'We hold these truths to be self-evident, that all men are created equal.'" Playing (or signifyin') on that most clichéd of phrases ("the American dream"), King's reiterated "I have a dream" comes to have some of the same aggressive, ironic, even caustic, force one could hear in Walker, Fern, and Douglass (though King's performance stuck to tones of righteousness and avoided pronouncing the bitterness of the speech's content). In asserting that he, too, has a dream, King both contests the exclusion of African Americans from the American dream and insists rhetorically on their place within it (a place that has often been imagined by whites as the scene of a haunting nightmare). The integrationist, appropriative terms of King's dream of racial harmony and transcendence ("I have a dream that my four little children will one day live in a nation where they will not be judged by the color of their skin, but by the content of their character") so expertly express the dogmas of official American idealism that he leaves the white audience watching on TV with few authorized means of resistance. At the same time, his image of the promissory note implies an ambiguity in "the American dream": Is it a dream of civil and political freedoms, or a dream of economic possibilities? Given the economic infrastructure of racism, can it be both? Since a promise belongs to the realm of moral action, what kind of ethos does the "promissory note" of "the American dream" require? To whom was that note issued? And what will it take to pay the debt? Do we have the economic, cultural, and spiritual funds, or are they insufficient? The shape of multicultural America's dilemmas in subsequent decades has its roots in these questions.

King would come down from the mountain only to be assassinated while assisting a sanitation workers' strike in Memphis as part of his "poor people's campaign." By 1968 his "American" credentials were in dispute because of his opposition to the Vietnam War and his emphasis on economic issues rather than civil rights. Criticism from black militants and harassment from J. Edgar Hoover's FBI further eroded King's capacity to hold together an American dream capacious enough to unite people across races. For his part, Ellison never did finish his much-awaited second novel. The "yes" Ellison pronounced in *Invisible Man* gave voice to a dream he found it hard to fulfill, as if the energy expended in upholding his *belief* in freedom robbed him of what force he needed to achieve something more in art (or politics). Ellison did write a series of powerful and problematic essays on literature, art, and cultural politics (collected in *Shadow and Act* and *Going to the Territory*) which, together with *Invisible Man,* deeply influenced the development of African American criticism and such practitioners as Houston Baker and Henry Louis Gates Jr. In retrospect, however, it is not surprising that it was the black nationalist, black aesthetic, and women's liberation movements that predominated in black cultural and literary studies from the 1960s to the 1990s, rather than any vision growing out of the work of

King and Ellison. In the dialectic of cultural struggle, their integrationist work in the arenas of political idealism and artistic universalism would inevitably have to make way for the claims of the particular and the material—of the *differences* that came to be the chief theme of contemporary cultural studies.

Of course, King and Ellison were always there alongside Malcolm X, Alice Walker, Amiri Baraka, Toni Morrison, Jesse Jackson, Albert Murray, Cornel West, and the others. It has just been difficult of late to know where to place King and Ellison, since the liberal tradition they belong to has been subject to so much critique in the less idealistic years since King's death. In trying to move the dialectic again and to pick up the thread of their legacies, I think we can borrow profitably on the promissory note of the tradition, as this essay has tried to show. The various calls for a "rainbow coalition," for "intercultural dialogue" and "the politics of recognition," and even for "multiculturalism" are symptomatic of an effort to declare a new "we the people," though there remain good reasons to fear any rush to revive patriotic community unless it is built on a foundation of historical memory and mutual care.

Meditating in *Shadow and Act* on the black writer's contradictory relation to the American dream and its fictional tradition, Ellison observes that "though as passionate believers in democracy Negroes identify themselves with the broader American ideals, their sense of reality springs, in part, from an American experience which most white men not only have not had, but one with which they are reluctant to identify themselves even when presented in forms of the imagination" (25). As I see it, the tradition of radical reform in American literary and cultural studies says "yes" to democracy in just the double-edged way Ellison describes. This affirmation obligates us to engage in complex and difficult acts of identification and imagination. On occasion we will need to affirm that which we have not experienced or, in politics, say "yes" even when the Supreme Court, from Dred Scott to yesterday, says "no." Although the America of which many dream has yet to be born, and may exceed the boundary of any nation-state, the outlines of its ethos have already begun to form as the cultural struggles of the late twentieth century take their next turns. One of those is the "ethical turn" now apparent in various arenas, from academic theory to the political marketplace. If an ethos is a way of life, combining the certainties of knowledge with the uncertainties of ideals and beliefs, what ethos follows from today's struggles for representation? Looking back to 1776 and forward beyond 1996, I think this ethos could be one that is accountable to history's horrors, that dreams of a community of stories, that is merciless in exposing the practices of injustice, that emphasizes the responsibility of individuals to each other, and that acknowledges that power without a vision of the good is a hollow goal.

Notes

1. The faculties of rationality and the moral sense were often used to construct this subjectivity (and to define those groups outside its borders). The essential study here is certainly Garry Wills's *Inventing America*. But Wills, in my judgment, often goes a bit far in exonerating Jefferson for his prejudices and racism. (See chapter 15, for example, where Jefferson's often prurient remarks on the inferiority of Negroes are implausibly balanced by his sentimental respect for the moral sense of slaves.) As I shall show, Wills exaggerates the "obscurity" into which the Declaration fell and underestimates the degree of influence its ideas immediately had among disenfranchised portions of the new American population.

2. For an account of the speech's context, see McFeely, *Frederick Douglass,* 172–73. For the complete text of the address see Blassingame, *Douglass Papers* 2:359–88. The tradition of ironically citing the Declaration continued into the twentieth century, as can be seen in depictions of the Fourth of July in Audre Lorde's *Zami* and Alice Walker's *The Color Purple.* Martin Luther King Jr.'s invocation of the Declaration will be examined later in this chapter.

3. History has a way of continuing to ignore these voices. In his marvelous volume on *Lincoln at Gettysburg,* Garry Wills focuses most of his attention on the centrality of the Declaration of Independence to Lincoln's political thought, and Wills presents detailed reviews of how white politicians in the era appropriated Jefferson's document. Unaccountably, there is no mention of Walker, Douglass, the Declaration of Sentiments, or any other instances from the counter-tradition I have sketched. Wills's analysis of how Lincoln interprets the Declaration as an idealistic promise would have been strengthened (and made more historically accurate) had he included a more diverse set of sources for his study. Lincoln's interpretation appears less novel when one considers how long it had been articulated by African Americans protesting slavery.

4. The speech King delivered was based on a carefully written and revised text, though King appeared to depart from it when he improvised the final section containing the "I have a dream" passages. This and other sections, however, represented reworkings of material King had been using for a number of years. Published versions of the speech are based on the delivered one, though the speech has often been reprinted with minor discrepancies. Some of these originate in the first publication of the speech in the *Negro History Bulletin,* which presumably drew on the prepared as well as the delivered text. For background and analyses see the essays collected in Calloway-Thomas and Lucaites. The edition of 1993 authorized by King's wife and daughter carries this note: "Disclaimer: The words that appear here are the original words written by Martin Luther King Jr., and are slightly different from the words Reverend King spoke on August 28, 1963." But King and his biographers confirmed that the latter part of the speech departed from the "original" written text; perhaps the Kings are referring to the written version King gave to the *Negro History Bulletin.* A still different version, closer to but not exactly the same as the delivered one, is available from the Martin Luther King Jr. Papers Project Web site at Stanford University. I have used this version and checked it against videotape of the speech.

Works Cited

Aptheker, Herbert, ed. *From the Colonial Times through the Civil War.* Vol. 1 of *A Documentary History of the Negro People in the United States.* New York: Citadel, 1951.

Bardes, Barbara and Suzanne Gossett. *Declarations of Independence: Women and Political Power in Nineteenth-Century American Fiction.* New Brunswick, NJ: Rutgers UP, 1990.

Berlant, Lauren. "The Female Woman: Fanny Fern and the Form of Sentiment." *American Literary History* 3 (1991): 429–54.

Blassingame, John W., ed. *The Frederick Douglass Papers. Series 1: Speeches, Debates, and Interviews.* New Haven: Yale UP, 1982.

Brown, William Wells. *Clotel, or The President's Daughter* (1853). Ed. William Edward Farrison. New York: Carol Publishing Group, 1989. Also reprinted in William L. Andrews, ed., *Three Classic African-American Novels.* New York: Mentor, 1990.

Buhle, Mari Jo and Paul Buhle. eds. *The Concise History of Woman Suffrage: Selections from the Classic Work of Stanton, Anthony, Gage, and Harper.* Urbana: U of Illinois P, 1978.

Calloway-Thomas, Carolyn and John Louis Lucaites, eds. *Martin Luther King, Jr., and the Sermonic Power of Public Discourse.* Tuscaloosa: U of Alabama P, 1993.

Chevigny, Bell Gale. *The Woman and the Myth: Margaret Fuller's Life and Writings.* New York: Feminist Press, 1976.

Derrida, Jacques. "Declarations of Independence." *New Political Science* 15 (1986): 7–15.

Ellison, Ralph. *Shadow and Act.* New York: Random House, 1964.

———. *Invisible Man.* New York: Vintage, 1952.

———. *Going to the Territory.* New York: Random House, 1987.

Fern, Fanny (Sara Payson Willis Parton). *Ruth Hall and Other Writings.* New Brunswick, NJ: Rutgers UP, 1986.

Fliegelman, Jay. *Declaring Independence: Jefferson, Natural Language, and the Culture of Performance.* Stanford: Stanford UP, 1993.

Gitlin, Todd. "On the Virtues of a Loose Canon." *Beyond P.C.: Toward a Politics of Understanding.* Ed. Patricia Aufderheide. St. Paul, MN: Graywolf Press, 1992. 185–90.

Hollinger, David A. *Postethnic America: Beyond Multiculturalism.* New York: Basic Books, 1995.

King, Martin Luther, Jr. "I Have a Dream." *Negro History Bulletin* 21 (May 1968): 16–17.

———. *I Have a Dream.* 1963. San Francisco: Harper Collins, 1993.

Lauter, Paul. *Canons and Contexts.* New York: Oxford UP, 1991.

Lauter, Paul, ed. *The Heath Anthology of American Literature.* 2nd edition. 2 vols. Lexington, MA: D.C. Heath, 1994.

Lind, Michael. *The Next American Nation: The New Nationalism and the Fourth American Revolution.* New York: Free Press, 1995.

McFeely, William S. *Frederick Douglass.* New York: Norton, 1991.

Morrison, Toni. *Playing in the Dark: Whiteness and the Literary Imagination.* New York: Random House, 1992.

O'Connell, Barry, ed. *On Our Own Ground: The Complete Writings of William Apess, A Pequot.* Amherst: University of Massachusetts Press, 1992.

Reising, Russell. *The Unusable Past: Theory and the Study of American Literature.* New York: Methuen, 1986.

Shumway, David. *Creating American Civilization: A Genealogy of American Literature as an Academic Discipline.* Minneapolis: U of Minnesota P, 1994.

Tise, Larry E. *Proslavery: A History of the Defense of Slavery in America, 1701–1840.* Athens: U Georgia P, 1987.

Walker, David. *David Walker's Appeal, in Four Articles, Together with a Preamble, to the Coloured Citizens of the World, But in Particular, and Very Expressly, to Those of the United States of America* (1829). Ed. Charles M. Wiltse. New York: Hill and Wang, 1965.

Watts, Jerry Gafio. *Heroism and the Black Intellectual: Ralph Ellison, Politics, and the Afro-American Intellectual Life.* Chapel Hill: U of North Carolina P, 1994.

Wills, Garry. *Inventing America: Jefferson's Declaration of Independence.* New York: Random House, 1978.

———. *Lincoln at Gettysburg: The Words that Remade America.* New York: Simon and Schuster, 1992.

2 "Not in the Least American": Nineteenth-Century Literary Regionalism as unAmerican Literature

Judith Fetterley
University at Albany, SUNY

My title comes from a book called *Deephaven,* published in 1877 by a writer named Sarah Orne Jewett. In this book Jewett describes the experiences two young women have when they choose to spend the summer in a little town in Maine rather than remaining in Boston or traveling with friends or family. The summer in Deephaven becomes the occasion for a pause in the lives of Kate and Helen, taken before the presumptively inevitable plunge into marriage and motherhood, irreversible adulthood. Yet for one of the women, the narrator Helen, the pause provides the opportunity to interrogate, however indirectly, conventional wisdom on the subjects of marriage and motherhood, the definition of adulthood, and the value of the characteristics associated with it. For Jewett, who chose not to marry, who chose in one crucial sense not to grow up as her culture defined this process for women, writing *Deephaven* may have helped her acknowledge and understand this difference and may have enabled her four years later to enter into a life-long relationship with Annie Adams Fields, widow of James T. Fields, the man who made the *Atlantic Monthly,* founded Ticknor and Fields, and for twenty years served as the arbiter of what would be called American literature. Was Jewett's choice unAmerican? Is her book unAmerican?

Deephaven, Jewett's narrator declares, "was not in the least American. There was no excitement about anything; there were no manufactories; nobody seemed in the least hurry. The only foreigners were a few standard sailors. I do not know when a house or a new building of any kind had been built" (84). I take this text as my starting point in proposing the term "unAmerican" as a way of thinking about a particular body of nineteenth-century texts and as a way of describing a particular critical stance, for when Jewett refers to the town of Deephaven as "not in the least American" I read her as thus marking the difference of her own text from what even in the 1870s could be considered American literature. In this context we might note the choice of another writer, Henry James, who appropriated the term "American" for the novel he published in 1877, the same year as Jewett published *Deephaven,* and who thus signaled his ambition to write a specifically American novel, perhaps even "the great American novel" (see Spengemann 98–114).

While the term "unAmerican," like all terms constructed in opposition, is problematic by virtue of its connection to the very thing it opposes, it has the advantage of foregrounding the degree to which the term "American" in the context of American literature has always referred to certain thematic content and to the values associated with that content. "American" has in this sense always been political. Thinking of texts as unAmerican has the added advantage of moving the question of the canon beyond tokenism; for it suggests that the controversy over what we teach cannot be resolved by merely adding a woman and/or a minority male writer to our syllabi since not all texts by women or minority males challenge the values currently associated with the term "American" in the context of American literature. While adding texts by women and minority males to our courses and syllabi is necessary political work, it is not sufficient, for we may well ask how much has been gained if black men establish personhood through invoking sexism or if white women establish personhood through invoking racism. It is, for example, no accident that I have sought to recover the tradition of American literary regionalism as opposed to, say, the body of anti-Tom texts written by white Southern women in the years following the publication of *Uncle Tom's Cabin* and preceding the Civil War. For in the texts of literary regionalism I find the values that lead me to critique the canon in the first place; that is, in regionalism I find a literature that models a subjectivity attained by standing up for others, not on them. Invoking the concept of "unAmerican" thus helps focus attention on the significance of which texts by minority males and women we choose to include. Finally, figuring one's critical stance as unAmerican provides a way of thinking about one's activity that does justice to its political intent and recognizes the dangers which attend it.

In this essay, I wish to model what Paul Lauter has labeled canonical criticism, a criticism that focuses on "how we construct our syllabi and anthologies, on the roots of our systems of valuation, and on how we decide what is important for us to teach and for our students to learn" (134), and specifically that form of canonical criticism which, in the words of Jane Marcus and Lillian Robinson, takes treason as its text. "Canon critique," a term I prefer to "canonical criticism" (which can perhaps be misread as traditional interpretation of the current canon), has been from the outset overtly political, concerned with issues of power and aligned with certain values. As an overtly political criticism, canon critique has sought to expose the political nature of the processes of canon formation and literary valuation, asking such questions as these: By what specific historical processes have certain texts become canonical? What politics have informed these processes? What politics inform the definitions of aesthetic value that accompany such processes? Lending still greater urgency to these questions is a context of increasing pressure to "get back to basics," and to create a set body of texts that will define what is American and who is literate. Indeed, as Paul Lauter comments, "it would not be too much to say that canonical criticism constitutes a part of a broader effort to reconstruct our society, and particularly our educational institutions, on a more democratic and equitable basis" (144–45).

In the field of American literature canon critique has sought to expose how the term "American" has been used to create a literary canon so hegemonic in the privileging of certain subjectivities as to make the term unAmerican not simply politically useful but actually meaningful. The equation of American literature with a handful of texts written by white men, primarily of Anglo-Saxon ethnicity and middle or upper middle-class backgrounds, with formal and thematic coherence sufficient to enable a theory of the "Americanness" of American literature, began in the early decades of the nineteenth century (see Baym, "Early Histories," and Brodhead, *Hawthorne* 48–66). Paul Lauter, Nina Baym, and Elizabeth Renker, however, have focused our attention on the middle decades of the twentieth century—when American literature became fully institutionalized as a field of study in colleges and universities—as the period which produced the map of American literature still operative today. Nina Baym has aptly labeled the canon established during these decades "melodramas of beset manhood" and has demonstrated how this paradigm ensures "that stories about women could not contain the essence of American culture" and thus "that the matter of American experience is inherently male" ("Melodramas" 130). Elizabeth Renker, in tracing how the First and Second World Wars created a context in which American literature could be read as engendering masculinity, has provided an additional context for understanding our current situation and in particular for understanding the connection between what we currently identify as American literature and certain formulations of our national interest.

To the degree that the analyses of Baym, Lauter, and Renker are correct, that what we currently accept as American literature implicitly and explicitly defines as American only certain persons and only the stories that serve the interests of those persons, then those of us who challenge the value of those texts and seek to disrupt the hegemony of the canon by recovering texts with different definitions and different stories are engaging in a process that could itself be described as unAmerican. And to the degree that the fictions we recognize as American serve the interests of those who also represent the state, the feminist critique of the American literary canon can be seen as a form of treason—a connection that explains the not-so-strange career of Lynne Cheney, perhaps the most politically motivated appointment in the history of the National Endowment for the Humanities, whose goal was to delegitimate, if she could not eradicate, the unAmerican activity of feminist canon critique. To put it another way, one can reasonably argue that American education at every level is currently organized to serve the needs of "boys" (here understood as a synecdo-che for Baym's "beset manhood") and that through what is taught and how it is taught our educational system ratifies boys' sense of agency, primacy, and sub-jectivity, particularly as defined against the objectivity of girls. Thus those of us who seek to place the needs of girls first—in our classroom practices, in our determination of course content, in our criticism—can be considered to be act-ing in an unAmerican, even treasonous fashion. For those of us who engage in feminist canon critique do so from a complex set of assumptions about the relation of identity to reading and writing practices. To put it simply, we assume a connection between the self-concept of a reader and the self imagined by and in a literary text. Thus, extrapolating again from Baym's argument and from my own argument in *The Resisting Reader,* the classic tradition of American litera-ture, by excluding women from the definition of "American," constructs the girl reading this tradition as herself unAmerican. To the degree, then, that our litera-ture cannot imagine the American as other than male, to that degree we who are women are already unAmerican. So indeed let treason be our text.

I wish to use as my example of the "unAmerican," and as my basis for ex-ploring the political utility of this term, a body of texts produced in the United States primarily by women writing during the second half of the nineteenth century which Marjorie Pryse and I call literary regionalism and which we have gathered together in a Norton Anthology, *American Women Regionalists, 1850–1910 (AWR).* The obligatory use of the term "American" to describe this anthol-ogy for marketing purposes itself provides a rich context for thinking about the difficulties and even contradictions of our enterprise. For while some of the writers in this tradition may be familiar to readers—e.g., Chopin, Dunbar Nelson, Freeman, Jewett—most are marginal to, if not absent from, current American literary history. Absent as well is any concept of the tradition of nineteenth-century regionalist writing as we understand it. Though some of the writers and texts included in our anthology come into the field of American literature through the rubric of "regional realism" or "local color," understood as subsets of "real-ism" (see, for example, Berthoff 90–102, and Sundquist), these categories de-rive from a history of American literature based on the writing of men, one which privileges their work as the source of its definitions. Indeed, certain re-cent texts have sought to establish the specifically masculinist nature of real-ism, the dominant term in virtually all writing about American literature after the Civil War (see, for example, Habegger and Bell). While in the case of Michael Bell in *The Problem of American Realism,* this identification has the effect of allowing him to ask the question, "what Jewett made of American realism" (179), and thus of positioning Jewett as a potential alternative to the values of realism, he reads her only within the context of her entanglement with what he calls "realist thinking." Thus he concludes, not surprisingly, that the ambitious Nan Prince of *A Country Doctor* (1884) is "free" to defy tradition only by embracing it and that once Jewett left behind the ambition projected into the story of Nan Prince "she would appear to have left herself with no clear rationale or counter rationale to put in its place, and after *The Country of the Pointed Firs* there was no obvious direction for her career to go" (204). Hence the fall in 1902, which effectively ended her life as a writer, was for Bell "fortunate." Bell fails to recognize that Jewett's work derives from a tradition of women's writing that goes back at least as far as the end of the eighteenth century and Maria Edgeworth, a tradition developed through the first half of the nineteenth century by writers such as Mitford, Stowe, Cary, and Cooke, and practiced by Jewett's contemporaries and acquaintances such as Thaxter, Murfree, and Freeman. In Bell's version of American literary history Jewett appears as an isolated individual struggling to create an alternative to oppose to the dominant discourse of realism and failing precisely because of her isolation and because realism is finally the only game in town. In a different version of American literary history, but perhaps not called that, Jewett might appear as a particularly talented practitioner of a long-established tradition, seeking to critique the self-consciously masculine "new" realism from a larger historical perspective.

And here I might observe that the elegiac tone Michael Bell adopts for his discussion of Jewett finds echo in Eric Sundquist's chapter in the *Columbia Literary History of the United States*. Sundquist subsumes regionalism under the rubric of local color and identifies it as "a literature of memory" (508), a memory, he observes, "often lodged in the vestiges of a world of female domesticity" (509). This reading bears an uncanny resemblance to the process Laura Romero has analyzed in "Vanishing Americans: Gender, Empire, and New Historicism," a process in which the elegiac mode of cultural and literary history performs the "historical sleight of hand" of representing "the disappearance of the native as not just natural but as having already happened" (385). Both Michael Bell in *The Problem of American Realism* and Richard Brodhead in *Cultures of Letters* position their reading of Jewett in relation to what they see as an overtly feminist effort to recuperate Jewett for contemporary readers (see Bell 197 ff. and Brodhead 142–144), and both participate in a process I would call the "re-vanishing" of Jewett—Brodhead by seeking to dismantle the conceptual framework which has led to her recuperation and Bell by suggesting that she can not finally be distinguished from the masculinist enterprise of realism. In Sundquist's chapter the palpable politics of the discourse over Jewett is itself "vanished" to re-emerge as a description of her disappearance as "having already happened."

While Marjorie Pryse and I retain the term "regional" in our name for this tradition, in part to focus attention on the significance of place to the production, reception, and content of this writing, and in part to avail ourselves of whatever recognition currently obtains from its present usage, we seek primarily through this term to create a category parallel to and thus potentially of equal importance to that of realism. And we seek as well to create a framework that will enable us to see connections, origins, and aims that remain obscure if we continue to subsume the work of regionalist writers under the category of realism. In creating the category of regionalism, then, we seek to model the effect on our understanding of American literature of deriving our map of American literary history from an analysis of the work of women. That this constitutes an unAmerican activity may be inferred from the fact that presentation of our work invariably leads to the question, "Weren't there any men writing regionalist fiction between 1850 and 1910?"— a question which barely contains the anxiety that men might be excluded from an American tradition or that certain male writers (for example, Charles Chesnutt) might best be understood in a context created by the work of women and subsumed within a category primarily female.

In asking readers to engage with the tradition of regionalist writing and in identifying the stakes of this engagement, I seek to provide a context within which the concepts of "unAmerican" and "treason" have meaning. For one can perhaps understand the intent of the effort to write Jewett out of history before she is even in, to "re-vanish" her, if one considers the effect of choosing Jewett's *The Country of the Pointed Firs* as *the* required American text for an eighth grade English class or a freshman introductory literature course; or of organizing an entire course in American literature around the issues it raises; or even of introducing it in an American literature survey. As my students like to point out, "This isn't an American book. It has no story and it is all about old women and a few old men. There isn't an American in it." Or consider the effect of defining Sylvy, the protagonist of "A White Heron," as an American cultural hero, a girl who comes to understand (hetero)sexuality as sexual harassment, the great red-faced boy who used to chase and frighten her in town reappearing in the form of the "nice" boy with a gun who seeks to kill and stuff "the very birds he seemed to like so much" (*AWR* 201); a girl who chooses to renounce the world, her chance of being an "American," perhaps even nationality itself, in favor of a bird's life. My students can't understand why she doesn't promise to marry the hunter when she grows up, and so we talk about domestic violence and why so much romance should end in so much battering.

My use of the term "unAmerican" presents one final question which I wish to raise here. In introducing literature currently considered unAmerican, is our goal to redefine the meaning of "American," to make it possible for girls to be Americans too? Or is the goal to replace the term "American" entirely? Can significant change be accomplished without renaming the field? Or has the term "American" become so profoundly associated with certain values that in order to introduce literature with different values into the field we will need to do nothing less than to cease using the term "American" and develop instead an alternative term, for example, "Writing in the U.S.," as Gregory Jay has suggested in "The End of 'American' Literature"? To put the matter another way, can the term "American" be recuperated for a different set of values or does its energy, its power, its eroticism derive from the values currently associated with it? Yet if we abandon the term are we not complicit in the very pattern we protest, and, by leaving all that power in the "wrong" hands, have we not made as well a major political error? On the other hand, can we have the power without a price? And is it possible that our very attachment to the term "American" derives precisely from those values which have precluded the participation of all but a few persons in the literary and cultural definition of the term in the first place? By playing with the terms "American" and "unAmerican," I seek thus to join the effort to identify the naming of the field of "American literature" as itself a site of contestation, not so much because I care what name we give it as because I care what values we promote through it. In seeking to gain readers for these texts, I seek nothing less than the creation of a citizenry committed to the values of inclusion, empathy, diversity, and community, and the cultural change which would follow upon the creation of such a citizenry. And in bringing attention to texts which have historically been excluded from the canon of American literature, I seek to model the process of inclusion and the change which it can accomplish, whether the end result be a redefined American literature or a new name for our enterprise.

If Huckleberry Finn, white boy on the run from the "sivilization" of women, provides the paradigm for how "our" literature has constructed the American, then a story like Mary Wilkins Freeman's "On the Walpole Road"—which opens with a description of a woman "who might have been seventy" with "a double bristling chin" (*AWR* 306), driving slowly along a road in company with another woman who was "younger—forty perhaps"—marks a difference, just as in *The Country of the Pointed Firs* Mrs. Todd, a woman of sixty-seven, and Mrs. Blackett, a woman in her eighties, pass on their knowledge to the younger generation defined as a woman in her forties, "perhaps." A literature which foregrounds old women rather than boys hardly seems American; it is as if the Widow Douglas were to take the story away from Huck.

But when we consider more closely that "bristling" chin, we realize that regionalism's understanding of story must be as different as its understanding of character, for women with bristling chins are not capable of generating those stories we have come to think of as American nor even those other fictions not quite so American, those novels whose business it is to negotiate the marriage of girls. Indeed, I would argue that literary regionalism occurs primarily in the form of the sketch or short story because this form made it possible to tell stories about elderly women with bristling chins, about women for whom the eventful means something other than marriage, about women in relation to each other, about women who take care of themselves. In "A New England Nun," one of the few regionalist texts that might be considered well-known, Freeman makes this feature of regionalist writing the subject of the fiction itself, for in this story Louisa Ellis comes to realize that her meaningful event is not the marriage she has awaited for fourteen years but the ritualized and sacramental life she has created during those years, feeding herself "with as much grace as if she had been a veritable guest to her own self" (*AWR* 356). Similarly, Jewett's "A White Heron," one of the few regionalist texts to feature a young girl as its protagonist, dramatizes Sylvy's instinctive swerve away from the seemingly inevitable heterosexual plot, her choice of her own life over the hunter's need. In that pause which halts the headlong rush, in that Deephaven time-out, regionalism creates its own "world elsewhere" which has yet to be recognized as American—no doubt in part because our current understanding of American cannot encompass the privileging of women's relations to themselves or other women over their relation to men. Indeed, since the literature we call American romanticizes the relation of boy to boy and man to man while it denies, if it does not vilify, the love of women for women and presents women primarily as rivals for the attention of boys and men, *Deephaven* deserves the accolade of unAmerican for its devotion to inscribing romantic love between women and the "deephaven" of female friendship.[1]

If the sketch provided the form which made it possible to talk about unAmerican women—women with bristling chins, women who love other women, women who love themselves, women who choose birds over boys—it did so precisely because such fictions could not be candidates for the accolade "great American novel." Indeed, the vexed relation of the form of regionalist writing to the definition of great American literature can best be demonstrated by *The Country of the Pointed Firs*. This text, which Jewett herself referred to as "papers," has defied efforts to define it as a novel and puzzled readers who have previously tried to label it. In concluding her preface to the edition of *The Country of the Pointed Firs* published in 1925, Willa Cather writes, "If I were asked to name three American books which have the possibility of a long, long life, I would say at once, '*The Scarlet Letter,*' '*Huckleberry Finn,*' and '*The Country of the Pointed Firs.*'" If Jewett recognized that she had to write a novel-length book in order to have a chance at the "immortality" predicted by Cather, she nevertheless refused in so doing to relinquish the essential identity of the sketch, no doubt one reason why her text has not in fact had the kind of life Cather predicted for it. And while Jewett's genius enabled her to find a way to write a novel-length regionalist text and thus to seek for regionalist fiction the status associated with length, the very fact that she needed to do this underscores the marginal status of the sketch in American literature. Yet if the marginal status of the sketch form was the price that had to be paid to gain the discursive freedom of regionalism, and if literary regionalists sold their birthright to be considered great American writers to gain that discursive freedom, they too, like Louisa Ellis, could be said not to "know it, the taste of the pottage was so delicious" (*AWR* 365). For, as Freeman suggests, pottage may be preferable to persons excluded from rights and required to cook.

In honor of the deliciousness of pottage, Marjorie Pryse and I have chosen the phrase "free to say" as the working title for our book on regionalist fiction. This title comes from a story by Rose Terry Cooke, "Miss Beulah's Bonnet," first published in 1880 in *Harper's*. In this story an elderly woman, having opened her house to her niece and her niece's children, Sarah, Janey, and Jack, finds herself "free to say I never did like boys. I suppose divine Providence ordained 'em to some good end; but it takes a sight o' grace to believe it: and of all the boys that ever was sent into this world for any purpose, I do believe he is the hatefulest" (*AWR* 130). Published four years after Mark Twain's *The Adventures of Tom Sawyer,* "Miss Beulah's Bonnet" can be read as an item in a dialogue about boys as a privileged subject of American literature and culture, and Miss Beulah's "free to say I never did like boys" can be read as Cooke's articulation of her desire to be free to write about women with "bristling" chins. Though Miss Beulah's "boy" refers to an actual Jack, we feel free to read "boys" as referring to a cluster of values associated with that word, and we see regionalism as originating in part in the desire to participate in a dialogue which challenges those values by doing something other than "liking boys."

Regionalist writers were themselves aware of the difficulties they faced in trying to create a space in American literature for stories which assert that bonnets matter more than boys, and they both addressed these difficulties in their fiction and developed strategies for circumventing them. For regionalist writers to be able to tell stories about bonnets rather than boys, they had to imagine audiences capable of hearing and reading such stories. In "Miss Beulah's Bonnet," Miss Beulah finds herself unable to attend church because her new bonnet, hidden under the cushion of a chair by Jack, gets smashed when the stout Mrs. Blake unwittingly sits on it during a visit. When the deacons come to interrogate Miss Beulah about her absence from church, they are confounded by her explanation:

> "Well, if you must know, I hain't got no bunnit."
> The deacons stared mutually; and Deacon Morse, . . . curious as men naturally are, asked abruptly, "Why not?"
> "'Cause Miss Blake sot on it."
> The two men looked at each other in blank amazement, and shook their heads. Here was a pitfall. Was it proper, dignified, possible to investigate this truly feminine tangle? They were dying to enter into particulars, but ashamed to do so; nothing was left but retreat" (*AWR* 135).

Because the culture associated with the church defines Miss Beulah's story as a trivial feminine tangle, hers is not a story that can be told or heard in church; and since the deacons are there in their official capacity as churchmen who must report back to their congregation, they cannot hear her story because they cannot imagine telling it. Indeed, within Cooke's fiction Miss Beulah's story only gets told by a woman to other women, within the separate sphere of the sewing circle, though we may suppose that the women go home and tell their husbands. In describing the deacons as dying to enter into particulars but ashamed to do so, Cooke herself constructs men as a rich potential audience for her story, just as she suggests that "girls'" stories may not get fully heard until men can imagine themselves telling them. In writing *her* story for a readership obviously comprised of men as well as women, she proposes that men in the privacy of reading can satisfy their desire to enter a truly feminine tangle without the loss of status that would attend a public acknowledgment of their curiosity. Yet such a proposition reveals men to be boys, governed primarily by the peer pressures of male bonding, formalized in such institutions as the church. In this context, male bonding, that holiest of holies in American culture (as witness the rituals of Superbowl Sunday), takes on a negative cast as Cooke challenges men to commit the treason of admitting in public in front of other men their interest in and connection to women's lives. In a culture obsessed with the question of why *Johnny* can't read and insistent on providing boys' stories to lure Johnny into literacy (since, as one elementary school teacher put it to me, girls will read stories about boys but boys won't read stories about girls), to ask men to hear and tell women's stories may indeed be unAmerican. Yet, as Cooke implies, what's truly shameful is a construction of masculinity that makes boys ashamed to read girls' stories.

For those of us interested in the unAmerican act of getting Janey to read, regionalism not only provides "girls'" stories but models as well the importance for women of having and telling their stories. In the figure of her own Janey, Cooke presents the situation of woman and story in a world of boys. Jack preserves the letter of his own honesty by making his little sister hide Miss Beulah's bonnet; he then terrifies her into silence with "wild threats of bears and guns" (*AWR* 126) and quickly distracts her so that she soon forgets what she has done. In creating women who come to recognize that they have a story and who become empowered to tell their story, regionalist fiction seeks to construct women as storyful rather than storyless and to connect having and telling stories to their sanity and survival. In "Sister Liddy," Freeman identifies having a story to tell as the one thing that maintains the sanity and dignity of the old women who are inmates of the county poorhouse. Polly Moss, whose physical deformity adds another dimension to her struggle, temporarily comes into her own in this strife-ridden community when she makes up and tells a series of stories about her imaginary sister Liddy. Similarly, in "The Praline Woman," Alice Dunbar-Nelson shows the significance of story to a working-class woman of color who is determined to share her stories with her customers and who exercises considerable ingenuity to find openings in the chatter of commerce for such an exchange. Of Jewett we could say that the entire art of *The Country of the Pointed Firs* lies in creating a written text that can identify women as a rich source of story and as storytellers, through characters such as Mrs. Todd but more importantly still through the narrator herself, who must find the way to write them down.

In seeking to empower persons made silent or vacant through terror to tell stories which the dominant culture labels trivial, regionalism seeks to change our perspective and thus to destabilize the meaning of margin and center. For including the story of one previously silenced and marginalized inevitably affects the definition of margin and center and calls into question the values that have produced such definitions. In *Deephaven* Jewett specifically associates this process with the category of the American, seeking thus to unsettle and destabilize our understanding of that term. In a chapter entitled "The Circus at Denby," Kate and Helen attend a circus. At the end of the day, their companion, Mrs. Kew, declares an interest in the side shows and they enter the tent containing the Kentucky Giantess, for, as Mrs. Kew says, "she never heard of such a thing as a woman's weighing six hundred and fifty pounds" (106). When Kate and Helen return from looking at the monkeys, an added attraction of this side show, they find Mrs. Kew engaged in conversation with the giantess who turns out to be someone Mrs. Kew used to know. In a quiet but momentous revolution, the freak turns out to be a neighbor with a story and a history and a secret and feelings, and as we read this account and experience this revolution we are forced to question definitions of center and margin, normal and freak, national and regional. Positioned as a spectacle for those who can afford to pay to see her and offered up as a subject for their conversation, the fat lady is not herself meant to speak. By placing cages of monkeys on the same platform as the giantess, the entrepreneur running the show seeks to rationalize the category of freak as somehow not really human and as therefore available for profit and use to exhibitor and viewer alike. Thus when the fat lady does in fact speak and the "freak" becomes "somebody's neighbor" (the title Cooke gave to her 1881 collection of regionalist fiction) the rationalization collapses and the category it has sustained no longer seems inherent. Once revealed as constructed, it can then be deconstructed.

In the second half of the chapter, Kate and Helen attend an evening lecture on "The Elements of True Manhood." Evoking here the Emersonian doctrine of self-reliance, Jewett associates this event with the issue of who is and is not included in the term "American." The young white man who comes to Deephaven to deliver this lecture assumes that in talking of and to himself he addresses everyone. His use of the stage as a place from which to speak at an audience expected to remain silent—so different from the arrangements of the fat lady—confirms his assumption of his own centrality. The lecture would seem to contrast with the circus, yet in Jewett's hands it comes to seem far more of a "show" than the circus itself. "You would have thought," observes Helen, "the man was addressing an enthusiastic Young Men's Christian Association. He exhorted with fervor upon our duties as citizens and as voters, and told us a great deal about George Washington and Benjamin Franklin, whom he urged us to choose as our examples" (110). And she continues, "If the lecture had been upon any other subject it would not have been so hard for Kate and me to keep sober faces; but it was directed entirely toward young men, and there was not a young man there" (110). As the lecture drones on, we come to see the lecturer himself as crazy for delivering a talk on the elements of true manhood to an audience composed entirely of old men, women, and children. Yet his failure to recognize his audience, and the arrogant solipsism implicit in this failure, reflects a larger cultural madness. For young men do not represent the majority of the population in Deephaven or anywhere else, and a culture that devotes itself entirely to the feeding of boys as if they constituted the whole human race, and that has nothing to say to old men, women, and children, is crazy if not malicious. After they have laughed long and hard, Kate and Helen come to see "the pitiful side of it all" (111) and send a contribution to the lecturer to help pay his expenses. Later they learn that he will repeat his lecture the following evening and, as Helen observes, "I have no doubt there were a good many women able to be out, and that he harvested enough ten-cent pieces to pay his expenses without our help" (111). While the chapter ends in anger, however subdued, we should memorialize Kate and Helen's laughter, their inability to keep sober during the lecture, as an instance of treason *in* the text and as a model of unAmerican activity.

Challenging and destabilizing the meaning of margin and center serves as a paradigm for regionalism's efforts to dismantle and deconstruct hierarchies based on the categories of gender, race, class, age, and region. While certainly not free itself of the infection of these hierarchies, regionalist fiction works toward dismantling the binary oppositions and the concomitant privileging of one item over the other that structures a culture dedicated to the elements of true manhood. Regionalist texts are astonishingly free of the dialect of gender that dominates most of nineteenth-century American writing by both men and women, for while regionalist fiction acknowledges gender differences, it recognizes these differences as the product of privilege, not biology. Jack is not so much born a nuisance as made one by the fact of living in a world run by deacons. And a story like Freeman's "A Church Mouse," which opens with the line, "I never heard of a woman's bein' saxton" (*AWR* 344), develops the position that such failures to hear exist not because of "nature" but because they help men maintain the privilege of not having to share the church with a "mouse" or the world with women. Hetty Fifield—old, poor, and homeless —fights for her own survival through pressing the revolutionary statement, "I dun know what difference that makes" (*AWR* 344).

Writing of a world inhabited by old men and women, Jewett creates a space to experiment with breaking down the rigid gender identities associated in her mind with the Emersonian definition of American. No figure in *The Country of the Pointed Firs* is more pathetic than Captain Littlepage, landlocked in the trivial feminine tangle of Dunnet Landing while longing for a world of high art, all lofty, lofty, and obsessed by the memory of another man's last voyage to the "end" of the world, the ultimately masculine adventure. Yet, ironically, those discoveries he has promised to pass on of "a kind of waiting place between this world an' the next" (*Firs* 26) are emblems of mediation, dissolution, blending—as if Jewett means to say, Go as far as possible toward one pole and you will arrive at a space that dissolves the idea of pole. For at the end of the world there seems to be a middle ground, a meeting place of this world and the next, emblematic of the dissolution of oppositional polarities. Yet while this space both obsesses and horrifies Captain Littlepage, for other characters and perhaps for Jewett herself this space functions as a desired goal. Thus Elijah Tilley places stakes in his fields to indicate, like buoys, the presence of rocks, declaring that "one trade helps another" (*Firs* 120), and in the absence of his wife has become himself a careful housekeeper (*Firs* 120). And thus Mrs. Blackett declares that "William has been son an' daughter both" (*Firs* 41). Regionalism's intention to dismantle race and gender differences finds succinct expression in Alice Dunbar-Nelson's "The Praline Woman." Here a praline-colored woman speaks a dialect which renders such distinctions temporarily inoperative: "'Ah, he's fine gal, is Didele'" (*AWR* 481). If this were American language, maybe we might not have a problem with gays in the military.

In regionalist fiction, the impulse to dissolve binary oppositions and destabilize the definition of margin and center through shifting our perspective begins with a feeling that can best be described as empathy, the capacity to imagine how someone else might feel, and we see regionalism as a fiction characterized, indeed inspired, by empathy. Regionalism's commitment to empathy serves to distinguish it from the post-Civil War local color movement under which regionalist writers are often subsumed. In local color writing, genteel narrators present regional characters to urban readers as instances of the quaint or queer. Such characters form a literary circus which serves to ratify readers' sense of their own normalcy and normativeness. Despite the gesture toward the local, then, local color writing in effect ratifies the hegemony of the "national" as a standard against which the local can be measured and found wanting. Regionalism, however, as we have seen from the instance of *Deephaven* and "The Circus at Denby," deconstructs the "national," revealing its presumed universality to be in fact the position of a certain, albeit privileged, group of locals.

In valuing empathy, regionalism proposes alternative behaviors to those which characterize the world of boys and, to the extent that boys are equated with the national, models behaviors not in the national interest. In "Miss Beulah's

Bonnet," Jack gets the reputation of a nuisance for his harassment of the hens, the cat, Nanny Starks, and even Miss Beulah herself, all creatures relatively defenseless against him. While empathy can obtain in a context of peers (as witness the impassioned defense of Beulah Larkin by Mary Jane Beers, the milliner who made her bonnet) regionalist fiction presents empathy primarily as a model for the relationships of "persons" with differing amounts of cultural power. By modeling an alternative mode of relating to that evinced by the "boy," regionalist fiction seeks as well to convert the boy and by such conversion to redistribute cultural power. When Sylvy in "A White Heron" refuses to "tell the heron's secret and give its life away" (*AWR* 205), we are left to wonder how different her life might have been had the boy looked at her the way she looks at the bird. A further instance of this phenomenon can be found in Stowe's *The Pearl of Orr's Island,* a text which Jewett identified as the origin of her own career as a writer of regionalist fiction. In this story, Stowe describes a boy and a girl, Moses and Mara, growing up together in early nineteenth-century New England, and analyzes the social structures which lead the boy to view the girl as an inferior being and to treat her with contempt. Mara, watching Moses prepare for his first fishing voyage, protests, however faintly, her own exclusion from the event:

> "How I do wish I were going with you!" she says [sic]. "I could do something, couldn't I—take care of your hooks, or something?"
> "Pooh!" said Moses, sublimely regarding her while he settled the collar of his shirt, "you're a girl—and what can girls do at sea? you never like to catch fish—it always makes you cry to see 'em flop." (136)

While Moses reads empathy as disqualifying Mara for life—Mara will later literally die for lack of the air and exercise such a voyage might give her—and as justifying his contempt for her, Stowe reads Moses' lack of empathy as a far more serious disqualification. In Moses we recognize a version of Tom Sawyer, the American bad boy who can do no wrong in the nation's eyes, despite the cries of tormented cats and aunts. Thus when we realize that Stowe's text intends to convert this boy into a "girl," to bring him to the point of feeling pain when she gasps so and thus to be more like her, we have a context for reflecting on the unAmericanness of empathy.

Empathy can characterize narrator as well as character, and in creating empathic narrators regionalist writers also propose a different model of storytelling from that "American" tradition begun by Washington Irving and developed through the genre of the tall tale, and in particular by the humorists of the old Southwest. In "In the Name of Wonder: The Emergence of Tall Narrative in American Writing," Henry B. Wonham provides evidence of the gendered nature of "American" in this explicitly American genre, not simply through the masculinist content of the tales or the masculine identity of the teller. More significantly, it occurs, as Wonham notes, because the audience for such tales is composed of boys (303), because the action of such tales involves the humiliation of a naive outsider frequently figured as female, and because "her victimization becomes a patriotic victory for American wit" (297). In "The Legend of Sleepy Hollow," Irving poses the question, Who will be given possession of Sleepy Hollow, that imaginative space which inspires our stories, and who will be driven out? In answering this question, Irving identifies the masculine Brom Bones as the decisive victor, the effeminate Ichabod Crane as the figure to be driven out, and the tall tale as the best way to tell a story about winning and losing because its very telling enacts a similar drama. Indeed, in his postscript to this story Irving suggests that the quintessential American story will be a tall tale circulated among men for the purpose of establishing dominance. The good reader is the one who gets the joke; the bad reader is the one who doesn't get it or refuses to find it funny, perhaps because the joke is on her or him; and telling stories about winning and losing becomes itself an act of winning and losing, of inclusion and exclusion, with character, teller, and listener all invited to identify with each other and against someone else, everyone a Brom Bones getting rid of an Ichabod Crane. As Wonham puts it, the tall tale serves an audience of "cultural insiders" (288) whose enjoyment depends upon the exclusionary practices of a narrative form appropriately characterized as "a sort of inside joke" (305).

Regionalist writers provide a different model of storytelling. Constructing women as storytellers, they also present storytelling as an activity designed to include rather than exclude, to heal rather than harm. In *The Country of the Pointed Firs,* the long anticipated visit of Susan Fosdick creates the occasion for an evening of storytelling. The narrator has invited Mrs. Todd and Susan Fosdick to her room, and as storytelling ensues from this invitation Jewett suggests the connection between storytelling and hospitality, just as she connects storytelling and healing through the narrator's references to the season of the year being the "time of syrups and cordials" (see Romines 63). Telling the story of Joanna serves as a way of keeping Joanna, the one "driven" out, connected in some way to her community and of easing the pain of those who feel they have lost her. Indeed, it continues the efforts Dunnet Landing folk made to stay connected with Joanna while she was still alive as "one after another ventured to make occasion to put somethin' ashore for her if they went that way" (*Firs* 77). Storytelling as one mode of staying connected thus participates in creating the community of Dunnet Landing as one in which far islands and scattered farms are linked together through "constant interest and intercourse . . . into a golden chain of love and dependence" (*Firs* 90). Moreover, in elaborating Joanna as a symbol of that place "in the life of each of us . . . remote and islanded, and given to endless regret or secret happiness" (*Firs* 82), the narrator indicates that in hearing this story she has come not simply to empathize but to identify with the exile.

In her last published story, entitled "The Foreigner," however, Jewett chose to critique the limits of regionalist empathy and in so doing to complicate still further the question of the American and the unAmerican, a gesture appropriate to a tradition which takes the critique of cultural values as its particular province. Yet it would be a mistake, I think, to read Jewett's critique as in fact arguing for a recuperation of the American, for the question her final story asks—How could Mrs. Todd have missed the foreigner and her story?—suggests that such losses occur through creating the category of the foreigner, a category which has meaning only in the context of the American and not-American. Indeed, anticipating the arguments of Virginia Woolf in *Three Guineas* against the value of nationalism for women, Jewett's regionalist fiction implies that the ancient knowledge women need to learn and inherit, and the stories we all need to hear, can be unfolded only in a space which refuses to participate in the masculinist notion of nation. Thus I would like to conclude this essay with a brief meditation on Jewett's "The Foreigner," a story which helps me think about the value of the term "American" in the global context of the twenty-first century. Deephaven, Jewett tells us, was not in the least American in part because "the only foreigners there were a few standard sailors." Here Jewett identifies Deephaven, and by extension the Dunnet Landing of her later work, as ethnically and racially homogeneous, an observation which prepares us for a story which seeks to extend the range of empathy to include those constructed as foreign.

"The Foreigner" tells the story of a woman, French by birth and Jamaican by residence, rescued from poverty and sexual harassment through marriage to a Captain Tolland, who brings her home to Dunnet Landing, a community which has no more ability to hear her story than the deacons do Miss Beulah's, and which lacks the curiosity of the deacons. As Mrs. Todd recounts to the narrator her story of Mrs. Tolland's life in Dunnet Landing and of the circumstances of her death, she reveals as well the limits of her own empathy, her failure to extend herself to include this woman in her definition of community.

Jewett's critique of the limits of Mrs. Todd's empathy becomes even more pointed when we consider how she has constructed the foreigner whom Mrs. Todd belatedly accepts. In creating her foreigner, Jewett hints at dimensions of otherness that might have made it impossible for Mrs. Captain Tolland to live in Dunnet Landing at all. She comes to Dunnet Landing by way of the West Indies, yet she herself is white and French, not colored or even native to those foreign islands. In this severely Protestant community, she seems foreign in her Catholicism, but she is neither Jewish nor atheist nor a practitioner of voodoo. Though the captains rescue her from a bar full of drunken men, she has not been raped, she is not a prostitute, and she does not arrive pregnant or with an illegitimate child. If Dunnet Landing cannot extend itself to include a white French Catholic who, duly married, still loves to sing and dance, what, Jewett

makes us wonder, would they do to a black unwed mother who practices voodoo?

Belatedly, Mrs. Todd finds common ground with the foreigner. Through her
love for her own mother, Mrs. Todd can "see" the foreigner's mother and assure
her that her mother is indeed present in the room where she lies dying. While
we are all familiar with the cliché "as American as apple pie and Mom," nothing is in fact more foreign to our literature than "seeing" mother or listening to
her story. To return for a moment to Freeman's "On The Walpole Road" and the
woman with the "bristling chin," we might equally locate this story's
unAmericanness in its celebration of the resurrection of "mother," for when
Mis' Green discovers that the funeral she has been called to attend is not for
Aunt Rebecca, the woman who has been like a mother to her, but for Uncle
Enos, she becomes "kinder highstericky" and laughs "till the tears was runnin'"
down my cheeks, an' it was all I could do to breathe" (*AWR* 310). "I thought you
was dead," she explains to Aunt Rebecca, "an' there you was a-settin" (*AWR*
310).

Throughout this essay I have used the term "unAmerican" to refer to a body
of literature that challenges the values currently understood as "American" in
order to provoke reflection about what we are doing when we teach American
literature. For, to me, the question of values constitutes the "To what end?" of
rethinking American literature, the title I gave to the 1993 NCTE Summer Institute for Teachers of Literature, where this paper was first presented. We suffer
today from a national narrative that valorizes violence, that defines masculinity
as the production of violence and defines the feminine and the foreign as legitimate recipients of such violence. We need different narratives and different
identities, whether we locate these in a field named "American literature" or
"writing in the U.S." or "literatures of America" or "literatures of the Americas" or "post-colonial writing." It is my argument here that we can find such
narratives and such identities in certain texts, of which the work of nineteenth-
century literary regionalists serves as one instance, that have been systematically excluded from the definition of American literature precisely because they
do not reproduce the national narrative of violence or the definitions of "masculine" and "feminine," "American" and "foreign," which such a narrative presents as our national interest. It is time, then, to take treason as our text and to
begin reading "unAmerican" literature.

Note

1. See Marjorie Pryse, "Archives of Female Friendship and the 'Way' Jewett Wrote,"
New England Quarterly 66 (March 1993), 47–66; and Judith Fetterley, "Reading
Deephaven as a Lesbian Text," in *Sexual Practice, Textual Theory: Lesbian Cultural
Criticism,* eds. Susan J. Wolfe and Julia Penelope (Oxford: Blackwell, 1993), 164–83.

Works Cited

Baym, Nina. "Early Histories of American Literature: A Chapter in the Institution of New England." *American Literary History* 1 (1989), 459–88.

———. "Melodramas of Beset Manhood: How Theories of American Fiction Exclude Women Authors." *American Quarterly 33* (1981), 123–39.

Bell, Michael. *The Problem of American Realism: Studies in the Cultural History of a Literary Idea.* Chicago: Chicago UP, 1993.

Berthoff, Warner. *The Ferment of American Realism: American Literature 1884–1919.* New York: Free Press, 1965. Reprint Cambridge: Cambridge UP, 1981.

Brodhead, Richard. *Cultures of Letters: Scenes of Reading and Writing in Nineteenth-Century America.* Chicago: Chicago UP, 1993.

———. *The School of Hawthorne.* New York: Oxford, 1986.

Cather, Willa. Preface. *The Country of the Pointed Firs and Other Stories.* By Sarah Orne Jewett. Boston: Houghton Mifflin, 1925.

Fetterley, Judith, and Marjorie Pryse, eds. *American Women Regionalists, 1850–1910.* New York: Norton, 1992.

Habegger, Alfred. *Gender, Fantasy, and Realism in American Literature.* New York: Columbia UP, 1982.

Jay, Gregory. "The End of 'American' Literature: Toward a Multicultural Practice." *College English 53* (1992), 264–81.

Jewett, Sarah Orne. *Deephaven.* Boston: Osgood, 1877. Reprint New Haven: College and University P, 1966.

———. *The Country of the Pointed Firs.* Boston: Houghton Mifflin, 1896. Reprint ed. Marjorie Pryse. New York: Norton, 1981.

Lauter, Paul. *Canons and Contexts.* New York: Oxford, 1991.

Renker, Elizabeth. "Resistance and Change: The Rise of American Literature Studies." *American Literature 64* (1992), 347–65.

Robinson, Lillian S. "Treason Our Text: Feminist Challenges to the Literary Canon." *Tulsa Studies in Women's Literature 2* (1983). Reprinted in *Feminisms.* Eds. Robyn Warhol and Diane Price Herndl. New Brunswick, NJ: Rutgers UP, 1991. 212–26.

Romero, Laura. "Vanishing Americans: Gender, Empire, and New Historicism." *American Literature 63* (1991), 385–404.

Romines, Ann. *The Home Plot: Women, Writing and Domestic Ritual.* Amherst: U of Massachusetts P, 1992.

Spengemann, William C. *A Mirror for Americanists: Reflections on the Idea of American Literature.* Hanover: UP of New England, 1989.

Stowe, Harriet Beecher. *The Pearl of Orr's Island.* Boston: Ticknor and Fields, 1862. Reprint Hartford: Stowe-Day Foundation, 1979.

Sundquist, Eric J. "Realism and Regionalism." *Columbia Literary History of the United States.* Ed. Emory Elliot. New York: Columbia UP, 1988. 501–24.

Wonham, Henry B. "In the Name of Wonder: The Emergence of Tall Narrative in American Writing." *American Quarterly 41* (1989), 284–307.

3 Transcendentalism Then and Now: Towards a Dialogic Theory and Praxis of Multicultural U.S. Literature

AnaLouise Keating
Eastern New Mexico University

> To make a claim for multi-culturalism is not, therefore, to suggest the juxtaposition of several cultures whose frontiers remain intact, nor is it to subscribe to a bland "melting-pot" type of attitude that would level all differences. It lies instead, in the intercultural acceptance of risks, unexpected detours, and complexities of relation between break and closure. Every artistic excursion and theoretical venture requires that boundaries be ceaselessly called to question, undermined, modified, and reinscribed.
>
> —Trinh T. Minh-ha

It is by now a commonplace among many Americanists to acknowledge the multicultural nature of U.S. American literature. All too often, however, multiculturalism is defined simply as the coexistence of a variety of distinct literary and cultural traditions, or as what Trinh Minh-ha describes in my epigraph to this essay: "the juxtaposition of several cultures whose frontiers remain intact." Although these explorations of ethnic-specific literary traditions have played an important role in expanding contemporary views of U.S. literature, they rely on a rhetoric of cultural authenticity that reinforces the belief in self-contained ethnic identities. Rather than develop new forms of identity, this rhetoric of authenticity is based on a politics of location that essentializes textuality by equating it with biological "roots." When readers focus almost exclusively on the differences between these supposedly distinct cultural identities, they inadvertently reinscribe inflexible boundaries that foreclose possible common ground in the discussion of works by apparently discrete ethnic/cultural groups. Thus, for example, African American literature is associated only with writers of African descent while Chicano/a writings are identified only with people of Mexican ancestry. Although scholars often examine the intersections between these distinct cultural traditions and canonical Euro-American literature, they rarely expand their studies to explore the similarities and differences among the various ethnic-specific traditions themselves. Reduced to a series of binary oppositions between ethnic-specific literary traditions and "mainstream" canonical U.S. texts, multiculturalism becomes another form of separatism.[1] But this conception of self-contained cultural/ethnic identities and literary traditions is far less accurate than it seems. If identity is always (already) relational, then it's never self-contained. However, by focusing almost entirely on the differences between cultural identities and literatures, we often overlook their commonalities.

In this chapter, I explore the pedagogical and theoretical implications of establishing transcultural dialogues, alternate forms of multicultural theory and practice that go beyond recent emphases on ethnic-specific literary texts and identities without becoming immersed in benign celebrations of "American"[2] identities and themes. More specifically, I suggest that dialogic patterns of reading can transform the boundaries between apparently distinct literary traditions into thresholds opening up new definitions of "American" literature and identities which neither erase nor reify the many differences among the various texts we read.

Given the central role Ralph Waldo Emerson and Henry David Thoreau have played in constructing an "American" self and an "American" literary tradition, canonical Transcendental texts like "Self-Reliance" and *Walden* offer a useful point of departure for these explorations in multicultural thinking. By rereading these nineteenth-century classics in conversation with contemporary works by June Jordan, Gloria Anzaldúa, Paula Gunn Allen, or other self-identified African American, Chicana, and Native American writers, I argue that static, universalized notions of an authentic "American" self can be transformed into flexible models of literary and cultural identity that deconstruct monolithic notions of difference and similarity. Let me emphasize: My goal is not to erase the differences between the various ethnic-specific traditions that make U.S. literature multicultural. Nor do I attempt to demonstrate that Anzaldúa, Jordan, Allen, or other contemporary writers marked by gender, ethnicity, or sexuality "should be" considered twentieth-century inheritors of Transcendentalist traditions and on those terms incorporated into the U.S. literature canon. Instead, I want to develop alternate reading practices that go beyond separatist multiculturalism to open up new narratives of "American" selves and "American" literary traditions.

Despite the many differences among them—differences which include but are not limited to gender, ethnicity, skin color, region, and historical era[3]—the nineteenth- and twentieth-century writers I examine in this chapter share a number of striking similarities: Their willingness to position themselves as outsiders to dominant U.S. cultural standards, their desire to challenge existing social conventions, their faith in each individual's untapped potential, their attempts to create nondual metaphysical systems which locate the spiritual in material and intellectual life, and their confidence in language's transformational power.

Although each point of similarity opens up new areas of exploration leading to alternate definitions of "American" literatures and identities, in this essay I will focus primarily on the various ways their quests for independence and self-definition play themselves out in their texts. My reasons for doing so are two-fold. First, Emerson and other nineteenth-century Transcendentalists have played a key role in shaping the highly celebrated belief in "American" individualism. Second, this celebration of self-reliance and personal autonomy is deeply in-grained in contemporary U.S. culture and viewed as an essential, uniquely "American" theme as well as a distinguishing mark of U.S. literary classics. Thus, for example, Joyce Warren argues that the works of Emerson, Thoreau, Melville, and other nineteenth-century Euro-American male writers illustrate what she calls the "American Narcissus," a radically solipsistic subject who denies the existence of other human beings in his quest for complete self-defi-nition and control:

> Emerson and Thoreau were writing in the American tradition, the tradition that glorifies the individual and insists upon the sanctity of the self. Such a philosophy forces the individual to protect himself by projecting a persona that exhibits all of the traits he feels he must live up to. With all of his energies devoted to the development of this inflated self, the American Narcissus can allow no room for the reality of other selves. That Ameri-cans have adopted this philosophy wholeheartedly and continue to endorse the writings of Emerson and Thoreau with such enthusiasm indicates how much this belief in the totality of the self remains a part of our culture. (69–70)

In this binary configuration, individualism entails a hierarchical relationship between subject and object, where the individual and society occupy mutually exclusive poles. For Warren's American Narcissus, nature and all other human beings are objectified and denied independent existence; they serve "only as objects to be ignored or destroyed (if they are undesirable) or to be made use of or absorbed into the self (if they are desirable)" (17).

To be sure, these binary oppositions between self and other or between sub-ject and object have played a central role in canonical descriptions of American individualism. As Nina Baym points out, during the 1940s and 1950s F.O. Matthiessen, Henry Nash Smith, Charles Feidelson, and other well-known schol-ars constructed a literary canon centered around their own highly individualis-tic "myth of America." This myth, associated almost exclusively with texts by "white, middle-class, male" writers

> narrates a confrontation of the American individual, the pure American self divorced from specific social circumstances, with the promise offered by the idea of America. This promise is the deeply romantic one that in this new land, untrammeled by history and social accident, a person will be able to achieve complete self-definition. Behind this promise is the assur-

ance that individuals come before society, that they exist in some meaningful sense prior to, and apart from, societies in which they happen to find
themselves. The myth also holds that, as something artificial and secondary to human nature, society exerts an unmitigatedly destructive pressure
on individuality. To depict it at any length would be a waste of artistic time;
and there is only one way to relate it to the individual—as an adversary.
(71)

As Baym's description of the adversarial relationship between the individual
and society indicates, canonical descriptions of "American" individualism rely
on a radical distinction between individual and collective identities. In this highly
celebrated "myth of America," the individual is viewed as an autonomous, independent human being, alienated from a society which requires repressive,
mind-numbing conformity. Like Warren, Baym argues that this literary drive
for self-expansion and independence relies on a restrictive definition of the individual that excludes far more people than it includes. Euro-American women,
African Americans, Native Americans, and other marginalized peoples have
been denied the freedom and independence associated with this solipsistic version of "American" individualism.

Yet I would argue that this "myth of America" can be enacted in other ways
as well, ways that illustrate and perhaps even extend Emersonian self-reliance.
Like canonical forms of "American" individualism, these alternate, multicultural
forms reject external sources of authority and underscore the importance of
self-trust, yet they do so without reinforcing narcissistic, self-enclosed concepts of identity. Instead, they replace the belief in isolated individual human
beings with a more flexible theory of identity, where self-development occurs
always in the context of others. By positing the interconnectedness between
each individual and society, these intersubjective models of individualism break
down the exclusionary, dualistic divisions between personal and communal identities found in conventional interpretations of an "American" self. In short, self-
reliance becomes a highly democratic endeavor that simultaneously extends
canonical interpretations of "American" individualism outward to include previously ignored groups and reconfigures the relationship between personal and
communal identities.

June Jordan's politics of self-determination—which I would describe as a
theory and praxis of intersubjective identity formation where self-development
occurs in the context of other equally important individuals—illustrates one
form these alternate, multicultural models of individualism can take. Throughout her work, Jordan emphasizes the importance of self-trust by insisting that
all human beings must have the freedom to define themselves and choose their
own courses of action. In "Civil Wars," for example, she challenges all external
forms of authority, including the "professional leadership" guiding the Black
Power Movement, the Women's Movement, and other politicized groups. Ac-

cording to Jordan, no matter how democratic such leadership seems to be, it cannot replace the authority and guidance she associates with each person's inner desires: "The only leadership I can respect is one that enables every man and woman to be his and her own leader: to abandon victim perspective and to faithfully rely upon the truth of the feeling that is his or hers and then to act on that, without apology" (186–87). As this emphasis on inner-directed leadership implies, Jordan bases her politics of self-determination on the non-elitist belief that each person has the ability and the wisdom to control his or her own life. In this essay and others, she attempts to share this belief with her readers. By rejecting the rhetoric of victimhood that denies personal agency, Jordan urges her readers to take responsibility for their own lives. Because she believes that each person has an infallible source of guidance located within him or herself, she encourages her readers to explore their hidden needs and desires and begin speaking out.

In many ways, this confidence in each individual's inner potential resembles canonical versions of self-trust seen, for example, in Emerson's assertion in "Self-Reliance" that "[n]othing is at last sacred but the integrity of your own mind. Absolve you to yourself, and you shall have the suffrage of the world" (149) or in Thoreau's confidence that by simplifying his life and relying entirely on himself he would discover universal truths about human existence.[4] Like Jordan, these nineteenth-century Transcendentalists reject external forms of authority and underscore each individual's ability to think for him or herself. Yet in Jordan's politics of self-determination, this belief in intellectual integrity and personal power has a distinctive, highly complex social dimension rarely seen in Emerson or Thoreau. Thus in "Thinking about My Poetry" she associates the self-trust she requires as a writer with the development of a personalized yet collective voice. This perspective enables her to avoid the solipsistic withdrawal or escape from society generally associated with canonical versions of American individualism. Instead, she can insist that self-reflection leads to the discovery of new forms of intersubjective identity. By looking within, she recognizes her interconnections with others which she then explores in her work. She explains that she sees herself and other Black and women poets as

> all of us working on the same poem of a life of perpetual, difficult birth, and . . . therefore, I should trust myself in this way: that if I could truthfully attend to my own perpetual birth, if I could trace the provocations for my own voice and then trace its reverberations through love, Alaska, whatever, that then I could hope to count upon myself to be serving a positive and collective function, without pretending to be more than the one Black woman poet I am, as a matter of fact. (126)

By locating the source of social change within each individual, Jordan opens up an intersubjective space where self-reflection, self-definition, and the creation of transformational collective identities can converge. Similarly, in "Civil Wars" she associates each individual's ability to think for him or herself with the construction of collective identities capable of bringing about radical social change. She maintains that "the ultimate power of *all the people* rests upon the *individual* ability to trust and to respect the authority of the truth of whatever it is that *each of us* feels, *each of us* means" (187, my emphasis).

As this oscillation between individual and communal identities indicates, Jordan's politics of self-determination relies on an intersubjective matrix where personal interests work in conjunction with the interests of others. Again in "Waking Up in the Middle of Some American Dreams" Jordan challenges conventional forms of individualism, or what she describes as the "beloved, national myths about you and me as gloriously rugged, independent individuals" (15). According to Jordan, these "national myths" of limitless autonomy and freedom are far less empowering than they seem, for they inhibit self-growth by preventing us from recognizing the ways our individualized needs intersect with those of others. Seduced by visions of uniqueness, each person becomes isolated and unable to attain his or her personal desires and goals. Drawing on the rhetoric of democracy embedded in U.S. culture, she insists that

> our American dreams of "the first" and "the only" produce an invariably mistaken self-centered perspective that repeatedly proves to be self-defeating and, even, antidemocratic. *Demos*, as in democratic, as in a democratic state, means people, not person. A democratic nation of persons, of individuals, is an impossibility and a fratricidal goal. Each American one of us must consciously choose to become a willing and outspoken part of *the people* who, together, will determine our individual chances for happiness, and justice. (19, her emphasis)

Jordan does not establish a binary opposition between the individual and society. Nor does she deny the validity of each individual's private needs and desires. Instead, she invents new forms of personal agency acknowledging the interconnections among apparently separate human beings. More specifically, she incorporates a communal dimension into her definition of the personal and establishes a model of identity formation where self-development requires each individual's interaction with others. By thus emphasizing the reciprocal, intersubjective nature of each individual's autonomy and self-growth, Jordan constructs an agent-centered collective subjectivity that unites inner direction with outward change.

Jordan's self-naming process in her 1989 collection of poetry, *Naming Our Destiny*, illustrates one form this model of interactional identity formation can take. Throughout the poems collected in this volume, she uses her own experiences as a twentieth-century bisexual woman of Jamaican descent to underscore the importance of personal and communal self-determination. As she examines the interconnections between her own destiny and the destinies of a wide variety of national and international groups, she rejects restrictive versions of isolated, self-enclosed individualism. Exploring a diverse set of private and public issues—including her relationships with female and male lovers, homophobia, Black English, racial violence in Atlanta, South African apartheid, and the Palestinian crisis—Jordan demonstrates that her own self-determination entails recognizing and affirming both the similarities and the differences between herself and others. For instance, in "Poem About My Rights," written in response to her experience of being raped, she alternates between personal, national, and international concerns. By so doing, she illustrates how the specific forms of oppression she experiences as a single black woman living in the United States intersect with South Africa's invasion of Namibia and Angola, U.S. imperialism, sexual violence against women, and unjust rape laws. In this poem and others, Jordan synthesizes personal and communal agency by drawing analogies between her own rights and the rights of all women, colonized countries, and other supposedly disparate groups.

As Jordan's willingness to identify herself with a variety of apparently dissimilar peoples implies, her complex self-naming process represents a significant departure from the rhetoric of authenticity found in many forms of ethnic-specific literary and cultural studies. In her politics of self-determination, individual and collective identities cannot automatically be based on ethnicity, gender, nationality, or other restrictive, naturalized categories of meaning. As she explains in "Civil Wars," "Neither race nor gender provides the final definitions of jeopardy or refuge. The final risk or final safety lies within each one of us attuned to the messy and intricate and unending challenge of self-determination" (187).[5] By rejecting ethnic- and gender-specific collective identities without denying their temporary historic significance, Jordan exposes the limitations in contemporary forms of separatist multicultural thinking.

Like Jordan, Gloria Anzaldúa enacts a variety of to-and-fro movements in which individual and collective identity formation are interconnected and occur simultaneously. Throughout her poetry, fiction, and prose she draws on her experiences as a Chicana growing up in south Texas and employs a highly personalized, assertive voice to invent new forms of intersubjective identity. Thus, for example, in "*Cihuatlyotl,* Woman Alone," she adopts a paradoxical position enabling her to redefine the personal and communal components of her own self-identity. Although she associates herself with *Cihuatlyotl,* a precolonial Mexican Indian creatrix figure representing the collective, ethnic-specific dimensions of her identity, she insists on her ability to define herself according to her own needs and desires. After exploring the various ways her family and other Mexican Americans have attempted to control her, she boldly asserts her independence without severing all ties to her ethnic community:

```
                              I refuse     to be taken over      by
things              people              who fear that hollow
aloneness         beckoning            beckoning.         No self,
only race *vecindad familia.*         My soul      has always
been yours         one spark      in the roar of your fire.
We Mexicans    are collective animals.                 This I
accept        but my life's work         requires autonomy
like oxygen.              This lifelong battle has ended,
*Raza.*                 I don't need to flail against you.
```

(Borderlands/La Frontera 173)

Even the style—the jarring line breaks and the unexpected, irregular spaces within each line—indicates the difficulties Anzaldúa experiences in her attempts to negotiate between the personal autonomy she desires as a writer and the sense of connection she desires as a member of her ethnic community. Yet as her shifts between singular and plural first-person pronouns suggest, she does not create a binary division between these conflicting desires. Instead, by locating her "soul" both in the beckoning "hollow / aloneness" she requires as a writer and in the collective Mexican *familia*, she destabilizes the binary opposition between them. This oscillation between individual and collective identities enables her simultaneously to accept and reject both her need for autonomy and the demands placed upon her by other Mexican Americans.

In many ways, this rejection of social convention resembles the emphasis on nonconformity found in nineteenth century Transcendental writers. Like Emerson, Anzaldúa exposes the paralyzing effects society's dictates have on each individual. And like Thoreau, she openly refuses to live her life according to the codes of behavior established by others.[6] However, by specifying the many various forms these social conventions can take, she adds increasing levels of complexity and sophistication to conventional interpretations of "American" individualism. More specifically, she uses the conflicts she experiences as a Chicana writer to enact a complex, multi-layered dialogue between a variety of groups, including the mainstream assimilationist U.S. culture which attempts to impose a single standard on all citizens, the Mexican American community which imposes its own ethnic-specific standards on its members, and her own personal desires. Thus in *Borderlands/La Frontera: The New Mestiza* she deliberately breaks with all negative religious and cultural belief systems and boldly declares:

> No, I do not buy all the myths of the tribe into which I was born. . . . I will not glorify those aspects of my culture which have injured me and which have injured me in the name of protecting me. So, don't give me your tenets and your laws. Don't give me your lukewarm gods. What I want is an accounting with all three cultures—white, Mexican, Indian. I want the freedom to carve and chisel my own face, to staunch the bleeding with

ashes, to fashion my own gods out of my entrails. And if going home is
denied me then I will have to stand and claim my space, making a new
culture—*una cultura mestiza*—with my own lumber, my own bricks and
mortar and my own feminist architecture. (*Borderlands/La Frontera* 21–
22)

By replacing the two-way conversation between the individual and society
found in canonical interpretations of "American" individualism with this multi-
layered discourse, Anzaldúa generates flexible, open-ended forms of individualized collective identity, or what she describes as the "new mestiza." As the
term suggests, Anzaldúa's new mestiza represents a hybrid, a complex mixed-
breed who can neither be reduced to a single category nor rigidly classified
according to a specific set of traits.[7] The product of two or more cultures—each
with its own value system—Anzaldúa's new mestiza draws from these various
traditions yet reorganizes them according to her own needs, desires, and beliefs. As she explains in "To(o) Queer the Writer," her "new *mestiza* queers have
the ability, the flexibility, the amorphous quality of being able to stretch this
way and that way. We can add new labels, names and identities as we mix with
others" (249).

Anzaldúa's "new mestiza" represents several remarkable departures from
previous interpretations of *mestizaje* found in Chicano literature. By feminiz-
ing the term "*mestizo*," her *mestiza* provides an important intervention into twentieth-century Chicano literary and theoretical movements which have been
dominated by male-centered issues.[8] And by extending conventional definitions
of the *mestizo* as a member of a specific biologically-based cultural group to
encompass the experiences of non-Mexican, non-Indian peoples as well,
Anzaldúa de-essentializes and pluralizes culturally-specific notions of identity.
As Marcos Sanchez-Tranquilino points out, Anzaldúa's theory of *mestizaje* represents an innovative alteration of earlier views: "Her interpretation goes beyond the traditional concept of *mestizaje*. For Anzaldúa, that concept cannot
ever again be thought of as a simple mixing of blood or cultures, but rather that
what has always been in effect a mixing of identities many times over—beyond
the old dualities be they gender, historical, economic, or cultural, etc." (568). I
want to underscore the radical implications of Anzaldúa's new *mestiza*: By rejecting essentialized conceptions of identity that rely on blood quantum, physical appearance, or other biologically-based components, she constructs a
transcultural theory of hybrid subjectivities.

In short, Anzaldúa replaces the rhetoric of authenticity found in many ethnic-specific traditions with new forms of communal identity based on each
individual's experiential knowledge and personal choice. Like Jordan, she creates highly personalized yet collective identities that go beyond gender- and
ethnic-specific categories of meaning. Take, for example, her self-positioning
in "La Prieta," an early autobiographical essay. As in *Borderlands/La Frontera*,

she acknowledges the numerous forms of conflict she has experienced in her interactions with Mexican Americans, other people of color, feminists, and lesbians and gay men, yet refuses to sever her ties with these various groups. Instead, she confidently insists on her ability to define herself as she sees fit and locates herself on the thresholds between these diverse groups:

> I am a wind-swayed bridge, a crossroads inhabited by whirlwinds. . . . "Your allegiance is to La Raza, the Chicano movement," say the members of my race. "Your allegiance is to the Third World," say my Black and Asian friends. "Your allegiance is to your gender, to women," say the feminists. Then there's my allegiance to the Gay movement, to the socialist revolution, to the New Age, to magic and the occult. And there's my affinity to literature, to the world of the artist. What am I? *A third world lesbian feminist with Marxist and mystic leanings.* They would chop me up into little fragments and tag each piece with a label. (205, her emphasis)

Significantly, Anzaldúa's threshold location includes ethnic- and gender-specific worlds she could be said to have entered by virtue of appearance and birth, as well as other worlds she has more consciously chosen to enter. Although each group makes full membership contingent on its own exclusionary sets of rules and demands based on ethnicity, gender, sexuality, class, ideology, or beliefs, Anzaldúa refuses these terms without disassociating herself from the various groups. By rejecting the need for unitary identities and exclusive, single-issue alliances, she challenges her readers—no matter how they identify—to reexamine and expand their own personal and social locations.

For Paula Gunn Allen as well, self-definition occurs only in the context of others. But unlike Anzaldúa and Jordan, who rely extensively on their personal experiences to create an intersubjective matrix where these new constellations of individual and collective identities can occur, Allen relies extensively on literature and myth.[9] More specifically, she builds on the radical holism she finds in traditional Native cosmologies and invents a transformational model of identity formation synthesizing the personal and communal dimensions of each individual's life. By locating this transformational model within the oral tradition, Allen develops a dialogic theory of tribal literatures that draws on language's performative effects to generate personal and social change.

Based on a relational model requiring participation by both storyteller and listeners, oral traditions reinforce the communal, creative dimensions of human existence. As Richard Bauman points out, this conversational structure can lead to the creation of new social systems. He associates the "distinctive potential" found in oral narratives with a performative, interactive model of language use and explains that verbal art's communal nature potentially establishes a unique bond between an individual and a group:

> It is part of the essence of performance that it offers to the participants a special enhancement of experience, bringing with it a heightened intensity

> of communicative interaction which binds the audience to the performer in
> a way that is specific to performance as a mode of communication. Through
> his [sic] performance, the performer elicits the participative attention and
> energy of his audience, and, to the extent that they value his performance,
> they will allow themselves to be caught up in it. (43)

Throughout her scholarly writings, Allen draws on this interactive model of
performative language to argue that oral narratives function simultaneously as
the expression and the active fulfillment of each individual's social needs. Yet
by incorporating a transcultural perspective into her description of oral traditions, she attempts to expand conventional anthropological definitions of the
term. According to Allen,

> [t]he oral tradition of all tribal people—whether Native American, Hindu,
> Greek, Celtic, Norse, Samois, Roman, or Papuan is best seen as psychic
> literature. It cannot adequately be comprehended except in terms of the
> universe of power, for it speaks to the relationships among humans, ani-
> mals of all kingdoms, supernaturals, and deities in a landscape that is sub-
> ject to influences of thought, intention, will, emotion, and choice.
> (*Grandmothers* 22)

This transition from oral to psychic literature underscores the intersubjective
dimensions of Allen's transformational model of identity formation, for she
associates these communally-based knowledge systems with a spiritualized mode
of perception located within each individual.

Allen provides one of the most extensive discussions of her dialogic theory
of literature in "The Sacred Hoop: A Contemporary Perspective," where she
draws from a wide variety of tribal mythic systems, including Cheyenne, Hopi,
and Keres, to distinguish between western literature's highly individualistic bias
and the communal dimensions she finds in American Indian literatures. Whereas
the former celebrates solipsistic, self-enclosed forms of individualism leading
only to isolation, separation, and loss, the latter does not. Instead, the oral narratives embodied in traditional tribal literatures posit an underlying dynamic
intelligence—or what, borrowing from the Hopi, she describes as "what lives
and moves and knows" (61)—enabling us to create communal identities based
on a shared worldview. By associating this holistic worldview with language's
transformational effects, Allen can insist that the mythic stories conveyed in
oral narratives utilize participatory, performative speech acts to unify individuals with communities and bring about radical change:

> The tribes seek—through song, ceremony, legend, sacred stories (myths),
> and tales—to embody, articulate, and share reality, to bring the isolated
> private self into harmony and balance with this reality, to verbalize the
> sense of the majesty and reverent mystery of all things, and to actualize, in
> language, those truths that give to humanity its greatest significance and
> dignity. To a large extent, ceremonial literature serves to redirect private

emotion and integrate the energy generated by emotion within a cosmic framework. (55)

As this synthesis of personal power and cosmic communal experience indicates, Allen does not reject all forms of individualism. Instead, she locates each individual's personal integrity and power within communally-based oral traditions, thus destabilizing the binary opposition between individual and collective identities.

In many ways, Allen's discussion of oral narratives' unifying effect resembles Thoreau's discovery of patterned, perpetual rebirth in *Walden*[10] or Emerson's theory of the imagination. Like Allen, Emerson locates the source of each person's individual power within a larger, communal context and a holistic worldview. As he explains in "The Poet,"

> [i]t is a secret which every intellectual man [sic] quickly learns, that beyond the energy of his possessed and conscious intellect he is capable of a new energy (as of an intellect doubled on itself), by abandonment to the nature of things; that beside his privacy of power as an individual man, there is a great public power on which he can draw, by unlocking, at all risks, his human doors, and suffering the ethereal tides to roil and circulate through him; then he is caught up into the life of the Universe, his speech is thunder, his thought is law, and his words are universally intelligible as the plants and animals. (233)

Just as Emerson's theory of imagination gives thinkers access to a "great public power" uniting them with all that exists, Allen's dialogic theory of tribal literatures underscores each individual's interconnections with a communally-based "universe of power" (*Grandmothers* 22). However, her emphasis on the particular forms this all-inclusive power can take gives her work a transculturally universal dimension not found in Emerson's more generalized universalism. In a sense, she translates the "universally intelligible" words of his poet into a variety of gender- and ethnic-specific forms.

Allen illustrates one form this transcultural translation can take in *Grandmothers of the Light: A Medicine Woman's Sourcebook*. Composed of an introductory section containing her reinterpretation of North American Indians' holistic worldview, her versions of Pueblo, Mayan, Cherokee, and other tribal mythic stories, and a brief overview of ten North American peoples' pre- and post-colonial histories, *Grandmothers of the Light* is targeted at a wide, multicultural female audience. In many ways, this text represents a radical departure from Allen's earlier, more scholarly works, for it can easily be viewed as a mainstream self-help book. And indeed, Allen implies that—read from the proper mythic perspective—the Native American myths she retells function as a guidebook for any woman interested in learning to "walk the medicine path . . . to live and think in ways that are almost but not quite entirely unlike our usual ways of living and thinking" (3). As she asserts in an interview with

Jane Caputi, "The stories are guides and a handbook on how to be spiritual if you want to be spiritual. [*Grandmothers of the Light*] gives you stories you can use like recipes on how to act, what to do. These stories are about being medicine women" (66).

More specifically, the stories are about women's ability to attain personal and collective agency. As Allen explains in the preface, the mythic tribal stories she retells demonstrate "the great power women have possessed, and how that power when exercised within the life circumstances *common to women everywhere* can reshape (terraform) the earth" (*Grandmothers* xvi, my emphasis). In other words, she implies that by fully participating in the "sacred myths" collected in her anthology, twentieth-century English-speaking women of any ethnicity or cultural background can become "medicine women" by developing a spiritual mode of perception that empowers them to bring about psychic and material change.[11]

> You say my name is ambivalence? Think of me as Shiva, a many-armed and legged body with one foot on brown soil, one on white, one in straight society, one in the gay world, the man's world, the women's, one limb in the literary world, another in the working class, the socialist, and the occult worlds. A sort of spider woman hanging by one thin strand of web.
>
> Gloria Anzaldúa

In this passage, Anzaldúa positions herself on the thresholds—simultaneously inside and outside a number of what seem to be mutually exclusive groups—and develops flexible models of intersubjective identity formation enabling her to establish points of similarity and difference among people of diverse backgrounds. Similar comments can be made about Allen and Jordan as well. By rejecting the belief in self-enclosed identities and the rhetoric of authenticity based on naturalized concepts of culture, ethnicity, gender, or other systems of difference, all three writers replace the celebrated versions of "American" individualism that rely on an authentic core self with alternate, more flexible forms. As they engage in multiple dialogues simultaneously, they enact a series of displacements that confound binary oppositions between personal and communal identities.

These to-and-fro movements between individual and collective identities resemble the "*fort/da* of the symbolic process of political negotiation," or translation, Homi Bhabha associates with the invention of new forms of social subjects. As he explains in "The Commitment to Theory," the construction of cultural meaning relies on an ambivalent movement which fragments claims of authentic, unitary, cultural identities from within (117). Drawing on discourse analysis and psychoanalytic theory, he outlines a transformational process of cultural translation based on his contention that all forms of identity are hybrid creations rather than pre-existing, organic discoveries; they are "symbol-forming and subject-constituting, interpellative practices" ("Third Space" 210). He maintains that the slippage between signifier and signified occurring within literature and other types of cultural representation opens up an ambivalent space where new political subjects and pluralized cultural identities can be articulated.[12] As he explains in an interview with Jonathan Rutherford, cultural translation indicates a twofold process of internal division, or self-alienation, and imitation:

> By translation I first of all mean a process by which, in order to objectify cultural meaning, there always has to be a process of alienation and of secondariness *in relation to itself*. In that sense there is no "in itself" and "for itself" within cultures because they are always subject to intrinsic forms of translation. . . . Developing that notion, translation is a way of imitating, but in a mischievous, displacing sense—imitating an original in such a way that the priority of the original is not reinforced but by the very fact that it *can* be simulated, copied, transferred, transformed, made into a simulacrum and so on: the "original" is never finished or complete in itself. The "originary" is always open to translation so that it can never be said to have a totalised prior moment of being or meaning—an essence. ("Third Space" 210, his emphasis)

As this rejection of static, self-enclosed identities implies, translation is an ongoing, de-essentializing process that relies on yet problematizes "authentic" representations of present and past cultural traditions, as well as the notions of authority and truth all such representations reinforce. Indeed, it's the recognition of difference within apparently unified cultural identities—or what Bhabha describes in "The Commitment to Theory" as "a Third space," a "split-space enunciation" (131)—that destabilizes apparently stable authoritative claims, thus making transformation possible. He maintains that

> [t]he intervention of the Third space of enunciation, which makes the structure of meaning and reference an ambivalent process, destroys this mirror of representation in which cultural knowledge is customarily revealed as an integrated, open, expanding code. Such an intervention quite properly challenges our sense of the historical identity of culture as a homogenising unifying force, authenticated by the originary Past, kept alive in the national tradition of the people. (130)

In short, although cultural meaning often relies on what seem to be unitary notions of an authentic core self, cultural identities are created, not discovered.

But what does this process of cultural translation and intervention have to do with reading and teaching U.S. literature? As a number of theorists suggest, the narratives we read—the stories we tell ourselves and our students—play an important role in constructing "American" identities and themes.[13] Thus, for example, the highly celebrated belief in a radically independent, solipsistic "American" self explored in this paper has, to a great degree, shaped the ways we see ourselves and our world. Seduced by the rhetoric of "American" individualism, we view ourselves as unique, fully autonomous human beings with distinct boundaries separating us from all others. Although we often believe these identities to be marked by gender, sexuality, and ethnicity, we generally view these components as authentic, stable attributes and assume that cultural identities are permanent categories of meaning based on biology, family, history, nationality, and tradition. In such instances, the boundaries between various groups of people—and, by extension, the theoretical perspectives designed to represent them—become rigid, inflexible, and far too restrictive. Yet as Bhabha's theory of cultural translation suggests, these self-enclosed, isolated identities are themselves produced by a rhetoric of authenticity that covers over internal contradictions, antagonisms, and gaps. Transcultural dialogues activate these internal contradictions, thus demonstrating that this belief in autonomous, self-contained identities is far less accurate than it seems. As Stuart Hall asserts, "[i]dentity is not as transparent or unproblematic as we think. Perhaps instead of thinking of identity as an already accomplished fact . . . we should think, instead, of *identity as a 'production,'* which is never complete, always in process, and always constituted within not outside, representation" (222, my emphasis).[14]

In the classroom, this view of identity as a fluid ongoing process continually reinvented by literature and other forms of representation serves at least two interrelated purposes. First, by challenging the rhetoric of authenticity associated both with canonical descriptions of an isolated "American" self and with the creation of ethnic-specific literary traditions, it provides us with more flexible forms of multicultural thinking. Unlike separatist multiculturalism—which reinforces apparently discrete ethnic traditions—these alternate types of multicultural thinking illustrate the hybridity in all U.S. literary forms. By reading ethnic-specific texts in dialogue with each other, students learn that the different literary traditions they explore are far less self-contained than they seem, for they're constructed through a complex process of appropriation and transformation in dialogue with "mainstream" U.S. canonical texts and themes. This insight takes them—takes us—beyond issues of inclusion to redefine existing knowledges and beliefs, such as "American" individualism, separatist multiculturalism, and the rhetoric of authenticity they rely on.

This fluid model of identity serves another purpose as well: By unsettling fixed notions of selfhood, it opens up the transformational possibilities contained within any apparently self-enclosed subject. Because each subject is composed of multiple parts and located at the intersection of diverse—sometimes overlapping, sometimes conflicting—discourses, no identity is or ever can be entirely stable and fixed. Instead, identity is always in process and we are always open to further change. This potential openness provides an important challenge to students' generally more stable, essentialized notions of subjectiv-

ity and selfhood, for it compels them to reexamine their own personal and social locations. More specifically, by disrupting the restrictive networks of classification that inscribe each "American" self as a racialized, en-gendered subject,
it creates psychic spaces where alterations in consciousness can occur. As they
begin recognizing the ways the highly celebrated belief in self-enclosed "American" individualism has (mis)shaped their sense of personal and communal identity, they enact flexible models of identity formation, where self-definition and
self-growth occur in the context of others.

I want to underscore the radical possibilities opened up by the dialogic theory
and praxis of multiculturalism I'm advocating in this paper. By reading nineteenth-century canonical texts in conversation with texts by Jordan, Allen,
Anzaldúa, or a number of other writers,[15] we—whatever color, class, ethnicity,
or sex "we" are—recognize contradictions and antagonisms within our own
pre-existing knowledges, self-perceptions, and beliefs. This recognition trans-
forms us. We engage in a series of convers(at)ions—transformational dialogues—
that destabilize the rigid boundaries between apparently separate individuals,
literary traditions, and identities. Like Jordan, Allen, and Anzaldúa, we invent
new intersubjective spaces where transcultural identifications—*mestizaje* connections—can occur.

Notes

1. Jack Salzman, Director of the Columbia University Center for American Culture
Studies, makes a similar point in a recent interview:

> "What first astounded me here was the lack of interest that people in vari-
> ous ethnic communities have in other ethnic communities. If I do a panel,
> whether fairly low-keyed or high-powered, let us say on the African Ameri-
> can community, the audience will be, for the most part, African Ameri-
> cans. There will be very few Hispanics, very few Asians. If I do a panel on
> Asian Americans, almost no one who is not Asian American will show up.
> We use terms such as *discourse* and *dialogue* all the time, but, in fact, there
> seems to be relatively little interest in dialogue between and among vari-
> ous communities." (qtd. in Kroeber 56)

2. Throughout this paper I have put the word "American" in scare quotes in order to
emphasize the mythic/metaphoric dimensions of the term as it is often used in literary
and cultural discourse. When I'm referring specifically to the United States, or to literature written in the United States, I use the term "U.S.," rather than "American." As I see
it, the latter term is too general for my purposes, for it incorporates Canada, Mexico, and
all of Central and South America. For insightful discussions of the difficulties with the
various ways the term "American" is used, see Jay and Fetterley.

3. Even the sketchiest biographical information indicates some of the many differences among the writers examined in this paper: Ralph Waldo Emerson, born in 1803 in
Boston, Massachusetts to a long line of ministers who first came to this country from

England in the 1630's; Henry David Thoreau, born in 1817 in Concord, Massachusetts to a second-generation French-American father and a mother of Scottish descent; June Jordan, daughter of Jamaican immigrants, born in 1936 in Harlem, New York; Paula Gunn Allen, born in 1939 on the Cubero Spanish-Mexican land grant in New Mexico to a Laguna-Sioux-Scottish mother and a Lebanese-American father; and Gloria Anzaldúa, born in the Rio Grande Valley of south Texas in 1942 to sixth-generation *mexicanos*.

4. For another fascinating parallel between Emerson and Jordan, consider Emerson's description of leadership in his journal:

> I have been writing & speaking what were once called novelties, for twenty-five or thirty years, & have not now one disciple. Why? Not that what I said was not true; not that it has found no intelligent receivers but because it did not go from any wish in me to bring men to me, but to themselves. I delight in driving them from me. What could I do, if they came to me? They would interrupt & encumber me. This is my boast that I have no school & no follower. I should account it a measure of the impurity of insight, if it did not create independence. (qtd. in Porte 434)

5. For another example of Jordan's rejection of the rhetoric of authenticity, see her self-positioning in "A Short Note to My Very Critical Friends and Well-Beloved Comrades" where she defiantly outlines the numerous ways her well-meaning friends and comrades have tried unsuccessfully to classify her according to color, sexuality, age, and ideology and asserts that their inability to do so indicates their own limitations rather than her own.

6. For Emerson's description of the personal paralysis that occurs when we attempt to follow society's dictates see, for example, "Self-Reliance." For Thoreau's rejection of social standards see the first chapter of *Walden*.

7. Anzaldúa discusses the new mestiza throughout *Borderlands/La Frontera,* but see especially Chapter 7, "*La concienca de la mestiza*: Towards a New Consciousness."

8. For critiques of the male bias in Chicano literature and theory, see Ramón Saldívar and see Anzaldúa in "To(o) Queer the Writer."

9. As I explain in *Women Reading Women Writing*, Allen does occasionally draw on her personal experiences. However, she does not include the types of intimate details found in Jordan's and Anzaldúa's writings.

10. See, for example, the final chapter in *Walden*.

11. For Allen, participation entails fully entering into the mythic tales. She explains that any reader who enters the stories "as a room is entered . . . moves into mythic space and becomes a voyager in the universe of power" (*Grandmothers* 109). Similarly, in *The Sacred Hoop* she states that "entry into the narrative tradition . . . lets people realize that individual experience is not isolate but is part of a coherent and timeless whole, providing them with a means of personal empowerment and giving shape and direction to their lives" (100).

12. Ernesto Laclau and Chatal Mouffe describe this process of articulation in *Hegemony and Socialist Strategy: Towards a Radical Democratic Politics*.

13. See, for example, Peter McLaren's "Multiculturalism and the Postmodern Critique: Toward a Pedagogy of Resistance and Transformation" and McLaren and Tomaz Tadeu da Silva's "Decentering Pedagogy: Critical Literacy, Resistance and the Politics of Memory."

14. Anzaldúa makes a similar point in "To(o) Queer the Writer" where she insists that identity cannot be reduced to a compilation of discrete categories or to "a bunch of little cubbyholes stuffed respectively with intellect, race, sex, class, vocation, gender. Identity flows between, over, aspects of a person. Identity is a river, a process. Contained within the river is its identity, and it needs to flow, to change to stay a river" (252–53).

15. Other dialogic combinations of nineteenth- and twentieth-century "Transcendentalist" writers might include Emerson, Alice Walker, and N. Scott Momaday on the poet and imagination; Walt Whitman and Leslie Marmon Silko on landscape and "American" identities; or Emerson, Thoreau, and Ralph Waldo Ellison on self-reliance.

Works Cited

Allen, Paula Gunn. *Grandmothers of the Light: A Medicine Woman's Sourcebook.* Boston: Beacon, 1991

———. *The Sacred Hoop: Recovering the Feminine in American Indian Traditions.* Boston: Beacon, 1986.

Anzaldúa, Gloria. *Borderlands/La Frontera: The New Mestiza.* San Francisco: Spinsters/Aunt Lute, 1987.

———. "La Prieta." *This Bridge Called My Back: Writings by Radical Women of Color.* Eds. Cherríe Moraga and Gloria Anzaldúa. New York: Kitchen Table: Women of Color Press, 1983. 198–209.

———. "To(o) Queer the Writer—*Loca, escritora y chicana.*" *Inversions: Writing by Dykes, Queers, and Lesbians.* Ed. Betsy Warland. Vancouver: Press Gang, 1991. 249–64.

Bauman, Richard. *Verbal Art as Performance.* Prospect Heights, IL: Waveland P, 1984.

Baym, Nina. "Melodramas of Beset Manhood: How Theories of American Fiction Exclude Women Authors." *The New Feminist Criticism: Essays on Women, Literature, and Theory.* Ed. Elaine Showalter. New York: Pantheon, 1985. 125–43.

Bhabha, Homi K. "The Commitment to Theory." *Questions of Third Cinema.* Jim Pines and Paul Willeman. London: British Film Institute, 1989. 111–31.

———. "The Third Space: Interview with Homi Bhabha." Rutherford 207–21.

Caputi, Jane. "Interview With Paula Gunn Allen." *Trivia* 16 (1990): 50–67.

Emerson, Ralph Waldo. *Selections from Ralph Waldo Emerson.* Ed. Stephen E. Whicher. Boston: Houghton Mifflin, 1957.

Fetterley, Judith. "Nineteenth-Century Literary Regionalism." *College English* 56 (1994): 877–95.

Hall, Stuart. "Cultural Identity and Diaspora." Rutherford 322–37.

Jay, Gregory S. "The End of 'American' Literature: Toward a Multicultural Practice." *College English* 53 (1991): 264–81.

Jordan, June. "Civil Wars." *Civil Wars.* Boston: Beacon, 1981. 178–88.

———. "A Short Note to My Very Critical Friends and Well-Beloved Comrades." *Naming Our Destiny: New and Selected Poems.* New York: Thunder's Mouth, 1989. 98.

———. "Thinking about My Poetry." *Civil Wars.* Boston: Beacon, 1981. 122–30.

————. "Waking up in the Middle of Some American Dreams." *Technical Difficulties: African-American Notions and the State of the Union.* New York: Pantheon, 1993. 11–24.

Keating, AnaLouise. *Women Reading Women Writing: Self-Invention in Paula Gunn Allen, Gloria Anzaldúa, and Audre Lorde.* Philadelphia: Temple UP, 1996.

Kroeber, Karl. "An Interview with Jack Salzman, Director of the Columbia University Center for American Culture Studies." *American Indian Persistence and Resurgence.* Ed. Karl Kroeber. Durham: Duke UP, 1994. 50–57.

Laclau, Ernesto, and Chantal Mouffe. *Hegemony and Socialist Strategy: Towards a Radical Democratic Politics.* London: Verso, 1985.

McLaren, Peter. "Multiculturalism and the Postmodern Critique: Toward a Pedagogy of Resistance and Transformation." *Between Borders: Pedagogy and the Politics of Cultural Studies.* Eds. Henry Giroux and Peter McLaren. New York: Routledge, 1994. 192–222.

McLaren, Peter, and Tomaz Tadeu da Silva. "Decentering Pedagogy: Critical Literacy, Resistance and the Politics of Memory." *Paulo Freire: A Critical Encounter.* Eds. Peter McLaren and Peter Leonard. New York: Routledge, 1993. 47-83.

Porte, Joel, ed. *Emerson in His Journals.* Cambridge: Harvard UP, 1982.

Rutherford, Jonathan, ed. *Identity: Community, Culture, Difference.* London: Lawrence & Wishart, 1990.

Saldívar, Ramón. *Chicano Narrative: The Dialectics of Difference.* Madison: U of Wisconsin P, 1990.

Sanchez-Tranquilino, Marcos, and John Tagg. "The Pachuco's Flayed Hide: Mobility, Identity, and Buenas Garras." *Cultural Studies.* Eds. Lawrence Grossberg, Cary Nelson, and Paula Treichler. New York: Routledge, 1992. 556–70.

Thoreau, Henry David. *Walden.* 1854. New York: Bantam, 1962.

Trinh T. Minh-ha. *When the Moon Waxes Red: Representation, Gender and Cultural Politics.* New York: Routledge, 1991.

Warren, Joyce. *The American Narcissus: Individualism and Women in Nineteenth-Century American Fiction.* New Brunswick: Rutgers UP, 1984.

II Crossing Cultural Boundaries

4 A Fusion of Cultures: The Complexities of the Caribbean Character in Literature

Elizabeth Nunez
Medgar Evers College, CUNY

When I was in high school at St. Joseph's Convent in Port of Spain, Trinidad, my literature teacher introduced my class to the concept of the coexistence of irreconcilable opposites. She was trying to get us to understand the odes of the nineteenth-century English poet John Keats. For reasons that were unclear to me then but are somewhat clearer now, I found immediate empathy with Keats and his point of view. And so too, I must add, did my Trinidadian teacher. Indeed, if there were a way for us to penetrate the heart of this frail English poet from another time and another place, it was through this notion of the coexistence of irreconcilable opposites. For there we were—the daughters of the enslaved and indentured from Africa, India, China, and the vast extinct empires of the Amerindians—all now living together in a tropical island where the heat and the sea were constant, speaking the language of our British conqueror and slave master and loving it, defending it. We aspired to his culture, his way of life, while remaining secretly comfortable with our own. We praised his achievements and accomplishments while celebrating with relish our own rituals—Hosay, Carnival, Duvali, baptisms, weddings, funerals—in our own way, in our own style.

It was also in that high school class that I first fell in love with the word "paradox," again for no reason that I was aware of at that time. Our teacher had asked one of my classmates to read her essay to the class. I don't remember the specific subject, that is, which of Keats's poems she was analyzing. I vaguely remember our teacher praising her paper. I remember her saying something about its brilliant insights, but nothing specific except the word that my classmate had used: paradox. The word resounded in my head. I was to use it over and over again, sometimes totally out of context, sometimes without apparent context, as though hearing it was enough; for it was a word that described me, bonded all of us in that multiethnic class, all the Trinidadians I knew.

I never stopped to ask why. It seemed a truth that did not require explaining or deconstructing. It simply was. But then in 1993 in Stockholm, Derek Walcott was to make the reason eminently clear to the world in a way only a master poet could. In his acceptance speech for the Nobel Prize in Literature, "The Antilles: Fragments of Epic Memory," Walcott told us what we Caribbean people already sensed: that paradox, contradiction, is the essence of Caribbean identity.

Walcott began his speech by describing his reactions to the Indian religious festival of Ramleela in the village of Felicity in Trinidad. Commenting that his first instinct was to view that ceremony as some watered-down version of the original epic, he admitted that "out of the writer's habit," he was "polluting the afternoon with doubt and with the patronage of admiration" (6). He was seeing the Caribbean as a purist might: "illegimate, rootless mongrelized" (7). He had failed to see it as the "celebration of a real presence," the "perpetuation of joy" (8). He had failed to recognize what he already knew: that the paradox of the Caribbean identity was that perfection and wholeness arrived out of contradiction and fragmentation. Finally, evoking the analogy of a broken vase that has been repaired with glue, Walcott declared:

> It is such a love that reassembles our African and Asiatic fragments, the cracked heirloom whose restoration shows its white scars. This gathering of broken pieces is the care and pain of the Antilles, and if the pieces are disparate, ill-fitting, they contain more pain than their original sculpture, those icons and sacred vessels taken for granted in their ancestral places. Antillean art is this restoration of our shattered histories, our shards of vocabulary, our archipelago becoming a synonym for pieces broken off from the original continent. (9)

Musing on these shards, he said wistfully, "I am only one-eighth the writer I might have been had I contained all the fragmented languages of Trinidad" (9).

This is the paradox of the Caribbean character—this containment of fragments, many irreconcilably opposed to one another—and thus the challenge of the Caribbean writer. For in order to portray the Caribbean character truthfully, the writer must be able to convey this complexity of the Caribbean identity, this coexistence of fragments from many diverse and sometimes contradictory sources. It is a challenge that novelist and critic Wilson Harris, in his *Tradition, the Writer and Society,* claims is very difficult to assume, because such a perspective does not yield "to consolidation of character" (28). As Harris puts it, the Caribbean writer is faced with the problem of how "to reconcile the broken parts of an enormous heritage, especially when those broken parts appear very often like a grotesque series of adventure, volcanic in its precipitate effects as well as human in its vulnerable settlement" (31). But broken, volcanic, even grotesque as these parts are, Harris stresses, as does Walcott, that it is in the gluing and joining of these parts that one discovers the Caribbean identity. It is this which Harris calls "remarkable about West Indian personality in depth," this sense of a "series of subtle and nebulous links which are latent within him" (28). For the writer then to portray one fragment without the other, to condemn or to praise one aspect of personality without acknowledging the coexistence of its opposite, is to distort the truth of the Caribbean person; for these competing fragments are as ever present in the Caribbean personality as are the many and varied ingredients in a *sancoche* soup which give it its distinctive flavor.

Perhaps V.S. Naipaul provides us with the clearest example of the dire consequences of this myopic view (though I hope to point out that Naipaul is not the only Caribbean writer who appears to find it difficult to deal with the paradox of Caribbean character). In his collection of essays *The Overcrowded Barracoon,* Naipaul says frankly that though every writer is, in the long run, on his own, "it helps, in the most practical way, to have a tradition." The English language he says, "was mine; the tradition was not" (25). As a Caribbean writer, then, Naipaul confronted his particular problem of possessing attitudes, values, and beliefs that were transmitted to him through the language of the British, a language which, though he claimed it as his own, originated with a people whose vision was not his. Indeed, Naipaul contends that the English way of seeing was alien to his own: "It diminished my own and did not give me the courage to do a simple thing like mentioning the name of a Port-of-Spain Street" (25).

Unfortunately, Naipaul does not extend this complexity of personality and the containment of paradox to his portrayal of Caribbean character. For when he attempts to mirror the West Indian in his writings, he sees only fragments that are reductions and distortions of the original. And he views the "glue" that bonds the parts not as Walcott urges us to—as that which creates a new and stronger symmetry—but rather as mimicry of the original, the parody of a foolish people ridiculously imitating that which they could never hope to attain. Thus it is that the Caribbean cities of Naipaul's novels teem with corrupt philistines who mimic European customs and habits, prostitute the integrity of European ideals and values, and are themselves filled with self-contempt and loathing.

Singh, the East Indian protagonist of Naipaul's novel *The Mimic Men*, is presented as "justifiably alarmed" that on the island he was now claiming as his, he found himself "now committed to a whole new mythology, dark and alien, committed to a series of interiors I never wanted to enter" (188). He can empathize with Hok, of mixed Chinese and Negro parentage, who refused to acknowledge his Negro mother in public, because it "wasn't only that the mother was black and of the people, though that was a point; it was that he had been expelled from that private hemisphere of fantasy where lay his true life" (97). And where is that "private hemisphere of fantasy"? It is for Singh located in the legacy of Europe, that fragment of civilization that can be glimpsed in the midst of Caribbean corruption. It is to be found in *The Heroes*, the last book Hok was reading. "What a difference," Singh bemoans, "between the mother of Perseus and that mother!" (97).

How then to reconcile these opposing fragments—that of the legacy of the conqueror (by implication the superior) and that of the conquered, the enslaved, the indentured (by implication the inferior)? One approach could be that of those writers, the novelist George Lamming in particular, who use the paradigm of the Prospero-Caliban relationship as a means of explaining and interpreting Caribbean character. Thus for these writers, as Caliban learned language from Prospero, so did the Caribbean acquire a new language from the English. As Caliban was generous to Prospero, showing him which streams were fresh, which poisonous, which land barren, which fertile, so was the Caribbean to the English, cultivating Caribbean lands for the Englishman's profit. As Prospero betrayed and enslaved Caliban, so did the English repay the Caribbean for kindness by imposing a state of political and economic dependence. As Caliban revolted against Prospero's attempt to denigrate his past, so must the Caribbean resist the seductive lure of the English that would encourage rejection of Africanness. The Caribbean person, then, may contain fragments of the English personality, but these fragments are not to be embraced or celebrated. Rather, they are to be rejected and reviled. There can be no coexistence of these irreconcilable opposites.

In Lamming's novel *The Emigrants,* a man gives advice to Collis, a fledgling writer who is "running away" from his own country to seek exile in England. He says:

> A writer's work is public property. That's not my fault nor yours. It's as it
> should be. But you remember: every word you use can be a weapon turned
> against the enemy or inward on yourself, and to live comfortably with the
> enemy within you is the most criminal of all betrayals. (100)

What does it mean "to live comfortably with the enemy within you"? Lamming's entire oeuvre can be viewed as an attempt to respond to this question. In his first novel, *In the Castle of My Skin*, the young boys are taught in Sunday school that "it would be better to belong to the empire and in the end to get back to the garden. After all there was nothing to lose by belonging to the empire" (73). But when they grow up, they discover there is everything to lose: self-esteem, self-rule, dignity, manhood. In their struggle for political independence from England, these young nationals begin to understand the consequence of allegiance to and love for the British empire. For it is the older generation who have accepted the inferior status accorded them by the British, who are their greatest obstacles. These adults regard their island as Little England, an essential part of Big England: "Like children under the threat of hell-fire, they accepted instinctively that the others, meaning the white, were superior" (21).

Ultimately in his final novel, *Natives of My Person,* Lamming makes it clear that the survival of Caribbean identity depends on the Caribbean ability to resist European influence. The Caliban one meets in this novel is not a creature in the "process of becoming" who depends upon Prospero for his identity. Rather, this Caliban resists Prospero, preferring death to surrender. Indeed, in no other work does Lamming make it clearer that these contradictory aspects of Caribbean character (fragments of the Old World of Europe and shards of the Americas, Asia, and Africa) cannot coexist. The very environment of the tropics works against this coexistence and rejects the European "fragments." Tropical breezes carry an infection that seeps into the brains of the Europeans, driving them to madness or self-destruction. Tropical birds crash into the ships of the colonizers, piling dead bodies on the deck so that the Europeans are forced to "run for cover." After the birds come the crocodiles turning the water blood red. By contrast, the Caribbean landscapes provide the natives with underground caves to protect them from the European invasion.

It is not surprising, then, that in the Caribbean novel, the crisis in the life of the Caribbean character is more often than not caused by the character's growing awareness that Caribbean identity is shaped by fragments of opposing cultures. This awareness is further complicated by a sense of shame and embarrassment about aspects of the Caribbean character which are rooted in Africa or Asia.

Let us take, for example, the bildungsromans of Merle Hodge and Jamaica Kincaid. In Hodge's novel *Crick Crack Monkey*, Tee, the main character, moves in two worlds, the world of Tantie and the world of Aunt Beatrice. In Tantie's rural world, the children of the inheritors of England's policy of slavery or indentured servitude live in harmony with each other and the tropical landscapes. Tee is at home with her Indian friend, Doolarie, and Tantie has ongoing amicable disagreements with the Chinese shopkeeper. While no specific references are made to Africa, African beliefs in the spirit and the ancestors permeate everyday life and provide explanations for occurrences such as the frequent breaking of the swing under the mango vert tree ("there was a jumbie living in the tree" [5]), or the winning of so many scholarships by the students in the Roman Catholic school ("It was all on account of their nuns and Fathers working obeah with Mary-statues and candles in the Catholic Church" [52]).

In this world where the "air smelt brown and green," Tee and her friends are free to run "as if [they] would always be wiry-limbed children whose darting about the sun would capture like amber and fix into eternity" (18). This Eden begins to shatter when Tee goes to the Big School and learns there is punishment for not giving due reverence to the British King. Her teacher informs the class that "not an eyelid must bat not a finger must twitch when we honor the Mother Country" (26).

Tee wins an academic scholarship to the best high school in the city, where she enters the middle-class world of Aunt Beatrice. Here Mr. Hinds's lessons are reinforced. Tee is admonished for her "ordinariness" and her "niggerness" for eating with a spoon; for liking tropical fruits and Caribbean food; for wanting to go to Doolarie's wedding, which her aunt dismisses as a "coolie affair"; and for wanting to wear her best dress, which her aunt discards as "niggery-looking." She begins to understand that she is expected to be ashamed of her

African roots and that her dark skin represents "the rock-bottom of the family's
fall from grace" (82).

She is taught that the European fragment of her identity is the better part and
that she would do well to suppress the other part. Soon she becomes confused
by her feelings of resentment toward her Tantie and her shame for finding herself thinking that way. On a seaside holiday with her Aunt Beatrice and her
cousins, she is troubled by a vision of her relatives on her Tantie's side of the
family:

> I saw us coming up out of the water with our petticoats and panties and old
> trousers clutching at our bodies, and some of us who hadn't bothered to
> find a piece of tattered clothing to bathe in, naked. And then Ma. Ma who
> sold in the market. Ma who was a market-woman. I wondered if Auntie
> Beatrice were aware of this fact. Then I thought with bottomless horror
> *suppose Bernadette and Carol and Jessica* came to know of this! It was not
> a thought to linger upon for one second. Frantically I swept it out of my
> mind, and into the vacuum floated Auntie Beatrice, leaning on the bannis-
> ter, looking out to sea, as I was crouching there looking out at the sea. I was
> irritated at the sea. I considered it had no right to roll itself to and fro, to
> and fro, in such a satisfied manner, as though nothing at all was wrong.
> And the sea-birds and the jumbled footprints in the sand and the dead leaves
> insulted me, too. (88–89)

Later Tee begins to feel that her "very sight" is "an affront to common de-
cency," and she wishes that her body could "shrivel up and fall away," that she
could "step out new and acceptable" (97). Ultimately, she concludes that the
only way to alleviate her distress is to run away, to leave the island. When her
father invites her to visit him in England, Tee desires "with all my heart that it
were next morning and a plane were lifting me off the ground" (111).

Jamaica Kincaid's *Annie John*, the main character of her novel of the same
name, responds in very much the same way as Tee to this clashing of the contradictory heritages that form her identity. She tells us of the "paradise" she lived
in as a child when she felt no conflict between the African world of obeah and
the spirits and the Judeo-Christian world of her Sunday school class. But once
she enters the big school, she begins to experience discomfort with the slave
master's culture, and she struggles to reconcile her sympathy for her English
classmate with the rage she knows she should have for "the terrible things her
ancestors had done." She concludes:

> Of course, sometimes, what with our teachers and our books, it was hard
> for us to tell on which side we really now belonged—with the masters or
> the slaves—for it was all history; it was all in the past, and everybody
> behaved differently now; all of us celebrated Queen Victoria's birthday,
> even though she had been dead a long time. But we, the descendants of the
> slaves, knew quite well what had really happened. (76)

It is this knowledge of what *really* happened that makes it difficult for Annie John to feel at ease in the world she finds herself loving more and more. In a scene uncannily reminiscent of that in Naipaul's *The Mimic Men* where Singh empathizes with Hok's yearning for "that private hemisphere of fantasy where lay his true life," Annie John tells that her frequent daydreams are of scenes in Belgium, a place she had picked because Charlotte Brontë, the author of her favorite novel, *Jane Eyre*, had spent a year there. More and more, she longs to be where "at last" she could understand the books she read (92).

Confused by these contradictory feelings, Annie John—like Tee, who admits that "at times she resented Tantie bitterly"—begins to resent her mother and the world she represents, with its "everlasting blue sky" and "everlasting hot sun." She, too, wants to run away. She says, "The things I never wanted to see or hear or do again now made up at least three weeks' worth of grocery lists. I placed a mark against obeah women, jewelry, and white underclothes" (135).

This, of course, is the peculiar dilemma of the Caribbean person: How to live comfortably in the castle of the skin, when within the walls of that castle are opposing forces which nevertheless claim equal rights to ownership of the castle. The shock of the awareness of this paradox propels both Kincaid's Annie John and Hodge's Tee into desperate flight to escape the horror of their acceptance of the "enemy" and the shame of their rejection of the "victim." How much more interesting it would have been for the reader had Kincaid and Hodge dared to develop their characters beyond this point, to present us with characters that every Caribbean person knows exist: those who live comfortably with irreconcilable opposites, those like Walcott, who says of himself, "I'm just a red nigger who love the sea,/ . . . I have Dutch, nigger, and English in me,/ and either I'm nobody, or I'm a nation" ("The Schooner Flight" 346).

Yet Walcott's work, in spite of his bold assertion, does not always reflect his ease with these "shards," as he calls them, these fragments from "disparate cultures" and "partially remembered customs," held together by a glue that makes the person whole and distinctly Caribbean. I attended a reading Walcott gave of *Omeros* at Queens College on November 23, 1993. At the question-and-answer period, a student with all the fresh innocence of his youthfulness, asked, "Mr. Walcott, was *Omeros* your attempt to make an analogy between the characters of Homer's *Odyssey* and the people of St. Lucia?"

Walcott seemed ready for the question. He cleared his throat and asserted that it would be foolish of him to write some sort of Black *Odyssey*. He said that some people were under the erroneous impression that that was what he was trying to do, as if a fisherman or fisherwoman in St. Lucia could not be heroic in his or her own right. He then mused on his own childhood and the admiration he had for the courage of the fishermen who risked their lives every day on a fickle sea. These are the true heroes, he said. If one were called Achilles, another Hector, another Helen, it was certainly not because they were aware of a literary and cultural connection to Homer's characters. In fact, he said, it is arrogance on the part of Plunkett, the Englishman living on the island where *Omeros* is set, to think that he could only admire the Caribbean Helen by comparing her to the Homeric Helen. Walcott quoted from *Omeros*:

> Helen needed a history
> that was the pity Plunkett felt towards
> her.
> Not his, but her story. Not theirs,
> but Helen's war.
> The name, with its historic hallucination,
> brightened the beach (31)

After reading these lines, Walcott murmured into his microphone something to the effect that, of course, one must question not only Plunkett but the author of *Omeros* who chose to write his poem from this frame of reference.

It is indeed that very specter of doubt Walcott raised by the comment mumbled under his breath that has been the source of criticism of his work by some Caribbean writers and critics. For despite Walcott's passionate condemnation of those who dismiss every West Indian endeavor as imitative (which many read as a veiled rebuke of Naipaul), there are as many who suspect Walcott of not being sufficiently Afrocentric, of placing more worth on the contributions of his European ancestors than on those of his African forefathers.

Be that as it may, this debate will surely go on. There will always be people who will demand that the Caribbean person not be at ease with contradiction; who, like Rochester in Jean Rhys's *Wide Sargasso Sea*, will require that the Caribbean person choose; who will not be able to understand that an Antoinette can feel a sense of belonging both to the African world of obeah and to the world of her English slave-owning ancestors. So, like Rochester, they will rename Antoinette, try to remake her, take her back to the home of her English forefathers. Then, like Rochester, they may call her insane when she chooses to plunge toward the freedom she finds in the moment of suspension between the fiery English mansion and the illusion of Tia's beckoning hands. If only Rochester could have accepted what he saw so clearly: "Creole of pure English descent she may be, but they are not English or European either" (67).

The challenge for the Caribbean writer is to portray this paradox, to insulate herself from the politics of the moment so that she can recreate the true image of the Caribbean person—fragments of original sources with histories of violence and antipathy towards each other, but fragments which nevertheless now coexist to form a whole identity that, to quote Walcott, is "not decayed but strong" (*Antilles* 11). The challenge is to render the contradictions in the Caribbean character in the way Gabriel García Márquez has done for us with Caribbean settings so that we see how something new and unique has been created out of parts of different cultural histories.

Early in his novel *Love in the Time of Cholera,* García Márquez describes the home of Dr. Juvenal Urbino. He tells us that though the reception rooms were furnished with European pieces from the late nineteenth century, "that European coherence vanished in the rest of the house, where wicker armchairs were jumbled together with Viennese rockers and leather footstools made by local craftsmen. Splendid hammocks from San Jacinto, with multicolored fringes along the sides and the owner's name embroidered in Gothic letters with silk thread, hung in the bedrooms along with the beds" (19). In the dining room there are Turkish rugs on the tiles, a Manila shawl on the piano. And, as if this eclectic mix were not enough, García Márquez tells us that Fermina Daza, the wife of Juvenal Urbino, "was an irrational idolator of tropical flowers and domestic animals" (21), so that all sorts of tropical flowers and trees and animals could be found in their garden and in their house: curlews and swamp herons eating anthuriums in flowerpots, an Amazonian monkey chained to a mango tree, an anaconda with free rein in the house to frighten the bats, salamanders, and the countless species of harmful insects that could be found everywhere during the rainy season. It is against this setting where symmetry is achieved out of apparent chaos that García Márquez wants us to judge his characters. Like the home of Dr. Urbino, like his colonial city which he refers to as "an illusion of memory," these Caribbean people are not European, Asian, African, or Amerindian, but contain parts of them all and are shaped by their many perspectives.

"Caribbean genius," Walcott tells us, "is condemned to contradict itself" (*Antilles* 21), and the critic of Caribbean literature must be open to this paradox. She must be able to appreciate what Caribbean sociologist Anthony Maingot calls upon his non-Caribbean colleagues to understand: One cannot predict in the Caribbean how things will turn out by simply basing one's conclusion on empirical evidence of origins. (Discussion at a Caribbean Studies conference at the University of Florida at Gainesville, 22 October 1994). The critic must bring a way of seeing to the interpretation of Caribbean literature that will allow her to find coherence in seeming inconsistencies in the thinking and behavior of Caribbean characters. She must be willing to divest herself of traditional criteria that might make it impossible for her to understand that the Caribbeans can celebrate the old plantation system while condemning it; they can rejoice in the rich heritage of their African or Asian past while extolling the beauty of their European cultural connections; they can dance through the streets at Carnival to the rhythms of the steelpan, an instrument forged out of the slave experience, while costumed as characters from Milton's *Paradise Lost.*

Works Cited

García Márquez, Gabriel. *Love in the Time of Cholera.* New York: Knopf, 1988.

Harris, Wilson. *Tradition, the Writer and Society.* London: New Beacon, 1967.

Hodge, Merle. *Crick Crack Monkey.* 1970. London: Heinemann, 1987.

Kincaid, Jamaica. *Annie John.* New York: Farrar, 1983.

Lamming, George. *The Emigrants.* 1954. New York: McGraw Hill, 1955.

———. *In the Castle of My Skin.* New York: Collier, 1953.

———. *Natives of My Person.* 1972. London: Picador, 1974.

Naipaul, V. S. *The Mimic Men.* 1967. Middlesex: Penguin, 1967.

———. *The Overcrowded Barracoon.* New York: Knopf, 1972.

Rhys, Jean. *Wide Sargasso Sea.* 1966. New York: Norton, 1982.

Walcott, Derek. *The Antilles: Fragments of Epic Memory.* New York: Farrar, 1993.

———. *Omeros.* New York: Farrar, 1990.

———. "The Schooner Flight." *Collected Poems, 1948–1984.* New York: Noonday, 1986.

5 Teaching and Learning across Cultures: The Literature Classroom as a Site for Cultural Transactions

Joyce C. Harte
Borough of Manhattan Community College, CUNY

Tradition has never favored the woman. (Jason)

Society dictates how women should live, what they should do and should not do. Fortunately, there are always women who rebel against these oppressive demands, and look for their own self-realization even if it means risking their own lives. (Nora)

Where there is oppression, there is resistance. (Linda)

Any human being should . . . have choices and not be locked into roles. (Jon)

Thank you for self-growth through literature. (Anne)

I strongly believe that one of the major functions of literature is to expand the reader's experience. This belief comes as a result of the ways in which literature has touched my life. I share the beliefs of Maxine Greene and Louise Rosenblatt in the power of literature to help readers transcend their own existence by opening themselves to the lived realities of people outside their own immediate culture. But, as Jane Tompkins reminds us, literature is also a vehicle of cultural definition. It should offer readers an opportunity to learn about and affirm themselves.

When I was a young girl growing up in British Guiana, now Guyana, books allowed me to imaginatively cross the boundaries of time and place. The childhood image most vivid to me is of a twelve-year-old girl lying flat on her stomach on the floor reading a book. This was my favorite place and position. It was where I would transport myself into other worlds, other possibilities. It was from this position that I would gradually become aware of my mother's voice calling me to run some errand or do some chore I had promised to do long hours before. Only after a threat would I get up from my book.

I was an avid reader and I often finished at least two books per day. I would then walk about five miles to the colonial public library, return them, borrow more, and hurry home in the dimming sunlight to read again, and again lose myself in a world of language. But what were those worlds to which I was transported in my reading? What were the books I read, and whose language was I absorbing? Although I was unaware of it at the time, the language, beliefs, and customs of my life-world lay far outside the boundaries of that culture represented by the books I read at school and at home. A critical part of my relationship to literature meant identifying with the culture and ideologies of a foreign white world. In other words, I, in the castle of my black skin, learned to read and write the world as an English person with a white Western yardstick.

In our classroom, with the tropical sun blazing down upon its roof, we were offered English culture through English literature and history. Our literary diet consisted of Shakespeare, Milton, Austen, and Keats. I recited and sang "with expression" my aesthetic delight in Wordsworth's daffodils and Shakespeare's "Song to Silvia." I memorized the lineage of English royalty. I learned about the Battle of Hastings and William the Conqueror. I analyzed, parsed, and wrote précis of poetry and prose passages. I remember my headmaster giving us "who steals my purse, steals trash /'Tis something, nothing/ . . . and has been slave to thousands." Long after I forgot that these lines were from *Othello,* I remembered that *he* was understood as the subject of the verb *steals.* And finally, I along with all the children in my classroom, descendants of slaves, sang confidently of our belief that as Britons, we "never, never shall be slaves."

In none of these cross-cultural encounters with literature was there any acknowledgment of the people who inhabited my landscape, my reality. It was as if we did not exist.

Part of what underlies my teaching has to do with my own experience as a reader/learner in a colonial context. The function of English education in colonial classrooms was to create a community of "common readers" (Hirsch) of one set of literature, one set of knowledge. The literary standard was fixed and held true for all readers. Differences were denied. Absent from my school experience was any admission of the dimensions of race, gender, sex, or class. Learning was a one-way transmission of knowledge from an English literary text which was projected, in the words of Ania Loomba, as "an amalgam of universal value, morality, truth, rationality" (1) and which we, as passive reader/learners, accepted and internalized unquestioned.

We acquired the language and culture of the British academy at the expense of our own cultures, our own selves.

My first consideration as a teacher who has been shaped by a colonial history is to recognize that which has previously been marginalized or excluded. I offer my students texts that not only reflect their lives, their landscapes, their realities, but that also reflect the wider culture of the world in which we live. My second consideration has to do with how those texts are taught. I want students to be active participants who engage with and reflect on texts and who question and criticize using their own backgrounds and experience in the production of knowledge. Thus, I have tried to create what Frances Maher calls "an interactive pedagogy, a pedagogy which integrates student contributions into the subject matter" (9).

I teach in an urban community college composed of mainly working-class students of African American, Latino, and Caribbean cultures. They are overwhelmingly female. Many of them have gained access to college through open admissions at the City University of New York. They see education as a vehicle to change their lives, which are often lived on the borders of society. Their responses, the meanings they construct, the ways they approach literature, and their ways of knowing are often based on their life experiences and their membership in particular communities.

Maxine Greene has written:

> In the culture of the United States, because of its brutal and persistent racism, it has been painfully difficult for Afro-American young people to affirm and be proud of what they choose as personal history. Poverty, hopelessness, the disruption of families and communities, the ubiquity of media images—all of these make it difficult for Black youth to place new conceptions against a past too often made to appear a past of victimization, shadows, and shame. (256)

It is perhaps because of this victimization, shadows, and shame that my students are often reluctant to read novels that only depict painful cultural experiences. They also want to read texts that affirm and empower them as men and women, that allow them to negotiate their own histories and to articulate their own realities and their own ways of being in the world, that allow them to grow, as Phoeby puts it in *Their Eyes Were Watching God*, "ten feet higher." In Adrienne Rich's words, my students want to read "with belief that what they read has validity for them" (65).

In the spring and summer of 1994, I taught an English elective course entitled "Women in Literature." My theme was a cross-cultural perspective on women's quest for personal freedom and self-definition. The novels I used were Kate Chopin's *The Awakening*, Zora Neale Hurston's *Their Eyes Were Watching God*, Zee Edgell's *Beka Lamb* and Mariama Bâ's *So Long a Letter*. The novels depict in a global way the cultural forces that seek to oppress women and the women's struggle not only to define a self, but also for the right to live their lives to the fullest potential. My aim was to give visibility and voice in the literature classroom to women authors and writers of color. My use of these texts draws on a paradigm suggested by the work of Henry Louis Gates Jr. (1991), who asserts that "the challenge facing America in the next century will be the shaping, at long last, of a truly common public culture, one responsive to the long-silenced cultures of color" (712). Gates suggests that we rethink education so that our teaching becomes an invitation to our students to enter into "conversation in which we learn to recognize the voices, each conditioned by a different perception of the world" (723). These novels provided the opportunity for my students, men and women of mixed ethnic and cultural backgrounds, to enter into conversation with these texts as they examined the thought, feeling, opinion, and lived experience of these literary women who refused "to keep their tongue between their teeth" *(Beka Lamb* 35).

The course derived its theoretical and pedagogical framework from a combination of reader-response, cultural, and feminist pedagogies. In *The Feminist Classroom,* feminist educators Frances Maher and Kay Thompson Tetreault define feminist and liberatory pedagogies as those which "aim to encourage the students, particularly women, working-class students, and members of underrepresented ethnic groups, to gain an education that would be relevant to their concerns, to create their own meanings, and to find their own voices in relation to the material" (9–10). As well, Louise Rosenblatt opens *The Reader, the Text, the Poem* (1978) with the statement: "The premise of this book is that a text, once it leaves its author's hands, is simply paper and ink until a reader evokes from it a literary work—sometimes, even, a literary work of art" (i). The experience of reading is an interactive, dialectical process whereby readers transact with texts using their own lives and experiences as men and women in society to help them construct meaning and knowledge from the experiences of the texts. However, as Patrocinio Schweikart indicates, reader-response criticism has tended to be utopian and has overlooked "the issues of race, class, and sex, and [has given] no hint of the conflicts, sufferings, and passions that attend these realities" (35). This leads Schweikart to assert that "reader-response criticism needs feminist criticism" (36).

I asked students to keep journals of their reading. Their responses served as springboards for class discussions. I began the course by having students read a few selected traditional and feminist versions of fairy tales which I supplied as a way of exploring traditional and changing perceptions of women and their roles in society. After the fairy tales and before starting discussion of the novels, the students and I also read the title essay from Alice Walker's *In Search of Our Mothers' Gardens* and Virginia Woolf's "If Shakespeare Had Had a Sister" from *A Room of One's Own.* These essays placed in historical perspective some of the issues and tensions affecting women's lives and the constraints their particular cultures imposed on them. Students wrote journal responses to lines or ideas they found significant. These responses were discussed in class and the issues raised formed a framework for discussion of not only the novels, but also for the two films we later saw: *Madame Bovary* and *Thelma and Louise.*

In "Toward a Black Feminist Criticism," Barbara Smith states that "the Black Feminist critic would find innumerable commonalities in works by Black women . . . and would assert the connections . . . of all Black women" (164). However, while in teaching we generally examine the commonalities in the texts of women of the African diaspora, seldom do we explore and examine the commonalities of experience between black and white women in literature. As Alice Walker states, "black and white writers seem to be writing one immense story . . . with different parts . . . coming from a multitude of different perspectives." She suggests that it is only when we open ourselves to these multiple realities that we understand "the whole story." While it is imperative that we first give students an intact sense of their own humanity, a sense of their own traditions, this does not mean a rejection of other cultures. We must be careful to avoid closing our students off from other diverse melodies and avoid perpetuating those "fixities" that Maxine Greene cautions us about (256).

In this essay I would like to give voice to and celebrate my students, those "academic outsiders" who engaged with these texts. The snapshots I offer here of student responses, taken from their papers, demonstrate that while students inevitably focused on race, gender, class, and religion as social forces which have a negative impact on women's lives and which serve to repress their voices, their journals and essays show concern with the broader concepts of freedom and the true worth of human life. As Nora, a Salvadoran woman, asks, "Is not freedom something we would all like to have?" They see this need for freedom as no easy fight because "the opinion of society is like a strong tidal wave knocking against the person who wishes to get through it without drowning" (Anne).[1]

It was mentioned continually in class discussion that the one who has power does not relinquish it easily. Students saw women's struggles as reflective of the larger fight against injustices that society perpetuates. In Jean's words, "Society doesn't like sudden change. It prefers to keep doing the same tired things and holding the same tired beliefs, even if they are wrong." She also recognizes that it is these forces that sometimes give rise to a process of accommodation: "Unfortunately social forces make us accommodate to situations that many times we do against our will."

The first two novels my students read were Kate Chopin's *The Awakening* and Zora Neale Hurston's *Their Eyes Were Watching God*. After journal writing and class discussion of our responses to the individual texts, I asked students to write an essay in which they compared Edna of *Awakening* and Janie of *Eyes*. I asked them to define the nature of each woman's search for personal freedom and self-definition. They were to consider the protagonists' worlds, and their particular circumstances—the time, place, way of life, and codes of conduct, etc., that govern their lives.[2] That is, they were to consider the relationship of individuals to their cultural contexts.

"The Rebellious Conviction of Their Spirits"

Many students expressed the view that "self-realization, self-definition and . . . personal freedom are processes that everyone aspires to." They also asserted that for women the process is much more difficult because of the way "they have been socialized." Students acknowledged that "gender roles, ethnicity, societal views, pressures and the time in which a person lives affect this process" (Jon).

Students read, discussed, and wrote about *The Awakening* and *Their Eyes Were Watching God* as the stories of two women: Edna Pontellier, a white woman who, in the words of Linda, an Asian American young woman, "lived in a world in which man's expectations and morals override woman's personal inclinations and desires" and Janie Starks, a black woman who "is pushed into her first marriage by a grand historical scheme called slavery." Nevertheless, these two women want to "discover themselves as women, as human beings through their own choices; not anyone else's" (Nora).

Students described many commonalities between Edna and Janie, such as their similar personal needs. Each woman seeks freedom, personal growth, and sexual passion. Alice asserts that both Janie and Edna "experience a general oppressiveness and lack of nurturance and understanding in their marriages" because "they both are with men that see them as figures and possessions." Similarly, for both of them, Anne says, there is an "early lesson in the futility of dutiful marriage." Marriage serves to deaden and stifle the voices of these women. Léonce Pontellier and Joe Starks treat their wives as if they cannot think, talk, or make decisions on their own: "Léonce reproached his wife with her inattention, her habitual neglect of the children. . . . If it was not a mother's place to look after children, whose on earth was it?" (Chopin 5). As Nora asserts, "he does not think he is part of the commitment." Jody Starks deemed Janie less than human: "Somebody got to think for women and chillun and chickens and cows" (Hurston 67). But, Janye says "Janie knew it wasn't true. . . . She knew Jody only got his power as a 'man' because he didn't dare come up against another man."

In addition, Edna and Janie have hidden talents—Edna for painting and Janie for shooting (hunting), and they both have trouble swimming. And, Alice says, "If the ocean offers the contemplation that brings answers to the questions of the soul then it is symbolic that the two protagonists find themselves confronting the water."

As adolescents, both Edna and Janie were questioning, and both authors use images of nature to describe the dreams of Edna and Janie for personal and sexual liberation. Janie was a "questioning young girl wondering about love and seeing it symbolically in bees, flowers, and blooming pear trees," Nora says. And Jon concurs: "Janie is an adolescent who is full of hopes, dreams, romantic notions and questions." At sixteen, Janie was "seeking the beauty of blossoming sexuality":

> She was stretched on her back beneath the pear tree soaking in the alto chant of the visiting bees, the gold of the sun and the panting breath of the

breeze. . . . She saw a dust-bearing bee sink into the sanctum of a bloom;
the thousand sister-calyxes arch to meet the love embrace and the ecstatic
shiver of the tree from root to tiniest branch creaming in every blossom
and frothing with delight. (Hurston 11)

Janie seeks this vision of fulfillment.

Similarly, in *The Awakening* when Edna talks about her childhood, she expresses her desire for freedom when she ran away from the oppression of a
church service:

I was just walking diagonally across a big field. My sun-bonnet obstructed
the view. I could only see the stretch of green before me, and I felt as if I
must walk on forever, without coming to the end of it. I don't remember
whether I was frightened or pleased. (16)

Edna kept this adolescent view of open possibilities buried deep within her. In
the words of Debbie, she "chiseled into the conventional cores of her stiffling
[sic] society" in search of that dream, and failing, "enhanced the flavor of her
life with the salted waters of the sea."

Students also commented on the women's "unusual circumstances" concerning fertility and motherhood. Alice remarks that "Janie has three marriages and
no children, all the while being symbolized with blooming and fertile pear trees.
Edna ends up killing herself because she cannot have the complete personal
freedom that she wants because of her children." Florence agrees with this view,
saying that "Edna viewed the . . . kids in her life as a burden and an infringe
ment on her freedom."

Yet while Edna and Janie both ask "Who am I?" and while both are "striking
in their similarities," due to the circumstances and prevailing conditions, they
are "just as dramatic in their differences" (Alice). These differences are evident
in the social tones pervading the novels. Two aspects of these differences that
student responses focused on were class and racial identity.

Edna and Janie's socio-economic backgrounds are different even though students acknowledged that both "move either down or up in social and/or economic class" (Alice). According to Florence, a Senegalese student, Edna, an
"upper crust lady, and the daughter of a father who owned a Mississippi plantation, had many opportunities. . . . She was opportuned [sic] with the basic necessities . . . for a white southern middle class woman." Edna's position in the
society is one of privilege. As a white Anglo-Saxon woman, she never questions her privilege and status in the society. Her search for self is not complicated by the color of her skin. Anne's response illustrates this view:

Edna indulges in her lifestyle as a birthright, and although she moves to the
tiny apartment, she rejects social mores through adultery, not through giving up a lot of financial security.

Meanwhile, students saw Janie's struggle "to come into her own" as complicated by the fact that she is black. She must struggle against the historic and
social realities of her world and against her grandmother's stifling view that
"De nigger woman is de mule uh de world so fur as Ah can see" (14). Janye
says: "Nanny wanted Janie to see there is no such thing as love for the black
woman and that she better be smart and marry a 'rich' man." Florence agrees:
"As an African American in the depths of Florida, Janie is born into poverty as
a granddaughter of a black ex-slave." Her life "is one of pain and struggle."
Alice, an African American young woman, observes, "Growing up black in a
white household being called everything but her name (which is even a slave
name by circumstance) . . . Janie has to fight against being 'de mule of de
world.'" Janie lacks status and economic security. At Nanny's insistence, she
marries Logan Killicks and moves into the economic security of "sixty acres
and a house" (20).

Janie does move up in socio-economic status, but in her search for growth
and self-actualization, she is willing to give up economic status. With Tea Cake,
Nora says, Janie "is able to learn a little of everything about life, such as poverty, love, and survival." They do so within a "rich environment where they
share different experiences with different kinds of people." Anne shares this
view. She says that "Janie . . . is much more soulful to me, much more of a
mentor spirit. . . . She shuns the materialistic view her grandmother placed on
her. . . . Janie walks her road . . . corougeously [sic]."

It was in how each woman sought to define self and personal freedom that
students saw the greatest difference between these heroines. Students were also
divided in their allegiances; some admired Janie, some admired Edna. Some
students saw Janie's quest as the more traditional, since she finds the personal
freedom that comes with self-realization and empowerment through love and
community:

> At the end of the novel Janie is experienced and wise, she finds out "about
> living fuh herself." She is contemplative and comfortable with herself. She
> had loved. And that was what she wanted. (Alice)
>
> Janie was an inspirational character because she reached her goal without
> being dragged through the gutter as a black prostitute or as a mammy clean-
> ing some white person's house. (Sanya)

Janie is

> conditioned by a desire to break poverty and subjugation and yet in spite of
> this she sustains a romantic vision of life. (Linda)

Two responses crystalize the positions of the students. Anne says that Edna
"has her experiences, her awakening, and decides that the only way to honor its
insistence is through a drowning freedom." But Anne sees the main difference
between these "rebels" as being one man, Tea Cake:

> Vergible Woods saved Janie and Edna had to save herself. Did Edna ever find a man to stroke her hair, look at her other than [as] a lace doll-woman? The answer is no. Edna had herself and autonomy in the end. Yet her society wouldn't condone, and "the children appeared before her like antagonists" so she took the final gutsiest exit, sans love, without an ultimate sharing of that autonomy . . . Edna never finding her Teacake, dies stunted through her awareness, pained in her own truth . . . Janie has the strength to persevere because . . . a man had looked at her at the same exact level and loved her anyway. . . . Janie had the memory of that bliss of shared equality to keep her strong, to imprint a constant and secret smile upon her face, and she receives the gift of sharing it with Phoeby.

Jason, on the other hand, has a different perspective on the two women's quests. Even though he acknowledges similarities, he feels that "they do not compare overall in the development of themselves and in the way they define selfhood." He thinks (and several of the women also share his view) that Janie appears to be "hung up on her sexual wants and needs as a gross misrepresentation of love." Jason believes that "had Janie and Joe remained sexually active . . . it would have taken a longer time for [Janie] to develop her emotions and herself." Jason argues that with Jody Starks's death Janie grows somewhat self-reliant, but it is only when Tea Cake steps into Janie's life that the process is consummated. He recognizes that "the friendship between them was essential in their development as lovers." With Tea Cake, Janie literally and figuratively lets her hair down. He allows her to express, feel, and think for herself. He encourages her to be her own person. She finds her "pear blossom" love with Tea Cake.

But Jason admires and "respects" Edna Pontellier because as a "Virginia Woolf type, she needed space and time to develop and define herself." He sees Edna as "a victim of a common syndrome in which a person runs blindly from one bad situation into . . . another . . . [that] is not necessarily bad, but . . . is not suited for who she is . . . and who she will become." He quotes from the novel to support his point of view.

Edna's children are important to her, but not as important as her self. When the motions of marriage cease to exist, she, like Janie, finds her voice and asserts herself. From this point on, Edna knows that her obligation is to herself "first and foremost," prompting her husband Léonce to say, "She's got some sort of notion in her head concerning the eternal rights for women" (Chopin 65). Jason says that it was with these words that

> I realized how I respect Edna so much more than Janie. Janie was prepared to be a wife and succumb to the standards set for a woman as long as she had love. Even if her preconceived notion of love (which led her to marry Joe Starks) didn't exist, she still played the woman's role while she was with Tea Cake. Granted she was a stronger person and more thoughtful, but she was still the wife and homemaker standing by her man's side.

Edna, on the other hand, he argues,

> was not willing to give in. She needed to spread her wings and soar . . .
> being a housewife didn't fit in. Edna needed to define herself for herself,
> not for Leonce, her father, sister or Robert. There comes a point when a
> person has to stop what there [sic] doing and look at what it is they're
> doing and ask themselves if they're doing it for themselves. . . . Edna de-
> fined Edna and would be someone that I would like to know.

But Anne embraces both of these "rebels" whom she considers as the "leaders yesterday, today, and tomorrow." She chooses two quotes from the text that
she feels exemplify the "grit" and the "rebellious conviction of their spirits."
Edna speaks to Mademoiselle Reisz:

> "Painting!" laughed Edna. "I am becoming an artist. Think of it! . . . Show
> me the letter and play me the Impromptu. You see that I have persistence.
> Does that quality count for anything in art?" (68)

And Janie finds the voice to speak up and out to Joe Starks:

> "Naw, Ah ain't no young gal no mo' but den Ah ain't no old woman nei-
> ther. Ah reckon Ah looks mah age too. But Ah'm uh woman every inch of
> me, and Ah know it." (74)

The next two books we read were Mariama Bâ's *So Long a Letter* (Senegal)
and Zee Edgell's *Beka Lamb* (Belize). These two novels portray females (one
older and one younger) who struggle to find a voice and redefine a self against
traditional customs and norms such as religion and oppressive colonial values.
As the assignment for these two novels, I asked students to focus on one of the
characters that they found interesting or relevant. I asked them to describe the
ways in which the modern or the traditional worlds affected the character's
behavior, paying attention to the differing expectations about marriage, family,
and the roles of men and women.

Bâ's short epistolary novel depicts Ramatoulaye, a Muslim woman, mother,
and schoolteacher of Senegalese descent who is mourning her husband's death,
which according to Islamic custom she must do for four months. According to
Carmen, a Hispanic student, "this religious custom keeps women under a man's
foot. A woman can revolt against a man but how can a woman revolt against
God?" Through her long letter to her best friend Aissatou, Ramatoulaye "rum-
mages through her life as she tries to interpret her status as a wife, mother, and
woman in a culture dominated by strong patriarchal Islamic values" (Carmen).

In her letter, Ramatoulaye, who is described by one student as "beautiful,
noble, courageous, wise, loving, intelligent, educated," recounts how, after
twenty-five years of marriage, her husband Modou leaves her and takes a co-
wife who is the same age as their teenage daughter and how Ramatoulaye chooses
to stay in the marriage. Student responses revealed that despite the man's "subtle

intelligence . . . embracing sensitivity . . . readiness to help . . . and ambition which suffered no mediocrity" (Bâ 40), according to Alice he is always "able to hold the idea of another wife as an option allowed by Islamic religion." It comes down to what is advantageous to the man and, "with his advancing age and Ramatoulaye's too, Modou needs someone like the young Binetou whose beauty and youth was advantageous to his maturing image" (Alice).

For this reason, students celebrated Ramatoulaye's coming to voice at the moment she rejects the proposal of marriage from her brother-in-law, Tamsir, and breaks the silence her "voice has known for thirty years" (Bâ 58). Jason says: "When Ramatoulaye speaks up and out at Tamsir, it reminded me of Janie finally giving it to Joe Starks. The only thing I could think of, as it excited me, was 'YOU GO GIRL.'"

But not everyone applauded Ramatoulaye's decision to remain Modou's wife. They viewed her act as one of conformity. Nora says:

> With Ramatoulaye I was disappointed and in some moments annoyed. Although she refuses two marriage propositions after her husband abandons her, she gives too much credit to Modou. . . . From my point of view a man like him does not deserve to be mentioned by his wife. This is something so common in our daily lives. Many women do not separate from their husbands even if their relation is in chaos, because they believe that this is a cross that God has given them.

Aissatou, on the other hand, whose husband Mawdo also takes a young co-wife, chooses not to stay. She divorces her husband and leaves with her children. Several students liked her uncompromising stance and decision to break away from the traditional ways of doing things. Nora commented:

> Aissatou shows through her strong decision that she deserves respect. She does not allow herself to have pity for a man who had no respect for their union, commitment, and love. I admire her integrity, intelligence, and her pride for detaching herself from a sick environment and succeeding on her own.

Florence, a Senegalese student, agrees. She identifies with Aissatou because she herself is a child of a polygamous marriage. Florence says:

> Personally, as a product of a culture and society where polygamy was practiced, I greatly admired the strength, courage and personality of an African woman to resist the norms, customs and traditions of the village. . . . Polygamy should not be encouraged because it helps to destroy families, creates rifts between loved ones, breaks up relationships, dehumanizes women, enslaves and above all, treats women as objects of bed instead of human beings.

While Ramatoulaye faces her crisis in mid-life, *Beka Lamb* depicts a young Belizean girl whose struggles to define a sense of self parallel her country's struggle to break the yoke of oppressive colonial ideals. The colonialists' effort to create a "better society" through imposition of their religious and cultural values lead to a clash of ideas and cultural beliefs. Fourteen-year-old Beka struggles to find her own identity between the traditional creole culture represented by her Granny Ivy and the new imperialist culture represented by the Catholic Academy. Student responses focused on how the colonial world offered education which "served to expand the opportunities available to Belizeans, but it took away more than it offered in the way of oppressive values and oppressive religion which affected ...the whole country negatively." At one point, Beka says to Sister Gabriela, one of her teachers: "Sometimes I feel bruk down just like my own country, Sister. I start all right but then I can't seem to continue" (115). Students discussed some of the reasons for this feeling of "bruk down," which they recognized as stemming from the race and class discrimination inherited from colonialism and illustrated in the following exchange:

> "You think Milio will marry you when you graduate, Toycie?"
> "He said so," Toycie replied.
> "Panias [Hispanics] scarcely ever marry creoles like we, Toycie." (46)

Student responses and discussion also focused on gender issues and the way traditional religion is again used to socialize girls into rigid conformity. Sister Virgil, the European principal of the Academy, is there to instill the colonial values and standards of morality for the girls: "As young ladies you must walk always with an invisible veil about you so as not to unleash chaos upon the world" (Edgell 91).

One student, Angela, described Sister Virgil as "the stonewall of traditional belief." Such a belief said that girls must be virginal in order to avoid hellfire— a result of Eve's sin. This colonial world of high moral values offers to exchange the image of Eve, a sinner, for the Virgin Mary, an acceptable role model. Thus, when Beka's friend Toycie becomes pregnant, she not only feels "ashamed and dirty" (90), she is also expelled from school. Toycie suffers a nervous breakdown and attempts suicide. Emilio, the boy responsible for the pregnancy, is not expelled from school. As Nora explains, "Beka sees her friend Toycie betrayed by the man who made her pregnant and by the traditional society rules that blame a woman instead of giving her support."

The novel shows that among the Belizeans pregnancy outside of marriage is common. This, however, is not seen as a social stigma in the eyes of the people. As Granny Ivy says, "It's sad if you lost your virginity unmarried and to the wrong man, but if you lose it, you lose it. There's no need to degrade yourself" (Edgell 135).

But for Sister Virgil, Angela argues, "Religion has instilled a dark cold reality . . . which doesn't seem realistic, since . . . it may be understood that the sheltered life a nun leads, gives way to a sheltered interpretation of life." In this interpretation women are the ones who must learn to control their emotions. Angela goes on:

> A nun is the traditional and most ancient of submissive roles a woman can opt for. . . . Her sheltered, parish-maintained world did not expose her to the ever changing situations of the world. For example, financial strife, the obligation to family (with or without offspring), the effects of being a woman in a small town without any strings to pull. Sister Virgil has never experienced the painful struggle everyday women experience. By taking [the] habit, I believe she gave that all up before she really knew what being a woman was about. Therefore on the subject, Sister Virgil loses creditability [sic].
>
> . . . .
>
> It seems that Sister Virgil's conscience is composed [of] everything but her own. Throughout the novel, Sister Virgil never expressed an idea that was conceived from personal experience or belief. Her submission to the catholic blinders made her fail to see the modern problems . . . which . . . not only concern the modesty of a young girl. It concerns the education of young people as a whole, to be more aware, not modest and naive. This modern day happening is the true cause of the vulnerability that women experience.
>
> Sister Virgil's submission to a male based ideology (Catholicism) shadowed any effort she might have had [sic] to understand the women of Belize. Her traditional way of thinking is really just a male interpretation of the proper conduct of women. Structure, discipline, shame, obedience, are the male influenced teachings Sister Virgil holds dear. Teachings that contradict the struggle and progress of modern day communities and especially modern women.

In the final assignment for the course, entitled "Perspectives and Insights," I wanted students to take a new critical stance towards the events in the novels. I wanted them to synthesize the experiences reflected in the novels and write an essay in which they made some general point about the ability of society to impose behavior and the power women have to shape the conditions of their lives. I asked them to draw on the essays of Alice Walker and Virginia Woolf to enhance their perspectives.

While student responses focused on varied social forces controlling women's lives across cultures, I will quote selected snapshots from Anne's paper that I think demonstrate the personal and liberatory value of these novels for students:

> There are three closely-knit themes that tie these readings together: courage, wisdom and the satellite [sic] for truth . . . they go beyond the suffering that was birthright for each character, the pains, the struggles. These stories have purpose...they teach the woman reader that it won't be easy, but perseverance is the only catalyst for change, and change must happen for woman united to become whole.
>
> . . . .

They tell the reader of woman's ultimate need for equality and personal
power...they tell the woman reader to fight for herself yet makes it clear
that it is up to her to do, and no one else can suffer for her or gain her
dignities.
. . . .
Freedom is a collective movement. . . . Truth, through the wisdom of these
amazing authors, is personal. Once fought for it may be shared, just like
Janie and Phoeby, Ramatoulaye and Aissatou, Edna and Mademoiselle Reisz
(then the ocean), Alice Walker and her mother, Shakespeare's sister and us
. . . . That is why these novels impacted with affirming knowledge project
the reader, prod the reader, to find her (or his) own force; power and truth
in her (his) time and place. These stories don't hand it over. They force it
into hungry hands.

Conclusion

I began this essay by drawing on my own experience as a colonial reader of
English canonical texts. Because of the hallowed status of those "great books"
from which our realities were erased and a pedagogy which demanded awe and
reverence for the authority of these texts, we were constructed as passive students who imbibed literature unquestioningly. Education was indeed, in novelist Beryl Gilroy's apt description, "suitable indoctrination" (195).

As America continues to expand and become more global, we can no longer
afford to allow education to be indoctrination. We have to be cognizant of Freire's
reminder that in order to demythologize and demystify what counts as tradition
and knowledge, the learning experience must be "an invitation to make visible
the languages, dreams, values and encounters that constitute the lives of those
whose histories are often actively silenced" (65).

As the excerpts show, my students engaged and critically responded from
perspectives that were uniquely their own. They empathized, actively questioned,
and identified the cultural and historical forces that silence and repress. As they
read these women's texts, my students reflected on and tried to clarify their own
beliefs. They felt empowered to make changes in their own lives and in the
world. One young woman came to my office to discuss the impact of these
women's texts on her personal life. She informed me that she had decided to
leave her married lover. Another told me that she had been in an abusive marriage, but had never found the courage to leave. The courage of the women in
our readings allowed her to find her own. The sole young male student in my
class wrote a note thanking me for introducing him to these texts.

I do not know if these young women followed through with their decisions,
but I do know that when texts are not treated as static containers of "timeless"
truths which students are to approach as awed communicants, and when they
are given the freedom to test their assumptions and respond to texts in a
variety of ways and from the diversity of their lives, then they become active,

conscious, and aware human beings striving for change. They can now meet, connect, and enter into conversation with Austen, Faulkner, Shakespeare—not with blindness but with critical awareness and expanded visions. They can now identify aspects of their own humanity.

In order to transform our classrooms into interactive places, we can draw on a variety of socio-cultural theory and teaching practices. I use a reader-response combined with a feminist approach because it enables students to begin articulating and integrating their life experiences with texts. Feminist theory in particular stresses the need for classrooms to be places of collaborative, cooperative, and interactive dialogue where students are enabled to use their personal locations and intellectual experiences to transact with literature.

Notes

1. All excerpts are from students' writing, and I have preserved students' exact forms. See epigraphs.

2. My assignments are adapted from Schriner (in Berlin and Vivion).

Works Cited

Bâ, Mariama. *So Long a Letter.* Portsmouth: Heinemann, 1981.

Berlin, James, and Michael J. Vivion, eds. *Cultural Studies in the English Classroom.* Portsmouth: Boynton/Cook, 1992.

Chopin, Kate. *The Awakening.* New York: Avon, 1982.

Edgell, Zee. *Beka Lamb.* Portsmouth: Heinemann, 1982.

Freire, Paulo. *Education for Critical Consciousness.* New York: Continuum, 1969.

Gates, Henry Louis Jr. "Goodbye Columbus? Notes on the Culture of Criticism." *American Literary History* 3 (1991): 711–12.

Gilroy, Beryl. "I Write Because . . . ." *Caribbean Women Writers: Essays from the First International Conference.* Ed. Selwyn R. Cudjoe. Wellesley: Calaloux; Amherst: U of Massachusetts P, 1990. 195–201.

Greene, Maxine. "The Passions of Pluralism: Multiculturalism and the Expanding Community." *Journal of Negro Education* 61 (1993), 250–261.

Hirsch, E.D. Jr. *Cultural Literacy: What Every American Needs to Know.* Boston: Houghton, 1987.

Hurston, Zora Neale. *Their Eyes Were Watching God.* New York: Harper and Row, 1990.

Loomba, Ania. *Gender, Race, Renaissance Drama.* New York: Routledge & Kegan Paul, 1989.

Maher, Frances, and Kay Thompson Tetreault. *The Feminist Classroom.* New York: Basic, 1994.

Rich, Adrienne. "On Teaching Language in Open Admissions: A Look at the Context." *The Uses of Literature.* Harvard English Studies 4 (1973): 257–273.

Rosenblatt, Louise. *Literature as Exploration.* 1937. Reprint New York: Barnes and Noble, 1968.

————.*The Reader, the Text, the Poem: The Transactional Theory of the Literary Work* Carbondale: Southern Illinois UP, 1978.

Schriner, Delores. "One Person, Many Worlds: A Multi-Cultural Composition Curriculum." In Berlin and Vivion. 95–111.

Schweikart, Patrocinio. "Reading Ourselves: Toward a Feminist Theory of Reading." *Gender and Reading.* Ed. Elizabeth A. Flynn and Patrocinio Schweikart. Baltimore: Johns Hopkins UP, 1986.

Smith, Barbara. "Toward a Black Feminist Criticism." *All the Women Are White, All the Blacks Are Men, But Some of Us Are Brave.* Eds. Gloria T. Hull, Patricia Bell-Scott, and Barbara Smith. New York: Feminist Press, 1982.

Tompkins, Jane. *Sensational Designs.* New York: Oxford UP, 1985.

Walker, Alice. *In Search of Our Mothers' Gardens.* Orlando: Harcourt Brace Jovanovich, 1983.

Woolf, Virginia. "If Shakespeare Had Had a Sister." *A Room of One's Own.* 1929. New York: Harcourt, Brace and World, 1957. 43–259.

6 Remembering as Resistance in the Literature of Women of Color

Brenda M. Greene
Medgar Evers College, CUNY

Writers (especially American writers) . . . often disavow the notion of a "literary duty" of political consciousness . . . but I do have a duty, beyond telling a good story or drawing a convincing character. My duty is to give voice to continents, but also to redefine the nature of American and what makes an American. In the process, work like this by myself and others will open up the canon of American literature.

—Bharati Mukherjee, "A Four-Hundred-Year-Old Woman"

Woman, African American, mother, teacher/scholar, I live in multiple worlds, multiple spaces. I am an American but I do not see myself at the center of the American experience. I find myself reflecting on what it means to be an American, for as an African American woman in higher education, I do not see myself represented in America's perception of itself. I experience that amorphous space which Latina scholars call "the borderlands" and that dilemma which Du Bois calls a "double consciousness." Constructed by my race, I am constantly reminded that I cannot be at the center of America's reality, and as such I have felt a sense of duality and a sense of alienation from the world of my cultural roots, the world of mainstream America, and the world of academia. This duality and alienation began to manifest themselves when I entered primary school, the real world of school. During those years, I moved back and forth between these multiple worlds and spaces, and I searched for others, who like me, lived on the borderlands. As I now reflect on those years, I realize that this searching was the result of my unconscious attempt to reconnect those fragmented parts of myself.

I was able to articulate the double consciousness and marginalization I felt when I entered college and encountered other black students who had had similar experiences. I recognized in these students the multiple spaces and worlds they occupied. Through their stories, I learned how they had explored the historical, spiritual and cultural dimensions of their roots to transform their realities into ones which placed them at the center rather than on the margins of society. As I read history, literature, philosophy, psychology, and sociology, I began to see myself represented, and I began to understand the complexity of my role as an African American woman in this society. I began to understand that I lived what bell hooks calls "a particular reality" (*Feminist Theory* 2), a reality which enabled me to look both from the outside in and from the inside out.

Like me, female writers of color live "particular realities." In their roles as women of color, they live in multiple spaces, spaces which are not constricted by boundaries, spaces which overlap and shift, spaces which are defined and redefined by constructs of race, ethnicity, gender, and/or geographical locations. Bharati Mukherjee's quotation above expresses the challenges facing these writers. In these multiple spaces, they create fiction which provides America with multiple perspectives of itself.

The characters created by female writers of color cross cultural boundaries and live complicated lives which symbolize the conflicts experienced by those who live on the borderlands. These characters live in worlds where they move from the center to the margin and back again, worlds where the boundaries of gender, race, ethnicity, and geographical space shift as characters embark on personal journeys and face issues such as the lingering legacies of colonialism and slavery, the pervasiveness of racism and sexism, and the survival of their peoples in a world which exploits and oppresses them economically, socially, and politically. As these characters confront these issues, they find themselves drawing on their history and remembering their religious and cultural roots, and like the students I encountered when I first entered college, they come to realize that the reconstruction of their multiple selves and their survival as well as the survival of their peoples are tied to looking within and beyond to embrace the historical, spiritual and cultural dimensions of their lives.

bell hooks's concepts of "critical fiction" and "marginality as site of resistance" offer a critical framework for reading the fiction of women of color. In her essay, "Narratives of Struggle," hooks describes critical fiction as that fiction which seeks to deconstruct 'conventional' ways of seeing reality and to challenge dominant and hegemonic ways of reading by compelling audiences to read and respond in ways that will transform the way they think (57). It is a fiction which provides America with a lens to view itself critically, to see itself from the perspective of those who because of politics, racism, sexism, and ethnocentrism have been labeled the "other." The characters in critical fiction create "sites of resistance" and live "particular realities." These sites of resistance, as stated in hooks's essay "Marginality as Site of Resistance," nourish one's capacity to resist and provide one with the critical perspective to see, create, and imagine alternative worlds. Thus, a reading paradigm framed around the constructs of "critical fiction" and "sites of resistance" enables us to examine the extent to which complicated characters in the fiction of women of color challenge and transform their reality and provide readers with alternative perspectives for viewing the world.

The writers selected for discussion in this paper call themselves African American, Caribbean American, Native American, and Chinese American and have all written at least one work in the last twenty years which reveals a concern with "remembering." Their narratives illustrate how women use the construct of remembering as a way to reconnect their fragmented selves and as a form of resistance. Each writer portrays female characters who cross geographical, racial, and ethnic boundaries and who grow, persist, and survive by drawing on the history, traditions, and stories of their cultural backgrounds. However, these stories should not be viewed as the representative sample of a particular body of work from one ethnic group; rather they should be examined as representative of voices which have been marginalized from the American literary canon and which provide alternative renderings of the American literary experience. These are voices which after years of invisibility, repression, and silencing are demanding to be heard, voices which must now be included as we move towards a redefinition of American literature. Although each of these writers has written several texts, I have chosen for the purposes of this paper to discuss only one text of each author. The writers are Marita Golden and Octavia Butler, (African American), Michelle Cliff, Elizabeth Nunez, and Cristina García (Caribbean writers), Linda Hogan (Native American), and Amy Tan (Chinese American).

Marita Golden's *Migrations of the Heart*

Writer Marita Golden begins her memoir *Migrations of the Heart* with the following acknowledgments:

> To my father, who told me the stories that matter.
> To my mother, who taught me to remember them.

These words establish for the reader the value of remembering for Marita, who is the narrator and protagonist. In her words, her father bequeathed to her "gold nuggets of fact, myth, legend" (3). He armed her with the conviction to remember, "unfolded a richly colored tapestry," and warned her "never to forget its worth" (3). When her father dies, Marita reflects on how his death stripped her "of a connection to the past, made it impossible to dare think of the future" (51). Her mother's death, however, strengthens her spirit. She reflects on how her mother had left her with "no houses but had bequeathed instead the legacy of a restless, courageous spirit" (39). This courageous spirit enables Marita to endure the migrations of the heart.

Marita's migrations of the heart continue throughout her college years. The memories of her father and mother guide her, and as she reaches young adulthood at the height of the black cultural nationalist movement, she immerses herself in reading and studying the history and culture of African peoples. Upon her completion of college, she enters graduate school as a journalism major at Columbia University, and her need to connect with her past and culture continues to manifest itself when she begins a relationship with a Nigerian student. Marita marries this student and migrates to Nigeria, a place that symbolizes for her a journey "home." Ironically, in Nigeria she finds herself faced with the dilemma of being "the other." An African American in a country where the majority are African, she feels connected because of her ancestral roots and race yet alienated because of her culture and gender. The conflicts that emerge as she attempts to adjust to life in Nigeria reveal the complexities that arise when one crosses boundaries of ethnicity, culture, and language.

Although Golden's text is autobiographical, it does not simply recount her past life. It follows a narrative structure which uses dialogue, tension, and conflict to reveal the paradoxes faced by many African Americans who traveled to Africa in the 1960s and 1970s in search of their roots and home. A knowledge of the socio-cultural context of that period is helpful in understanding the issue with which Golden was dealing. African Americans had participated in the civil rights struggle and during the black cultural nationalist movement had asserted their rights and demanded to be heard. They renamed themselves personally, and as a collective group they took trips "home" to Africa in search of their roots. Golden was in the midst of this black cultural revolution, and her story exemplifies the stories of many who attempted to reconnect with their past.

Marita, like many who took the trip "home," realizes how American she is. Living in America as an African American woman, she has lived in multiple worlds. She embodies both the culture of African Americans and mainstream American culture. In moving to Nigeria, she attempts to adapt to another culture—one where attitudes concerning family, relationships, and the role of women differ. However, because she cannot give up her American self, she feels marginalized in Nigeria. In America, her cultural framework is defined by the intersections of race, ethnicity, class, and gender in an American culture. In Nigeria, these elements come together and create a Nigerian cultural framework of which she cannot be a part. Marita's husband, Femi, warns her:

> It's not enough for you to love me. You can't love me alone. You must love my mother, my father, my family. . . . It will not be easy. . . . Americans do not know this love. In my family we owe everything to everyone else. . . . Can you accept that burden? . . . Honor me with that kind of love? (56–7)

She comes to realize that she cannot do what Femi asks. Her experience in Nigeria enables her to connect with her past and to look at herself without the constraints defined by white America. In Nigeria although she is a black woman in a country where the majority are black, she refuses to allow herself to be defined by the role adapted by many Nigerian women, one which is subordinate to men. She realizes that she is in a cultural environment where male children, in particular, are valued and belong to the father. In short, she defines the role of the male/female relationship and the role of the child differently.

Faced with not being able to adjust to different cultural values and norms, Marita returns to America where the particularity of her existence immediately confronts her. She finds herself in Boston, a place where racial tensions have flared and where the divisions by ethnic groups remind her of the tribal divisions within Nigeria. These racial tensions and conflicts exist in America and are a continual part of Marita's reality. She has tried to escape from this reality, but she cannot. She must live with difference and face racism.

Marita's migrations bring her face to face with what it means to be a single, black, professional, woman/mother in white America. She examines her migrations to Africa and her return to America, and she confronts her fears of being alone and emotionally and spiritually disconnected from herself and from her past. In doing so, she realizes that she cannot fill the emotional and spiritual void in her life by escaping to another place or by living in the shadow of another person. Africa offers her a tie to her ancestral roots and America situates her in a complicated present. Her connection of the fragmented parts of her life occurs when she comes to terms with the fact that being an African American woman means that she has to live with paradoxes (as described by Nunez in her essay in this volume). She has had to search for her roots and come to the realization that as an American black woman, she lives in multiple spaces and endures a particular kind of reality. She cannot be defined by one culture. Remembering the history, traditions, and stories passed on to her enables her to acknowledge all parts of herself.

Octavia Butler's *Kindred*

bell hooks's aphorism, "Remembering makes us subjects in history; it is dangerous to forget" ("Narratives" 54) provides an excellent premise for reading and interpreting Octavia Butler's novel *Kindred*. This novel takes the form of a slave narrative; however, Butler moves beyond the traditional slave narrative by creating a character who lives in 1976 Los Angeles and who travels back in time over a span of years which range from 1815 to 1865. Dana, the central character, is called back in time when Rufus, her master and her ancestor who fathers a child who will become her great aunt, needs her. In her travels, Dana participates in the lives of her future ancestors and witnesses the inhumanity and brutality of slavery.

Butler uses the slave narrative genre to illustrate why Dana must remember. In going back, Dana comes to understand herself and to resolve the dilemmas she feels in her personal life. By remembering and playing a role in the family of her ancestors, she ensures the survival of her ancestors and thereby her own survival.

While in slavery, Dana is subjected to emotional and physical abuse. The first words in the prologue of the novel establish the extent of this abuse. "I lost an arm on my last trip home. My left arm. And I lost about a year of my life and much of the comfort and security I had not valued until it was gone" (9). Dana's need to continue to return to Rufus is revealed when she asks herself: "Was that why I was here? Not only to insure the survival of one accident-prone small boy, but to insure my family's survival, my own birth?" (29). Her survival is necessary and the final words in the epilogue epitomize why Dana must undergo this experience. When visiting the site of the plantation where her ancestors lived, Dana questions her husband Kevin: "Why did I even want to come here. You'd think I would have had enough of the past." Kevin replies: "You probably needed to come for the same reason I did . . . To try to understand. To touch solid evidence that these people existed" (264).

Butler complicates this slave narrative prototype in many ways. Unlike traditional slave narratives where one primarily gets a first-hand account of the brutal and inhuman treatment of slaves by their masters, this one presents alternative perspectives for why so many appeared to have withstood slavery. Dana comes to understand that silence was a weapon for survival. By observing what happens to the slaves on the plantation, she questions her assumptions about those slaves whom the militants of the 1960s would have labeled "passive" or "Uncle Toms."

Tess, the house slave who has been in the family for years, survives because she does not want to die. Dana notes that Tess "had done the safe thing—had accepted a life of slavery because she was afraid" (145). Tess avoids what happens to Alice, Dana's future aunt. After running away, Alice is brought back "bloody, filthy, and barely alive" (145). Alice responds to Dana, who is nursing her back to health: "Think you know so much . . . Why didn't you know to let me die" (160). Thus, in reflecting on the actions of Tess and Alice, Dana realizes that the ability to survive in the midst of the horrors of slavery takes a special kind of courage—a courage which involves the personal sacrifice necessary for her and her family to survive into the twentieth century.

Dana's symbiotic relationship with Rufus further complicates the narrative. Rufus is both her master and future ancestor. Furthermore, when Kevin, her white husband in twentieth-century Los Angeles travels back with Dana and is placed in the position of master, he begins to resemble Rufus and to talk like him. This blurring of the roles of Kevin and Rufus symbolizes both the possible conflicts experienced by Dana and by those in interracial relationships as well as the anguish and anxiety experienced by those black women who were forced to succumb to the desires of white men/masters. The ultimate oppression experienced by these women was rape; when Dana is confronted with this violation, she resists and makes a choice to end the oppression that Rufus bestows upon her and her future ancestors. In making this choice, she liberates herself and ensures the survival of her family. She also appears to resolve the conflicts that she feels with respect to her white husband Kevin.

Butler's placing of Dana in a biracial marriage foreshadows the exploration of black and white relationships during the time of slavery and into the 20th century. It allows us to see the interdependent nature of these relationships. Although she is black, Dana's roots can be traced back to a white plantation owner who depends on her for his survival. His survival is connected to her and the other slaves, just as her survival depends on keeping him alive. The lives of blacks and whites are intertwined, and as Toni Morrison points out in *Playing in the Dark: Whiteness and the Literary Imagination,* when one reads the literature of America, one is reading stories which reveal the nature of racial relationships in this society. The presence or absence of blacks in American literature underscores the ways in which race is constructed by both black and white writers.

In remembering her past, Dana comes to understand her present. She learns to live with what Nunez (in this volume) calls a "paradox of irreconcilable differences." Her identity is not fixed but fluid, and she learns to live in multiple worlds which cross boundaries of race, time, and geographical space. Because of her first-hand experience with American slavery, she gains a deeper understanding of this "paradox of irreconcilable differences" and of what it means to be a black woman in America. She realizes that her remembrance of the past has created a site for surviving in the present and for resisting the destruction of her people.

Michelle Cliff's *Abeng*

The title of Michelle Cliff's novel *Abeng* immediately situates the story and the reader in the past and on the island of Jamaica. "Abeng" is an African word meaning conch shell. The *abeng* was used to call in the slaves from the fields and was also used by the Maroon armies to pass messages. Cliff, through her nonlinear manipulation of time and space, moves the reader back and forth through time as she provides an historical perspective for understanding the struggles of the peoples of Jamaica from pre-slavery through colonial times and as she recounts the coming-of-age story of Clare Savage, a twelve-year-old middle-class mulatto girl in colonial Jamaica.

The presence of multiple spaces in Clare's life and the dilemmas facing her become readily apparent at the beginning of the novel. Clare and her family attend the morning service of the Presbyterian church (Mr. Savage's place of worship), which has a black and white middle-class congregation, and the evening service of the Tabernacle of the Almighty (Mrs. Savage's place of worship), which has a predominantly black congregation. These places of worship symbolize the paradox with which Clare lives. She is caught between two ways of worshipping God and her parents symbolize two races and two ways of looking at the world.

Clare's father, James Arthur Savage (Boy), views himself as white and is the descendant of a white plantation owner who, upon learning that freedom for his slaves is forthcoming, decides that he would rather burn than free his slaves—so he sets fire to the plantation. "Boy" Savage is mesmerized by things related to the supernatural. He turns to religion at an early age and loves to tell stories of the great exploits and adventures of peoples from other lands. In the words of Clare, "Mr. Savage was caught somewhere between the future and the past—both equal in his imagination" (22).

Clare's mother, who is black, descends from the Freemans. The Freemans have lived close to the land and have worked it. Clare's grandmother (Mrs. Freeman) lives in the deep country. She owns land and is well-respected in her village. She has a knowledge of traditional songs, rituals, and herbs used by African peoples, and she passes this knowledge on to her daughter. Thus, the Savages and the Freemans represent opposite ends on a continuum of Caribbean lifestyles.

The selection of the names "Savage" and "Freeman" also symbolizes the conflicts that permeate Clare's life and the lives of many in her culture. "Savage" symbolizes the harsh treatment which whites inflicted upon their slaves. In addition, Clare notes how the Savages have perceived themselves:

> The definition of what a Savage was like was fixed by color, class, and religion, and over the years carefully contrived mythology was constructed, which they used to protect their identities. When they were poor, and not all of them white, the mythology persisted. (29)

Clare's father, thus, represents a group of people who distinguish themselves from those who are of a different race, class, and religion. Yet he marries a Freeman, foreshadowing the conflicts and paradoxes of Clare's life. "Freeman," on the other hand, connotes freedom, civility, and humanity; it is a name which symbolizes the desired goal of those who were enslaved. Clare, a Freeman and a Savage, must live with the connotations of these two names.

Clare's conflicts are heightened by her friendship with Zoe, a girl from the back country who symbolizes all that Clare is not. Zoe is dark skinned and of the low-income working class. Clare comes to love Zoe, and in so doing she confronts that part of herself which has been insensitive to the ways, attitudes, and values of people who come from a different class. In loving Zoe, it is as if Clare confronts her alter ego.

Cliff's interweaving of the history of the island adds another dimension to this coming-of-age novel. Throughout the novel, we get historical accounts of the struggles of the Arawaks and the Maroons as they attempt to resist slavery and colonialism. We see how slavery and colonialism affect the psyche of Caribbean peoples—people like James Arthur Savage and other middle-class mulattos who have difficulty accepting their mixed identity and acknowledging how their people and island have been exploited. We see how class and race affect the ways in which students in school are treated. Those of darker complexions attend different schools. Clare is kept apart from her dark-complexioned friend Zoe who is from the country and whose mother is a market woman. Cliff's text thus provides us with an alternative historical perspective on the slavery and colonialism practiced in those countries of the Americas which were "discovered." Her perspective, a critique of slavery and colonialism, reminds us that although many Indians and Africans were killed, there were also many who resisted.

The protagonist Clare also carries within her a history of struggle. Like her ancestors who persisted and resisted, she must persist and acknowledge all parts of herself. Like Marita in *Migrations of the Heart* and Dana in Butler's *Kindred,* Clare must learn to live with contradictions. She must learn to live on the borderlands, and she must cross the boundaries which her parents have established. She must confront both parts of herself in order to grow. If she does not accomplish this, she will be silenced like her mother or live on the edge of fantasy and reality like her father.

The novel closes with a dream in which Clare and Zoe are fist-fighting and Clare hits Zoe in the eye, an act that symbolizes Clare's struggle with that other part of herself. In struggling with Zoe, her alter ego, she confronts the black part of herself. The narrator, in describing Clare's dream, informs us that "she had no idea that everyone we dream about we are" (166). Thus, although Clare is not consciously aware of why she has a fight with Zoe, this dream and fight foreshadow the internal struggle which she must engage in if she is to connect those fragmented parts of herself. Cliff reminds us that Clare's identity, like Marita's and Dana's, is not fixed, but formed and represented by multiple spaces.

Elizabeth Nunez's *When Rocks Dance*

Elizabeth Nunez, like Cliff, creates a novel which depicts the effects of slavery and colonialism on the peoples of early twentieth-century Trinidad. In her novel *When Rocks Dance,* slavery has ended, but British colonialism and racism ensure that its legacy remains. Over time the peoples of Trinidad—Arawaks, Caribs, East Indians, Africans, and Chinese—have struggled to gain wealth and power. Although sugarcane is a major staple, the plantations continue to be the havens for poverty and oppression. Cocoa, also a staple central to the economy, is displaced with the discovery of oil. The path out of this poverty is the acquisition of land; this quest for land and what one must do to acquire it becomes a major theme in Nunez's novel.

Nunez begins her novel with an epigraph from John Oliver Killens's *Black Man's Burden:*

> We need our own myths and legends to regain our lost self-esteem, our regard for each other as a people capable of working together to move the mountains that stand before us. (7)

Myths and legends have for centuries been the means by which peoples carry their cultural traditions, rituals, and values. These myths and legends cross ethnic and racial boundaries and come in many forms. What is considered myth in one culture is viewed as religion in another. This need for people to have their own myths and legends provides a framework for reading and interpreting Nunez's novel.

The central character, Marina, is the daughter of a British plantation owner and a black Trinidadian woman, Emilia. Marina and Emilia must learn to go back to the "old ways," to follow the laws of their ancestors. They must not forget nor ignore the past, for this knowledge will help them to gain control over their future. Emilia is determined that her daughter Marina should inherit her father's land, and when she finds herself still landless and in poverty after the death of the British plantation owner, she resolves that her daughter should marry someone who will enable her to acquire land. Thus, Marina marries Antonio, a biracial man who faithfully practices Catholicism and who is the son of a defrocked Jesuit priest and a black woman. This marriage comes to symbolize the conflict between traditional African religion and Western Catholicism, a conflict which Marina must face as she chooses to fulfill her mother's dream and desperately attempts to conceive children who will inherit their father's land.

In her determination to have children and to acquire land, Marina defies the boundaries of Western Catholicism and seeks the counsel of a Warao Indian and *obeah* woman. Her seeking of advice from those connected with the spiritual world and with the rituals of African religion illustrates the journey that Marina must take. Like Clare in *Abeng,* who is also a person of mixed blood, Marina must recover that part of herself which is black. In acknowledging the power of *obeah,* she accepts its presence in her life. This acceptance of *obeah,* a traditional religion practiced in the Caribbean by people of African descent, enables her to resist the forces which have kept her and her mother landless and to ultimately regain her land. Her remembrance of things past ensures her survival into the future.

Like Cliff, Nunez weaves into her narrative a description of the historical causes and consequences of slavery and colonialism in Trinidad. In doing so, she provides an alternative view of the history of the island. The reader learns how the Portuguese who came to the island were not only seeking religious freedom, but were attempting to escape the plagues that were raging throughout their land. Further, their ships often carried cargoes of slaves. Thus, the Portuguese who were escaping religious persecution were participants in the slave trade and brought to the Caribbean not only slaves, but diseases such as cholera and yellow fever.

Nunez also describes how slavery and colonialism upset the spiritual balance between nature, the land, and people. She notes:

> The island was populated then and was to be populated later by a people who approached life's mysteries not with an intellect disengaged from their oneness with nature, but with minds opened to truths whispered to them from the sea, the earth, the animals, the birds, the fish. (119)

Nunez's novel is, thus, both a critique of slavery and colonialism and a story of the ways in which people transform their reality by establishing sites of resistance. Marina is representative of those who approach life's mysteries with a sense of the spiritual balance between nature, the land, and the people. In order for Marina to regain her land, she opens her minds to the "truth" and remembers the myths and the legends of her people. Thus, despite the legacies left by slavery and colonialism, she is able to establish a site of resistance and transform her reality.

Cristina Garcia's *Dreaming in Cuban*

Cristina Garcia's novel *Dreaming in Cuban* is the story of several generations of the del Pino family. Through dreams, letters, poems, monologues, and flashbacks of different members of the family, Garcia uses the theme of remembering to weave the family's story together. The story begins with a dream. Celia del Pino, the matriarch of the del Pino family, sits in her wicker chair on a beach in north Cuba and scans the horizon. Having just learned that her husband has died, she watches as he emerges from the water and invites her into the water. As she grieves for him, she reflects on the lives of three generations of her family, a family which has suffered emotionally and physically, endured many losses, and been divided as a result of the politics of the Cuban revolution.

The Cuban revolution is the catalyst that fragments the family and sends it in varying directions. Each member of the family goes his/her way and charts his or her own individual course for survival. Throughout the years of her marriage, Celia has held on to the memories of her lost lover by writing letters to him. When she and her husband become more and more estranged, he places her in a mental institution, and upon her release she actively becomes involved in the revolution. Lourdes, Celia's daughter, emigrates to New York, opens up several bakeries, and becomes excessively overweight, using food to attempt to restore the losses she feels in her life. Celia's daughter Felicia turns to men and then to *santería,* a traditional, syncretic religion practiced by the Cuban people. Javier, Celia's only son, turns to the world of the academy and subsequently loses himself, his wife, and his daughter. Celia's granddaughter Pilar, an artist, rebels against the capitalist attitude adopted by her mother and turns to music and art to address the emptiness she feels in her life.

By providing the reader with the dreams and reflections of individual members of the del Pino family, Garcia gives us alternative perspectives on the revolution and on the varying ways in which it has impacted the lives of the Cuban people. The character who emerges as the most complicated and paradoxical is Pilar.

Pilar symbolizes the person on the borderlands. She lives with contradictions. Frustrated by her life in New York, she dreams of her grandmother, and heads for Cuba to see her. The following words epitomize her despair in New York and her relationship with Celia, her grandmother.

> Even though I've been living in Brooklyn all my life, it doesn't feel like home to me. I'm not sure Cuba is, but I want to find out. If only I could see Abuela Celia again, I'd know where I belonged. (58)

Pilar's dreams of her grandmother and her longing to see her grandmother symbolize a psychic relationship between the two women. When Pilar is finally able to return to Cuba, she reflects on the idea that her grandmother leaves her a legacy, "a love of the sea and the smoothness of pearls, an appreciation of music and art and a disregard for boundaries" (176). Her grandmother instills confidence in her, and she in turn provides her grandmother with a desire to pass on her memories to her granddaughter. Celia cannot form this connection with her daughters, but with her granddaughter she is able to form a spiritual bond. She tells her granddaughter, "Women who outlive their daughters are orphans. . . . Only their granddaughters can save them, guard their knowledge like the first fire" (222).

Garcia's depiction of the psychic relationship between Pilar and her grandmother reveals the cyclical nature of life, a concept also found in Native American literature. In this novel, Celia's last letter to her lover clearly illustrates that the memories of the grandmother will live on in the granddaughter and that the granddaughter will continue the tradition of the grandmother.

> My dearest Gustavo. . . . My granddaughter, Pilar Puento del Pino, was born today. It is also my birthday. I am fifty years old. I will no longer write to you, my amor. She will remember everything. (245)

Pilar, the child of contradictions, the child on the borderlands, cannot resolve her inner conflicts until she connects with her grandmother. And to do this, she must cross the boundaries of space and time. She must capture that Cuban part of herself and merge it with an American self to form a new identity, one which cannot be defined by one culture, race, ethnicity, or religion. Like Marita in *Migrations* who travels to Africa, Dana who travels to nineteenth-century America in *Kindred,* Clare in *Abeng* who psychologically travels to the time when Jamaica was peopled with Arawaks and Maroons, and Marina who travels to the *obeah* woman in *When Rocks Dance,* Pilar must go back to her roots in order to go forward and understand all aspects of her multiple selves.

Pilar's site of resistance cannot be created in Cuba; it must be created in America, a place where she must struggle with the dilemmas of living in multiple spaces. Remembering her Cuban roots enables her to create a site of resistance in America, and to thereby transform her reality.

Linda Hogan's *Mean Spirit*

The reasons for remembering take on a different nature in Linda Hogan's novel *Mean Spirit.* In this historical novel, we see how the white man's ravishing of the land and Osage peoples affects their spiritual and physical world and results in their destruction. Her novel is a true testament to bell hooks's statement that "remembering makes us subjects in history; it is dangerous to forget" ("Narratives" 54). Through Hogan's story, we see how the oil-rich lands of Native Americans were systematically taken away through corruption, murder, and arranged marriages. The central characters of this novel, the Graycloud family, in attempting to hold onto their land, call upon their ancestors and seek the advice of elders.

Hogan uses an episodic, circular structure to tell her story. There are no divided chapters, and Hogan moves the reader in and out of the lives of the Osage people. The reader watches as the Osage people in the valley begin to learn the ways of the white man and return to the ways of the "Indians" when they re-enter the hills. Through this nonlinear structure, we come to understand the importance of harmony between the land, people, and nature and to know that the "Indians" of the Osage community understand that their survival depends upon maintaining a harmony between their spiritual and physical worlds.

The narrative follows the story of the Graycloud family as they resist attempts to have their oil-rich land taken from them. The setting is 1922 Oklahoma, and the collective spirit and efforts of this family work to ward off the total downfall of their peoples. They refuse to accept the prophecy that the white man will infringe on their peace and take everything away, and in their attempts to preserve themselves, they believe that they must learn the ways and adapt some of the customs of the white man. Lila Blanket, one of the Osage "Indians" from the Hills, tells her daughter, "Some of our children have to learn about the white world if we're going to ward off our downfall" (6). This strategy, however, undermines Native American values, for it violates the "Indian" belief that the natural balance between man and earth must be respected and maintained. A statement by Reverend Joe Billy epitomizes the catastrophic results that this thinking brings. In a sermon, Reverend Billy states that "the Indian world is on a collision course with the white world" (13). Thus, although the "Indians" attempt to adapt to the ways of the white man, the results are devastating, and Reverend Billy's warning becomes prophetic, symbolizing the future of the Osage peoples as a tribal nation. The tragic consequences of their adaptation to the white man's value system become magnified when Grace Graycloud, the richest "Indian" woman among the Osage peoples, is murdered.

As the novel continues, we see how the combined forces of deceit, greed, and corruption in the government contribute to the exploitation of Native American rights, more murders, mysterious fires, and deep extended grief among the "Indian" people. The "Indian" response to this is silence. They have learned that this is the key to their survival. When the government cheats one of their tribal members out of his money there is silence, for the

> "Indians" knew, from history itself, that it was a smart thing to keep silent on the affairs and regulations of Washington, to be still and as invisible as possible. They might be cheated, but they still had life, and until only recently, even that was not guaranteed under the American laws, so they remained trapped, silent, and wary. (63)

Throughout the novel, the visions and forces of the spiritual world serve as guides for the "Indians," who face continuous obstacles. As they confront these obstacles, they seem to garner more strength and more perseverance to do what they can to ensure their personal and collective survival. Horse, the elder who keeps an historical account of the trials and tribulations of his peoples, decides that he will add to the Holy Bible what is missing. The words which he adds are a message to the Osage people and to those who have mistreated them. He warns the people to live gently with the land and to remember that their spirits are in harmony with nature and with the universe.

Hogan's novel provides the reader with an alternative historical perspective for how and why Native Americans were made invisible. Hers is a story which seldom gets told and which powerfully illustrates the need to remember. Those who do not remember will fail to break the silence and the pattern of self-destruction. As in the novels of Golden, Butler, Cliff, and Nunez, the Hill "Indians" of Hogan's novel realize that their survival depends on acknowledging their past, a past which their peoples must draw upon to define their mission and to continue their journey into the present. It is a journey which cannot defy the laws of land and nature.

Amy Tan's *The Joy Luck Club*

Amy Tan's *The Joy Luck Club* is a journey in remembering. In this novel, the central characters use the telling of stories as a way to overcome the obstacles they face in their current lives. Thus, remembering through the sharing of memories becomes a way that immigrant Chinese American women create sites of resistance which ensure that their first-generation Chinese American daughters will survive.

Jing Mei Woo, the daughter of Ann Mei, takes her mother's place in the Joy Luck Club, an act that affirms their spiritual connection; as her mother's daughter, Jing Mei Woo symbolizes an aspect of her mother's own true nature and self. Placed in this situation, Jing Mei Woo realizes that she does not truly know her Chinese mother, and we see how, through remembering her mother's stories, Jing Mei comes to know her mother and thereby to know another aspect of herself.

Tan's novel is cyclical in structure, beginning and ending with Jing Mei taking the place of her mother. She has the task of telling her long lost sisters the story of her mother's life. When she protests to her aunts and to her mother's friends that she does not know her mother, they reply:

> Not know your mother? . . . How can you say? Your mother is in your bones! . . . Tell them stories she told you, lessons she taught, what you know about her mind that has become your mind. (31)

According to feminist critic Trinh T. Minh-ha, "Storytelling, the oldest form of building historical consciousness in the community, constitutes a rich oral legacy, whose values have regained all importance recently, especially in the context of writings by women of color" (481–82). Tan enriches her novel by the telling of stories. Through the stories told by mothers to their daughters, daughters learn to avoid the pitfalls of greed and selfishness, to be respectful and patient, and to persevere despite pain. Through the daughters' stories, we learn what it is like to grow up as a hyphenated American and to live in multiple spaces, culturally, ethnically, and geographically. We see how the Chinese American identity is not static, but fluid. Like other persons of color, Chinese Americans must live with contradictions, and remembering the stories of the past helps give them the ability to persist and resist.

This ability is the enduring characteristic that most women in Tan's novel possess. Linda Jong recounts how she sacrifices her life to keep her mother's promise of accepting the village matchmaker's choice of the son of a family more wealthy than hers. She sacrifices herself for a period of time and devises a plan that will help her to regain her lost self. Waverly Jong, her daughter, recounts how she was six when her mother taught her the art of invisible strength. Waverly learns that the strongest wind cannot be seen and thereby learns to focus on the acquisition of an invisible strength as she competes in chess matches. Rose Hsu Jordan also learns to be strong like the wind. Her mother tells her that a girl is like a young tree and carries a strength within her. Like the young tree, the girl will grow straight and tall if she listens to her mother who is beside her. Her mother warns her, however, that those who listen to others grow crooked and weak and fall to the ground with the first strong wind. These women do not survive; they retreat to the innermost part of their minds where they live out the remainder of their days. This is what happens to Ying Ying St. Clair. Ying Ying recounts how she kept her mouth closed so that her selfish desires would not fall out. She recognizes at an early age that in order to survive, she must hide her true and real self; however, the result of her hiding causes her to lose both her voice and her mind. Those who are strong and who hold on to their true nature survive. They are the ones who are able to create sites of resistance, places where they can imagine and plan for alternative worlds, dream of their future and the future of their children, and escape the oppression resulting from planned marriages in a traditional patriarchal Chinese society which continually devalues women.

The construct of remembering in Tan's novel bridges the gap between two worlds, those of the past and the present. Through bringing the past to the present, the immigrant Chinese mothers are able to exist in two worlds and to endure the complexity of living in two cultures. Through the use of story, each Chinese immigrant mother symbolically transfers an awareness of the complexity of living in two cultures. As each daughter recounts and relives the stories told to her by her mother, she gains new insight into her mother and into the relationship between her mother and herself. In doing so, she comes to appreciate the value of her mother's stories and is able to attempt to define ways in which her life can be made more meaningful by this knowledge. Like the characters in the narratives of Golden, Butler, Cliff, Hogan, Nunez, and García, remembering causes the mothers and daughters of Tan's novel to confront themselves and thereby to confront their true strengths and weaknesses.

Conclusion

In her text *Black Women, Writing, & Identity: Migrations of the Subject*, Carole Boyce Davies writes that black women's writing "should be read as a series of boundary crossings and not as a fixed, geographically, ethnically or nationally bound category of writing" (4). Boyce Davies maintains that to attempt to interpret or theorize about black women's writing in relation to specific geographical or ethnic states is to define this writing from narrow and marginalized spaces. Black women exist all over the world, and the word blackness has different connotations in different parts of the world. In the United Kingdom, for example, blackness is not solely related to skin color or race. In addition, it has to do with class, position, or marginality in society and includes Asians, Arabs, and Latinos. Therefore, if one recognizes that black women's writing crosses geographical boundaries, then interpretations about the subject of black women's texts will involve more complex and more complicated theories.

Boyce Davies's concept of black women's writing as fluid and shifting across boundaries also applies to writing by women of color. The writers discussed in this paper come from different races and ethnic groups and create texts that may be read and studied as narratives which form a nexus where race, class, gender, and history converge to create situations whereby characters use remembering as a way to gain knowledge of themselves and as a form of resistance to oppression, exploitation, racism, colonialism, and sexism. The characters in these texts transform their realities into ones which acknowledge the fragmentation, marginalization, and spiritual and emotional voids in their lives. They create sites of resistance which enable them to live with contradictions and dilemmas, with what Nunez calls paradoxes. In living their lives on the borderlands, they exist in multiple spaces and move back and forth between the center and margins of society. Although they exist in these multiple spaces and worlds, they have a common need to tell their stories, to tell the truth, to resist—as the Latin American writer Claribel Alegria puts it, to "assume and take on the role of historians, politicians, sociologists, and teachers" (106).

By entering the texts of these writers into a conversation on rethinking American literature, we validate the need to include and expand our reading, discussion, and study of female writers of color in our English classrooms and the need to rethink, redefine, and reshape our paradigms for interpreting the literature of contemporary women of color. The texts discussed here provide readers with a framework to perceive American literature in more complicated ways. American literature is not bound by the borders of the United States; it includes the Caribbean, Central America, South America, and all of North America. These texts cannot be defined by one genre, structure, theme, or form. They are nonlinear and shift across history and geography. Some have ambiguous endings and are cyclical in nature. Others provide alternative perspectives on history. They center women's lives and focus on subjects who cross cultural boundaries of race, ethnicity, class, and gender. These texts cause us to rethink American literature.

Works Cited

Alegria, Claribel. "Latindad and the Artist." *Critical Fictions: The Politics of Imaginative Writing.* Ed. Philomena Mariani. Seattle: Bay Press, 1991. 486–91.

Butler, Octavia. *Kindred.* 1979. Boston: Beacon, 1988.

Cliff, Michelle. *Abeng.* New York: Penguin, 1984.

Davies, Carole Boyce. *Black Women, Writing, & Identity: Migrations of the Subject.* New York: Routledge, 1994.

Garcia, Cristina. *Dreaming in Cuban.* New York: Ballantine, 1992.

Golden, Marita. *Migrations of the Heart.* 1983. New York: Ballantine, 1987.

Hogan, Linda. *Mean Spirit.* 1990. New York: Ballantine, 1992.

hooks, bell. *Feminist Theory from Margin to Center.* Boston: South End, 1984.

———."Marginality as Site of Resistance." *Out There: Marginalization & Contemporary Culture.* Eds. Russell Ferguson et. al. Cambridge: MIT, 1990. 341-43.

———."Narratives of Struggle.*" Critical Fictions: The Politics of Imaginative Writing.* Ed. Philomena Mariani. Seattle: Bay Press, 1991. 58–61.

Morrison, Toni. *Playing in the Dark: Whiteness and the Literary Imagination.* Cambridge: Harvard UP, 1992.

Mukherjee, Bharati. "A Four-Hundred-Year-Old Woman." *Critical Fictions: The Politics of Imaginative Writing.* Ed. Philomena Mariani. Seattle: Bay Press, 1991. 24–28.

Nunez, Elizabeth. "A Fusion of Cultures: The Complexities of the Caribbean Character in Literature." *Rethinking American Literature.* Eds. Lil Brannon and Brenda M. Greene. Urbana: NCTE, 1997. 71–80.

———. *When Rocks Dance.* New York: Ballantine, 1986.

Tan, Amy. *The Joy Luck Club.* New York: Ballantine, 1989.

Trinh T. Minh-ha. "Grandma's Story." *The Woman That I Am: The Literature and Culture of Contemporary Women of Color.* Ed. D. Soyini Madison. New York: St. Martin's, 1994. 486–91.

7 Crossing Cultural Boundaries with Leslie Marmon Silko's *Ceremony*

Robert O'Brien Hokanson
Alverno College

In today's classroom, as in today's society, "multiculturalism" is a loaded term, one whose meaning depends on who is invoking it and to what end. For my purposes here, I want to talk about multiculturalism not so much as a theoretical concept or political agenda, although it surely is both, but as a fundamental reality of life in the dynamic and diverse society of the United States. As Shelley Fisher Fishkin, author of *Was Huck Black?*, observed in a column for *The Chronicle of Higher Education,* "'Traditional' American culture has always been multicultural. Our teaching must take into account our increasingly complex understanding of what our common culture is and how it evolved." Given this reality—and this challenge—the key question for teachers and students is not, "Are you 'for' or 'against' multiculturalism?" but rather, "How can we best understand and respond to our shared circumstances?"

It is in addressing this question—the *real* question that we all (students, teachers, citizens) face—that I've turned to Leslie Marmon Silko's novel *Ceremony* (1977). I've found *Ceremony* to be a particularly valuable text not only because it vividly depicts contemporary Native American culture but also because it is *about* the broader phenomenon of crossing cultural boundaries. Critics like Paula Gunn Allen, Kenneth Lincoln, and James Ruppert have done some excellent work on the role of Pueblo Indian tradition in Silko's novel, but less attention has been paid to its representation of the interaction among Native, Anglo, and Mexican cultures. It is in this interaction that *Ceremony* models ways of understanding and responding to the "multicultural" world in which we all live, and I use Silko's novel to help my students learn not only about contemporary Native American literature but also about the dynamics of multiculturalism in literature and society.

Through Tayo, a young WW II veteran, and those who help him in his quest to heal himself and the land, Silko presents an image of an Indian culture that is rooted in tradition but constantly changing and adapting to the contemporary world. These changes are principally represented in terms of the intersection and interaction of cultures. Tayo himself is a "half breed"—Laguna, white, and perhaps part Mexican—and his mixed and multiple identity mirrors that of the American Southwest, where three cultures (and more) have clashed, blended, and sometimes co-existed for hundreds of years. In this, Tayo's story is a microcosm of the broader story of historical and cultural change. "You are part of it now," the Mexican dancer Night Swan tells Tayo after their sexual encounter, confirming his role as one who crosses cultural boundaries. As the novel unfolds, it becomes clear that it is only through recognizing and then affirming his role in the wider multicultural drama of the Southwest—and beyond—that Tayo can regain a sense of himself and restore the land around him. Like the overlapping cultures it presents, the text of *Ceremony* is also a hybrid, mingling songs and stories from Pueblo Indian tradition, the style and techniques of contemporary American fiction, and the conventions of the coming-of-age novel into a rich weave of storytelling.

As a writer, Leslie Marmon Silko herself embodies the dynamics of a multicultural society. Silko is of mixed ancestry (Laguna, white, and Mexican), and she has written forcefully about the multicultural reality of life in the United States. In an essay entitled "Fences Against Freedom," she critiques the notion of "race" as a fixed, absolute category and its use as a political tool in shaping immigration policy and the policing of the U.S.-Mexican border. Recalling her upbringing at Laguna, she contrasts the contemporary politics of race with the inclusive worldview she learned as a child:

> My parents and the people of the Laguna Pueblo community who raised me taught me that we are all one family—all the offspring of Mother Earth— and no one is better or worse according to skin color or origin. . . . It was not so easy for me to learn where we Marmons belonged, but gradually I understood that we of mixed ancestry belonged on the outer edge of the circle between the world of the Pueblo and the outside world. (9)

This place on the margin between worlds is also where Tayo resides. Through Tayo and other figures who embody cultural interaction, *Ceremony* shows us that no borders are permanent and impermeable, and that only through recognizing this fact can we fully understand the world and our place in it.

In this way, Silko's novel helps students see "multiculturalism" as a dynamic process rather than an either/or proposition. *Ceremony* demonstrates how distinctions blur and boundaries shift—not into a melting pot of forgetfulness but into a wider, more comprehensive vision. These are vital insights for my students and me as we work toward a fuller understanding of what "American" literature is and has been. The interplay among a multiplicity of cultures and cultural forms in *Ceremony* makes it clear that we need to register the complex cultural matrix of texts as completely as we can rather than simply pigeonholing them as "Native American" or "Mexican American" or "white." *Ceremony* also works against the tendency of readers to either reduce difference to sameness or dismiss what is "other" as foreign and unintelligible, a tendency that Helen Jaskoski has observed in her teaching of Native American literature (53). By keeping Tayo, and the novel as a whole, rooted in the belief system of the Pueblo peoples, Silko maintains a sense of what is unique to his outlook and circumstances even as he embarks on the kind of quest for identity that is found throughout literature. Students can then compare their own sense of identity to Tayo's without losing sight of the fact that his predicament is neither identical to or entirely different from theirs.

In teaching *Ceremony*, then, I aim to engage the students in my American literature course in a process of reading that opens up notions of culture and identity in the way Greg Sarris describes in his discussion of how to promote critical thinking and cultural understanding among diverse students:

> Reading, like all classroom activity, must be seen and promoted as something that continues and recreates culture both in the ways its practices alter and maintain previous methods for continuing and recreating culture and in the ways it helps individuals negotiate personhood "in a world of multiple and conflicting demands." (196–97)

As Sarris and many others have noted, such a process is rarely simple and often uncomfortable, but because *Ceremony* itself models a dynamic conception of individual identity and cultural tradition, it can do much to help students understand the dynamics of diversity throughout American literature and culture.

———————

As the prose narrative of *Ceremony* opens, Tayo's life—and that of the Pueblo generally—is dangerously out of balance. He has returned from the war in the Pacific deeply troubled by his experiences, and the crippling drought at Laguna reflects his individual dis-ease. The holistic worldview of Pueblo tradition has become a nightmare, it seems, as he can't shake the vision of his Uncle Josiah among the Japanese soldiers his unit killed in the Philippines or the feeling that his prayer for the jungle rain to end has been fulfilled on the parched reservation. The depth of Tayo's estrangement from Pueblo beliefs is registered in his reaction to seeing Japanese American women and children at the Los Angeles train depot after his release from the Veterans' Hospital: "'Those people,' he said, pointing in the direction the women and children had gone, 'I thought they locked them up'" (18). The connection with the Japanese he had sensed in the Philippines is now abhorrent to him, and he falls back on distinguishing himself from "those people" as a refuge from such an inclusive vision. Tayo's challenge in *Ceremony* is to (re)discover what he is a part of—and then to act on this knowledge. Over the course of the novel, he learns that he is indeed part of a larger cultural process, a larger story, that encompasses and even goes beyond embracing his Native American heritage.

Two key figures in Tayo's process of learning and healing are Night Swan and Betonie, each of whom represents a departure from "pure" Indian blood-lines and traditions yet proves to be a crucial catalyst in preparing him for the part he will play in the unfolding story. Tayo first meets Night Swan because his Uncle Josiah is having an affair with her—with the disapproval of Tayo's aunt and the gossips of Laguna and to the derision of the people of Cubero, where Night Swan lives. Night Swan appears to be merely an aging whore who's come to the end of her road in the flat above Lalo's bar, but she is clearly much more than that to Josiah—and to Tayo.

In an encounter before he goes to war, Night Swan gives Tayo a glimpse of the larger process he fully understands much later. She has noticed that, like herself, Tayo embodies the crossing of cultural boundaries:

> "I have been watching you for a long time," she said. "I saw the color of your eyes."
> Tayo did not look at her.
> "Mexican eyes," he said, "the other kids used to tease me." (99)

Like his lighter skin, Tayo's eyes have always marked him as a "half-breed," drawing whispers and ridicule from both Indians and Anglos. Night Swan counters his shame with the novel's first statement of a multicultural ethic:

> "They are afraid, Tayo. They feel something happening, they can see some-thing happening around them, and it scares them. Indians or Mexicans or whites—most people are afraid of change. They think that if their children have the same color of skin, the same color of eyes, that nothing is chang-ing." She laughed softly. "They are fools. They blame us, the ones who look different. That way they don't have to think about what has happened inside themselves." (99–100)

Tayo doesn't respond to this insight, but Night Swan insists on its importance: "You don't have to understand what is happening. But remember this day. You will recognize it later. You are part of it now" (100). Tayo's sexual encounter with Night Swan affirms his role in the process of cultural interaction and change that his own mixed ancestry represents. Her multicultural vision also gives him an alternative to the shame and confusion he feels as a "half-breed." Rather than an individual aberration or outcast, Night Swan would have Tayo see himself as part of a larger, inexorable tide of change. As Kenneth Lincoln has noted, in *Ceremony* "the mixed breed is living testimony to the transitions, the changes, the old ways evolving consistently into new variables" (248). Helping my stu-dents recognize this process in Silko's novel helps them better understand the thoroughly "mixed" quality of American literature and culture generally because they come to see change and diversity as the norm rather than the exception.

For Tayo, however, the multicultural vision Night Swan expresses is blurred by the horrors of his experiences in the war, just as the knowledge of Indian beliefs Tayo gained from his Uncle Josiah as a child is obscured by the pressure to conform to the white world view he faced at school. It is only after he returns to Laguna that these memories, and the lessons they hold, come back to him. Yet these recollections alone aren't enough to heal Tayo or the land. Neither is the Scalp Ceremony, the traditional way of reintegrating warriors into the fabric of the universe after they had killed or touched dead enemies. "There are some things we can't cure like we used to," the Laguna medicine man Ku'oosh tells Tayo. "Not since the white people came" (38). Tayo finds himself in a double bind: The traditional ritual has lost its power to heal warriors who fight a modern, mechanized war, but the connection between him and the land remains strong enough that his praying for the rain to end in the jungles of the Philippines has resulted in a drought at Laguna.

On Ku'oosh's recommendation, Tayo's family sends him to Betonie, a Navajo medicine man whose contemporary variations on traditional rituals have earned him both distrust and grudging respect among the Indians of the region. Like Night Swan, Betonie defies social conventions and cultural boundaries. He lives in a traditional hogan overlooking Gallup, site of the annual Indian Ceremonial staged for tourists and a "border town" where Indians come off the reservation in search of work and alcohol. Betonie doesn't talk or act the way a medicine man "should," but his explanation of why he lives where he does reveals a broader, more comprehensive perspective like the one Night Swan had also expressed:

> "It strikes me funny," the medicine man said, shaking his head, "people wondering why I live so close to this filthy town. But see, this hogan was here first. Built long before the white people ever came. It is that town down there which is out of place. Not this old medicine man." (118)

Tayo then recognizes something he shares with Betonie—hazel eyes. "Mexican eyes," Tayo had called them when Night Swan had noticed his, and Betonie acknowledges Tayo's glance by saying, "My grandmother was a remarkable Mexican with green eyes" (119). Like Tayo and Night Swan, Betonie is part of "it"—part of the process of cultural interaction and change that Tayo is only beginning to understand.

When Tayo steps into Betonie's hogan, he finds an array of "medicine," both traditional and contemporary, that overwhelms him. Along with bundles of roots and twigs and bags of dried herbs and tobacco, he sees bundles of newspapers, piles of telephone books from around the country, and a collection of Coke bottles carefully arranged around the circular space of the hogan. "He wanted to dismiss all of it as an old man's rubbish, debris that had fallen out of the years," Silko writes, "but the boxes and trunks, the bundles and stacks were plainly part of the pattern: they followed the concentric shadows of the room." Betonie sees Tayo's distress and reassures him:

> "Take it easy," he said, "don't try to see everything all at once." He laughed. "We've been gathering these things for a long time—hundreds of years. She was doing it before I was born, and he was working before she came. And on and on back down in time." (120)

Here Betonie is referring to the string of women and men who kept the ceremonies alive across the generations—men and women who also embodied the dynamics of cultural growth and change. Two of these people were his grandfather, the Navajo medicine man Descheeny, and his grandmother, the "remarkable Mexican" who gave him his green eyes.

Still torn between worldviews, Tayo nearly reaches the point of defying Betonie and denying the pattern that the medicine man says is unfolding around him, but he catches himself with an insight into his illness and that of the land around him:

> He wanted to yell at the medicine man, to yell the things the white doctors had yelled at him—that he had to think only of himself, and not about the others, that he would never get well as long as he used words like "we" and "us." But he had known the answer all along . . . . Medicine didn't work that way, because the world didn't work that way. His sickness was only part of something larger, and his cure would be found only in something great and inclusive of everything. (125–26)

Here Tayo begins to understand and embrace his role in the larger story, the "ceremony" Betonie has described to him. Like Betonie's ceremonies, this one brings together ancient elements and contemporary circumstances.

Betonie helps Tayo recognize that connections and change—not boundaries and stability—are the norm. He tells Tayo that his grandmother had in fact insisted he attend Sherman Institute, the Indian school in Riverside, California, as part of his education as a medicine man because "It is carried on in all languages now, so you have to know English too" (120). The ceremonies have always been changing, if only in subtle variations, Betonie explains, and the circumstances of the contemporary world make even more substantial changes necessary:

> "At one time, the ceremonies as they had been performed were enough for the way the world was then. But after the white people came, elements in this world began to shift; and it became necessary to create new ceremonies. I have made changes in the rituals. The people mistrust this greatly, but only this growth keeps the ceremonies strong.
>
> "She taught me this above all else: things which don't shift and grow are dead things." (126)

Betonie's vision is not only one of fluidity and change but also one that stresses the connections between things rather than boundaries or distinctions. He uses this comprehensive vision to explain to Tayo that his problems, and those of the Indian peoples generally, are part of a larger scheme that goes deeper than the clash of Native and Anglo cultures. The larger conflict, Betonie says, is between the "witchery," a fundamental force of evil and death, and those who would counter it:

> "That is the trickery of the witchcraft," he said. "They want us to believe all evil resides with white people. Then we will look no further to see what is really happening. They want us to separate ourselves from white people, to be ignorant and helpless as we watch our own destruction. But white people are only tools the witchery manipulates; and I tell you, we can deal with white people, with their machines and their beliefs." (132)

At this point, the text shifts to a story of how white people were the product of a contest among Indian witches—an ironic reversal of the notion of white primacy and superiority—and Betonie begins the rituals that will broaden and sharpen Tayo's vision of himself and the world. The narrative of Tayo's time with Betonie is also interwoven with a series of verse accounts of Indian myths. These stories of Hummingbird and Fly, Coyote, and the Bear People all involve transformation and the return of captives or exiles—themes that resonate strongly with Tayo's predicament and Betonie's healing rituals.

Tayo has a glimmer of a more comprehensive vision after Betonie's initial series of ceremonies. Looking out over the landscape, he senses connections he hadn't recognized before: "He took a deep breath of cold mountain air: there were no boundaries; the world below and the sand paintings inside became the same that night" (145). This sense of interconnection between inside and outside, between ritual and reality, is epitomized by the story of Descheeny, Betonie's grandfather, and that "remarkable Mexican woman" who was his grandmother. Their story is a kind of parable of what happens when different cultures meet, and it informs Tayo's situation as well as Betonie's.

As Betonie tells it, a group of Navajo hunters found a girl in a tree outside a Mexican settlement one night. They took her with them, but something about her hazel green eyes frightened them and they went to Descheeny for help. Despite the objections of his wives, Descheeny takes the Mexican girl in, and he soon discovers that she herself is working against the same cosmic witchery that he confronts—that she is part of the essential variation in the ceremony:

> "He had been watching the sky before she came, the planets and constellations wheeling and shifting the patterns of the old stories. He saw the transition, and he was ready. . . .
>
> "He reasoned that because it was set loose by witchery of all the world, and brought to them by whites, the ceremony against it must be the same.

> When she came, she didn't fool him for long. She had come for his cer-
> emonies, for the chants and the stories they grew from.
>   "'This is the only way,' she told him. 'It cannot be done alone. We must
> have power from everywhere. Even the power we can get from whites.'"
> (150)

This is the pattern, the story, that Betonie, Night Swan, and Tayo enact. Each of
them, like Descheeny and the Mexican girl, represents a transgressive Other or
outsider who crosses cultural boundaries, and it is this figure that keeps the
culture vital and helps it adapt to a changing, even threatening, world. This is
another point where *Ceremony* is particularly valuable as a model of multicultural
practice. Silko's novel makes it abundantly clear that change is the norm—that
borders won't hold—and that our best response is to try to understand and embrace our role in it.

    At the end of his ceremonies for him, Betonie reasserts the role Tayo must
play in the larger story: "This has been going on for a long long time now. It's
up to you" (152). With this, Tayo returns to Laguna and finds himself on another drinking binge with his buddies Leroy and Harley. Only this time he is
able to put his actions, and theirs, in a broader context—the fundamental sense
of loss and broken connections that no amount of alcohol can fully obliterate.
"Old Betonie might explain it this way," Tayo thinks, "there were transitions
that had to be made in order to become whole again, in order to be the people
our Mother would remember" (170). Following this insight, the narrative shifts
to the story of Kaup'a'ta, the Gambler, who tricks his victims into gambling
away all that they have, even their lives, until he is outwitted by the Sun, who
succeeds in freeing his children, the storm clouds, from Kaup'a'ta. Like the
other myths of recovery and renewal in the novel, this one parallels Tayo's
individual circumstances and connects them to a wider cultural context.

    With a fuller sense of his place in the traditional and contemporary "story,"
Tayo begins to fulfill Betonie's vision of his role in the new ceremony by setting out to recover Josiah's Mexican cattle, which disappeared while he was at
war. These cattle—a cross between a tough Mexican variety and the meatier
Hereford of the North—are also "half-breeds," ones Josiah hoped would adapt
well to the conditions at Laguna, and another symbol of cultural interaction and
change. Tayo finds the cattle on land owned by Floyd Lee, a white rancher who
has attempted to cordon off "his" land with a steel fence. Cutting this fence so
he can drive his family's cattle through becomes an extended metaphor of breaking through the stereotyped distinctions and divisions from which he and so
many others have suffered:

> Why did he hesitate to accuse a white man of stealing but not a Mexi-
> can or an Indian? . . . He knew then he had learned the lie by heart . . . only
> brown-skinned people were thieves. . . .
>   The lie. He cut into the wire as if cutting away at the lie inside himself.
> The liars had fooled everyone, white people and Indians alike; as long as

> people believed the lies, they would never be able to see what had been
> done to them or what they were doing to each other. . . . He stood back and
> looked at the gaping cut in the wire. If the white people never looked be-
> yond the lie, to see that theirs was a nation built on stolen land, then they
> would never be able to understand how they had been used by the witch-
> ery. (190–91)

In cutting through Floyd Lee's fence, Tayo not only opens a way to regain his
family's cattle but also aligns himself with the inexorable process of change
that works against fixed boundaries and distinctions.

Tayo's decision to embrace his role in the ceremony Betonie had envisioned—
his decision to pursue the missing cattle—also leads him to a deeper sense of
himself as an Indian through his relationship with the mountain spirit Ts'eh.
Like his fleeting encounter with Night Swan, Tayo's more extended relationship with Ts'eh teaches him about the connections between himself and the
world around him. This time, however, he more fully understands the significance of his lessons, and Ts'eh offers him more thorough, intimate knowledge
of Native traditions. These insights range from where and how to gather roots
and plants to the workings of the cosmic witchery manifested in Emo, the most
brutal of the embittered war veterans at Laguna, who has renounced his Indian
heritage in favor of a twisted combination of flag-waving and machismo.

When Tayo chooses to confront the evil Emo represents, he plays out his
role in the larger story, the larger ceremony, of the struggle between the forces
of change and life and those of stasis and death. This climactic episode takes
Tayo to an abandoned uranium mine and, mindful of the proximity of Los Alamos
and White Sands, to an insight that broadens his understanding to encompass
not only his Indian heritage and his role in the story of cultural change in the
Southwest but also the common predicament of all human beings in the nuclear
age:

> There was no end to it; it knew no boundaries; and he had arrived at the
> point of convergence where the fate of all living things, and even the earth,
> had been laid . . . . From that time on, human beings were one clan again,
> united by the fate the destroyers planned for all of them, for all living things;
> united by a circle of death that devoured people in cities twelve thousand
> miles away, victims who had never known these mesas, who had never
> seen the delicate colors of the rocks which boiled up their slaughter. (246)

For Silko, this widest circle of connection is a final rebuttal to any notion of
"us" and "them," and it is a chilling reminder of what is ultimately at stake in
our attempts to understand and live with each other.

———

The multicultural ethic of *Ceremony* is a legacy of its roots in Native American
tradition as well as a mark of its place in the "American" story of an emergent
national culture that encompasses a multiplicity of ethnic traditions. Silko

challenges us to take this notion of cultural pluralism seriously, and to embrace the changes it entails rather than continue to fool ourselves about who and what we are. In this respect, she, like Betonie, plays the role of what Cornel West calls a "critical organic catalyst," someone who stays "attuned to the best of what the mainstream has to offer—its paradigms, viewpoints, and methods— yet maintains a grounding in affirming and enabling subcultures of criticism" (36). Beyond this, however, Silko also helps us understand that a multicultural ethic is about more than mainstream and subculture. Here she addresses the concern raised by John Mentzos that too much multicultural work centers on the two-way relationship between "mainstream" white society and some "Other," rather than examining and promoting relationships among various communities of color. In *Ceremony*, the dynamics of cultural interaction play out among three cultures which themselves prove to be mixed and various. As we've seen, the novel works against fixed notions of "us" *vs.* "them," stressing instead the multiple and shifting layers of individual and cultural identity. David L. Moore examines this dynamic sense of identity and culture from a poststructuralist perspective in an essay on *Ceremony* and the poetry of Ray Young Bear. He characterizes the "postcolonial praxis" of these writers as being marked by relationality rather than dichotomy, agency rather than determinism, and positionality rather than marginality (393). Though my American literature students tend not to discuss *Ceremony* in such terms, our work with the novel does leave them with an understanding of the possibilities the novel presents for broader connections, action, and change.

For my students and me, a key element of the cultural awareness *Ceremony* promotes is not only this kind of multicultural ethic but also a multicultural aesthetic. We've learned that we're not necessarily doing anything "wrong" if we find hints of Eastern philosophy or Christian imagery in a novel by and about a Native American. Likewise, we've learned that we can talk about such elements of the text as its time shifts, Tayo's sense of alienation, and his quest for wholeness in terms of both "white" and "Native" cultural traditions—but that the cultural matrix of a work like *Ceremony* is more than a two-way street. Equally productive lines of inquiry also include considering the role of Mexican culture (which is itself a hybrid of indigenous and European cultures) in the novel and the Southwest generally and examining the role of gender in the book in the light of Paula Gunn Allen's thesis about the feminine in American Indian traditions.

The nature of *Ceremony*'s multicultural aesthetic makes me wary of approaches to the novel that too rigidly oppose Native and Western traditions—or that would take Silko to task for being too closely tied to the forms and ideology of the dominant culture. Shamoon Zamir, for example, has criticized *Ceremony* for adopting a transcendent, ahistorical sense of myth that "aligns Silko's narratives not so much with their traditional sources of Pueblo oral culture as with Western high modernism's reactionary appropriation of a global mythology of sacrificial rejuvenation" (400). He goes on to compare the novel's climactic scene of Tayo resisting the urge to kill Emo with the mythological method of T. S. Eliot's *The Waste Land*. Rather than find fault with Silko for such intertextual connections, I encourage my students to consider them in the light of the novel's multicultural aesthetic. It is certainly worthwhile to discuss the risks of Silko's incorporating "Western" notions of myth and the quest plot into her multicultural method, and it is essential to be clear about what defines Native American belief systems and how they are different from Western ones, but the ultimate point of a work like *Ceremony* is that such distinctions inevitably break down. The broader lesson I want my students to learn from this is that although we need to be informed and precise about cultural differences, *Ceremony* teaches us that such distinctions, and the cultural forms we associate with them, constantly shift and blur.

One way I've tried to reinforce this point has been to draw on the work of other contemporary artists who share an aesthetic that crosses multiple cultural boundaries. We've listened to recordings by John Trudell, a former American Indian Movement activist who performs socially engaged songs/poetry with the backing of a rock band and traditional Native American singers, and watched an "MTV Unplugged" poetry slam featuring performers who speak from and about a multiplicity of cultural traditions. These "multicultural" works not only demonstrate the interaction of cultures but also cross borders between genres as well as elite and popular culture.

Another fruitful approach to *Ceremony* in my classes has been to highlight the process of cultural mediation that James Ruppert describes in his work on the novel. Ruppert has shown how the juxtaposition of the prose narrative of Tayo's story with Pueblo myths in verse form results in "not only an increased appreciation of the Native worldview by non-Native audiences but also an evolution of Native worldview through that 'constant interaction between meanings' which characterizes Bakhtinian dialogism" ("Dialogism and Mediation" 130). For Ruppert, *Ceremony* challenges its readers to transform their cultural frameworks in much the same way that Tayo learns he must transform his outlook in order to adapt to a dynamic and diverse world ("Reader's Lessons" 84–85). I, in turn, challenge my students to think of this kind of mediation as a three- or four-dimensional process, rather than one that is necessarily limited to the intersections of Native and Anglo cultures, and to focus on those moments in the novel that present scenes of such cultural interaction.

The challenges, rewards, and frustrations of "multicultural" work are ever present in my teaching of *Ceremony*, and I try to remember that my approach to teaching needs to address not only the diversity of the material I present but also the diversity of my students. As Greg Sarris notes in recounting his use of storytelling in teaching Native American literature, no one approach will work, or work the same way, for every classroom setting (157). By concentrating on the dynamics of crossing multiple cultural boundaries, I aim to open up our discussions of *Ceremony* to the wide range of students I find in my classes. Although my students tend not to be very well acquainted with Native American culture, they do know a lot, often more than they realize, about living in a multicultural society. Making room for their knowledge of and experience with "multiculturalism" in our work with Silko's novel has proven well worth the time and effort. I've also found it tremendously helpful to learn from my colleagues, either through hall conversation or such valuable sources as Mary A. Dilg's essay "The Opening of the American Mind: Challenges in the Cross-Cultural Teaching of Literature," which deals directly and practically with issues of preparation, classroom dynamics, and the role of the white teacher in the culturally diverse classroom.

Whatever the challenges and conflicts inherent in crossing cultural boundaries in the classroom, Silko's "Fences Against Freedom" reminds us what's at stake in the attempt. Her essay recalls not only the inclusive worldview she learned as a child but also the realities of racism in her life today. As a person of mixed ancestry, Silko herself has had several run-ins with the Border Patrol, and she now travels the southern route between Tucson and Albuquerque with apprehension—and anger (59). This anger is reflected in her latest novel, *Almanac of the Dead* (1991), an encyclopedic account of life along the border that tempers *Ceremony*'s promise of renewal and wholeness. Indeed, Silko's more recent work serves as a useful counterpoint to *Ceremony*—a reminder of how far American society has yet to progress in making the ideal of cultural pluralism a reality.

Whether we live on the border or not, as "Americans" in the 1990s, we, like Tayo, are all part of "it" now. The drama of crossing cultural boundaries is one we can and must enact each day. Through its mixing of cultural forms and its story of individual growth and cultural change, Silko's novel provides students and teachers with a model of "multiculturalism" that is both more vivid and more deeply meaningful than abstract lectures or media sound bites. With models such as this, we can continue to rethink American literature in profound and fruitful ways.

Note

I would like to thank my students at Alverno College for continuing to enrich my understanding of "multiculturalism" and "American" literature.

Works Cited

Allen, Paula Gunn. *The Sacred Hoop: Recovering the Feminine in American Indian Traditions*. Boston: Beacon, 1986.

Dilg, Mary A. "The Opening of the American Mind: Challenges in the Cross-Cultural Teaching of Literature." *English Journal* 84.3 (1995): 18–25.

Fishkin, Shelley Fisher. "The Multiculturalism of Traditional Culture." *The Chronicle of Higher Education* 10 March 1995: A48.

Jaskoski, Helen. "Teaching with *Storyteller* at the Center." *Studies in American Indian Literature* 5.1 (1993): 51–61.

Lincoln, Kenneth. *Native American Renaissance*. Berkeley: U of California P, 1983.

Mentzos, John. "Hypocrisy at the Heart." *Colors* (September–October 1994): 14–17.

Moore, David L. "Myth, History, and Identity in Silko and Young Bear: Postcolonial Praxis." *New Voices in Native American Literary Criticism*. Ed. Arnold Krupat. Washington: Smithsonian Institution, 1993. 370–95.

Ruppert, James. "Dialogism and Mediation in Leslie Silko's *Ceremony*." *The Explicator* 51.2 (1993): 129–34.

———. "The Reader's Lessons in *Ceremony*." *Arizona Quarterly* 44.1 (1988): 78–85.

Sarris, Greg. *Keeping Slug Woman Alive: A Holistic Approach to Native American Texts*. Berkeley: U of California P, 1993.

Silko, Leslie Marmon. *Ceremony*. 1977. New York: Penguin, 1986.

———. "Fences Against Freedom." *Hungry Mind Review* 31 (Fall 1994): 9, 20, 58–9.

West, Cornel. "The New Cultural Politics of Difference." *Beyond a Dream Deferred. Multicultural Education and the Politics of Excellence*. Eds. Becky W. Thompson and Sangeeta Tyagi. Minneapolis: U of Minnesota P, 1993. 18–40.

Zamir, Shamoon. "Literature in a 'National Sacrifice Area': Leslie Silko's *Ceremony*." *New Voices in Native American Literary Criticism*. Ed. Arnold Krupat. Washington: Smithsonian, 1993. 396–415.

8 Mirrors, Windows, and Prisms: Teaching Asian American Literature in the P.R.C. and the U.S.A.

Mary Louise Buley-Meissner
University of Wisconsin–Milwaukee

The transformative power of Asian American literature makes it one of the most dynamic literatures in the ongoing cultural development of this country. As novelist Cynthia Kadohata asserts, "The main obligations writers have are to learn their craft and to keep themselves on fire. Only by fulfilling these obligations can they tell stories that burn" (xv). Stories, I would add, that burn through our minds to change how we know the world, that make us see and feel—from the inside out—what human beings are capable of doing (at their best, at their worst, in the everyday drama of their lives). As Garrett Hongo observes in his introduction to *Under Western Eyes: Personal Essays from Asian America,* the most compelling narratives often are "written against social silencing, but emerging from deep personal silences dedicated to reflecting on moral, political, and identity issues" (22). What does it mean to be an American of Asian heritage? To be a second- or third- or fourth-generation American who is regarded as a "foreigner" in this country? To be an American whose history is missing from this country's grand narratives of its destiny—with little or no mention in standard history books of Angel Island, the Chinese Exclusion Act, antimiscegenation laws, labor strikes, internment camps, court appeals for justice, and so on? How does it feel to be "raced" by others whose superiority depends on your inferiority? To be "erased" by others who say, "Now that I've gotten to know you, I don't think of you as Korean (or Indian or Laotian)"? Asian American literature incisively addresses such issues, burning through stereotypes to confound and challenge us with its redefinitions of identity, difference, and community.[1]

Yet Asian American literature is compelling for another, equally important reason. In Garrett Hongo's words, it often enacts "an arrest of the practical mind so that the mind of memory and imagination can then be engaged, calling forth the purpose of taking pure pleasure in the meditative act of writing itself" (22). Pure pleasure, yes, that is also what animates Sui Sin Far's essays, Hisaye Yamamoto's short stories, and the work of so many other authors. Their integrity is inseparable from their artistry. Whatever insights they offer, they depend on us to be attentive to silences within stories, stories within silences, the languages of the emotions and the senses. Recollecting experience, they re-form it through storytelling that transcends (yet is made true by) the characters who come to life on the page.[2] When we enter into that life, anything can happen. And that is why I would like to tell you about my experiences teaching Asian American literature in both the People's Republic of China and the United States.

My main purpose will be to show how students come to appreciate that literature through an approach emphasizing its artistry, rhetoricity, and historical background. By artistry, I mean the conceptual and stylistic interrelationship of the fundamental elements of fiction: point of view, characterization, plot, scene, and theme. As King-kok Cheung (*Articulate*) remarks, Asian American literature rarely has been given the "close reading" accorded canonical literature, so that its deconstruction seems counterproductive—a point reinforced by other scholars such as Elaine Kim, Amy Ling, and Sau-ling Cynthia Wong. By referring to the rhetoricity of that literature, I mean to highlight its intentionality—its persuasive appeals and strategies. For I believe that Asian American authors—like all authors of world literature[3]—transform our perceptions of self, society, and culture. In "The Politics of Knowledge," Edward Said observes, "The attempt to read a text in its fullest and most integrative context commits the reader to positions that are educative, humane, and engaged" (312). Reading in that way, inevitably we are guided by the choices authors have made in creating the word-woven worlds we are invited to enter. As to the historical background of Asian American literature, I realize that it is crucial to any serious study of authors' achievements. Elaine Kim emphasizes that fact in her pioneering work *Asian American Literature: An Introduction to the Writings and Their Social Context,* explaining that sociohistorical knowledge "can mean the difference between understanding a work and completely misunderstanding it" (xviii). In sum, I believe that students have much to gain from attention to the texts and contexts of Asian American literature—to the artistry, rhetoricity, and historical background which make it uniquely appealing and worldly.

This essay describes the reading experiences of students at Shanghai International Studies University (where I recently taught multicultural literature as a Fulbright professor of American Studies) and the University of Wisconsin–Milwaukee (where I regularly teach Asian American literature). For cross-cultural comparison and contrast, I also will refer more generally to Chinese and American students' attitudes toward literature, based on four years of teaching at Chinese schools and eight at UWM.[4] One of the most striking differences between the two groups of students relates to their basic conceptualization of literature's value. The Chinese students that I have met consistently describe "serious" literature as significant because it "mirrors" life in objective, realistic, verifiable terms.[5] They respect authors who "stand outside" society in order to reflect its problems and progress back to citizens in need of enlightenment and moral instruction. "Great" authors are those who go beyond "personal" interests to address issues affecting society as a whole. They encourage ordinary people to face the hardships of life without losing heart; no matter how much they themselves have suffered, they are not bitter. Perhaps the most important lesson they offer is that of learning from experience. Thus, "world-class literature" inspires readers to confront their own reflections and realize what they must do for society's advancement. The most influential literary doctrine in China remains Mao Zedong's "Talks at the Yan'an Forum on Literature and Art," which demands that literature serve politics in carrying out the Party leadership's aims (Duke, *Blooming;* Link, *Stubborn*). Of course, innovative writers have tested the limits of that dictum (Barmé and Minford; Kinkley; Lee, "Beyond"; Wang), but it remains powerful in determining what is published, taught, and accorded official respect. In addition, Chinese students tend to accept the classical Chinese view of literature as a subset of history (Plaks), therefore subject to assessments of its factuality and enduring truth-value. From ancient times through the present, "the fundamental affinity of literature, morality, and politics" (Link, *Roses* 17) has been the basic standard for determining literature's value.

My American students, in contrast, frequently regard literature as an array of "windows" through which they can observe other people's lives. Selecting various windows to open or close, they can maintain a certain distance from what they see. In their view, the transparency of literature makes it possible to "look through" books at the world—a distinctly different quality than the reflectivity admired by Chinese. If either the subject or style of literature seems "obscure," they tend to be skeptical about its significance. Unlike Chinese students, they do not look to literature for direct guidance in life. If authors seem to "moralize," American students are likely to be uninterested. In general, they appreciate portrayal of clearly motivated "characters in action" rather than illustration of socially instructive themes. Most American students that I have taught do not expect history or politics to be important in determining literature's value.

The closest Chinese word to the English "study"—*xue*—means "to analyze the merits of a meritorious person and model your behavior after his" (Schoenhals 25). "Great" works of literature are to be studied in China because they are exemplary in every way: politically, socially, morally, stylistically. "Popular" literature also should express "correct" attitudes, but its status is lower because it is not as ideologically or artistically refined. Only when Chinese students read "great" literature do they analyze word-by-word, line-by-line in order to explicate its lessons. Similarly, only in English classes do American students "take everything apart" to "dig out the meaning." Outside of school, Chinese and American students find reading much more enjoyable. As many have told me, they "get into books" which are believable yet unpredictable, surprising but nonetheless "true to life." Could that also happen in school? My experiences at

SISU and UWM suggest that it can—if students are given the opportunity to read in new ways.

At SISU, however, students initially were extremely resistant to reading the multicultural anthologies, *Visions of America* and *Imagining America* (Brown and Ling), which I had selected (and shipped from the U.S.) for an American Studies course, "Cross-Cultural Perspectives on American Experience." None of the students ever had heard of the authors whose work I planned to discuss. Names they recognized and respected in American literature were Stephen Crane, Mark Twain, F. Scott Fitzgerald, Ernest Hemingway—"major authors" whose books reflected "major social concerns" of their times. These and other "great men" exemplified "honesty and courage in showing us how to live." (The only books by American women that students knew were Alice Walker's *The Color Purple* and Margaret Mitchell's *Gone with the Wind,* both praised for exposing racism.) When students were told that we would be reading stories and essays by American authors such as Bharati Mukherjee (of Indian heritage), Bienvenidos Santos (Filipino), Kim Yong Ik (Korean), and Tahira Naqvi (Pakistani), they protested, "Are these authors really American? What's the point of reading their work if we've never heard of them before?" Students were certain that unknown meant inconsequential. In their view, "minority" authors necessarily were of "minor" importance. Because such authors did not belong to the "main culture," they were "too narrow" in outlook, inevitably biased and inescapably personal. They had no "widely applicable lessons" to offer, only descriptions of their own "small corner" of society. In sum, the entire enterprise of studying their work seemed suspect.

Here it should be noted that all of these students (eleven women and seven men) were enrolled in the American Studies program to earn an advanced teacher-training certificate. They had been selected and sent to SISU by their schools so that they could enhance their English language skills (reading, writing, listening, speaking) through a two-year program in literature, history, and economics. All of them were English teachers with two to ten years of experience at commercial colleges, technological and government institutes, teachers' colleges, or universities. As part of a national campaign to improve instruction in English (and other in-demand subjects), they were preparing to become "model teachers" (an official accolade), who would carry "advanced knowledge" back to their schools. With few exceptions, however, they had not studied—or practiced—English extensively since graduating from college. (It is not uncommon for Chinese teachers of English to use English infrequently, mainly because instruction tends to emphasize grammar and syntax.)

Throughout middle school and college, they had excelled in English through word-by-word, sentence-by-sentence analysis of the "language points" (particularly the grammatical rules) illustrated by their texts. In studying American literature, most had read only excerpts or summaries intended to highlight the authors' ideologies. For every book on the national standardized curriculum, these teachers had learned the "correct" interpretation. For example, Fitzgerald's *The Great Gatsby* reflected "the corruptness of the American Dream," and Hemingway's *The Old Man and the Sea* showed how "man must fight to survive." Through a series of increasingly competitive exams (only 5 percent of middle school students in China go on to college), they had proven their mastery of language and literature. Now I expected them to develop a new approach to new authors, emphasizing their own interpretations of characters, events, and themes. No wonder they protested, "You expect too much!"

Two Asian American authors evoked especially strong responses from the SISU students: Sui Sin Far (1865–1914) and Hisaye Yamamoto (b. 1921). These "minority" authors proved to be highly interesting to students as we analyzed themes and styles suggesting the interrelationship of artistry, rhetoricity, and history. In reading Sui Sin Far's autobiographical "Leaves from the Mental Portfolio of an Eurasian" (originally published in 1909), they were most impressed by her integration of personal and social concerns. Through class discussion of her essay, they concluded that she "reformed the meaning of 'personal' to make it powerful" by representing her own life as a catalyst for social change. In "Leaves," Sui Sin Far describes her evolving sense of bicultural identity through a series of increasingly painful episodes. The second oldest of fourteen children, she grows up in poverty, but suffers the most from doubting that anyone fully accepts her. With a Chinese mother and an English father, she soon realizes that others regard her as an "interesting little creature" (Brown and Ling, *Visions* 23). At six years old—when her family moves from England to the United States—she encounters the first Chinese person (other than her mother) that she has ever seen and "recoil[s] with a sense of shock." However, when she is taunted with "Chinky, Chinky, Chinaman, yellow-face, pig-tail, rat-eater," she fights back and proclaims, "I'd rather be Chinese than anything else in the world" (23–24). Yet even with this victory, she feels as if she is a stranger to both of her parents, who remain silent on the question of her identity. By age eighteen, Sui Sin Far has read every book she can find on China and the Chinese. By her early twenties, she establishes a successful career as an investigative reporter, becoming so well known in Chinese communities that they owe "an everlasting debt of gratitude to Sui Sin Far for the bold stand she has taken in their defense" (27). Throughout her life, however, Sui Sin Far realizes that she does not completely fit in anywhere. Chinese know that she is different because she does not speak their language; among other people, she feels even more out of place.

Sitting next to her at dinner, her employer remarks, "Somehow or other . . . I cannot reconcile myself to the thought that the Chinese are humans like ourselves. They may have immortal souls, but their faces seem to be so utterly devoid of expression that I cannot help but doubt." Other people at the table agree, adding: "A chinaman is . . . more repulsive than a nigger. . . .They always give me such a creepy feeling. . . .I wouldn't have one in the house." Sui Sin Far knows that her life will be easier if she remains silent—for everyone has assumed she is "white"—but her conscience forces her to speak out: "The Chinese may have no souls, no expression on their faces, be altogether beyond the pale of civilization, but whatever they are, I want you to understand that I am— I am a Chinese" (Brown and Ling, *Visions* 28). Before long, she leaves town for another job. Wherever she travels—America, Canada, Jamaica—Sui Sin Far hopes that people will accept her as an individual. But whether or not they do, she continues to speak out for the humanity of the Chinese.

Students were deeply impressed by Sui Sin Far's pride in her Chinese identity, pointing out to me that her 1909 essay was published when China itself was in great political turmoil. (The Republic of China was not formed until 1911; the People's Republic of China was established in 1949.) As one student speculated, "In China, Sui Sin Far might have joined the May Fourth Movement for democracy." They also shared her pride in Chinese culture's superiority to all other cultures—a superiority taken for granted by virtually all Chinese students that I have met. Thus, they were pleased to learn that Sui Sin Far led an extraordinary life in America, producing not only first-rate journalism (e.g., "The Chinese Woman in America" and "Chinese Workmen"), but also the first book of fiction by an Asian American, the short story collection *Mrs. Spring Fragrance*.[6] Her achievements stand out even more against the anti-Chinese racism of her era. To help students grasp the significance of her work, I explained that tens of thousands of Chinese men had emigrated to the United States in the 1850s through the 1870s to toil in gold mining, railroad construction, and agricultural development. These sojourners to "Gold Mountain" had left a country ravaged by civil war, foreign aggression, political corruption, and the natural disasters of flood and famine. As Ronald Takaki details in *Strangers from a Different Shore,* their labor supported their families in China and substantially contributed to America's growth as a self-sufficient nation. But when the stock market crashed in 1873 and an economic depression set in, the Chinese were blamed for soaring unemployment rates. The U.S. government's response was the 1882 Chinese Exclusion Act, the first national act to target and exclude immigrants by race. This legislation was criticized by civic and religious leaders (Baldwin; *The Other Side;* Townsend), but to no avail; in 1902, it was renewed for another ten years.[7] Chinese already in this country had virtually no legal rights or legal protection.[8] As the popular press editorialized and pulp fiction warned the American public, "[The Chinese are] poisoning the moral atmosphere, tainting society, undermining the free institutions of this country, degrading labor, and resisting . . . all efforts to remove them. . . . Good people, what shall be done?" (qtd. in Wu, 32).

In reading "Leaves" against its historical background—which was new and disturbing to everyone in class—students could see that Sui Sin Far's "personal" and "political" concerns are inseparable. Her narrative does not merely reflect social issues, but instead re-presents them imaginatively. For example, she recalls (as if it is a recurring experience) "meet[ing] a half Chinese, half white girl. Her face is plastered with a thick white coat of paint and her eyelids and eyebrows are blackened so that the shape of her eyes and her whole expression is changed" (Brown and Ling, *Visions* 30). Sui Sin Far explains that the girl is desperately trying to pass as Spanish in California, but one student interpreted the passage in this way: "Perhaps it is the author who has a split identity in a split society."

Throughout "Leaves," Sui Sin Far skillfully integrates artistry and rhetoricity, so that questions about her own life illuminate issues of cross-cultural significance. "Individuality is more than nationality" (33), she insists—not only for herself, but for any and all people denied their rights on the basis of their race. Reading "Leaves," students gained new understandings of the relationships between literature and politics, art and rhetoric, history and truth. As one of them suggested, "Literature tells the truth in its own way. It takes in history and politics. But it tells its own story."

———————

Why are you interested in reading Asian American literature? At UWM, I ask students this on the first day of a course that introduces them to American authors of Chinese, Japanese, Korean, Indian, and other Asian heritages. Most students have never heard of Sui Sin Far, Hisaye Yamamoto, or any other authors included in the course; most are enrolled to satisfy the university's "cultural diversity" requirement for graduation.[9] However, I am always curious to learn what they expect. Different groups of students provide different answers, of course[10], but here are some recurring responses: "Asia has always seemed mysterious to me, so I would like a glimpse of it. . . . I would like to understand how Asians think, especially because few Americans know anything about this minority. . . . I enjoy American literature courses because they let me look into other people's lives, and I expect this 'special interest' course to do the same. . . . I would like to find out why Asian American literature is becoming popular, even though I am not Asian myself." These responses suggest basic assumptions that students bring to the course: Asian American literature will reveal "East" to "West" (a division analyzed by Said in *Orientalism),* making a "mysterious" culture more familiar without taking away its exotic appeal. Moreover, it will explain to Americans what it means to be "Asian"—defined by ideas particular to that singular group. Students also assume that the experience of reading Asian American literature should conform to the already familiar experience of reading American literature (one being subsidiary to the other). No special knowledge should be required for a "special interest" course; anyone should be able to learn something from it, even though Asian American authors appeal mainly to "Asian" readers. Overall, "Asian" seems to stand in students' responses for alien and unassimilatable, defining the course as the study of "foreign" literature.

However, some students answer "Why are you interested in Asian American literature?" quite differently. Japanese, Indian, Laotian, and other Asian American students often remark, "I hope to learn more about my own identity, especially what 'Asian' and 'American' mean in my life." African American, Hispanic, and American Indian students frequently note, "It's important to me to learn more about what other minorities have experienced in this country, including how they have survived." In contrast to students hoping for a guided tour of "Asia," they want to see America (and their own place in it) more clearly. Of course, serious interest in the study of literature is not determined by ethnicity or race. In fact, I have found that students in China and America alike come to be remarkably flexible and creative in their thinking about literature—even if at first they might seem close-minded.

For example, a major revelation for many UWM students is that Asian American literature is written by *American* authors who address *American* experience (not exclusively, but predominantly). It is not written by Chinese about China, or by Japanese about Japan. Another surprise to many students is learning that Asian Americans are not a homogeneous group. As Lisa Lowe explains, "From the perspective of the majority culture, Asian Americans may very well be constructed as different from, and other than, Euro-Americans. But from the perspective of Asian Americans, we are perhaps even more different, more diverse among ourselves . . ."(27). The circumstances of emigration (historical, political, economic), identifications with the "homeland," degrees of assimilation, regions of settlement, social memberships, educational attainments—these and certainly other elements of experience defy any attempt to decide what is "essentially" Asian American. However, many scholars of Asian American literature and history are convinced that "National, historical, and even class distinctions recede in the light of the experience of difference within a white-dominated society" (Lim and Ling, *Reading* 4; see also Lowe; Sumida; Wong *Reading*). For some Asian Americans at some moments in American history, racial identity has been "involuntary, unerasable, full of burden," as it was for Japanese Americans during World War II (Lim, "Ambivalent" 26). In any case, that identity is irreducibly complex—varying from individual to individual, yet undeniably influenced by collective experience. So the term "Asian American" should be recognized as a strategic one, employed for intellectual and political resistance against oppression. As Sau-ling Cynthia Wong emphasizes, its application to literature serves "an emergent and evolving textual coalition" (*Reading* 9), extending from early immigrants' songs and poetry to contemporary novels and plays.[11]

It cannot be assumed, however, that history ever provides a "correct" reading of literature. History itself must be scrutinized for its biases and revised to incorporate new perspectives on our country's development. For example, although Asian Americans have been here for over 150 years, they have been rendered invisible and silent by their exclusion from far too many accounts of America's economic, cultural, and political advancement. To redress this injustice, scholars of Asian American history have documented the participation of Chinese, Japanese, Korean, Filipino, Indian, and other Asian Americans in shaping our national character (e.g., Chan *Asian;* Cordova and Canillo; Daniels; Lee *Asian;* Lee *Quiet;* Min; Okihiro; Takaki; Yung). Even revisionary history, however, cannot explain literature in any direct, incontestable way; nor does literature "prove" whether or not history should be accepted as true. Both are subject to interpretation; both are forms of storytelling (Canary and Kozicki; White). Yet literature is by nature more exploratory than investigative, more tentative than conclusive. It speaks to us more personally, and asks us to respond in kind.

As students become more familiar with Asian American literature, they soon realize its themes are meaningful across cultures. Students in both China and America, for example, have been deeply affected by Hisaye Yamamoto's "Seventeen Syllables," the tragic story of a Japanese American woman in the 1930s who briefly leads a double life. Living on an isolated California farm, Tome Hayashi has fulfilled her responsibilities as wife, mother, and worker for many years without protest. Every day she labors beside her husband in the fields, picking and boxing tomatoes for a cannery. Without fail, she quietly attends to Mr. Hayashi's needs, looks out for their fifteen-year-old daughter, Rosie, and keeps their house in order. But for three months, the dutiful Tome becomes the independent Ume Hanazono, eloquent writer of beautiful haiku. Late at night, sitting alone at the kitchen table, she tries her best to "pack all her meaning into seventeen syllables only, which [are] divided into three lines of five, seven, and five syllables" (Yamamoto 8). Without neglecting her family, she soon becomes "an extravagant contributor" (9) under her pen name to the haiku section of a Japanese-language newspaper. Mr. Hayashi never comments on her work, and Rosie (who knows as little Japanese as her mother knows English) cannot understand it. Then one day an unexpected visitor, the haiku editor of *Mainichi Shimbum*, arrives with news for Tome: she has won first place in a poetry competition. "Believing and not believing, pleased and overwhelmed" (16), Tome accepts her prize—an exquisite Hiroshiges print—and invites the editor to tea. But Mr. Hayashi only exclaims to Rosie, "Ha, your mother's crazy!" Soon he sends Rosie to bring her back to the fields. And when Tome asks for a minute more, Mr. Hayashi's anger explodes "exactly like the cork of a bottle popping" (17). He marches into the house, pushes the editor out, seizes his wife's prize, and throws it to the ground. To Rosie's shock, he smashes it with an axe, pours kerosene over it, and sets it afire. Certain that "his act of cremation [is] irrevocable," he then returns to the fields. Watching "the dying fire," Rosie cannot believe what has happened, but her mother calmly asks, "Do you know why I married your father?"

Rosie then hears that "Her mother, at nineteen, had come to America and married her father as an alternative to suicide" (18). Tome had been in love with the eldest son of a wealthy family; they carried on their affair secretly because her own family was poor (her father was a gambler and alcoholic). When she became pregnant, her lover already was engaged to someone else. Completely degraded in her family's eyes, Tome gave birth to a stillborn son. At that time, seventeen years ago, she wrote to a sister in America, threatening to kill herself unless she could leave Japan. The sister arranged a marriage with "a young man of simple mind [and] kindly heart," who never learned of Tome's past. Tragic as this story is, she tells it "perfectly," as if she has "memorized it by heart, reciting it to herself so many times that its nagging vileness [has] long since gone" (19). Rosie's only response, however, is "I would have liked a brother." Tome's final plea—"Promise me you will never marry!"—brings Rosie to tears, but not to understanding of what she has heard.

Discussing their initial reactions to "Seventeen Syllables," Chinese students sympathized with Tome because "she lost her dreams" and "she had to go back to a lonely life." Nonetheless, many thought Mr. Hayashi "deserved more pity because he suffered more." A majority of our class (five out of seven men and six out of eleven women) agreed on these points: the husband was "cheated out of a happy life" in his arranged marriage; his destruction of Tome's prize was "wrong but understandable"; and Tome should have tried harder to be "a good wife and a good mother." They also thought her life as Ume the poet was "fated to fail" because it was "too selfish, too private, just for herself." The other students also pitied Mr. Hayashi, but they did not believe Tome should be treated so cruelly. As one woman protested, "Tome did her best in a difficult situation. Writing haiku is not wrong! When her husband took away her prize, he took away the beauty of her life. Now what will she have left?" As we continued to discuss "Seventeen Syllables," I realized that no singleminded concept of "Chinese tradition" or "Chinese culture" could explain students' views. (For certainly tradition and culture always are in flux, always in the process of being formed.) They themselves had enrolled at SISU for reasons that could be considered "selfish": personal advancement, higher social status, the opportunity to qualify for study overseas. Those who had the most sympathy for Tome questioned whether or not their own hopes were too high. As one woman wondered, "If you want more than being a mother and a wife, will you always be lonely? Can poetry fill up Tome's life?" In contrast, those who criticized Tome most severely were determined not to let their own lives be disrupted. One student's remarks, for example, seemed to describe himself as much as Tome's husband: "He has to keep things in order. That is not his choice. It is his duty."

Reading "Seventeen Syllables," Chinese students initially were disappointed that Yamamoto did not explain how the characters should be judged. In effect, they wanted the story to reflect Yamamoto's lessons on life back to them. Her artistry and rhetoricity, however, are so tightly interwoven that the *experience* of reading the story finally seems more important than anything else. For example, the story is told not by Tome, but by her daughter, Rosie, who understands very little of her parents' unhappiness. The story is filled with silences external and internal: out on the tomato fields, where everyone works "as efficiently as a flawless machine" (16); inside the house, where the only sound is the mother's "midnight scribbling with pencil on scratch paper" (9); within the family, where words are measured against the risk of being misunderstood. Rosie does not question this way of life, but she tries to escape it through fantasy and infatuation. On the way home from visiting friends, when her parents do not speak to each other in the car, she pictures their "green pick-up crumpled in the dark . . . three contorted, bleeding bodies, one of them hers" (12). Kissed by seventeen-year-old Jesus Carrasco, a hired hand on the farm, Rosie falls "for the first time entirely victim to a helplessness delectable beyond speech . . . [a] terrible, beautiful sensation" (14). Ironically, Rosie has no idea that her mother's own emotional life is much more tumultuous. Even at the end of "Seventeen Syllables," when Tome confesses the shame of her loveless marriage, Rosie's thoughts return to Jesus's touch. Words fail to bring mother and daughter closer together, yet the silence between them has been broken. If Tome cannot escape her own fate, at least she has tried to change Rosie's.

Teaching in both China and America, I have found that when students carefully attend to Yamamoto's creative interplay of character, plot, and point of view, they recognize that the rift between mother and daughter is no less important than the tension between husband and wife. As one Chinese student observed, "When I reread the story, I see how desperate Tome is for Rosie to have a different life. Tome puts her whole life into seventeen syllables, but Rosie shouldn't have to." Noting that Tome's stillborn son would have been seventeen years old if he had lived, another Chinese student remarked, "When Tome watches her poetry prize burning up, she goes through her son dying again. She didn't get a new life in America. She didn't get a new life as a poet. She watches all of her hopes burning up." Making such connections, students could see that Yamamoto is centrally concerned with portraying Tome in her full complexity as mother/wife/poet. Judging Tome or her husband is not the point of "Seventeen Syllables."

American students, however, usually are initially critical of both characters. They expect to look through the "window" of the story into lives which can be evaluated by their own standards of "right" and "wrong" behavior. They castigate the husband for his "completely irrational actions," and they cannot understand why the wife is "so submissive, as if she has no will of her own." They want to know why she stays in such an unhappy situation: "If she wants a different life, she should pack up and get out." As for Rosie, "She should get out of there as soon as she can. She has to have her own life." Wherever I have taught, however, students have developed new insights as they have learned about the historical background of "Seventeen Syllables." Arranged marriages—such as that between Tome and her husband—were not unusual for the *issei*, the first generation of Japanese immigrants. Before the 1924 Asian Exclusion Act, young Japanese men came to work for plantations, farms, railroads, and canneries in the United States. When they had secured employment, they often sent for "picture brides" who had been matched with them through an exchange of photos and background information. Couples met for the first time in the United States, then settled down to raise families. As King-kok Cheung points out, by 1930, the American-born *nisei* (the second generation) outnumbered the *issei* (*Hisaye* 5). Japanese farms—such as the one depicted in "Seventeen Syllables"—substantially contributed to the country's agricultural development, but the Alien Land Law Act of 1913 barred "aliens ineligible for citizenship" from buying land or leasing it for more than three years. Anti-Asian racism culminated in the World War II internment of 110,000 Japanese and Japanese Americans (two-thirds of whom were U.S. citizens), confiscation of their homes and businesses, disintegration of families, and destruction of communities. Not until 1952 could Japanese become naturalized citizens. For many Japanese Americans, the internment symbolizes an alienation which has not ended (e.g., Houston; Murayama; Okada; Sone; Uchida; Yamada).

"Seventeen Syllables" is set in the 1930s, before Japanese families were forced into Manzanar, Tule Lake, and the other camps. Learning what lies ahead, however, Chinese and American students recognize the tragic desperation in Mr. Hayashi's life. No matter how hard he tries to make his farm as productive as possible, he will lose it. In fact, it is not his to own, regardless of his labor. His wife is a stranger to him; his daughter is by birth a citizen of the country calling him "alien." Thus, students realize that Mr. Hayashi is enraged not only by his wife's independence, but by all that he has lost in coming to America. Similarly, they realize that Tome is caught up in circumstances affecting many *issei* women in America. She cannot simply "pack up and get out." She has only one sister in America, few friends, and nowhere to turn if she leaves home. Rather than passivity, she demonstrates extraordinary strength of character in fulfilling her responsibilities as wife, mother, and worker. As for Rosie, students can see that many difficult decisions lie ahead for her. Like many other *nisei,* she must find her own way to be Japanese and American in a country where her parents can never fully belong.

Historical background to Asian American literature is useful to all students, but American students in particular are sometimes shocked by what they learn about their own country. In every class at UWM, comments like the following are common: "I never studied anything about the camps before. I feel angry about what happened and why I didn't learn about it before." (The average age of UWM students is 27.) Yamamoto herself was interned in Poston, Arizona, where she edited the camp newsletter. For fifty years, she has been writing short stories about Japanese American experience with a voice Cheung describes as "at once compassionate and ironic, gentle and probing" (Introduction xiv) in its exploration of ordinary people's lives. Yet an anthology of her stories was not published in the United States until 1985; and the first collection of scholarly essays on her work was not assembled until 1994.[12] In an interview, Yamamoto once claimed that she "didn't have any imagination" and "just embroidered on things that happened" (Crow 74).[13] However, she is now widely recognized as a pioneering author of the Japanese American literary tradition.

Attentive to artistry, rhetoricity, and history, we can read in ways that open up a spectrum of compelling possibilities. Each of us will learn something different, for each of us will hold the prism of literature up to a different light and at a different angle (according to when, how, and why we are reading). As the writer Tobias Wolff observes, "We need to feel ourselves acted upon by a story, outraged, exposed, in danger of heartbreak and change. Those are the stories that endure in our memories, to the point where they take on the nature of memory itself. . . . [The best stories] inscribe themselves forever on the reader's moral being, and bring the world into sharper focus" (viii). In that way, perhaps, literature becomes history, a re-collection or re-presentation of experiences that define our individuality and humanity. Authors such as Sui Sin Far and Hisaye Yamamoto ask that we look again—more closely and carefully—at life's potential to enrage, exhilarate, or completely surprise us. Who we are, what we believe and why, how we hope to live with others—these are concerns drawing us into the study of Asian American and all world literature. As we read, we remember: bitterness tasted, hopes realized, silence endured . . . . Yet, as Wolff points out, "the experience of something read can form us no less than the experience of something lived through" (viii), literally changing our minds by weaving into our memories intricate, vivid images of other people's pains, joys, and sorrows. Reading Asian American literature, I believe, can unravel us—and it can help to make us whole.

Notes

1. For surveys of primary and secondary works, see Cheung and Yogi; Kim *(Asian)*; Ling *(Between)*; and Wong *(Reading)*. Two excellent introductory anthologies are *Growing Up Asian American* (with selections from 1912 through 1993), ed. Hong, and *Charlie Chan Is Dead: An Anthology of Contemporary Asian American Fiction*, ed. Hagedorn.

2. As my remarks suggest, I consider fiction and literary nonfiction (e.g., creative essays and memoirs) to be more alike than different in their narrativity. For discussions of this view, see Anderson, Eagleton, and Warnock.

3. World literature, in my view, appeals to readers across cultures, who will understand it in their own variously complex ways.

4. In China, I have taught as a "foreign expert" at Yangzhou Teachers College (1982–84) and as a Fulbright professor at Beijing Teachers College (1986–87) and Shanghai International Studies University (1993–94). During that time and in 1992, I lectured at other Chinese schools and conducted research on teacher education ("Teachers," "Teaching").

5. For ongoing research, I have kept detailed notes on class discussions at SISU and UWM. Other material quoted in this essay includes SISU students' midterm examinations, their final take-home examinations, UWM students' daily journals, their final take-home examinations, and notes from conferences with students at both schools. Students have given permission for this use of their work.

6. Amy Ling has done extensive research to give Sui Sin Far's work the critical attention that it deserves *(Between,* "Chinese," "I'm"). With Annette White-Parks, Ling recently edited *Mrs. Spring Fragrance and Other Writings*. The first full-length study of Sui Sin Far's work is White-Parks's *Sui Sin Far/Edith Maude Eaton: A Literary Biography*.

7. For comprehensive discussion of anti-Asian immigration policies, see Sucheng Chan's research *(Asian,* "Exclusion").

8. However, Asian immigrants and Asian American citizens have a long history of fighting for their legal rights in court (Chan, *Entry*; Okihiro; Takaki).

9. Undergraduates must take a three-credit "cultural diversity" course to satisfy the General Education Requirements for graduation; it can be selected from a wide range of humanities and social science courses addressing ethnic and/or racial issues.

10. Students at UWM, a Midwest urban university mainly drawing students from within the state, cannot be assumed to "typify" American students any more than those at SISU "typify" Chinese students. Students from different regions of the country, different social and economic backgrounds, and so on, may have different expectations in reading Asian American literature for the first time. By describing my students' changing attitudes, I hope to encourage the expansion of literary imagination among all students—and their teachers.

11. For commentaries on the early history of Asian American literature, see Chin ("Come"); Him et al.; Hom; Wong ("Politics").

12. The first anthology published was *Seventeen Syllables: Five Stories of Japanese American Life* (Tokyo: Kirihara Shoten, 1985). In 1988, Kitchen Table Women of Color Press published *Seventeen Syllables*, a collection of fifteen stories. In 1994, Rutgers University Press published *Hisaye Yamamoto: Seventeen Syllables*, a collection of critical essays edited by King-kok Cheung. For critical commentaries on Yamamoto's work, see also Cheung *(Articulate)*; Kim *(Asian)*; and Wong *(Reading)*.

13.   Yamamoto also has said that "Seventeen Syllables" is loosely based on her mother's life (Cheung, "Interview" 86).

Works Cited

Anderson, Chris, ed. *Literary Nonfiction: Theory, Criticism, Pedagogy.* Carbondale: Southern Illinois UP, 1989.

Baldwin, Mrs. S. L. *Must the Chinese Go?* 3rd ed. New York: H. B. Elkins, 1890.

Barmé, Geremie, and John Minford, eds. *Seeds of Fire.* Hong Kong: Far Eastern Economic Review Ltd., 1986.

Brown, Wesley, and Amy Ling, eds. *Imagining America: Stories from the Promised Land.* New York: Persea, 1991.

———. *Visions of America: Personal Narratives from the Promised Land.* New York: Persea, 1993.

Buley-Meissner, Mary Louise. "Teachers and Teacher-Education: A View from the People's Republic of China." *International Journal of Educational Development* 11.1 (1991): 41–53.

———. "Teaching American Literature in China: Learning How Students Read and Respond." *English Education* 22.3 (1990): 192–99.

Canary, Robert H., and Henry Kozicki, eds. *The Writing of History: Literary Form and Historical Understanding.* Madison: U of Wisconsin P, 1978.

Chan, Sucheng. *Asian Americans: An Interpretive History.* Boston: Twayne, 1991.

———, ed. *Entry Denied: Exclusion and the Chinese Community in America, 1882–1943.* Philadelphia: Temple UP, 1991.

———. "The Exclusion of Chinese Women, 1870–1943." In Chan, ed. 94–146.

Cheung, King-kok. *Articulate Silences: Hisaye Yamamoto, Maxine Hong Kingston, Joy Kogawa.* Ithaca: Cornell UP, 1993.

———, ed. *Hisaye Yamamoto, "Seventeen Syllables."* New Brunswick, NJ: Rutgers UP, 1994.

———. Interview with Hisaye Yamamoto. In Cheung, ed. 71–86.

———. Introduction. In Yamamoto, xi–xxv.

Cheung, King-kok, and Stan Yogi, compilers. *Asian American Literature: An Annotated Bibliography.* New York: MLA, 1988.

Chin, Frank. "Come All Ye Asian American Writers of the Real and the Fake." *The Big Aiiieeeee!: An Anthology of Chinese American and Japanese American Literature.* Ed. Jeffery Paul Chan, et al. New York: Meridian, 1991. 1–92.

Cordova, Joan May T., and Alexis S. Canillo, eds. *Voices: A Filipino American Oral History.* Stockton: Filipino Oral History Project, 1984.

Crow, Charles L. "A MELUS Interview: Hisaye Yamamoto." *MELUS* 14.1 (1987): 73–84.

Daniels, Roger. *Asian America: Chinese and Japanese in the United States since 1850.* Seattle: U of Washington P, 1988.

Duke, Michael S. *Blooming and Contending: Chinese Literature in the Post-Mao Era.* Bloomington: Indiana UP, 1985.

Eagleton, Terry. *Literary Theory: An Introduction.* Minneapolis: U of Minnesota P, 1983.

Hagedorn, Jessica. *Charlie Chan Is Dead: An Anthology of Contemporary Asian American Fiction.* New York: Penguin, 1993.

Him, Mark Lai, et al. *Island: Poetry and History of Chinese Immigrants on Angel Island, 1910–1940.* 1980. Seattle: U of Washington P, 1991.

Hom, Marlon K. *Songs of Gold Mountain: Cantonese Rhymes from San Francisco Chinatown.* Berkeley: U of California P, 1987.

Hong, Maria, ed. *Growing Up Asian American.* New York: Avon, 1993.

Hongo, Garrett, ed. *Under Western Eyes: Personal Essays from Asian America.* New York: Anchor Original Books/Doubleday, 1995.

Houston, Jeanne Wakatsuki, and James D. Houston. *Farewell to Manzanar.* San Francisco: Houghton Mifflin, 1973.

Kadohata, Cynthia. Introduction. *American Eyes.* Ed. Lori M. Carlson. New York: Holt, 1994

Kim, Elaine H. *Asian-American Literature: An Introduction to the Writings and Their Social Context.* Philadelphia: Temple UP, 1984.

Kinkley, Jeffrey C., ed. *After Mao: Chinese Literature and Society, 1978-1981.* Cambridge: Harvard UP, 1985.

Lee, Joann Faung Jean, ed. *Asian American Experiences in the United States: Oral Histories of First to Fourth Generation Americans from China, the Philippines, Japan, India, the Pacific Islands, Vietnam and Cambodia.* Jefferson, NC: McFarland, 1991.

Lee, Leo Ou-fan. "Beyond Realism: Thoughts on Modernist Experiments in Contemporary Chinese Writing." *Worlds Apart: Recent Chinese Writing and Its Audiences.* Ed. Howard Goldblatt. Armonk, NY: Sharpe, 1990. 64–77.

Lee, Mary Paik. *Quiet Odyssey: A Pioneer Woman in America.* Ed. Sucheng Chan. Seattle: U of Washington P, 1990.

Lim, Shirley Geok-lin. "The Ambivalent American: Asian American Literature on the Cusp." In Lim and Ling, eds. 13–32.

Lim, Shirley Geok-lin, and Amy Ling, eds. *Reading the Literatures of Asian America.* Philadelphia: Temple UP, 1992.

Ling, Amy. *Between Worlds: Women Writers of Chinese Ancestry.* New York and Oxford: Pergamon, 1990.

———. "Chinese American Women Writers: The Tradition behind Maxine Hong Kingston." *Rethinking American Literary History.* Ed. A. LaVonne Brown Ruoff and Jerry W. Ward Jr. New York: MLA, 1990. 219–36.

———. "I'm Here: An Asian American Woman's Response." *New Literary History* 19 (1987): 1–16.

Link, Perry, ed. *Roses and Thorns: The Second Blooming of the Hundred Flowers in Chinese Fiction, 1979–1980.* Berkeley: U of California P, 1984.

———. *Stubborn Weeds: Popular and Controversial Chinese Literature After the Cultural Revolution.* Bloomington: Indiana UP, 1983.

Lowe, Lisa. "Heterogeneity, Hybridity, Multiplicity: Marking Asian American Differences." *Diaspora: A Journal of Transnational Studies* 1.1 (1991): 21–44.

Mao Zedong. "Talks at the Yan'an Forum on Literature and Art." Trans. Bonnie S. McDougall. Ann Arbor: Center for Chinese Studies, U of Michigan P, 1980.

Min, Pyong Gap, ed. *Asian Americans: Contemporary Trends and Issues.* Thousand Oaks, CA: Sage, 1995.

Murayama, Milton. *All I Asking For Is My Body.* 1959. San Francisco: Supa, 1975.

Okada, John. *No-No Boy.* 1957. Seattle: U of Washington P, 1976.

Okihiro, Gary Y. *Margins and Mainstreams: Asians in American History and Culture.* Seattle: U of Washington P, 1994.

The Other Side of the Chinese Question: Testimony of California's Leading Citizens. San Francisco: Woodward, 1886.

Plaks, Andrew, ed. *Chinese Narrative.* Princeton: Princeton UP, 1977.

Said, Edward. *Orientalism.* New York: Vintage, 1971.

————. "The Politics of Knowledge." *Race, Identity and Representation in Education.* Ed. Cameron McCarthy and Warren Crichlow. New York: Routledge, 1993. 306–14.

Schoenhals, Martin. *The Paradox of Power in a People's Republic of China Middle School.* Armonk, NY: Sharpe, 1993.

Sone, Monica. *Nisei Daughter.* Seattle: U of Washington P, 1953.

Sui Sin Far (Edith Eaton). "Chinese Women in America." *The Land of Sunshine* 6.2 (1987): 62.

————. "Chinese Workmen in America." *The Independent* 3 July 1913: 56–58.

————. "Leaves from the Mental Portfolio of an Eurasian." *The Independent* 21 Jan. 1909: 125–32.

————. *Mrs. Spring Fragrance.* Chicago: A. C. McClurg, 1912.

————. *Mrs. Spring Fragrance and Other Writings.* 1912. Ed. Amy Ling and Annette White-Parks. Urbana and Chicago: U of Illinois P, 1995.

Sumida, Stephen H. "Afterword." In Hong, ed. 399–405.

Takaki, Ronald. *Strangers from a Different Shore: A History of Asian Americans.* New York: Penguin, 1989.

Townsend, L. T. *The Chinese Problem.* Boston: Lee and Shepard, 1876.

Uchida, Yoshiko. *Desert Exile: The Uprooting of a Japanese-American Family.* Seattle: U of Washington P, 1982.

Wang, David Der-wei. *Running Wild: New Chinese Writers.* New York: Columbia UP, 1994.

Warnock, John, ed. *Representing Reality: Readings in Literary Nonfiction.* New York: St. Martin's, 1989.

White, Hayden. "Introduction: The Poetics of History." *Metahistory: The Historical Imagination in Nineteenth-Century Europe.* Baltimore: Johns Hopkins UP, 1973.

White-Parks, Annette. *Sui Sin Far/Edith Maude Eaton: A Literary Biography.* Chicago and Urbana: U of Illinois P, 1995.

Wolff, Tobias, ed. *The Vintage Book of Contemporary American Short Stories.* New York: Vintage, 1994.

Wong, Sau-ling Cynthia. "The Politics and Poetics of Folksong Reading: Literary Portrayals of Life under Exclusion." In Chan, ed. 246–67.

————. *Reading Asian American Literature: From Necessity to Extravagance.* Princeton, NJ: Princeton UP, 1993.

Wu, William. *Yellow Peril: Chinese Americans in American Fiction, 1850–1940.* Hamden, CT: Archon, 1982.

Yamada, Mitsuye. *Desert Run: Poems and Stories.* Latham, NY: Kitchen Table Women of Color Press, 1988.

Yamamoto, Hisaye. *Seventeen Syllables.* Latham, NY: Kitchen Table Women of Color Press, 1988.

Yung, Judy. *Chinese Women of America: A Pictorial History.* Seattle: U of Washington P, 1986.

9 Father Martínez: Folk Hero or Dangerous Infidel? Rereading Willa Cather's *Death Comes for the Archbishop*

Judith Beth Cohen
Lesley College

> It is time to take *Death Comes for the Archbishop* off the shelf, out of the library hush reserved for masterpieces and read it actively as part of the multi-ethnic conversation it seeks to dramatize.
>
> —Bette Weidman, "Willa Cather's Art in Historical Perspective"

"That's the worst 'good' novel ever written," said New Mexican wood-carver Charles Carillo. "Willa Cather told many lies in that book about *nuevomexicanos.*"

I was in New Mexico to team-teach a new course titled, "Traditions and Cultures: The History, Literature, Arts and Ecology of the Southwest," developed as part of an Interdisciplinary Studies Master's program at Lesley College in Cambridge, Massachusetts. A midwesterner by birth and New Englander by choice, I, along with my Cambridge-based colleagues, would be learning with our students. Under the guidance of local experts, we would examine rare Indian pottery and weavings in the locked vaults of the School of American Research, climb the canyons of Georgia O'Keeffe's beloved Ghost Ranch, and watch mesmerized as the Santo Domingo Pueblo Indians celebrated their annual corn dance. Santa Fe and its environs would be our primary text, interpreted for us by New Mexican historians, artists, and ecologists. Along with our reading, we would experience the diverse cultures of the region first-hand.

We were sitting under the cottonwood trees at El Rancho de Las Golondrinas, a living museum of Hispanic culture outside Santa Fe, when Carillo attacked the novel I had assigned as a core text. Only the night before I had lectured on Cather's visual images, her use of historical sources, and her emphasis on the interaction between the land and the people who lived on it—precisely the themes of our course. At that unnerving moment of cultural collision, I was unprepared to defend my choice of this "despised" required reading.

Carillo, himself an anthropologist, *santero* (carver of wooden saints), and member of the Penitentes (a Catholic brotherhood), traced the history of folk art tradition that produces the colorful figures found in village homes and

146

churches. These doll-like weeping virgins and saints reminded me of the Native American *kachina* figures. The relationships Carillo described between New Mexican Catholics and their saints seemed similar in quality to the Pueblo Indians' attitude toward their spirits. Indeed, for many of mixed blood, and many converted Native Americans, traditional practices and Catholicism coexist without conflict. Carillo explained how the scarcity of priests in what was then northern Mexico led to the formation of these lay brotherhoods and sisterhoods, still active today. In Cather's novel, we'd encountered the schismatic Penitentes and their bloody rituals, presented as backward, ignorant and misguided. Yet this artist/academic represented the Brotherhood as a respected living tradition that merged art and spirituality.

In *Death Comes for the Archbishop* Cather recounts the story of French Bishop Lamy's drive to establish the Catholic Church in northern Mexico just after the territory was conquered by the United States in 1848. Cather's protagonist Jean Latour is a fictionalized version of the historical Bishop Lamy, whose statue stands before the Santa Fe cathedral. However, Father Martínez of Taos, the renegade priest who refuses to outlaw the Penitentes, has no fictional mask. It appears that Cather did not consider the indigenous figure important enough to merit the protection of an invented name. She treats Padre Martínez's subjugation and excommunication as the Bishop's "victory." In his talk, connecting New Mexican folk art with religion and history, Carillo insisted that Father Martínez was not the womanizing demon Cather had depicted, but an important leader who had educated the Mexican poor and had taken a strong stand against the U.S. invasion.

As we toured the nineteenth century farm's water mills, threshing houses, and Morada de la Conquistadora (meeting house of the Penitente Brotherhood) Carillo's complaint dogged me. Cather's stereotyped images of race and gender had given me ample opportunities for noting the limits of her perspective, but questioning her presentation of Father Martínez hadn't occurred to me. We New Englanders might know something about Native American culture; certainly we were eager to visit the pueblos, see the colorful rugs and pottery, and attend religious dances, but we were terribly uninformed when it came to Hispanic culture. My problem was not my failure to critique Cather's historical accuracy, for the questions themselves would never have formed had I not been immersed in the culture she wrote about. The awakening hit me: the classic trope of innocence lost. Now that my chosen text had become a weapon in the culture wars, I was faced with a conflict very much alive nearly seventy years after the book's publication.

As our students fanned out to work on their research, I had my project to do. While they interviewed present-day *santeros* about their craft, spent time with native women working to prevent wife battering on the San Il'defonso pueblo, or collected historical documents for an American Studies course on Colonial

New England, I searched for information about the real Father Martínez. In the critical accounts I had consulted before going to New Mexico I'd found no mention of the Martínez controversy. Reviewing the book for the *New York Times* in 1927, Henry Longan Stuart worried that Cather's fictionalized history could be "laying down snares for the feet of generations to come . . . quite ready to take the word of so fascinating a writer in matters of fact as well as of fancy" (Stuart 245). Interested in blurred genres myself, and more inclined to think of history as stories handed down by those in power, I dismissed this criticism as conservative grousing. But in New Mexico, Cather's deliberate distortion of history for her own artistic purposes became a moral issue. Her much praised novel had long been controversial in the Hispanic community, generating as much venom as Twain's *Huckleberry Finn* does for some African Americans. If Cather's account of Father Martínez was not simply unflattering, but full of inaccurate allegations capable of shaping readers' versions of New Mexican history, then it would be irresponsible not to offer competing views.

First, I reminded myself just why I had selected the novel. The course bibliography included readings in history, anthropology, art, and ecology, assigned by my colleagues, and I was limited to one literary selection. Cather's novel seemed perfect for a number of reasons. Her freewheeling use of history and her creation of a non-dramatic form she called "a narrative," composed of a prologue and nine distinct books (Woodress 399), gives her novel a collage-like quality that seemed almost postmodern to me. We were asking our students to understand history, artistic production, and the physical environment, not as separate subjects, but as fully interrelated. Hadn't Cather done just that herself, drawing from both historical and visual sources to produce her innovative novel? And didn't *Archbishop* contain material on the three cultures we would be exploring in New Mexico: Anglo/European, Native American, and Hispanic? True, Cather's protagonist might be a refined French priest, but she shows how ethnicities intermingled in the New World to produce a unique cultural fusion.

Soon after arriving in New Mexico, Father Latour finds the oriental sound of an old bell especially pleasing. When he learns that it was brought to Mexico from Spain and dates back to 1356, he comments on the Catholic appropriation of a Muslim custom: "The Spaniards handed on their skill to the Mexicans, and the Mexicans have taught the Navajos to work silver; but it all came from the Moors" (45). For most of us, this cultural layering becomes invisible. On my own travels through southern Spain, I learned that much "Spanish" architecture and design actually derived from a mixture of Moorish and Jewish Middle Eastern influences. Thus, I was especially pleased with Cather's attention to details that defy a monolithic or static interpretation of ethnicity.

Furthermore, Cather believed that *Archbishop* was her best novel. Both a critical and commercial success, the book is also a culmination of her long interest in the southwest (Woodress 391). Though not a Catholic herself, she used the story of the Church's establishment in northern New Mexico as a way of exploring themes that interested her—for example, how a refined individual can thrive in a remote, western landscape. She was also expressing the 1920s efforts to create a distinctive American culture from its many ethnic strands. The freshness of the American presence in New Mexico during this period gave her an open canvas for crafting a unified culture in what she considered to be a disorganized, wild place (Weidman 61). Her interest in the Church was not based on its religious beliefs but rather on its organizational unifying purpose (Weidman 55).[1]

In her visits to New Mexico she had heard stories about Bishop Lamy, the first Catholic Archbishop of the American territories, and felt as if he were "a personal friend" (Woodress 393). No doubt she identified with the cultured Frenchman who misses the gardens, cuisine, and comforts of his homeland. His lonely labor in devotion to his chosen vocation probably struck her as similar to her own life as a dedicated artist. Cather enthusiastically read an obscure account of *The Life Of The Right Reverend Joseph P. Machebeuf* by an admiring priest named Howlett. This book gave her the model for Father Valliant, Bishop Latour's warm, folksy, lifelong friend, who becomes his assistant in New Mexico (Woodress 393). Whereas Latour is depicted as formal, cool, and reserved, Valliant is more expressive and more connected to the humble people he serves. The idealized friendship between two men probably allowed Cather to inject autobiographical elements based on her relationship with her companion, Edith Lewis.

In addition to the Howlett book, Cather read letters written by the first French missionary priest in northern Mexico, and "at least eight or ten other volumes on the southwest" (Woodress 403).[2] Cather was often the guest of Mabel Dodge Luhan, the New York writer who relocated in Taos, married a Taos Indian and urged many artists and writers (D.H. Lawrence among them), to discover the wonders she found in her new home. Along with Cather's reading and her own observations, stories she heard from Tony Luhan also became incorporated into her book (Smith 105). Since Lois Rudnick, Mabel Dodge Luhan's biographer, would be lecturing our group at the Luhan house in Taos, here was yet another connection between the *Archbishop* and our course agenda.

Almost as strong as the novel's historical themes are its visual elements. My own images of New Mexico and the southwest come almost entirely from Georgia O'Keeffe's paintings of deserts and canyons, and Willa Cather's descriptions, as vivid as O'Keeffe's paintings. In *Archbishop*, Santa Fe is "a thin wavering adobe town . . . a green plaza . . . at one end a church with two earthen towers that rose high above the flatness" (22). Cather captures the spectacular desert/sky relationship: "The great tables of granite set down in an empty plain were inconceivable without their attendant clouds, which were a part of them, as the smoke is part of the censer, or the foam of the wave" (95). She takes readers inside a secret Indian cave, where Latour hears "one of the oldest voices of the earth" in "the sound of a great, underground river, flowing through a resounding cavern" (130). We're transported to the sky Pueblo of Acoma; here the Indians "born in fear and dying by violence for generations, had at last taken this leap away from the earth, and on that rock had found the hope of all suffering and tormented creatures—safety" (97). We travel to the Navajo's Canyon de Chelly and learn of their belief "that their old gods dwelt in the fastness of that canyon; like their Shiprock, it was an inviolate place, the very heart and center of their life" (293). Finally, Cather explains why the Catholic Cathedral in Santa Fe, built in 1861 and graced with its statue of Bishop Lamy, looks like a French church accidently dropped into the desert.

Cather mentioned three different visual sources that inspired the way she approached *Archbishop*. As a student in Paris, she was attracted to the frescos of Puvis de Chavannes in the Pantheon. In separate panels, they show the life of St. Genevieve, who led her people to victory over the Huns in 451. Cather's decision to write an episodic narrative showing the life of a "modern saint," full of little details rather than big dramas, was inspired by this work, painted in the 1870s (Woodress 399, Keeler 252). Another French painter, Jehan Georges Vibert's "The Missionary Story" gave her the idea for the book's prologue (Woodress 402). Finally, Hans Holbein's "The Dance of Death," a series of woodcuts from the end of the sixteenth century, shows how death comes to all no matter how high their station in life. It even pictures a skeleton coming to claim an archbishop. Cather's style is similar to that of a woodcut, which cuts away excess material, "leaving only clean, simple lines" (Woodress 403).

Since our course included the study of both indigenous art and the modernists drawn to the southwest, I had asked students to record the images they noted and compare their own to Cather's. I urged them to notice how her images worked on more than the pictorial level: monotonous red sand-hills the shape of haycocks, the priest kneeling before a cruciform tree, goats leaping from a stream like arrows speeding from a bow. I hoped they would see how meaning came from images, both in the lightning and animal motifs on Pueblo pottery, as well as the pages of novels.

I could forgive Cather for depicting Native Americans as childlike and primitive, or Mexicans as lazy and profligate. She was a product of the views and racial attitudes of the late twenties. In historical context, her insights about Native Americans seem progressive. Though he doesn't doubt his mission to bring the true light of the church to "antediluvian" Indians and wild, dissolute Mexicans, the Bishop is awed by the mystery and depth of the Indians' beliefs. When he celebrates mass at the Acoma pueblo, and again when he takes refuge in a cave with his Indian guide Jacinto, he questions his ability to bring Catholicism to these ancient people, so far beyond his reach. He admires their way of passing "through a country without disturbing anything; to pass and leave no trace, like fish through the water, or birds through the air" (233).

When Cather portrays Mexicans she is less generous, and when it comes to
Father Martínez she seems to have dipped her portrait brush in tar. A turning
point in Bishop Latour's mission to gain control of all the parishes comes in his
climactic confrontation with Father Martínez in Book Five (Woodress 398).
Cather depicts the "powerful old priest" as a devilish opponent. She pictures
him on horseback with high boots and spurs, a wide Mexican hat and great
black cape around his shoulders, "an enormous man . . . his head . . . set defiantly on a thick neck." He has "brilliant yellow eyes," "full florid cheeks," and
a mouth "the very assertion of violent, uncurbed passions and tyrannical self-
will; the full lips thrust out like the flesh of animals distended by fear or desire"
(141). "Dictator" of the parishes of northern New Mexico, he has the native
priests "under his thumb" (139). Cather repeats the rumor that Martínez insti-
gated the 1847 revolt of the Taos Indians in which American Governor Bent and
a dozen other white men were killed. She tells us that Martínez profited from
the affair by promising the captured Indian rebels he would intervene on their
behalf if they deeded him their lands. While he was away, they were hanged,
and Martínez "now cultivated their fertile farms which made him quite the richest man in the parish" (140). Cather also gives credence to rumors about the
priest's many illegitimate children. After Martínez cuffs a ten-year-old for his
failure to kneel or remove his hat, he excuses his rough treatment, calling the
boy "my own son" (143). Bishop Latour finds Martínez's disordered house
overrun by serving women and large yellow cats which the priest feeds from his
plate (144).

While she presents him as the stereotype of the sensual, dark "other," Cather
does allow Martínez to speak for himself. He argues with the Bishop about
celibacy, which

> "may be all very well for the French clergy, but not for ours . . . Celibate
> priests lose their perceptions. No priest can experience repentance and for-
> giveness of sin unless he himself falls into sin, is broken, experiences for-
> giveness and rises to a state of grace . . . Otherwise, religion is nothing but
> dead logic." (146)

Cather may side with the French Bishop, but she makes the native priest a
worthy opponent whose views merit our attention. He defends his living church,
which is not "a dead arm of the European church" but a religion "that grew out
of the soil" independent of Rome's authority (147). In a crucial passage, he
warns the Bishop:

> "You know nothing about Indians or Mexicans . . . If you try to introduce
> European civilization here and change our old ways, to interfere with the
> secret dances of the Indians...or abolish the bloody rites of the Penitentes,
> I foretell an early death for you." (148)

He advises Latour to study the native traditions before he begins his reforms. The dark things forbidden by your Church are a part of Indian religion.

You cannot introduce French fashions here" (148). Despite his "vulgar long teeth" (148), and his snoring "like an enraged bull" (149), Martínez nevertheless sings the mass beautifully. The Bishop even admits to himself that "rightly guided, this Mexican would have been a great man. He had an altogether compelling personality, a disturbing mysterious, magnetic power" (150). Like other powerful literary villains, Martínez is a complex man. Though Cather makes him livelier and more fascinating than the Bishop himself, her sympathies are clear. Another renegade priest, Martínez's crony Lucero, has a deathbed dream of his old friend burning in hell (171). Despite Cather's disdain for him, Martínez's anticolonialist warning has powerful resonance today. If his words reach beyond the confines of the text to comment on the folly of the Church's authoritarian position, why is Cather's portrait of Martínez so problematic?

When I turned to sources that considered the priest from a native New Mexican perspective, I found a very different story. That Cather's novel has been quoted by historians, and that her account of life in New Mexico during the American military occupation is considered accurate, outrages these scholars. (I recalled the 1927 reviewer's warning that I had so easily dismissed.) According to Ray John de Aragon, a New Mexico historian, Father Martínez was one of the most significant cultural figures of northern New Mexico: "When the Padre's lips parted, it was said drops of compassion, love and justice spilled forth" (125). It galls de Aragon that Cather and the French Bishops were so ignorant as to think they were bringing Catholicism to New Mexico, when "the Catholic Church had been firmly entrenched in New Mexico for 350 years" (de Aragon 139). E. A. Mares, another New Mexican historian, has made it his mission to raise public awareness about the realities of Father Martínez's life. He was curator for an exhibit about Martínez at the Millicent Rogers Museum in Taos, which included the publication of an essay collection offering new perspectives on the priest's life (1988). Mares wrote and performed a one- man play, *I Returned and Saw Under the Sun: Padre Martínez of Taos* (1989), in which the priest takes on both Bishop Lamy and Willa Cather and insists on setting the record straight. These writers reject Cather's characterization of Martínez and present a context for understanding the Lamy/Martínez dispute on which the novel turns. The priest's rebellion, when viewed through indigenous eyes, makes Cather's artistic treatment more than creative license. Though Latour is a stand-in for the historical Lamy, Martínez is himself in the novel; surely she would be sued for libel in today's climate.

To understand this dispute, we must step back from the mid-nineteenth-century setting. As I walked through the Taos pueblo, where Native Americans have lived continuously for more than two thousand years, I felt the same "religious silence" Cather noted. She describes the two communal houses "shaped like pyramids, gold-colored in the afternoon light, with the purple mountain lying just behind them," and the "gold colored men in white burnouses . . . still as statues," the people whom "Coronado's men . . . described . . . as a superior kind of Indian" (150–151).

I could imagine the place in the sixteenth century, when Juan de Onate led his mixed band of soldiers and friars north into this remote territory and disturbed seventy pueblos of indigenous people speaking four distinct language groups. (Today only eighteen pueblos remain.) Following the establishment of Santa Fe in 1610, the Franciscan friars created a network of missions in the pueblos, determined to banish the native *kachina* dancing and *kiva* ceremonies they considered to besaw devil worship. While most Pueblo people accepted Catholicism, they wanted to retain their own faith as well, comfortable with a fusion that made sense to them. Gradually, the treatment they received became intolerable: forced labor, paid tributes, and violence against their Indian Holy Men led to an Indian rebellion unique in the New World. The independent, unorganized pueblo peoples united under Pope, a Tewa religious leader who had been imprisoned by the Spaniards. In 1680, they drove the Spaniards out of Santa Fe all the way back to the El Paso area (Simmons 47–57). For the first time in the colonial world, an indigenous people had successfully rebelled against an occupying power. Though Don Diego de Vargas reconquered New Mexico twelve years later, the Spanish colonists had learned from their errors. Under the new regime, they allowed the native peoples more autonomy and left the ceremonial kivas undisturbed (Mares, "Many Faces" 21). Compared to the fate of Native Americans in New England, who had undergone wholesale slaughter and defeat in King Phillip's War (1675–1676), the Pueblo people fared better, which helps explain why they are still such a strong cultural presence in New Mexico (Simmons 73).

From these early days, intermarriage between the indigenous people and the Spanish settlers was creating a distinctive New Mexican Indohispanic people, a fusion of Native American, and Mexican/Spanish Catholic cultures. Father Martínez lived through three distinct historical periods in New Mexico—Spanish rule, Mexican rule, and finally U.S. possession and military occupation. The historical evidence shows him to be a community leader, concerned for the welfare of the poor, who understood and defended grass roots Catholicism (Mares, "Many Faces" 18). He was born to a ranching family in Abiquiu, New Mexico, in 1793, a time when the Spanish Empire was on the verge of collapse and the successful American and French revolutions were stimulating a new sense of democratic possibility. Martínez married as a young man, but after his wife died in childbirth, he went off to a seminary in Durango and was ordained a secular priest in 1822 at age twenty-nine (de Aragon 127). With Mexico now independent of Spain, Martínez returned to open a coeducational school in his home in 1826 when educating girls was very unusual. With his own printing press, he advocated for the rights of the native peoples, defending them against exploitation by American trappers. He called for the preservation of the buffalo, so the Indian people would have their own source of livelihood (de Aragon 137).

With the Franciscan friars almost gone, priests were scarce. To fill the void, the Penitente Brotherhood and its women's equivalent, the Carmelitas, were founded. The Brotherhood met in their secret *moradas.* Each year they carried out the bloody practice of self-flagellation during Holy Week as a form of penance, a ritual that continues today. When Bishop Lamy demanded that they be disbanded, Martínez, who understood their origins, defended the Brotherhood. They'd learned these traditional rituals from the Franciscan friars, but the practice of self-flagellation can be traced back to St. Anthony of Egypt in 356 A.D. (de Aragon 131). To the native Indohispanic people, these rites were part of the landscape, much like the secret dances and rituals observed by the Pueblo peoples.

Just as he defended the Penitente rituals, Martínez also resisted the Bishop's efforts to destroy the wood-carved *santos* that decorated the village churches. Like the Pueblo artisans, the traditional *santeros* produced their work anonymously. The purpose of their art was spiritual, and individual artists did not seek recognition—another concept that must have seemed strange to the European clergy. Mares faults Bishop Lamy for destroying much of this folk art because of his personal repulsion for the crude, bloody figures. Many were replaced with bulky plaster-of-paris statues which Mares calls "bathrobe art" (Mares, *I Returned* 51). In village churches like the Sanctuary at Chimayo the colorful *bultos* (three-dimensional figures) and *retablos* (flat figures) are vivid and memorable. Collectors now pay large prices for sad looking Christ figures and red- cheeked virgins, each figure with its own distinct personality. In regard to the *santos,* Cather's fictional Bishop is more tolerant than the historical Lamy. Latour finds them "more to his taste than the factory-made plaster images in his mission churches in Ohio" (Cather 28), surely a reflection of Cather's own taste.

Lamy's cathedral, seen by Willa Cather as his triumphant achievement, contributed to the struggle between the Bishop and Father Martínez. Mares points out that people were used to a barter economy and would trade corn or animals in exchange for Baptism or marriage ceremonies. During the time of the early Church fathers, church leaders were expected to subsidize the Indian and Mexican communities, rather than exacting money from the poor. After Mexican independence, a general anti-clerical feeling caused resentment against tithing and Martínez wrote against the practice. Bishop Lamy issued a Circular in 1854 imposing a new tithe under pain of excommunication. Mares sees this demand as the Bishop's way of forcing poor Catholics to finance his new cathedral, an architectural venture the local people could not understand or support. To them, the old adobe Cathedral of St. Francis ("a mud-pie palace," to Lamy) was beautiful to its worshipers (Mares, *I Returned* 50).

De Aragon rejects the charges that the Taos priest was a sensualist or fathered illegitimate children. In fact, he claims that Martínez used his own publications to denounce immorality and cohabitation (130). Mares speculates that the reason there are so many people with the surname of "Martínez" around Taos is that the Padre adopted many orphans and gave them his own name. Furthermore, there is no historical evidence that Martínez was associated with the Taos rebellion and execution of Governor Bent in 1847 (Mares, "Many Faces" 27). The priest actually served on the Territorial Assembly and was elected its president after the Taos uprising (Mares, *I Returned* 45). It would have been preposterous, Mares argues, to make the fomenter of such a rebellion head of a government council. Furthermore, Padre Martínez was such an expert on canon law that Bishop Lamy consulted him often and asked for his assistance on legal briefs (de Aragon 142). It would be more accurate to represent Martínez as a peacemaker and healer than an instigator. These New Mexico historians argue that he justly opposed the American military occupation Bishop Lamy supported, for under its policies people lost their landgrants, their native clergy, and centuries of tradition (de Aragon 144). They see Martínez as a liberator in the tradition of other great Mexican liberators.

Another glaring historical discrepancy concerns Cather's representation of Father Vaillant, the Bishop's assistant, depicted as a loveable, rough-hewn charmer:

> Even the thick-blooded Mexican half-breeds knew his quality at once. If the Bishop returned to find Santa Fe friendly to him, it was because everybody believed in Father Vaillant—homely, real, persistent, with the driving power of a dozen men in his poorly-built body. (Cather 38)

The real Machebeuf abused his authority and violated canon law by revealing secrets disclosed in the confessional. Though Martínez brought this to the Bishop's attention, he ignored the complaints (de Aragon 141). Finally, feeling his age at sixty-three, Martínez offered to resign over his many conflicts with Lamy provided that he be allowed to pick his own successor, a request the Bishop also ignored. Lamy sent Machebeuf to Taos to read the excommunication orders before Martínez's own congregation. The Padre's refusal to be defrocked and his defiance as he continued to serve his parishioners must be seen in this context. What Cather represents as the Bishop's triumphant victory over a local heretic, these revisionist historians see as an unjust colonialist usurpation.

Cather's treatment of another historical figure shows how easily she forgives evil if the doer is an American as opposed to a Mexican. She presents the scout Kit Carson as "thoughtful and alert"; he is "reflective, has a capacity for tenderness" (75). Carson's Mexican wife is devout, and if he is illiterate it is probably an accident. To Bishop Latour, Carson is a man like himself, with standards and loyalties, who lives by a code, and the two men have "a long friendship" (75). As for Carson's savage slaughter of the Navajos trapped in Canyon de Chelly, Cather calls it "misguided," but she justifies it thus: "Carson was a soldier under orders, and he did a soldier's brutal work" (294). Hispanic readers may see a further unintended parallel here, that the Bishop himself is another soldier doing his own "brutal work" for a greater cause. Though Martínez's alleged crimes of rebellion and profligacy seem insignificant by comparison, Carson remains a hero in the novel, while Father Martínez burns in hell (171).

The research on Father Martínez, prompted by post-1960s concerns over racial equality and civil rights, was clearly unavailable to Willa Cather. Should we then assume that she was limited entirely by the perspective of her own sources? Patricia Clark Smith of the University of New Mexico at Albuquerque argues that Cather could have known there were two sides to the Martínez/ Lamy controversy. Mabel Dodge Luhan, in her 1937 memoir *Edge of Taos Desert,* wrote about a later French priest who nearly spoiled the beautiful adobe church in Taos. Fortunately, this Father Joe was unable to touch the lovely church in Rancho de Taos or we would never have had O'Keeffe's powerful images of that adobe building (Luhan 84). There the community still gathers each year to put a fresh coat of the mud-mixture on their beloved church. Luhan repeats many of the same stories about Father Martínez that appear in Cather's novel: that he was a lady's man who might have incited the Taos revolt and benefitted from the Indians' land. But her critical picture of Father Joe—so similar to Lamy in his coldness, insistence on tithes, and dislike of the *santos*—make him seem closer to the historical Lamy than to Cather's invented Bishop (Luhan 88– 90; Smith 104). If Cather absorbed stories from Luhan, she was selective, for Luhan reveals a very different attitude toward the Penitentes than we get from Cather. Luhan wrote:

> There seemed to be a happiness in the Mexican life, due to the Penitente exorcisms, wherein they flayed themselves, unconsciously perhaps, to di- minish the accumulated bitterness and despair that they could not pour out upon us. They came out of these ceremonies refreshed. . . . they drew their own blood, identifying themselves with Jesus Christ, who died for them, and who is still dying for them in their flesh. (Luhan 81)

Mary Austin, a writer who had settled in New Mexico and lent Cather her house while she was working on *Archbishop*, was appalled by Cather's book. In her autobiography she wrote that the building of the French cathedral in a Spanish town was a calamity and that the local culture had never gotten over it (Smith 106). Though these differences may be about political rivalries between the writers, Smith feels that Cather's decision to take the French Archbishop's side was a conscious one, that she must have been aware of other views of Father Martínez (Smith 107).[3]

Despite Cather's clearly condescending stance toward people of color, Smith believes she underwent a change in attitude as she completed her novel. The book's conclusion shows a more ambivalent attitude toward the Bishop's mission in New Mexico. Archbishop Latour prefers to die in Santa Fe rather than return to France: "in the Old World he found himself homesick for the New" (274). At the end of his life, he expresses a nostalgic regret for the vanishing purity of the land he has helped to colonize. Just as the colonial forces he represented destroyed the culture it tried to "save," the cathedral he labored all his life to construct becomes his own tomb. Smith finds the irony here inescapable. Whether or not Cather intended it, Smith reads her celebration of this outsider's victory as an indictment of the colonization process (Smith 121–122). Cather's greater tolerance comes through as the Bishop rejoices that he "lived to see two great wrongs righted . . . the end of black slavery, and the Navajos restored to their country" (292). In his final return to Santa Fe, Cather pictures him entering the city on horseback, wrapped in his Indian blanket, gazing at his Romanesque Cathedral, an image of cultural fusion that seems closer to the multicultural reality of the southwest.

Cather's emerging ambivalence toward colonialism can be examined in light of the novel's quest to bring a unifying culture to New Mexico's various ethnic groups. Bette S. Weidman argues that by having the Bishop forsake his native France to die in the New World, Cather is rejecting the limits of the European past in favor of a new culture and new ethnicity. Though the Cathedral may be French in style it represents a fusion, made with stones from the New World (Weidman 61).

In the controversy over Father Martínez, I stumbled upon an ideal "contact zone" (to use Mary Louise Pratt's phrase). I was nudged into reading Cather's novel not as a simple narrative, but as a document of cultural collision between Europeans and indigenous Indohispanic people. The novelist must be free to exercise her imagination when dealing with history. As a fiction writer myself, I don't hesitate to play freely with memories and experience. However, the claim that allegiance to an artistic purpose frees one of any responsibility for accuracy crumbles. At the very least, through the simple gesture of an invented name, Cather could have given Martínez the same degree of literary respect she offered Lamy and Machebeuf.

The next time we ran the course, I prepared a packet of readings to accompany the novel. These included an excerpt from the E. A. Mares play with Father Martínez speaking in his own voice, and another from Mabel Dodge Luhan's memoir where we get a fuller view of local customs through the eyes of another outsider, an Anglo woman married to a native man. Students would read Cather's novel in context "as part of the multi-ethnic conversation it seeks to dramatize" (Weidman 68). By expanding the reading to include complicating texts, I could examine the novel's virtues while accurately presenting the passionate revulsion it inspired in generations of *nuevomexicanos*.

To help students focus on their own process of research and meaning-making in such a complex environment, I also assigned Jane Tompkins's article, "'Indians': Textualism, Morality and the Problem of History." She records her personal journey through secondary and primary sources, as she searches for a "true" account of Indian/Puritan relations in seventeenth-century New England. Her essay offers students a parallel view of their own region as a basis for comparison with the southwest. More important than content is the process Tompkins so clearly describes; she critiques her own poststructuralist skeptical perspective, coming to regard it as one more point of view as distinct and also as limiting as that of the Puritans or Indians. In discussing the shortcomings of a purely perspectival approach to history, she argues that we must piece together the story as best we can "believing this version up to a point, that version not at all, another version almost entirely, according to what seems reasonable and plausible, given everything else that I know" (76). Her honesty as she struggles to reconcile the many voices she encounters serves as a model for students in their own research projects.

Along with the Tompkins reading I shared my own discoveries about Father Martínez. My encounter with the material hinged on the mediating concept of *place*. With the place itself as my primary text, and indigenous people as my guides, my reading of Cather was altered, expanded, and challenged. I could better understand the ongoing dialectic between identity politics as expressed in the Hispanic community, and the fused multi-ethnic identity created from the diverse potpourri of Spanish, French, Native American, Mexican, and Anglo influences. Teachers may not have the luxury of traveling to Santa Fe to teach *Death Comes for the Archbishop*, but when assigning a novel so deeply embedded in an historical time and place, we can make the place itself a text by bringing visual and historical materials into the classroom. Above all, we can include the voices of those who have a stake in the material so we do not repeat the errors of colonialism in our teaching.

Notes

1. For a more complete discussion of *Death Comes for the Archbishop* as a novel of acceptance and reconciliation that views Cather as an inheritor of Hawthorne's art in her treatment of American themes, see Weidman. Weidman also suggests Native American N. Scott Momaday's novel *House Made of Dawn* (1966) as a good tandem reading along with Cather's novel. I would add novels by Hispanic writers: Rudolfo Anaya's *Bless Me Ultima* (1972) and Ana Castillo's *So Far From God* (1993).

2. Woodress mentions J. B. Salpointe's *Soldier of the Cross*, the *Catholic Encyclopedia*, H. H. Bancroft's *History of New Mexico and Arizona*, and books by Charles Loomis and Ralph Twitchell. Clearly, none of these writers is indigenous.

3. Smith offers a persuasive argument comparing Latour to Odysseus, and Father Martínez to Circe. She suggests that the Circe story "impelled [Cather] to turn Martínez into more of a sensualist" than any of her sources warranted (118).

Works Cited

Cather, Willa. *Death Comes for the Archbishop.* 1927. New York: Vintage Books, 1971.

de Aragon, Ray John. "Padre Antonio Jose Martínez: The Man and the Myth." In *Padre Martínez.* 125–151.

Keeler, Clinton. "Narrative without Accent: Willa Cather and Puvis de Chavannes." *Critical Essays on Willa Cather.* Ed. John J. Murphy. Boston: G. K. Hall, 1984. 251–257.

Luhan, Mabel Dodge. *Edge of Taos Desert: An Escape to Reality.* 1937. Albuquerque: U of New Mexico P, 1965.

Mares, E. A. "The Many Faces of Padre Antonio Jose Martínez: A Historiographic Essay." In *Padre Martínez.* 18–47.

Mares, E. A. *I Returned and Saw Under the Sun: Padre Martínez of Taos. A Play.* Albuquerque: U of New Mexico P, 1989.

Padre Martínez: New Perspectives from Taos. Taos, NM: Millicent Rogers Museum, 1988.

Pratt, Mary Louise. *Imperial Eyes: Travel Writing and Transculturation.* New York: Routledge, 1992.

Rudnick, Lois. *Mabel Dodge Luhan: New Woman, New Worlds.* Albuquerque: U of New Mexico P, 1984.

Simmons, Marc. *New Mexico: An Interpretive History.* Albuquerque: U of New Mexico P, 1988.

Smith, Patricia Clark. "Achaeans, Americanos, Prelates and Monsters: Willa Cather's *Death Comes for the Archbishop* as New World Odyssey." In *Padre Martínez.* 101–123.

Stuart, Henry Longan. Rev. of *Death Comes for the Archbishop* by Willa Cather. *New York Times Book Review* 4 September, 1927: 2. *Critical Essays on Willa Cather.* Ed. John J. Murphy. Boston: G. K. Hall, 1984. 244–247.

Tompkins, Jane. "'Indians': Textualism, Morality and the Problem of History." *'Race,' Writing and Difference.* Ed. Henry Louis Gates Jr. Chicago: U of Chicago P, 1985. 59–77.

Weidman, Bette. "Willa Cather's Art in Historical Perspective: Reconsidering *Death Comes for the Archbishop.* In *Padre Martínez.* 48–70.

Woodress, James. *Willa Cather, A Literary Life.* Lincoln: U of Nebraska P, 1987.

III Negotiating Differences

10 Negotiating Difference: Teaching Multicultural Literature

Patricia Bizzell
College of the Holy Cross

I'm going to begin by assuming that we want to teach multicultural literature. That is, I don't want to try here to make the case for doing so. Also, I'd like to stipulate a definition of "multicultural" that is as broad as possible, to include diversities of gender, social class, and sexual preference, as well as race and ethnicity. I'd also like to define "literature" broadly, to include not only fiction and poetry but also sermons, eulogies, autobiographies, histories, and more.

My main goal in this essay is to address two of the problems that typically attend teaching multicultural literature: how to select and group multicultural readings, and how to integrate literary and rhetorical approaches in teaching multicultural literature (or, teaching literature in the writing class and writing in the literature class).

I

One problem concerns how to select and group multicultural readings in an English course. You might select solely on the basis of personal preference. This approach has the advantage of enabling you to teach to your strengths—I suspect most of us teach better when we are teaching texts that we like. But basing your selections on personal preference can give students the idea that reading multicultural literature is nothing but a matter of preference, so that if it happens not to appeal to their personal tastes, they are free to ignore it. On the contrary, I'd like to think that studying multicultural literature is a responsibility for citizens in a multicultural democracy. So I'm leery of selecting on the basis of my personal preference alone, although it may enter into a selection process that also involves other criteria.

Another option would be to select readings on the basis of the students' personal preference. It seems to be common wisdom in composition studies that students will be more seriously engaged with readings that they themselves select. Of course, one problem with this approach is the same problem I noted above in talking about choosing according to the teacher's personal preference. Elevating preference can seem to trivialize the objects of study.

Furthermore, I'm not sure that it is always true that students like their own choices best. Students do not always know about the texts that will most interest them. I've found, for example, that many African American students do not know the work of any antebellum Black writer other than Frederick Douglass—but they are very excited to discover Maria Stewart, David Walker, and more. Again, I'm leery of relying solely on the students' personal preference, although I would make it one factor in my selection process. I like the idea of presenting students with an array of texts that I've found, inviting them to contribute some choices of their own to the array, and then deciding collectively which ones we will study.

The basis of selection that I think is most important is local and national significance. That is, I would select on the basis of what cultures are represented in the school, and the town, and on the basis of what might be considered "major works" of multicultural literature of national significance, such as Frederick Douglass's autobiography. Choosing in this way has the great advantage of putting study on an appropriately serious and professional basis, while allowing for a very wide variety of texts to be read.

Of course, this approach also has several liabilities. It involves you in making potentially controversial decisions about course content—but I think it's our professional responsibility to make these decisions. Also, it may involve you in research to assemble the appropriate texts, but this, too, is our professional responsibility—and a task to which students might very well contribute.

Having decided on the criteria to govern text selection, however, we still have to consider how to group the texts we and our students have chosen. The traditional method of grouping, of course, is by literary period. For example, you might select readings from a traditional category such as "American Renaissance" and add several slave narratives. This has the advantage of enabling you to retain a structure that may be familiar from your own professional training, that may employ syllabi with which you are already comfortable—requiring only a few modifications—and that may allow you to continue to teach many "old favorite" canonical texts along with a few new, multicultural ones.

A major disadvantage here, however, is that this approach leads to a "tokenist" treatment of multicultural texts. It isn't only that you won't be likely to teach as many of them if you cling to traditional categories where they are not included; it's also that these categories are defined by aesthetic criteria that may not be best suited to appreciating the beauties of multicultural texts. For example, slave narratives such as Harriet Jacobs's *Incidents in the Life of a Slave Girl* have rhetorical designs on their audiences that are anathema in the critical consideration of canonical texts such as Nathaniel Hawthorne's *The Scarlet Letter.* To really appreciate what Jacobs is doing, the old critical categories must be busted up.

Furthermore, it doesn't really solve the problem to create new literary-period categories that focus on multicultural literature—replacing the "American Renaissance" with the "Harlem Renaissance," for example. Instead of tokenizing, such categories have a tendency to ghettoize multicultural literature and to disguise its profound influences on American literature as a whole.

Another approach to grouping readings—one that has been very popular in composition anthologies—is to arrange them by supposedly universal themes. You might choose a theme such as "coming of age," for example, and select a group of texts from different cultures that all appear to focus on this theme. In theory, this approach has the advantage of putting all the readings on an equal footing—unlike the traditional literary period approach, which tends to privilege the canonical—and it allows a very wide range of selection.

A serious disadvantage to this approach, however, is that it tends to minimize, or even trivialize, cultural difference. Students may indeed be encouraged to note differences in each culture's treatment of common themes, but the common theme itself pushes the ultimate conclusion that "underneath these differences we're all alike," a conclusion to which students often rush all too eagerly because it excuses them from dealing with the most profound aspects of cultural difference. Furthermore, the common theme itself might reflect one culture's preferences without acknowledgment—e.g., not all cultures are equally interested in discussing gender roles.

Some might wish to argue, though, that this approach encourages tolerance for cultural differences among the students. I'm not sure that this is always true. The "universal themes" approach has a tendency to produce collections of readings that focus on painful experiences, that often depict people of color as victims, and that can make a reader feel as if an emotional response is being extorted. Students who are members of the cultural group depicted in such a story can be acutely embarrassed by classroom discussion of these episodes; and students who are not group members can be severely alienated, depressed, and "turned off" to the point of rejecting, rather than embracing, any message of tolerance.

I think Mary Louise Pratt's concept of the "contact zone" offers the best paradigm for grouping multicultural readings. Pratt uses the term "to refer to social spaces where cultures meet, clash, and grapple with each other, often in contexts of highly asymmetrical relations of power, such as colonialism, slavery, or their aftermaths as they are lived out in many parts of the world today" (34). In "Contact Zones and the Structure of English Studies" (1994), I have commented on the usefulness of Pratt's concept to English studies, arguing that "this concept can aid us both because it emphasizes the conditions of difficulty and struggle under which literatures from different cultures come together (thus forestalling the disrespectful glossing over of difference), and because it gives us a conceptual base for bringing these literatures together, namely, when they occur in or are brought to the same site of struggle or 'contact zone'" (166). I've suggested that the United States is a "congeries of overlapping contact zones" and that "'multiculturalism' in English studies is a name for our recognition of this condition of living on contested cultural ground, and our desire to represent something of this complexity in our study of literature and literacy" (166).

Pratt also offers some specifics on kinds of assignments we'd give in teaching the literature of a contact zone:

> exercises in storytelling and in identifying with the ideas, interests, histories, and attitudes of others; experiments in transculturation and collaborative work and in the arts of critique, parody, and comparison (including unseemly comparisons between elite and vernacular cultural forms); the redemption of the oral; ways for people to engage with suppressed aspects of history (including their own histories); ways to move *into and out of* rhetorics of authenticity; ground rules for communication across lines of difference and hierarchy that go beyond politeness but maintain mutual respect; a systematic approach to the all-important concept of *cultural mediation*. (40, Pratt's emphasis)

Applying this concept to grouping multicultural texts, what you would do is, first you would pick your contact zone or historical moment, one particularly relevant to your town or region or one—like the internment of Japanese Americans during World War II—that clearly has national implications. Then, make your selections from among the texts already grouped there, brought to the contact zone by their authors. A contact zone is a historical moment when different groups contend for the power to say what's going on, what it all means, what should happen next; so you look at texts produced by these different groups *for* this contention and implicit (or often explicit) dialogue with each other.

For example, instead of teaching a course on the "American Renaissance," teach a course on fiction and non-fiction texts addressed to the antebellum debate over slavery or over "woman's place." You could include canonical texts such as Herman Melville's *Benito Cereno* or Nathaniel Hawthorne's *The Blithedale Romance,* but include them as *voices in a dialogue* with other writers from other perspectives, such as William Apess or Margaret Fuller.

It might be objected, however, that organizing a course around a contact zone amounts to propagandizing. By choosing scenes of unequal power struggles, we could be said to raise moral issues, and perhaps even to promote liberal political solutions, which might be regarded as out of place in the classroom. In response, I would argue that the main aim in teaching literature of a contact zone is not to prove that injustice took place, but rather to examine how all sides engaged issues rhetorically. And because the focus is on all sides, diverse views will be represented much more than they usually are in our liberal-biased anthologies—more selections will have to be included that are conservative or even racist or sexist.

I do not, however, disavow all designs on my students' moral and political development. As I have argued in "Power, Authority, and Critical Pedagogy"

(1991), I think there is a legitimate place for the teacher's authority to raise moral issues. I am willing to use my power as a teacher to urge students to consider the issues raised in a contact zone, and I would hope to be able not to indoctrinate but to persuade them to my values of social justice, as I have argued elsewhere (1992):

> I find myself in somewhat the same position as the ancient Greek rhetorician Isocrates. Like postmodern skeptics, he debunked teachers of his day who claimed to be able to foretell the future—that is, who claimed to give their students a set of values guaranteed to apply in all times and places. . . . Isocrates nevertheless did propose to teach virtue—virtue derived not from some transcendent realm but, rather, from the traditions of his community; indeed, according to postmodern skepticism, community should be the source of all values. Isocrates argued that while he could not guarantee to change—that is, to compel—his students, he could attempt to influence them—that is, to persuade them to adopt the values deemed most praiseworthy in his community. His authority as a teacher of virtue would thus be established rhetorically. (6)

Of key importance in this position is that I speak not for my own personal values but for values I try to show are sanctioned by the community I and my students share—and contingent on debate. I show this both by the historical record (choosing contact zones in the past) and by my own openness to being persuaded (for example, as a non-Catholic, I've been changed by my Catholic students' views on abortion).

II

Another problem in teaching multicultural literature has to do with its place in literature classes as opposed to composition classes. Actually, I don't think there should be any opposition here. I don't think there should be any difference between the way we teach our literature classes and the way we teach our writing classes. What I want students to do is to study rhetorical strategies of persuasion in readings from a variety of genres, fiction and non-fiction ("literature"), and also to practice rhetorical strategies in a variety of writings of their own ("composition"). To maintain this position, I have to make two arguments: that literature should be taught in the composition class, and that writing should be taught in the literature class.

The issue of literature in the composition class boils down to the issue of the "content" of the composition class—a much neglected subject. Let me begin by stipulating that "content," for purposes of this essay, means "what students in writing classes are writing about." I know it is a current truism in composition studies that insofar as writing courses have content, the "content" is information about writing processes. This truism implies that we think we can separate the teaching of writing from what students are writing about; and it is because of this supposed separation that we think we can avoid talking about what students are writing about, and teach "only" composing processes.

Contemporary theories of learning, reading comprehension, and composing all suggest that in order to write about something, students have to integrate it with what they already know and thus construct their own interpretation of it. This integration is what made classical rhetoricians such as Isocrates—whom I mentioned before on the topic of virtue—hope that exposure to good values would affect students' values; and it is also what made them think that effective rhetoricians would need to draw on knowledge that their audience shared. Now we would say that this process of integration is the very process of learning; without it, neither reading comprehension nor written composition can take place (see, e.g., Petrosky).

So whatever students are reading in the writing class, whether it be their classmates' papers or the selections in an anthology, they are perforce learning about it. If they weren't, they wouldn't be able to write about it. Another way to put this would be to say that writing teachers are teaching students the knowledge content of whatever they are reading, whether this is the teachers' intention or not. And teachers are commenting on the students' use of this content in their writing, unless teachers never comment on anything other than grammar mistakes. Even if the teacher is able to preserve a seeming separation between composing and content in comments such as, "You need more evidence here to make your argument about killing all homosexuals more convincing," even here, the teacher is commenting on how the student has handled the knowledge content of the essay.

So I think we should ask ourselves what we are teaching by the choices we make about what students are to write about. There seems to be a range of tacit answers to this question in the course contents currently in use. For example, some writing courses use anthologies that attempt to illustrate for students the conventions of academic discourse, with writing samples from various disciplines; or the knowledge content of academic literacy, with "great books" selections. I don't want to spend time here discussing the pros and cons of this approach, which has been subsumed in the lengthy discussion in composition studies over whether or not students should be taught academic discourse. Let me just say here that I find these kinds of readers rather elitist—too exclusionary of multicultural content and the students' own cultural resources.

To address this difficulty, you might take the approach that content should be whatever the students choose to write about. If the content is the students' choice, then presumably they can draw on whatever cultural capital they bring to class. No one will have a disadvantage based on the prior knowledge he or she possesses. This approach is sometimes pursued with the aid of anthologies that present content that all people, whatever their resources of cultural capital, are presumed to share, that is, selections about various aspects of personal life that "everyone" is presumed to have experienced, such as childhood or schooling; or more formal belletristic meditations on issues supposed to be of current concern to "everyone," such as gender relations or race relations. In other words, these anthologies are organized around what I called the "universal themes" approach (above), and exhibit some of the same problems I have already pointed out.

This reading does not seem to be assigned in order to convey necessary knowledge content, but rather simply to serve as a prompt for the students to develop their own writing. For example, an anthology selection on Native American marriage customs might be used to stimulate students to reflect on bonding patterns in their own communities, without much attention to whether this reading is teaching them anything about Native Americans.

True, these anthologies usually include selections from a variety of ethnic, racial, and cultural groups. There may be some intent to encourage tolerance by giving students more information about different social groups—but I have already discussed the problems with this hope. The most widely accepted theoretical justification for the diversity of these readers, however, is that they maximize the chances that all the diverse students in the class will see their cultural capital legitimated in the academy.

While this is a worthy goal, I am troubled by some problems here. For one thing, this is a somewhat essentialized approach to what students might want to read and how they might want to write. The assumption seems to be that although tolerance may be a valuable but secondary by-product, the main reason the selections by, let's say, Latina/o writers are there in the anthologies is to legitimate the cultural capital of Latina/o students, and so on. This approach tends to close off discourse possibilities for the students thus essentialized, as Victor Villanueva and bell hooks, for example, have both testified. They explain that their writing styles have been enriched by a variety of sources: Villanueva draws on classical sophistic rhetoric, which he links historically to his own Puerto Rican heritage; hooks asserts her right to speak in a variety of voices, not only the Black English Vernacular that a college writing teacher regarded as her "authentic" voice.

Moreover, in a class where the content focus is on the individual sensibility and on personal responses to experience, there is an inevitable tendency to teach students how to feel, teaching them what representations of their experiences are going to seem sophisticated and persuasive. For example, as Bruce Herzberg and I have argued, this tendency can be observed in the choices writing teachers made for what student essays to include in the anthology *What Makes Writing Good*. In some courses, the responsibility for responding to representations of experience is placed on the students themselves, but these situations may be no less oppressive, as majority views of how people should behave get imposed on

everyone in the class. This kind of schooling of the emotions borders on oppressive surveillance.

I would like to propose the contact zone concept, which I discussed above,
as a better approach to defining the content of the composition course, an approach that I hope meets some of these objections. I suggest that we attempt to
devise materials with the idea in mind of educating our students to be effective
communicators in a multicultural democracy.

One advantage to this approach is that it provides a rationale not only for
making the materials multicultural, but also for avoiding essentializing these
materials. Students will see their own cultural capital legitimated in the academy; but at the same time, they will have the opportunity to familiarize themselves with a wide range of materials, so that they will be able not only to
increase their own repertoire of discourse practices but also to increase the range
of practices, employed by others, that they can understand. The students will be
able to develop personal styles, but with both the freedom to range over a variety of cultural practices in developing these styles, and the responsibility to
communicate across cultural boundaries both within and outside the classroom.

Another advantage to this approach is that it is properly rhetorical, focusing
on strategies for communicating both within various groups and across cultural
boundaries. This approach encourages the study of discourse location or discourse community, a useful analytic tool in the variety of discourse situations a
multicultural democracy presents.

In addition to being multicultural and rhetorical, course content should also
be historical. The United States has always been a multicultural country, and
the rhetorical strategies of many groups have developed their richness over time,
through experiences of negotiating difference at various moments in American
history. Therefore, to appreciate the fullest range of these rhetorical strategies,
some attention to their historical development is needed—as can be gained by
grouping materials around a contact zone from the past. Moreover, I would
argue with Fredric Jameson that effective democratic communication, as well
as other forms of political action, require that people be able conceptually to
locate themselves in history, to see their relationships to their own and other
groups in the past, present, and future. (He calls this kind of knowledge "cognitive mapping.")

The materials for such course content could vary widely as to genre, from
argumentative public speeches to intimate personal narratives, and including
visual texts as well. I would want any collection to include contemporary materials, just to emphasize the relevance of course activities to contemporary life;
but I think it is necessary for rhetorical richness that contemporary materials be
linked to the powerful rhetorical traditions from which they have developed.
I've found in my own classes that it is especially empowering for student writers from oppressed social groups to learn that people like themselves have been

using language against oppression with eloquence, and some practical success, for a long time. This vista of a rhetorical tradition of their own can offer more courage for present struggles than exhortation to a misplaced middle class individualism, asking them to stand alone on bitterly contested contemporary rhetorical turf with no more protection than their "own opinions."

Let me illustrate by briefly describing a composition course I taught in the fall 1993 semester that employed materials of the kind I am describing. Most of the students in this class would be classified as basic writers if Holy Cross sorted composition students according to such categories (we don't). I assembled materials centering around the debate in antebellum America on the meaning of the phrase "all men are created equal" from the Declaration of Independence. This phrase became a bone of contention in the increasingly heated debates over slavery in the period. We read selections from the writings of both European American defenders and African American attackers of slavery, comparing their rhetorical uses of the Declaration and the ways they played off of each others' arguments. We also read materials supplied by the students: contemporary opinion pieces on race relations that echoed arguments found in the nineteenth-century readings.

For example, slavery defender David Christy argued that "all men are created equal" was never intended to mean *all* people, but only people like those who signed the Declaration, namely white men of the upper social classes. In contrast, abolitionist Charles Langston argued that African Americans' participation in the American Revolution testified to their inclusion in the promises of the Declaration, and that resistance to slavery actually built upon Revolutionary ideals. In effect, African American rhetoricians disinherited white defenders of slavery, and depicted themselves as the true descendants of the revered founding fathers. Rhetoric scholars Celeste Michelle Condit and John Louis Lucaites have argued that our contemporary interpretation of the phrase "all men are created equal" to include all people is in fact largely the result of the powerfully successful efforts of these African American rhetoricians.

My students wrote and shared a variety of assignments working over these difficult and lengthy readings: they summarized the arguments, analyzed and compared the writers' rhetorical strategies, and tried their own powers in writing assignments that challenged them, for example, to rewrite the opening paragraph of the Declaration of Independence as one of our authors would have done it, explaining the changes they made, or to explain how any writer should address the problem of speaking to two audiences at the same time, those who agree and those who disagree, illustrating from the work of one of our authors.

I won't say that we were always able to live up to my high hopes for the course, but still, there were some exciting moments in student papers. For example, when asked to compare the rhetorical strategies of slavery defenders Christy, George Fitzhugh, and Albert Bledsoe, Tawanya, an African American student, pointed out that these writers contradict themselves when, on the one hand, they claim that enslaved people are not well educated enough to take care of themselves if free, and, on the other hand, deny them access to education. She not only noted the failure of these writers' attempts to sound reasonable and humane, but she also commented on the intertextuality of the rhetoric. She attacked Christy, chronologically the latest writer, because he didn't notice the contradictions in the work of his earlier colleagues but repeated many of them instead.

Thus, the literature content of this course clearly helped my students to develop their rhetorical powers. Furthermore, this course is distinguished from courses I teach in American literature only by the proportion of reading to writing: in writing courses, we write more and read less, and in literature courses, vice versa. This brings me to my second argument, namely, that writing should be taught in every literature course.

It's everybody's job to teach writing, not just the writing faculty's (indeed, not just the English faculty's, as writing across the curriculum programs have shown). I know that some literature faculty still maintain that teaching writing is beneath them and should be "taken care of" in first-year composition courses, but they're simply wrong. For one thing, these literature faculty are teaching writing already, if they assign any writing at all. They may just be teaching it badly, if they don't give it any explicit attention informed by scholarship in composition studies. Furthermore, writing can and should be taught at any level, and even students who have excelled in a first-year composition course can still improve. Indeed, I think no one ever finishes learning to write; I know I haven't.

Some literature faculty are coming to recognize that they need the help of writing pedagogy. As confessed by Jane Tompkins in her 1990 essay "Pedagogy of the Distressed," literary scholars have usually taught lecture-fashion, maximizing their own dazzling performances, minimizing student discussion, and ignoring student writing altogether. Now Tompkins and others announce with great fanfare pedagogical discoveries that teachers in composition studies have been working over for years. (For excellent critiques of Tompkins's essay by Susan Jarratt and Elizabeth Flynn, see Olson.)

Composition studies has reversed the order of traditional literature teaching for some time, putting student writing first, encouraging student discussion, and finding ways to reduce our own authority and efface ourselves (indeed, almost too much so, as I suggested above in my discussion of authority and teaching "virtue"). Among the topics literature teachers need to learn are these: how to coach the writing process, especially how to generate ideas in response to reading; how to push the idea of writing processes as recursive, foregrounding revision; how to encourage collaborative work; how to sensitize students to different audiences and give them practice writing for different audiences; how to get students personally invested in research papers; and more.

This folding together of literature and composition is being facilitated, I think, by the emergence of "rhetoric" as a master term in both fields, as well as both fields' interest in cultural studies. I'd add that I'd like to see composition studies following literary studies' lead in new historicism, as well. But I don't have space to go into these topics here.

III

I believe we must teach multicultural literature organized according to historical-moment contact zones, and fully integrate teaching literature and teaching writing. My hope for the outcome of this project, on which literature faculty and writing faculty should collaborate, is that teachers and students alike will come to see difference more as an asset than a liability.

To illustrate what I mean, let me conclude with a rereading of the Bible story of the Tower of Babel. In those days, there was no cultural diversity—the story says human beings all spoke the same language. Agreeing so well, they were well able to mobilize their resources and build a tower reaching toward heaven. God was displeased by the arrogance of this project. To stop it, says the story, God made the people speak different languages. God created cultural diversity.

Now usually, we think of this creation of different languages as a *punishment* for an evil deed (building the tower). Presumably, it's a punishment because the change from pre-Babel linguistic unity is seen as a painful loss. That's like thinking of linguistic and cultural diversity in the United States today as a "problem" or "liability."

But what if we think of God's act of creating different languages for the people in the story not so much as a punishment, but as a *remedy?* They got into trouble because they agreed *too much.* There was no "outsider," no one from a different culture, to question what they were doing and to persuade for a different perspective. On this reading, God decided that what the people needed was diversity, to help keep them out of trouble, to provide moral checks and balances.

That's how I'd like for us to think of cultural diversity in the United States today—it's a remedy for social injustice, a tremendous creative asset. I hope we can convey this valuing of difference to our students by teaching multicultural literature as I've suggested, foregrounding the negotiation of difference. And maybe, through that, we can see social justice increase in the United States and the world—that's my biggest hope of all.

174 Patricia Bizzell

Works Cited

Bizzell, Patricia. "'Contact Zones' and the Structure of English Studies." *College English* 56 (1994): 163–69.

———. "The Politics of Teaching Virtue." *ADE Bulletin* 103 (Winter 1992): 4–7.

———. "Power, Authority, and Critical Pedagogy." *Journal of Basic Writing* 10 (1991): 54–70.

Bizzell, Patricia, and Bruce Herzberg. Rev. of *What Makes Writing Good: A Multiperspective*. Eds. William E. Coles Jr. and James Vopat. *College Composition and Communication* 37 (1986): 244–47.

Condit, Celeste Michelle and John Louis Lucaites. *Crafting Equality: America's Anglo-African Word*. Chicago: U of Chicago P, 1993.

hooks, bell. "'when i was a young soldier for the revolution': coming to voice." In *Talking Back: thinking feminist, thinking black*. Boston: South End Press, 1989. 10–18.

Jameson, Fredric. "Cognitive Mapping." In *Marxism and the Interpretation of Culture*. Eds. Cary Nelson and Lawrence Grossberg. Urbana: U of Illinois P, 1988. 347–57.

Pratt, Mary Louise. "Arts of the Contact Zone." *Profession 91*. New York: MLA, 1991. 33–40.

Petrosky, Anthony. "From Story to Essay: Reading and Writing." *College Composition and Communication* 33 (1982): 19–36.

Olson, Gary, ed. *Philosophy, Rhetoric, Literary Criticism: (Inter)views*. Carbondale: Southern Illinois UP, 1994.

Tompkins, Jane. "Pedagogy of the Distressed." *College English* 52 (1990): 653–60.

Villanueva, Victor. "*Inglés* in the Colleges." In *Bootstraps: From an American Academic of Color*. Urbana: NCTE, 1993. 65–90.

11 Teaching American Literature as Cultural Encounter: Models for Organizing the Introductory Course

Marjorie Pryse
University at Albany, SUNY

During the past decade I have created and revised a course guide for instructors that in its most recent version (1994) is titled *Teaching with the* Norton Anthology of American Literature, Fourth Edition[1]. Although I have imagined myself in armchair conversation with colleagues at geographically distant institutions, it was not until the 1994 NCTE Summer Institute for College Teachers at Myrtle Beach on "Rethinking American Literature" that I had an opportunity to meet face to face with instructors who reported that they had used the various editions of the course guide as part of their class preparation. In this essay I have expanded some of my thinking in *Teaching with the* Norton Anthology of American Literature, hoping to continue conversations from the Summer Institute and to address other colleagues who have never taught with the *Norton Anthology of American Literature (NAAL)* and therefore may not even know that *Teaching with the* NAAL exists.

In writing the first two editions of what I originally titled a "course guide" to teaching American literature, the model I used assumed that the instructor had already read the literature, knew the historical and critical "territory," and could serve as a knowledgeable guide for students entering that territory for the first time. In the late 1990s, such a metaphor for instruction in the American literature classroom no longer makes as much pedagogical sense as it did even five years ago, for two reasons. First, the range and diversity of texts taught in American literature classrooms across the nation (and increasingly included in the fourth edition of *NAAL* and other anthologies, such as the Heath) have altered our understanding of the territory of American writing, and the categories and characteristics of this writing are subject to debate. Which works should appear in any "canon" of "great American" texts? In a critical climate that promotes reexamination of the very body of knowledge that constitutes the teaching field of American literature, we would do our students a disservice by presenting authors and texts standard to anthologies published a decade or longer ago as if these anthologies still represented American literature. Second, in light of the changing shape of this body of knowledge, a pedagogy that required the instructor to maintain a fiction of expertise would carry with it several hazards. It would rule out introducing students to new or newly discovered works from the past or from writers who trace their literary and historical origins to non-Euro-American sources, at least to the extent that most instructors in the American literature classroom have not yet become experts in this literature. An American literature course built on the premise that the instructor serves as a guide remains useful only to the extent that we work to overcome our own limitations.

If we make it clear at the outset that the body of knowledge we know as American literature has changed and is in the process of further change and that we are willing to "get lost" with our students—to paraphrase Robert Frost's "Directive"—in order to "find ourselves" again, then the concept of instructor-as-guide is reinvented in a more vital and flexible way. Indeed, the exploration of American literature itself becomes an encounter in which students recognize both that the texts they read may alter their conception of "American" and that this altered sense may contribute to new configurations of what has been known as American literature.

The new "literature to 1620" sections in the fourth edition of *NAAL* and several other anthologies of American literature bring the concept of encounter directly into the pedagogy of the American literature course. Mary Louise Pratt uses the term "contact zone" to refer to "social spaces where cultures meet, clash, and grapple with each other, often in contexts of highly asymmetrical relations of power, such as colonialism, slavery, or their aftermaths as they are lived out in many parts of the world today." She observes that the Stanford University course Cultures, Ideas, and Values (CIV), which "centered on the Americas and the multiple cultural histories (including European ones) that have intersected here," itself became a contact zone in which students as well as texts brought "radically heterogenous" reception to the intersection of these multiple histories and various "American" stories. In such a course, she writes, "we were struck . . . at how anomalous the formal lecture became," at how "impossible" and "unimaginable" became "the lecturer's traditional (imagined) task—unifying the world in the class's eyes by means of a monologue that rings equally coherent, revealing, and true for all."[2] Pratt's description of "the arts of the contact zone" may characterize the experience of other classrooms in which the instructor takes seriously the concept of encounter. Ultimately, more is at stake than encounters on the page; what American literature reveals to students about their own lives, myths, and histories invites intellectual encounters in classroom discussion as well, and in the alchemical process of such discussion, the changing shape of American literature anthologies becomes a catalyst, not a fixative.

Organizing the American literature course, like the process of anthology revision, requires choice: what to add and what to delete to make room for new texts, new voices. These choices are themselves informed by the following factors: new scholarship, especially on women and minority men who have written American texts; developments in literary and critical theory; the extent of perceived relationship between cultural texts and social contexts; and increasing freedom to acknowledge the literary value of texts that traditionalists have not considered high culture—such as diaries, oral literatures, political writing, and regional fiction. Indeed, the very debates concerning the inclusion of certain authors and texts in the literary canon—and in the American literature classroom—may themselves be viewed as a struggle between the high culture of American literature traditionally defined and an increasingly populist sense of the function and value of American literary representations. The study of American literature demonstrates the series of radical inventions and interventions that produced government documents as well as creative texts, that constituted acts of autobiography as well as ethnography, that emerged as myths and counter myths reflective of their particular age and the aging of American culture. Like the society it in part reflects, the scholarly and teaching field of American literature is also an invention (initially, by turn-of-the-century historians[3]) as well as the site of national, cultural, and political intervention. Teaching American literature as an encounter between the inventions of the past and the cultural interventions of the present becomes a useful metaphor for pedagogy, building as it does from the earliest records of the encounter between native peoples and Europeans (the explorers and the exploiters, the recorders and the critics).

Conceiving of teaching American literature as an encounter for undergraduate students raises a series of questions. How do any of us create a course outline that will guide, but not dictate, students' approach to American literature; that will allow the instructor a sense of mastery without precluding exploration of new material; and that further makes it possible to manifest the pleasures we find in any given work, along with a collective sense of the aesthetic? How do we create a course that may be required for students who then enter the classroom without themselves having experienced choice? Are there ways to teach American literature that can help all students perceive themselves as members of a culture that includes them? Many students expect to be "taught" American literature as if it were a body of finite knowledge, a collection of accepted readings to be assimilated. Identifying the conceptual framework by which an instructor has chosen to organize the course encourages students to read, think, speak, and write from the perspective they bring with them, as they simultaneously learn to locate that perspective within a larger context. But the larger context always includes other perspectives, other ways of organizing an American literature course.

Over the years I have tried various models of course organization and have become convinced of the value of choosing some model—hoping to help students clarify what initially appears to be the "boggy, soggy, squitchy picture" of

American literature, especially as they experience it in a two-volume anthology.[4] A model of course organization provides the coherence of an organizing principle from which students may risk moving beyond the known to writers they might otherwise find alien—because they write in a different century, out of an ethnic background other than the students' own, from the point of view of another gender, or by means of experimenting with language or genre. The models by which I have variously organized American literature courses since the late 1970s include the historical approach, the "major authors" approach, the literary-traditions approach, and the inclusion approach. To someone from outside the profession, these four models might seem politically neutral and in some sense equally valid choices for course organization. But within departments and professional organizations like the National Council of Teachers of English, the American Literature Association, and the Modern Language Association, these approaches have come to be associated with points on a cultural spectrum of representation that spans from the more traditional and conservative models on the side of the historical and "major authors" approaches, to more liberal and even radical models of American culture on the side of the literary-traditions and the inclusion approaches. In light of the NCTE Summer Institute, I have reexamined the models I have used and suggest here ways in which the historical, "major authors," and literary-traditions approaches might all, like the inclusion approach, become cultural encounters in the classroom.

The Historical Approach

Most anthologies of American literature are organized according to the chronology of the authors' birth dates, and many of us write schedules of required reading that are more or less chronological and thus basically follow the order represented in the anthology. But mere chronology does not produce a perspective on literary history, and many instructors would argue that it is impossible to understand literature without placing it in its historical context. The historical approach makes room for students to ask questions that interest them about the writers' lives; about the ethnic, literary, geographical, and political environments within which they wrote; and about the ideologies or religious beliefs that influenced their cultural expression.

In practice, this can mean choosing texts that have a connection to specific historical events. The events themselves can generally inform the presentation of readings on the syllabus, provide a focus for background discussion, and give students the basis for asking questions in class or for selecting essay topics. One advantage to this approach for a course that may focus on the literatures of early encounter or the colonial period is that it allows students to locate literary works in the context of an American history course they may also be taking, or have taken, as part of a core or general education requirement. For the

post-Civil War period and into the twentieth century, in which American literature proliferates with a diversity of voices, themes, and degrees of connection
to historical moments, the instructor can focus on the development of an American literature and on both the individual writers and the aesthetic movements
that produced it as events of historical significance in their own right. Note,
however, that during the last twenty years the discipline of history has itself
become transformed by the social historians and the scholars who have created
the subdiscipline of women's history. Like these transformations in the discipline of history, the attempt to locate literature in its historical context actually
produces an effort that is far from traditional. Furthermore, in the context of
increasing awareness of the social construction of American literature itself as a
field of study[5], and of literary movements as equally socially constructed[6], an
unexamined historical approach may actually obscure for students the role that
social and cultural assumptions play in identifying what we understand as significant and "historical" events.

The historical approach does offer the coherence of parallelism; in the broad
sweep of a survey course, Puritanism and modernism become equivalent terms
to the extent that they form discrete sections in course organization. Such a
course sketches for students the "isms" of American literary study: from European colonialism to Puritanism, deism, transcendentalism, regionalism, realism, naturalism, modernism, and postmodernism. Questions emerge from such
a model: As they read specific works, what connections can students find between ideologies that suggest a worldview (such as Puritanism and deism) and
others that are more philosophical and aesthetic in their focus (such as transcendentalism and realism)? At the same time, to what extent do particular writers
enhance, subvert, or simply ignore the assumptions of their age? Class discussion and analysis of individual texts can usefully challenge the apparent subordination of writers and works to categories on a syllabus. Such a framework for
course organization can provide a set of definitions that students may be willing
to challenge. Puritanism, for example, becomes a useful umbrella concept in
discussing many of the writers in the 1620–1820 period; however, a number of
frequently anthologized writers in the same period had no relation to Puritan
thinking, and there are others—Hawthorne is the notable example—in later
periods who continued to examine Puritanism in their works. Similarly, coming
to terms with the concept of modernism can help students understand many of
the thematic and aesthetic choices writers make in the 1914–1945 period, but
what happens to the concept if you ask students to consider the "modernism" of
Whitman and Dickinson? Or if you ask them to explain the persistence of interest in traditional themes and lyric forms in many poets who wrote during the
"modern" period?

One difficulty the historical model creates rests in this same apparent parallelism of course organization. Writers who do not fit the general pattern

become more difficult to include in the syllabus unless the historical approach includes a counterpoint. The literature of witness and encounter in writers like Bartolomé de las Casas, Bernal Díaz del Castillo, and even Samuel de Champlain offers a different perspective than the mainstream accounts of the literature of colonial expansion in the writings of Christopher Columbus, Hernán Cortés, or John Smith. And while texts of witness and encounter truly "historicize" the literature of European colonialism, the status of such writers and works is effectively marginalized by the historical model, particularly the model that organizes a course around the series of ideologically and aesthetically marked categories (the "isms" listed above) that the scholarly and teaching field of American literature has, in its own creation, marked out as the mainstream.

A consideration of the list of other issues and categories around which American literature may be organized confirms the effective marginalization of certain writers and texts. Such a list includes, among others: Native American songs and oratory; "other" colonial writers such as John Woolman who were not Puritans; writers who considered the issue of slavery, the treatment of Native Americans, or the lives of American women over the course of two or more centuries; and the literature of the Harlem Renaissance. Furthermore, entire categories of writers and texts that might otherwise fit the model become marginalized, as instructors over the course of a survey have little time to differentiate between regionalism and "local color" writing, or even to include regionalism at all because realism includes several "major authors" (and long works of fiction that take up a lot of space on the syllabus).

Even a cursory discussion of the issues and specific problems involved in choosing a historical model of course organization reflects the difficulty in viewing it as a "traditional" or "default" model. Rather, the historical approach creates a number of opportunities for the instructor to call into question the inclusiveness of categories of American literary history as well as to raise other questions concerning the development of "American" writing that we may not have thought about when we were students. Why does the Declaration of Independence have the power it has? Does it reflect the power of particular groups as well as the disenfranchisement of others? To stimulate discussion on this question, the instructor may include Elizabeth Cady Stanton's 1848 "The Declaration of Sentiments," Frederick Douglass's "The Meaning of July Fourth for the Negro," and the Cherokee Memorials as part of a discussion of Jefferson's text. How might certain works believed to influence the course of history—such as Thomas Paine's "Common Sense," Harriet Beecher Stowe's *Uncle Tom's Cabin,* or W. E. B. Du Bois's *The Souls of Black Folk*—redefine our sense of *literary* history? Further, if we should all have been exposed to modernist and postmodernist thinking and writing by virtue of having been born in the mid- to late-twentieth century (as the chronological development of American literature may seem to imply to students), then why do some Americans still think, write, or read as Puritans or nineteenth-century women? To what extent does our national literature speak for all of us, and to what extent does it record the thinking of a very few?

The historical approach, carefully examined, helps undergraduates explore the possibility that what they are reading may have significance for the development of their own identity—or cluster of identities—as Americans. It helps them find their own place in the history of American expression as our literature reflects that history—and with a sense that the historical approach itself is simply one way of telling a story about the body of texts we loosely term American literature.

The "Major Authors" Approach

In terms of pedagogical choice, presenting the American literature course as a study of single figures or "major authors" makes it possible to read more of each writer's work, to spend more class time discussing each writer, and to encourage in students more sustained contemplation and appreciation of each writer—all powerful reasons to retain "major authors" as a model for course organization. It does not have to eliminate the historical context or the literary history within which any given writer wrote, although the course design does emphasize the development of each writer's individual career and relegates historical and cultural context to the background.

As part of choosing texts for a major authors course, an instructor might find it useful to think through his or her own criteria for "major." Some of these criteria might include the following: (1) appeals to a variety of readers ("universality"); (2) wrote works that influenced more than one other major author; (3) contributed an acknowledged "masterpiece" to American literature; (4) sustained a literary career beyond a single tour de force, or beyond middle age; (5) pioneered or innovated in subject matter, literary tradition, technique, or genre; (6) gained recognition as "major" by literary critics and historians; or (7) has "stood the test of time"—which may be decoded as having been regularly taught in undergraduate courses and thus would be removed from survey anthologies at the publisher's peril. However, scrutiny of these or any other criteria for establishing an author as "major" will demonstrate their arbitrariness.

The concept of the universal and wide appeal loses persuasiveness when we consider how readily and for how many centuries white males of European descent—many of whom have controlled the power of cultural definition and the means to create a mass market—have dominated the pattern for such universality. The concepts of influence (on other "major authors"), acknowledged "masterpiece," and recognition by critics all exist within a circular and circumscribed evaluative field. For these criteria, we are using unexamined and undefined concepts of "major author" in effect to establish the category. And the concepts of sustained literary career and pioneering innovation merely allow for critical fashions to dictate who is "in" and who is "out" of the canon. Herman Melville's *Moby-Dick* is canonized for its innovation and critics have established their own reputations debating the question of whether or not the work may be considered a novel. Other American fictions, such as Sarah Orne Jewett's *The Country of the Pointed Firs* or Mary Austin's *The Land of Little Rain* raise similar questions—but do not achieve Melville's length and do not embed their segments in a short narrative about hunting and killing a mythic animal. (The prospectors for gold in Austin's work encounter only mirage.) White American women writers and African American writers rarely achieve canonical status. Even Ralph Ellison, despite the acknowledgment that *Invisible Man* is long and innovative, may be questioned because his total lifetime production was small. Toni Morrison, with her Nobel Prize and her novel *Beloved,* achieves "major author" status among her contemporaries—but she is still alive. Some of the words we might casually use to explain our choices of certain writers over others—*great, universal, enduring*—can actually obscure the process of literary evaluation or the critical and political construction of an author's reputation. For illuminating insight into the politics of construction or reconstruction of a "major American author," see Jane Tompkins's discussion of the politics of Hawthorne's literary reputation in *Sensational Designs*[7], and Lawrence Schwartz's book, *Creating Faulkner's Reputation.*

To work critically, a major authors model should also raise questions concerning the process by which an author becomes "major"[8]: How does an author become "major"? Who decides? Is the question open to debate? Is there a handbook that establishes the criteria for nomination to the canon of "major authors," or does the acceptance of a particular author reflect the opinions of readers over time? If so, which readers? Why do there appear to be so many major authors in one period (such as 1820–65) and so few in others (such as 1620–1820)? Why, in a period where so many authors wrote from such a wide range of identities and geographic regions (such as 1865–1920), do we continue to focus on only a few (e.g., Clemens, Howells, and James)? How do students discover authors not included in the anthology or the course? Can we be certain that we would not consider any of them "major"? To what extent does the term "major author" imply *size*—length of novels or poems, number of novels or poems over a lifetime? What does a writer of short works such as stories or lyric poems have to do—or more likely, what do the critics have to do for such a writer—in order to earn for him or her the distinction "major author"?

The very process of trying to construct a list of "major" American authors for consideration in the classroom reflects the challenge—as well as the possibilities—of teaching with the "major authors" model. The smaller the number of authors to be included in the course, the greater the difficulty of making the justification to traditional colleagues for including white women or minority men or women writers. For example, if we survey the entire field of American literature and want to choose only five writers on whose "major" status scholars would agree, we might end up with the following list: Hawthorne, Melville, Clemens, James, and Faulkner. Such a list omits poetry and drama as genres— as well as significant works by many other authors arguably considered "major." A more profitable approach to choosing a list for a "major authors" course would include expanding the number of authors as much as time permits, thereby making room for alternatives. Another approach would involve rethinking the category of "major" altogether, recognizing the arbitrariness the category represents, and choosing some writers for such a course that not only challenge assumptions about the phrase "major author" but also introduce students to minority and women writers whose work indeed has become capable, especially by the late twentieth century, of "major" influence on American culture.

Rethinking not only American literature but also the category of "major author" produces a wider list of writers from which to choose in constructing a "major authors" course. Such a list would include the five writers I have cited above as well as many other European American males—Emerson, Whitman, Frost, Eliot, O'Neill. Such a list might also include, in addition to Dickinson and Wharton (often the only women included in a "major authors" course), Stowe, Jewett, Chopin, Chesnutt, Cather, Hurston, Hughes, Brooks, Wright, Malamud, Ellison, Welty, and Rich among still others. Complicating the notion of "major author" calls into question the very category—and yet, such complication brings the "major authors" model to life in the classroom. Perhaps one of the ultimate challenges in teaching the "major authors" course is helping students break down any associations they may have that *major* always equals "European American" or "male" and that white women or Native American or African American writers—because they appear as a numerical minority in the anthology, or because they wrote only short works in short forms—are always "minor" authors.

The Literary Traditions Approach

Implicit in the framework of the literary-traditions approach is a certain plurality: students will study more than one tradition because American literature as we understand it in the late twentieth century has combined several, sometimes recognized as the cultural productions of predominantly women writers ("woman's fiction," regionalism, sentimentalism)[9] or of particular racial or ethnic groups (the slave narrative; literary expression of the Harlem Renaissance; Jewish and immigrant fiction; labor, protest, and populist literature).

This approach raises its own questions: How does any given tradition begin? How do historical, social, political, and market forces contribute to or inhibit the formation and development of the tradition? Is the tradition imitative or self-invented? What are its distinctive genres? Who are its exemplary figures? What constitutes its range of themes? What is its relation to oral or folk traditions? What formal, cultural, or thematic connections exist between any two literary traditions? And how do we define the boundaries of single traditions? To what extent does any given American writer express a self-conscious sense of inclusion within or exclusion from a particular literary tradition? Is the concept of literary tradition (and the concept of a plurality of literary traditions) invented by the writer or by the teacher-critic? While racial or ethnic origin and regional identity, gender, and class experience may define boundaries or categories of authors and works in particular literary traditions, how permeable are these boundaries, and are there some writers who defy (or reject) categorization—either by their own disclaimers or by their thematic concerns? Are there some writers who belong to more than one literary tradition in such a way as to call into question the usefulness of the very concept of literary tradition? (African American women writers, in particular, may belong to several literary traditions at once.) And after we have examined the disparate parts that form the whole of American literature, does it still make any sense at all to talk about "an" American literature?[10]

The approach problematizes the concept of the universal. Without denying the existence of human commonalities that cross boundaries of ethnic, gender, or regional perspectives, the implied pluralism of the literary-traditions approach may challenge the existence of any central point of view by which many students define their own value and identity. Such an approach shifts the center of classroom discourse away from the European American male tradition, challenges the concept of mainstream, and invites new questions. The experience of reading as integral to a literary tradition writers whom literary historians have referred to as "minor" or "minority" may initially disconcert students who identify themselves as members of a cultural mainstream, who value "universals" in literature, or who insist that humanism ought to erase the ethnic, gender, regional, or class identity of the author. Perhaps it is particularly difficult for European American students eighteen to twenty-two years old to participate in an intellectual process that will require them to entertain a "minority" perspective at a time in their lives when they are trying to achieve their own intellectual and emotional maturity (their "majority"). But even European American and male authors have written some of their best work from within the perspective of marginality. In *The Mark and the Knowledge: Social Stigma in Classic American Fiction,* I examined works by Hawthorne, Melville, Faulkner, and Ellison to show how American writers often achieve their capacity for vision through the experience of feeling marked, alienated, or stigmatized. Such writers, along with Thoreau, Whitman, and Clemens, suggest that, beginning in the nineteenth century, being a poet or a fiction writer was itself enough to marginalize an American white man, and one concept of literary tradition might include those white male writers who focused on themes of marginality.

An instructor might want to discuss the differences between, for example, Henry David Thoreau's choice to write from the isolation of Walden Pond and to embrace eccentricity and Frederick Douglass's imposed outsider perspective as slave and heroic fugitive. For European American men, choosing marginality often helps them focus their individual vision. But they begin to write with a sense of their literary authority that minority writers do not share. Minority writers, on the other hand, must work to transcend the apparent limitations of marginality—that they do not see themselves as possessing literary authority and, instead, feel silenced by European American male culture—in order to write at all. Who knows what individual writers within minority literary traditions might have accomplished in American literary history without the burden of social stigma? In the literary traditions of African American male and female writers, Charles Chesnutt and Zora Neale Hurston are significant figures, for both of these writers were able to locate some other source than the Christian God for their own creativity; the same holds true for Native American writers. For Chesnutt and Hurston, writing out of the perspective of black folk life (or, for Native Americans, of myth and spirituality) allowed them to imagine a source for storytelling authority that was accessible to them—through the traditional figure of the story-telling conjure woman or man in the black community—and, thereby, to disengage the silencing function of Puritan and patriarchal typology.

Engaging students in comparative discussions of the sources of literary authority available to European American male writers and to writers from other traditions represented by American literature can help them break pervasive associations, inherited from the Puritans, that only white males have the authority to speak—for others as well as for themselves. It can also lead them to think in new ways about their own nascent authority—as thinkers, speakers, and writers in the classroom. When they see African American and European American (and in contemporary literature, Latina and Asian American) female authors finding the authority to write, they locate the models they may need to break their own silence. The classroom discussion that results when students reflect on the struggle for expression in others can ease the isolation and alienation white women and minority students often feel, and it can dissolve the indifference to literary study for many students enrolled in a "required" course. Students—whatever their gender or ethnic origin—learn to view cultural power as something they may not necessarily inherit, but can discover in themselves.

In practical terms, the literary-traditions approach initially involves identifying the particular traditions the instructor wishes to present and the relative amount of syllabus space to allot to each. Once that decision is made, then within each tradition, the instructor makes choices of specific writers for inclusion and exclusion. This framework eliminates the necessity of weighing the relative significance of, say, Hurston and Hemingway. The instructor may need to choose among Faulkner, Fitzgerald, and Hemingway, or to teach shorter texts because of the limitations of classroom time. But the instructor can reserve the question of Hurston's significance for that part of the course in which students can read Phillis Wheatley, Harriet Jacobs, Nella Larsen, Alice Walker, and/or Toni Morrison; or she can locate these writers among a plurality of women's traditions in poetry and prose.

Another practical question involves how to order the traditions on the syllabus. If an instructor begins with the white male tradition, will that once again set up white male experience and expression as the norm, all others as marginal? White women, and men and women from minority traditions, have written in full awareness of the literary productions of European American men, and one way to organize the course is to remain roughly chronological but to discuss the earliest writers in each literary tradition as they emerge. For example, early readings can introduce students to all of those texts that established origins in several literary traditions: Native American creation stories, and works by William Bradford or Edward Taylor, Anne Bradstreet, Phillis Wheatley, and Frederick Douglass.[11] Later, the instructor may group polemical or political writers from several traditions: Jonathan Edwards and Thomas Jefferson, Margaret Fuller and Elizabeth Cady Stanton, William Apess and Zitkala-Sä (Gertrude Simmons Bonnin), Booker T. Washington and W. E. B. Du Bois or Anna Julia Cooper. At any point in the course, the instructor may group writers from several traditions according to genre or theme. This method does not preclude students from making specific connections between writers from different traditions who wrote at about the same time, and it does create a literary context within each tradition that will help students avoid setting minority and women writers "against" white male writers or viewing the European American male tradition as seminal simply because white males were granted (or granted themselves) cultural authority at an earlier historical moment.

However an instructor decides to present the literary traditions—chronologically or by means of groupings—it may help students to create a visual mapping of individual writers within their historical period. As an example based on available texts within one anthology (*NAAL*), Figure 1 organizes major figures in European American, African American, Native American, Hispanic/Latino(a), and Asian American literary traditions both by tradition and according to chronology.

The Inclusion Approach

In examining each of the previous approaches to organizing the American literature course, I have already raised a number of questions that teaching from the inclusion approach foregrounds. Even so, adopting inclusion as a model of organization does differ even from the literary-traditions approach by assuming that literary texts are written within social, historical, political, and economic contexts—indeed, that social and material conditions affect the writing of the text as much as if not more than the individual character of the author. Conversely, the inclusion approach also asserts that literary texts themselves affect the very social and cultural contexts from which they emerge. Therefore, much more is at stake than simply including a few white women writers, or a few writers—men and women—from minority groups, if the instructor is committed to presenting an inclusive American literature. In effect, the inclusion approach becomes a survey of the ways in which gender, race, class, region, and sexual orientation intersect in the literary work, as well as the way in which the text, in its representations of these categories of cultural analysis, thereby constructs the reader. Gender, race, class, region, and sexual orientation become categories by which society organizes hierarchies of status and value and which literary texts either inscribe or critique.

The approach assumes that literary texts contribute to constructing these cultural hierarchies, that this occurs even if the literary work (or author) appears to be unconcerned with politics or ideology, and that students read from within structures of value whether or not they are aware of doing so. The approach leads to its own questions: How does a given work represent the material lives of the lyric voices or the characters it depicts? What cultural ideologies underpin this representation, and what interests does the representation serve? How might the voices or characters in the literary work have responded to their own representation? Teaching an inclusive American literature moves considerably away from the formalism of the New Critics' "close reading" approach to criticism and pedagogy, but argues that students still need to read closely and that the study of writers and texts develops their ability to "read" their culture critically. Ultimately, the inclusion approach sets up an encounter between students and the culture in which they live as represented by American literary texts.

The approach further assumes that any exploration of the question "What is American literature?" requires helping students bring into focus the particular strategies by which U.S. society has established and maintained its social hierarchies. What is "American" about American literature thus becomes the extent to which these literary texts both reflect and construct—and more rarely, critique—social and cultural values that privilege Americans of Anglo-European origin, the masculine gender, propertied persons of some wealth, and the perspectives of the Northeast region and heterosexual orientation over all others. The "inclusion" approach both adds writers to the syllabus and makes it possible to explore the social construction of white male subjectivity in texts by male writers of Anglo-European origin—a theme that traditional studies of American literature have obscured.

VOLUME 1

Tradition	To 1620	1620–1820	1820–1865
Euro-American Male	Columbus Barlowe Champlain Smith	Bradford or Taylor Edwards Franklin de Crèvecoeur John Adams Jefferson	Irving Emerson Hawthorne Poe Thoreau Whitman Melville
Euro-American Female		Bradstreet Rowlandson Ashbridge Abigail Adams	Fuller Stowe Dickinson Davis
African-American Male		Equiano	Douglass
African-American Female		Wheatley	Jacobs
Native Americans	Stories of the Beginning of the World	Occom	Cherokee Memorials Apess
Hispanic Male	Casas Cortés Díaz del Castillo Cabeza de Vaca		

VOLUME 2

Tradition	1865–1914	1914–1945	American Prose since 1945	American Poetry since 1945
Euro-American Male	Clemens Howells or Dreiser or Adams James Crane	Frost Stevens Williams or Eliot O'Neill Fitzgerald Faulkner Crane	Williams Malamud Bellow Miller Mamet	Warren Berryman Lowell Merrill Ashbery or Wright

Tradition	1865–1914	1914–1945	American Prose since 1945	American Poetry since 1945
Euro-American Female	Jewett Chopin Freeman or Austin Gilman Wharton	Cather Stein Lowell Yezierska Moore Porter Taggard	Welty O'Connor Oates Beattie	Bishop Levertov Rich Plath
African-American Male	Washington Chesnutt Du Bois	Toomer Brown Hughes Wright	Ellison Baldwin A. Wilson	Hayden Baraka Harper
African-American Female		Grimké Hurston	Walker	Brooks Lorde Dove
Native American Male	Native American Oratory Eastman Oskison Chants and Songs	Black Elk	Momaday	Ortiz
Native American Female	Bonnin Chants and Songs		Silko Erdrich	
Latino				Ríos
Latina			Chávez	Cervantes
Asian-American Male				Lee
Asian-American Female				Song

Figure 1. Suggested Readings: Organized by Race, Nationality, and Gender. Reproduced from *Teaching with the* Norton Anthology of American Literature, Fourth Edition (1994). Copyright © 1994 by W. W. Norton and Company, Inc. Reprinted with permission of the publisher.

One of the controversial features of the inclusion approach is that it calls into question the idea (proposed by E.D. Hirsch among others) that to be culturally literate, readers must read certain "classic" works that other readers will also have read.[12] The conceptual framework for such a course moves into the foreground writers and texts as well as themes and genres that literary criticism and history have marginalized. Such themes might include, for example, the immigrant experience; family relationships and attitudes toward children; race, segregation, and slavery; and gender issues of women's lives, work, and vision. Such genres might include recognition of literary modes and forms indigenous to the United States and its particular history, for example, the literature of witness and encounter in the pre-colonial period, the slave narrative, folk literature, feminist writing, nineteenth-century regionalism, African American fiction and poetry, Jewish fiction, Southern fiction, Beat poetry, feminist poetry, and protest and political poetry. Some indigenous genres are more problematic in terms of critique and sometimes, if not always, work to reinforce cultural stereotypes. For example, to problematize the concept of indigenous genres as resistance, introduce students to humor of the old Southwest, Indian captivity narratives, and "local color" fiction. The very concept of lesbian or gay literature is itself contested at the end of the twentieth century. Does the category include writers believed to be lesbian or gay, whether or not the writers themselves ever discussed sexual orientation? Does it include any writer whose work raises questions concerning what Adrienne Rich has called "compulsory heterosexuality," or who has produced specific works of interest in the study of cultural representations of lesbian and gay experience?

Rethinking American literature clearly requires us to rethink our models of course organization as well. It also asks us to contemplate the role of the American literature classroom in helping our society to confront and resolve its social and cultural dilemmas. American literature may not directly address public policy issues, but it provides formative ground within which readers of all ages and especially undergraduate students—who enter our classrooms before they fully enter society—can develop a perspective concerning the significance of literature and the humanities to American life. Any American literature course becomes provisional to the development of such perspective, representing less what Robinson Jeffers called in his poem "Shine, Perishing Republic" a "thickening to empire" and more what Adrienne Rich describes in "Diving Into the Wreck" as "a book of myths / in which" more and more "our names [do] appear." Or it represents what Michael Harper has termed "History as Apple Tree" (in a poem of the same title), in which American myth becomes "my own myth: / my arm the historical branch, / my name the bruised fruit, / black human photograph: apple tree." Models for organizing an inclusive American literature course—however that principle becomes interwoven with historical features, with notions of "major author" and literary tradition—add the image of cultural encounter to the book of myths and human photographs that depict what "American" literature has come to mean at the turn of the twenty-first century.

Notes

1. This article draws on and expands from Marjorie Pryse, *Teaching with the* Norton Anthology of American Literature, Fourth Edition, copyright © W.W. Norton & Company, Inc. 1994. The entire course guide, which includes detailed syllabi and questions for student papers and exams, is available from W. W. Norton. This excerpt/reworking is reprinted with permission of the publisher.

2. See Pratt, 34, 39.

3. See Shumway.

4. This phrase, which appears early in *Moby-Dick* when Ishmael arrives at the Spouter-Inn, locates indeterminacy as part of Herman Melville's vision. I like to think that Melville, along with several other "classic" and "canonical" American writers, would himself have refused to participate in canon-formation—except, of course, as it has produced a market for his work.

5. See Shumway.

6. See, for example, Kaplan, and Trachtenberg.

7. See especially chapter 1.

8. This question is related to the larger question of the canonization process, one raised widely by critics and scholars during the past twenty years; for a useful discussion of these issues, see Lauter.

9. See Baym, *Woman's Fiction*; Fetterley and Pryse; and Dobson. See also Fetterley's essay in this volume.

10. See Gregory Jay's essay in this volume and "The End of 'American' Literature."

11. The fourth edition of *NAAL* has included Native American creation myths as part of its "Literature to 1620" section, even though these myths cannot be "dated" as such—thereby offering the opportunity to begin an American literature course with the expression of the people who first inhabited the Americas.

12. See both Hirsch and the challenge to Hirsch by Knoblauch and Brannon.

Works Cited

Baym, Nina. *Woman's Fiction: A Guide to Novels by and about Women in America, 1820–1870*. Ithaca: Cornell UP, 1978.

Baym, Nina, et al., eds. *Norton Anthology of American Literature*. 4th ed. New York: Norton, 1995.

Dobson, Joanne. "Sex, Wit, and Sentiment: Frances Osgood and the Poetry of Love." *American Literature* 65 (1993): 631–48.

Fetterley, Judith, and Marjorie Pryse. *American Women Regionalists 1850–1910: A Norton Anthology*. New York: Norton, 1992.

Hirsch, E. D. *Cultural Literacy: What Every American Needs to Know.* Boston: Houghton Mifflin, 1987.

Jay, Gregory. "The End of 'American' Literature: Toward a Multicultural Practice." *College English* 53 (1991): 264-80.

Kaplan, Amy. *The Social Construction of American Realism.* Chicago: U of Chicago P, 1988.

Knoblauch, C.H., and Lil Brannon. *Critical Teaching and the Idea of Literacy.* Portsmouth, NH: Boynton Cook, 1993.

Lauter, Paul. *Canons and Contexts.* New York: Oxford UP, 1991.

Pratt, Mary Louise. "Arts of the Contact Zone." *Profession 91.* New York: MLA, 1991. 33–40.

Pryse, Marjorie. *The Mark and the Knowledge: Social Stigma in Classic American Fiction.* Columbus: Ohio State UP, 1979.

———. *Teaching with the* Norton Anthology of American Literature, *Fourth Edition.* New York: W. W. Norton, 1994.

Schwartz, Lawrence H. *Creating Faulkner's Reputation:The Politics of Modern Literary Criticism.* Knoxville: U of Tennessee P, 1988.

Shumway, David. *Creating American Civilization: A Genealogy of American Literature as an Academic Discipline.* Minneapolis: U of Minnesota P, 1994.

Tompkins, Jane. *Sensational Designs: The Cultural Work of American Fiction 1790–1860.* New York: Oxford UP, 1985.

Trachtenberg, Alan. *The Incorporation of America: Culture and Society in the Gilded Age.* New York: Hill and Wang, 1982.

12 But, Is It Good Enough to Teach?

Frances Smith Foster
Emory University

It was not very long ago that I had a hallway conversation with a colleague who told me that he was quite eager to add an African American text to his Modern American Fiction course, but he had been unable to identify a text that could compare favorably with those on his syllabus. It would be unfair (and it would certainly prove embarrassing to his African American students), he asserted, if his syllabus included writing by minorities that was obviously inferior to that of the other literature in the course. My colleague asked if I could suggest an author or a title that was good enough to teach in company of Fitzgerald's *The Great Gatsby,* Hemingway's *The Old Man and the Sea,* and Steinbeck's *The Grapes of Wrath.* At the time I was not taken aback by his request. I suggested Ellison's *Invisible Man.* "Too difficult," he replied. This class, he said, was designed to attract high enrollments of general-interest readers and thereby ensure that Spenser, Milton, and Chaucer would continue to be offered for the majors. I furrowed my brow and suggested Zora Neale Hurston's *Their Eyes Were Watching God,* Richard Wright's *Native Son,* James Baldwin's *Go Tell It On the Mountain,* or anything by Alice Walker or Toni Morrison. "Ah, Toni Morrison," he responded, "maybe she'll do. Can you recommend something of hers I can read over the summer? Maybe I can use her next year."

The building in which the English department offices were located was constructed as two squares connected by a single passageway on each floor. At the far extreme of one square was the "ladies'" restroom and at the far extreme of the other was the "men's," so there was by necessity a lot of passing in the hallways. I recall another corridor conversation with another colleague. He taught children's literature and was in the process of ordering his books for the coming semester when he discovered that *M.C. Higgins, the Great* was no longer in print. He was quite put out about it. How could one of the very few triple-crown winners—Newbery, Boston Globe/Horn Book, and National Book Awards— be allowed to go out of print? He wouldn't be able to include an African American text this semester. "Virginia Hamilton [the author of *M.C. Higgins*], has published at least twenty-five books—several others have won major prizes," I reminded him. "Are they all out of print?" He hadn't thought of that, he confessed; though he'd been teaching *M.C. Higgins, the Great* for several years now, he was not familiar with Virginia Hamilton's other books. He decided that he'd have to read more of her works sometime soon and perhaps, if *M.C. Higgins* were not reprinted, he would find a substitute.

I think I should hasten here to assure you—for what it's worth—that these conversations did not take place at my current academic home. Yet, these are not made-up incidents, and they are not atypical. There are many other examples I could recite. But these will serve to illustrate two things. One, these were the "good guys," professors who were competent, responsible, and innovative, colleagues who agreed that the curriculum should be diversified and who were not unwilling to try to do their part. And two, I "understood" and sympathized with their problem—it was one that I entertained when I constructed my courses in American autobiography, young adult fiction, introduction to literature, and other "mainstream" or semi-mainstream courses. I, too, was concerned about how to cover all that needed to be covered and still include previously ignored literary pieces, about how to identify a representative work that was "good enough to teach" instead of, or in concert with, *The Education of Henry Adams, The Chocolate War,* or *Oedipus Rex.*

I do not know exactly how or when it began to dawn on me that if we were not asking the wrong question, we were at least misinterpreting IT—that in trying to choose an African American text we were asking what we did not routinely ask about European American texts. We were adopting criteria which, if applied to all our syllabi selections, might totally change what we teach, how we teach it, and why. Now, this is *not* to say that "But, is it good enough to teach?" is an unacceptable or irrelevant question—on the contrary, perhaps we should ask of every selection not only is it "good enough" but is it "the best" text to teach? Actually, "But is it good enough to teach?" is a question long overdue and one with which we've had *limited* experience.

I do know that that question did not occupy a prominent place in my academic training. As a student I generally assumed that if a work appeared in the anthology, if it were by a particular author, or if it were being taught to us, it was "good enough." If it seemed odd or uninteresting, I looked to my professor to explain what assumptions underlay the text, what interpretative techniques I needed to learn in order to appreciate it. As a beginning professor, the texts I chose to teach were partly determined by what I thought I could teach with authority. I leaned toward the texts that I thought I knew best, which were mostly the genres, authors, and titles that I had been taught, or those that were similar enough to them that I could readily apply the methods and information I did know. For me, as for many, my syllabi were also determined by what was in the Norton anthology or what text was sort of simple enough to be "done" in one or two class meetings. Such pragmatism led me to include "A Rose for Emily" and

"Dry September" and not "The Bear" or *Absalom, Absalom!*, to select *The Scarlet Letter* over *Moby-Dick*. Sometimes, particularly before I got tenure, the question was "Which text is least likely to create controversy?" *Catcher in the Rye, Sons and Lovers,* and *Ulysses* were less likely to attract concern than *Are You There, God? It's Me, Margaret; Lolita;* or *Naked Lunch*. Had I been asked about my criteria, I would have answered, I think, directly from the first lecture in my introduction to literature course: I was about the business of presenting the best thoughts of the best minds complemented by representative examples of movements, trends, and concerns, and concluding with an example of a new and innovative writer—a "current classic," if you will. In practice, I was presenting what was available, what was familiar, and what fit the schedule.

I don't generally get requests for "an" author or "a" text these days. The Canon Busters have created anthologies sufficiently inclusive to include poems by Phillis Wheatley and excerpts of Frederick Douglass's *Narrative*. Publishers make available in paperback all of Hurston's and Wright's and Walker's and Morrison's works. And I suspect that these days "But is it good enough to teach?" would be considered a hostile question about writings by individuals from previously excluded groups. Yet I think that this question is an important one. It should be taken as a "leading question," an interrogative serve or an opening bid, perhaps. An appropriate response would be (1) What are you trying to teach? (2) What are the course goals? (3) Why do you want to teach it? and even (4) Why are you teaching? "Good enough" depends in part upon *how* you intend to use it. If it replaces a particular work, then why was that work in the course and can the new one fulfill that function as well or better? For example, if the goal is to demonstrate the progressive plot structure—exposition, rising action, denouement—one shouldn't use Jean Toomer's *Cane*. On the other hand, if one wishes to consider the interface between the "naturalistic" movements and imagism, or wants an episodic, 1920s text set in a particular region of the United States, exemplifying a carefully blended experimental mixture of realism, romanticism, local color, and Gothic, then *Cane* could easily replace *Winesburg, Ohio,* or it could work as a companion piece to compare and contrast ways in which Jean Toomer and Sherwood Anderson—two writers of the same ilk, writers who were in fact friends as well as colleagues—influenced one another. Similarly, Robert Hayden, Melvin Tolson, or Ralph Ellison works better in a unit with T.S. Eliot and Ezra Pound than would Countee Cullen, Angelina Grimké, or Chester Himes.

"Good enough" is also influenced by your own ability: Do you know enough to teach it? Are you willing to learn? Or from another side, "good enough" depends also upon the students in the class and which of their needs and attitudes you're trying to influence. And here I want to preach one small sermon! The proportion or the existence of particular "ethnic" or cultural representations in the curriculum should not depend upon the ethnic or cultural composition of the class. It is very curious to me that the appearance of African Americans, or Laotians, or Puerto Ricans, or other people of color triggers concerns that their absences do not. And yet, the percentage or existence of Jewish or Catholic students, Greek pagans, or Elizabethan playgoers does not determine whether one teaches Bellow, Joyce, Sophocles, or Shakespeare. If Jewish students can read and respond to *Paradise Lost,* if Protestants can appreciate *Portrait of the Artist as a Young Man,* if twentieth-century readers can learn from and love *The Odyssey, The Canterbury Tales,* or *The Bostonians,* then can they not also learn from and appreciate *Middle Passage, The House on Mango Street, The Kitchen God's Wife,* and *Farewell to Manzanar*? It is not the Mexican American students only who benefit from a consideration of the literary potential of code switching and the use of the vernacular. It is not the Native American student only who should recognize that repetition and indirection have aesthetic function and value or that the roles of the tricksters Coyote and Raven are not exactly like those of the tricksters Anansi and Br'er Rabbit. The Japanese American students are not the only ones who should know how the concentration camps of the 1940s affected the literary production of those who experienced that dislocation—or even the basic fact that such a travesty indeed occurred in these United States. In other words, it is not simply the traditionally excluded who need and have a right to learn about more than one culture, class, or condition. Students of the political and economic majority—even if their status as a numerical majority were not being seriously eroded—deserve to know themselves in relation to those who share and have shared this earth, this life, and this language. My title, my question, begins with "But" because I assume that folks attending this particular conference have, to some extent, accepted the idea (or certainly are willing to entertain the notion) that what we have traditionally been taught is not the total literary production, perhaps not the most artistic or technically sophisticated, maybe not even the best representative of the time, place, or circumstance. ("Buts" do not want to close off discussion, they invite it.) I want a conversation that reviews what "IT" means, that asks if "good enough" is too minimal a standard, and that identifies what we are teaching when we don't teach certain things. But first, I want to suggest that we may need to back up and ask ourselves again, "Do we really want to teach IT?"

I take as my theme the first words of Toni Cade Bambara's *The Salt Eaters:* "Are you sure, Sweetheart, that you want to be well?" (3). The idea that I want to explore is, why try a cure without considering the costs and side effects of the therapy unless it is a "life-threatening emergency"? Or to try another medical metaphor: When I tried to help my friends identify a "good enough" author or text without examining the origins and intensity of their concerns, I was applying a cold compress to an aching head. It was not necessarily wrong, but it may have masked symptoms and delayed recognition of a more fundamental dis-ease.

And yet, my impulse was the kind that is common to those of us who—for whatever reason—find ourselves—or want ourselves to be—part of the multicultural movement: we folks who know ourselves to be AGAINST censorship and FOR the politics of diversity; we good, brave, and clear-sighted individuals who know what *e pluribus unum* is really supposed to mean, who believe that the strength and the survival of the United States of America must come from all races, cultures, classes, creeds, genders, etc., working and living in harmony but keeping our integrity, composing together something like a quilt more aesthetically pleasing, larger, and more useful than any could be alone.

In training graduate students and consulting with English departments, and in being a teacher myself, I am becoming increasingly concerned about the implications of inclusive politics, about how the many attempts to rethink American literature are not working as well as they should—in part—because too many of us are trying to include each and all into the existing "center." I tried to think of efficient and effective ways to explain what I mean. (I considered appropriating scientific terminology—"we confuse admixtures with amalgams." I thought that a domestic metaphor would be appropriately subversive—my best was "The inclusive curricula as commonly practiced is rather like adding corn to biscuit dough and calling it cornbread.") It was fun, but I decided to be scholarly and just casually demonstrate my diverse reading patterns. In " 'Othered' Matters: Reconceptualizing Dominance and Difference in the History of Sexuality in America," Ann duCille states that we tend to employ a methodology which "merely appends the 'othered' to already existing analytical paradigms rather than fundamentally altering the ideological assumptions that inform those frameworks" (103).

In *The Salt Eaters,* the healer Minnie Ransom recognizes that what has made Velma sick won't be reversed with two aspirins, a more varied diet, or a summer of leisure. So she begins her healing session with the primary question: "Are you sure, Sweetheart, that you want to be well?" It holds for us, also. We cannot re-form American literature by consuming fewer words by dead white men, increasing our intake of women's texts, and adding a new category or two to our literary plates. Yet, as teachers and scholars, we have favored additives. Most of us have tried to ADD ONE, to ADD ON, and usually (as with my colleagues) planned to start this new regime—one day soon. (In frustration, a few have added, then subtracted, and returned to their old habits.) In "The End of 'American' Literature" Gregory S. Jay makes some cogent remarks on the problems of inclusion, and other essays in this volume raise other aspects of this issue. So, I think I can be brief on these points.

ADD ONE. "Inclusive" folk like, or feel obligated, to add one of each—or, if space or time is short, one to represent the others. So, Harriet Jacobs or Zora Neale Hurston, Toni Morrison or Terry McMillan, Audre Lorde or Angela Davis become "The" African American writer on the syllabi of women's literature classes and in the critical conversations. These "superblackwomenwriters" are sometimes expected to satisfy the requirements for diversity of class, race, politics, gender, and genre. Ann Plato, Anna Julia Cooper, Ann Allen Shockley, or Sherley Anne Williams are conflated in footnotes of "see also's." Poets, dramatists, writers for young adults, and many males are not even mentioned.

We may, and should, extend this example to include the ADD ONE COURSE concept. For African American literature, adding one course requires that we attempt to cover 250-plus years in one semester or quarter. We may consider also the ADD ONE FACULTY MEMBER idea, wherein the announcement of an opening or the call for recommendations hardly needs much deconstructing to understand that their ideal addition would be a black, woman-identified senior scholar or a Spanish speaking Native American from Minnesota. But I think the point is made: the ADD ONE approach is simply inadequate.

Next, by ADD ON I mean to include a text INTO a curriculum while excluding its literary context, its criticism, its theory or aesthetic. I also mean evaluating a text from another culture or from another perspective as if it were simply another effort to meet a universal objective, or judging IT by a set of assumptions inappropriate or marginal to its intentions, concerns, or expectations. As an example, consider the situation that Judith Fetterley describes in her introduction to *Provisions: A Reader from Nineteenth-Century American Women*. Remember her example of Lyle Wright's objection to the subjects "missed" in early U.S. fiction. As Fetterley points out, Wright's lament for the absence of stories concerning the "masted schooners and flying clippers, stagecoaches . . . railroads . . . The frontier pushing westward . . . Trails . . . being blazed to the Pacific, etc." (8) is predicated upon assumptions that are gender biased. Fetterley suggests that his comments can be useful because Wright does at least catalog some of the subjects about which most women did not write. But I believe it takes a resisting reader to do this, and too often our resistance is too low. Generally, when a bias is unmarked or is familiar—maybe even shared—we accept rather than analyze. We repeat rather than translate.

The problem of getting well is compounded when the treatment is inappropriate. And all too often in the case of scholarship on nontraditional literatures, prescriptions are too quickly and carelessly offered. Again, Fetterley has provided us with a close enough example when she describes the "contempt" implicit in

> the cavalier approach to facts when the subject is mid-nineteenth-century women writers. So pervasive is the sloppiness that one must perforce conclude that those who write on this material feel not simply that they will not endanger their reputation as scholars by such carelessness, but rather that were they to take this material seriously enough to perform even the most minimal tasks of scholarship, this accuracy would endanger their reputations. In brief, the material is too trivial for scholarship . . . . Particularly appalling is the combination of factual sloppiness with a tone of absolute authority. (21)

Yet, how are we to know when to question the doctor, especially when we are "the doctor"? One common mistake is to abandon too quickly or to fail to use standard diagnostic procedures or professional expertise. For example, one can argue that because Cassie in Harriet Beecher Stowe's *Uncle Tom's Cabin* hid in the attic and worked a diabolic plan to run her master crazy, then Cassie should be seen as the Gothic model for Linda in *Incidents,* which was published a few years later. However, one does this only by ignoring genre definitions (in this instance by conflating fiction with autobiography) and by failing to research even casually an author's life or aesthetics. Or one could cite Frances Harper's "Eliza Harris" as evidence that Harper was so moved by Stowe's portrayal in the novel that she tried to match it in poetic form. The assumption that Stowe is the ur-author and Harper is one of her apprentices falters, though, if we consider that both Harriet Beecher Stowe and Frances Harper were appropriating an actual—and often repeated—incident that occurred at Ripley, Ohio. To ADD ON with the assumption that we already know how to read, interpret, describe, or apply IT is dangerous and degrading.

An equally irresponsible stance is to abandon all responsibility for understanding and interpreting or to neglect to determine what relevant literary methodology there is for dealing with "Other" literatures because we've discovered that to Others we are also Others. Chagrined and apologetic, some of us murmur that "Since I'm not X, I can't possibly know." We resort to summarizing what a prominent "scholar" has said or to confiding our "feelings" about literary experience. While our personal feelings are important, sometimes even to the matter at hand, confessing is not professing. This stance betrays itself very simply, I think. How many of us are, or have students who are, nineteenth-century factory workers? How many of us are confused because our mother has married our father's murderer? Yet we know and expect others to appreciate *Life in the Iron Mills* and *Hamlet.* Or, how much credence would we allow men who say they can't teach Emily Dickinson, George Sand, or Katherine Anne Porter because they are not English, French, or Southern women? If that is too facile or simplistic a dismissal of what I consider fraudulent displays of positionality politics, then several essays in this volume discuss or demonstrate the problems of such an approach with more detail and more seriousness. It is my contention that exposure to noncanonical literature reacts with arrogance, ignorance, and rationalization to make great discomfort for us all. And it is my suggestion that whether it is indeed an insidious infection of ethnocentricity that makes us feel we need not learn any more about the subject we propose to teach, or if it is the press of programmatic concerns that pushes us to read too hastily or to rely upon inappropriate secondary sources—the result is about the same.

The decision to teach from a multicultural perspective—to rethink and to represent American literature—requires more knowledge than most of us have, and perhaps more extensive therapy than we're willing to endure. For example, how can we be expected to know that *Incidents* is a slave narrative that employs fictive strategies and not the historical romance that it resembles? How would we know to place both Stowe's and Harper's "Eliza Harris" within its larger historical and literary contexts when we did not know they existed? When noncanonical writers, the events of which they write, and the strategies and techniques by which they convey their visions are not included in the usual reference works, how do we educate ourselves? And since the politics of positionality are a distinct improvement over the professions of objectivity or universality that gave rise to them, how and when do we know whose authority to accept and the extent to which we must/should relinquish our own?

As a beginning, I suggest that we be very careful about privileging the readings and assumptions of European or European American theorists to interpret and assess the literary productions of those who are not of or about that Eurocentric enterprise. Assessing texts by "Others" using criteria based upon different models, showing no evidence of being acquainted with scholarly discourse in professional journals devoted to "Other" literatures, consistently ignoring the contributions of African American, Latino/Latina, Asian American, and Native American critics and theorists is indefensible. By the same token, rejecting the contributions of a twentieth-century white Southern male scholar on the literary productions of a black New England female slave is also biting off one's nose to spite one's face. It is—and here I am employing the African American rhetorical strategy called "signifying"—as indefensible as a graduate program that gives no serious consideration to any literary approaches or criticism practiced prior to 1980. Yet, look at the bibliographies and footnotes in most professional literature and see how extensive or diverse the textual samples or citations for such discussions are.

The third possibility that I mentioned—the procrastination syndrome of "intending to" or "being willing to, if . . ."—generally manifests itself in ADDING NONE or, even more embarrassing, TRYING ONE, then reverting to the habits of the past, teaching what is easier to serve up and to digest. This is to be less than honest with ourselves and our students; it is to abdicate our responsibility as scholars and critics. You see, we can no longer claim not to have realized that white educated men were not the only ones who wrote or were published. But each semester or quarter that we postpone diversifying our syllabi, our curricula, or our faculties is another quarter of allowing our students to persist in such ignorance—or perhaps more likely, allowing them to continue to believe that we are less knowledgeable than they are. For in reality, many of our students now see, live near, like, and even love at least one or two "Others." And in those pockets where personal contact with people of various races, classes, sexual orientations, etc., does not occur, popular media have introduced them to Arsenio, Geraldo, and Roseanne. In fashion and speech, in music and dance, even white heterosexual middle-class males are aware of and in fact imitating Others. Our students recognize that creativity in language and variation of social perspective do exist. They listen attentively to the commentary of rap and hip-hop artists. They memorize the narratives of storytellers such as Eddie Murphy as well as the multitude of verbal wizards that appear regularly on "Def Comedy Jam." Airport bookstores and supermarket checkout lines stock *The Color Purple, Beloved,* and *Waiting to Exhale.* The longer we procrastinate about diversifying our literature courses, the more evidence our students have of our own moribundity. So we've got to do something—if we want to be (and do) well.

But if not adding ONE or adding ON, then what? Hayden White and others have stated, we must "change our attitudes with respect, not only to our object of study . . . *and* to the methods of historical analysis and representation which we have inherited . . . but also to the whole question of the theories, methods, and modes of representation we should use in an inquest that is just as much into ourselves and our age as it is into" any enterprise, literary or otherwise (127). In theory I agree, but in practice it is not something most of us can do overnight. To change paradigms, to fundamentally alter the construction of our institutions is a task that seems to exceed my present abilities and inclinations. It certainly demands time and energy already seriously reduced by the demands of budget cuts, larger classes, and other measures. Just gearing up for new courses or getting ready to responsibly teach familiar books calls for more time than most of my days have.

To change our attitudes may require discomfort, maybe even reconstructive surgery. In my own case, I came to this profession via a love for and an attraction to literature as it was taught to me and as I understood it, even felt it. I recognized some overlooked areas and validated my own career choice by focusing upon African American literary productions. I'm doing well and making a contribution. Am I sure that I really want to be any more well than this? Even if I were to say "YES" loudly and sincerely, another question would remain: How much more can I learn and do and be well? Am I in danger of spreading myself so thin that I am not good enough to teach? I don't know. But I have begun my therapy by accepting the obvious.

The study of literature, like most areas of intellectual inquiry, has been irrevocably altered by social, political, economic, technical, and perhaps spiritual changes. We will never again be confident that we can recognize or "master" the best thoughts of the best minds. We can neither read nor can our libraries afford to buy *all* the good books available. As teachers and as scholars we need to shift our attention from passing on a tradition to focusing upon ways of knowing, from interpreting the symbols in a text to understanding the entire text as symbolic. In effect, we need to shift our attention to include methodology, process, production—and yes, even theory. *But* we must avoid mistaking process for product. We should not substitute discussion *about* literature for literature itself. (And if we really value and respect language, we've got to learn to read more accurately and to write and speak more clearly about what we are reading.)

One way that I'm trying to do this is to include my students more clearly in the process of the course. I present goals in the syllabus and invite them to record their own. From time to time we calibrate. I give ideas on how I intend to evaluate our success ("By the end of this course . . .") and I try to construct projects and exams that reflect these goals. I explain why I've selected certain texts and mention others I've excluded. I try to demonstrate or identify the literary approaches I'm using, explaining as best I can the various "rules" and assumptions we construct in this discipline.

I have also accepted the idea that no one group, professor, or reader can know or learn or convey all of the "ITs". I am drawn more and more to collaborative efforts, to literary study as a shared enterprise. This is not to be confused with the open classrooms of the 1970s, when all our feelings, opinions, fantasies were "equal." But it is influenced by some of that, because I am a product of those moments when New Criticism met historicism, when African American literature was being rediscovered and reinvented, and when teachers were students also. I talk to my colleagues more. I exchange syllabi and course visits. I read their exam questions and their publications and send notes: *What . . . ? Why . . . ? What about . . . ?* I assign writings and projects designed to incorporate investigation and analysis (the good ole research paper revisited). For example, introductory literature courses require two library projects; and toward the end of the course—as a final even—I ask students, given my goals for this course, which text should be replaced with what and why?

"But, is it good enough to teach?" I end by answering this question with another question, a question that for me must precede and accompany any others: "But, do you really want to (have to) teach IT?" Or, "Are you sure, Sweetheart, you really want to be well?"

Works Cited

Bambara, Toni Cade. *The Salt Eaters.* New York: Vintage, 1981.

duCille, Ann. "'Othered' Matters: Reconceptualizing Dominance and Difference in the History of Sexuality in America." *Journal of the History of Sexuality* 1 (1990): 102–27.

Fetterley, Judith, ed. *Provisions: A Reader from Nineteenth-Century American Women.* Bloomington: Indiana UP, 1985.

Jay, Gregory S. "The End of 'American' Literature: Toward a Multicultural Practice." *College English* 53 (1991): 264–81.

White, Hayden. "'The Nineteenth-Century' as Chronotype." *Nineteenth-Century Contexts* 11 (1987): 119–29.

13 Teaching the Rhetoric of Race: A Rhetorical Approach to Multicultural Pedagogy

John Alberti
Northern Kentucky University

In "What to the Slave Is the Fourth of July?", an address given significantly on July 5, 1852, Frederick Douglass turns aside from his anti-slavery argument to address a profoundly rhetorical question about the ultimate efficacy of that argument:

> But I fancy I hear some one of my audience say, it is just in this circumstance that you and your brother abolitionists fail to make a favorable impression on the public mind. Would you argue more, and denounce less, would you persuade more, and rebuke less, your cause would be much more likely to succeed. (369)

Douglass is speaking as a lecturer here; but every lecturer is also a teacher, and the point Douglass is making about the relation of logic and rhetoric, of argument and persuasion, has pedagogical implications for the multicultural literature classroom in general and for the discussion of race in particular. Douglass's rhetorical dilemma is shaped by what W. E. B. Du Bois would later famously characterize as the doubleness of African American identity, a sense of both belonging to and yet also standing as the antithesis to a dominant, Euro-centered American culture (Du Bois 8–9). The teacher in the multicultural classroom also encounters a question of doubleness relating to the perceived connections or disconnections between the diverse texts being taught and the instructor, between the students and the texts, and between the students and the teacher. This doubleness is nowhere more fraught with tension, but as a result also nowhere more important to confront, than in the matter of race. In this essay, I wish to argue for an approach to pedagogy I call "cultural rhetoric" as a means both of framing the analysis of race and ethnicity in the classroom and of understanding the roles pedagogy and the teaching of American literature itself play in the reification or resistance to constructions of race and racial oppression.

I first need to clarify my use of the term "rhetoric," a notoriously ambiguous term, both in denotation and connotation. An older, more institutionally traditional sense of the word calls to mind either conventional composition classes in "persuasive" writing or the scholarly study and compilation of forms and tropes, often using the classification systems developed by the great classical rhetoricians. From such a formalist perspective, the speech acts that Douglass places under scrutiny—"argue" and "denounce," "persuade" and "rebuke"— can and should be defined according to specific sets of formulae, devices, and tropes, each clearly discernible from the others and each in a sense transhistorical, so that a rebuke in ancient Athens can be understood as essentially the same phenomenon as in early nineteenth-century America. Over the last twenty years, however, "rhetoric" has been revived, transformed, and modified by developments in both composition and literary theory. No single new consensus definition has emerged, but my own use of the term follows those theorists who use it to refer to the study of language as social action rather than static construct. This is a poststructuralist view of rhetoric based on (1) an understanding of linguistic and other sign systems as both constitutive as well as expressive of human desires and ideas and (2) the deconstruction of the opposition between the individual and the social, between "personal" meanings and the linguistic code used to convey those meanings. Such a perspective starts from the proposition by M. M. Bakhtin that "verbal discourse is a social phenomenon—social throughout its entire range and in each and every of its factors, from the sound image to the furthest reaches of abstract meaning" (259).

The stress here is on language use as an activity, as a form of what Jane Tompkins calls "cultural work." Thus, such an approach focuses on intention and strategy in the analysis of language uses, but not in the sense of regarding language as simply a neutral tool used by a given speaker or writer to achieve certain predefined ends. Again, as Bakhtin puts it:

> There are no "neutral" words and forms—words and forms that belong to "no one"; language has been completely taken over, shot through with intentions and accents. For any individual consciousness living in it, language is not an abstract system of normative forms but rather a concrete heteroglot conception of the world. All words have the "taste" of a profession, a genre, a tendency, a party, a particular work, a particular person, a generation, an age group, the day and hour. Each word tastes of the context and contexts in which it has lived its socially charged life; all words and forms are populated by intentions. (293)

For Bakhtin, then, "As a living, socio-ideological concrete thing, as heteroglot opinion, language, for the individual consciousness, lies on the borderline between oneself and the other" (293). As we shape language, language shapes us in a dialectical process that is inherently social, diverse, and dynamic. Composition, whether we mean the encoding process we call writing or the decoding process we call reading, thus involves negotiation and conflict among what Gregory Jay refers to as "heterogeneous representational forces" ("American"

240). As a result, every speech act invokes not just the particular intentions and meanings of a single individual but the entire network of socially constructed values, identities, and world views we call ideology. The complex interplay of specific speech acts with the socially-constituted systems of linguistic meaning thus serves as the site of ideological conflict and transformation. As Terry Eagleton defines it, rhetoric refers to "grasping language and action in the context of the politico-discursive conditions inscribed within them" (168). Rhetoric in this sense means the active discursive manifestation and transformation of ideology.

A cultural rhetoric approach helps us to understand how the rhetorical frustrations Douglass expresses in his speech derive from ideological frustrations over the social construction of racial identity. The quote from Douglass above leads into a section where he works to expose for his audience the contradiction between the racial logic used to dehumanize the slaves ideologically and the judicial logic informing the slave laws used to maintain the practice of slave labor:

> Must I undertake to prove that the slave is a man? That point is conceded already. Nobody doubts it. The slaveholders themselves acknowledge it in the enactment of law, for their government. They acknowledge it when they punish disobedience on the part of the slave . . . . What is this but the acknowledgment that the slave is a moral, intellectual and responsible being? (369)

The legal apparatus of slavery excludes slaves from the body politic on the basis of a cultural belief system that excludes the slave from the category of "human." Yet, that very same legal structure includes sanctions on slave behavior dependent on the inclusion of slaves in the categorical definition of humanity. However, simply pointing out this seeming problem in logic is not to solve it; indeed, part of Douglass's point is that he is telling—or teaching, to reinforce the connection with pedagogy—his audience nothing new. ("That point is conceded already.") The problem is not one of insufficient knowledge but of repressed knowledge; more specifically, the problem lies at the connection between knowledge and power. The "truth" of black inferiority does not provide the foundation in reality for the erection of a system of slave labor; instead, the desire to maintain an oppressive social system drives the construction of racial identity. The construction of racial identity and racist thought is not a "mistake" easily corrected through better reasoning but a motivated rhetorical activity. Douglass's problem is, as a result, deeply rhetorical, rhetorical in the cultural sense, in that it hinges on the discursive processes of ideological maintenance and transformation. Systems of "logic" are themselves implicated in these discursive structures. Thus, Douglass collapses the distinctions between arguing and denouncing, persuasion and rebuke, "logic" and "emotion" and asserts that "At a time like this, scorching irony, not convincing argument, is needed" (371).

As Gregory S. Jay points out, however, Douglass's use of irony is not simply a function of language narrowly defined but is a component part of the entire performative context of Douglass's public appearances:

> As a speaking subject, Douglass constantly trades on the shock value of his eloquent literacy, on the *irony* of his appearance and speech. Dialectically, one cannot *understand* Douglass without recognizing his humanity, and to recognize his humanity is to transform the history and category of the "human" as his era conceives it. ("American" 241, emphases his)

As a result, there is no part of Douglass's performance or his argument which is not rhetorical in the cultural sense, both implicated in and transformative of socio-ideological constructions of race, humanity, logic, and justice. The terms "implication and transformation" are crucial, because in this speech Douglass both invokes a given sense of what humanity means to his audience ("moral, intellectual and responsible being") and attempts a total transformation of that sense. In the words of Valerie Smith, "Douglass . . . attempts to articulate a radical position using the discourse he shares with those against whom he speaks" (27). Smith also describes the dangers of this approach in her critique of Douglass's use of the rhetoric of the "self-made man" in his autobiography: "What begins as an indictment of mainstream practice actually authenticates one of its fundamental assumptions" (27). As Bakhtin points out, however, Douglass has no choice but to face these dangers, for he has available to him no discursive tradition and no language not already "shot through with intentions and accents." Any language he uses brings with it a complex and conflicted ideological history. Rhetoric involves not so much controlling as negotiating among these socio-ideological forces.

In deconstructing the logic of race slavery in order to assert the humanity of African Americans, for example, Douglass has to consider in what ways such an argument might potentially also reinscribe, simply through reference to them, the very categories of race that not only justify race slavery but that also reinforce the sense of social complacency and security certain members of his audience may feel in their "white" identity, whatever their personal attitudes about abolition may be. At the same time, the "scorching irony" produced by the entirety of his rhetorical performance threatens that complacency and thus risks alienating his audience by suggesting the instability of racial and even human identity. In her reading of Douglass's speech, Priscilla Wald argues that by foregrounding the reality of his disenfranchisement and contrasting it with his (self) evident humanity, Douglass brings about an anxious recognition in his white audience that the rights supposedly recognized by the government as "inalienable" and "self-evident" are in fact subject to government conferral and modification:

> Embodying the alienability of natural rights—and the consequent denial
> of his personhood defined by those rights—the disenfranchised pointed to
> the power of government to violate its sacred trust. The bestowal of citi-
> zenship and protection of liberties that were the recognized tasks of the
> law seemed to collapse into a *conferral* of personhood from which even a
> white native-born American man might well worry that he may one day be
> excluded as other groups were already excluded. (19)

This may well be a lesson his audience might not want to learn.

Douglass's self-reflexive consideration of his speech as rhetorical speech
act suggests that the pedagogical implications of the rhetorical approach I am
advocating here go beyond simply another version of textual analysis to a consideration of the rhetorical dimension of the pedagogical act itself, along with
the disciplinary and institutional structures which form the context for pedagogical performance. This self reflexivity is especially crucial in terms of teaching the rhetoric of race and ethnicity. If we regard race and ethnicity themselves
as rhetorical rather than absolute constructs—that is, as context-specific discursive practices operating within larger ideological frameworks—then race and
ethnicity become no longer issues of outside themes that we then bring to the
study of literature, but constitutive elements of the institutional study of literature. To teach literature is to engage in the construction of and critique of race
and ethnicity. By extension, as Wald makes clear, such an activity deals with
our and our students' most deeply-held beliefs and anxieties about our own
identities and social status, thus forcing a conscious awareness of our collective
implication in the construction and reproduction of a system of racial identity
and privilege that some may wish to keep repressed.

The academic study of American literature has from (before) the beginning
always already been a part of the larger ideological project of the construction
of a specifically racial/ethnic national identity, as David Shumway extensively
and persuasively documents in his *Creating American Civilization* (see also
Lauter). At the end of that work, Shumway considers various proposals to counter
these traditional discursive constructions of national racial identity. While
Shumway makes various critiques of such programs on theoretical grounds, his
main reservations seem, not surprisingly, to be more practical: the difficulty,
unlikeliness, and therefore undesirability of waiting for large-scale institutional
change; that is, a radicalizing of the entire disciplinary or university structure
(Shumway 345–59).

I certainly do not wish to argue against the drafting of long-term, radical,
and theoretically comprehensive manifestos for such change; indeed, such intellectual work is crucial if multiculturalism means to be more than another
version of curricular reform. But the rhetorical approach I am suggesting here—
the emphasis on pedagogy as provisional, strategic action conducted in the

context of larger ideological contests—serves as a way of following Douglass's example of considering the relation of the particular discursive act to these larger activist programs.

Again, by discursive act, I mean not just the texts listed on the syllabus but the entire pedagogical context, including the placing of the text on a syllabus, the very use of a syllabus and the pedagogical conventions implied by such a document, the assignment of the text and assignments related to the text, the demographics of the classroom, the institutional site of instruction, and so forth. If a certain version of poststructuralism questions the distinction between text and commentary, between "primary" and "secondary" texts, then that questioning extends to the classroom as well, where from the rhetorical perspective I am suggesting here, "teaching" the text is not supplementary to but a constitutive part of the "text" itself. For example, if I have assigned Douglass's speech in a literature class, the textual experience of the students, the experience relevant to the rhetorical analysis I propose, consists of Douglass's written text, those portions of the text I highlight as "significant" and therefore worthy of close attention, my pedagogical commentary on these significant passages, the institutional, historical, and social context, the reactions and commentaries of other students, as well as Douglass's text as material object—whether it is read in an anthology of "American" literature, African American literature, Great Speeches of the Nineteenth Century, or a photocopied duplicate.

Such an approach offers an important perspective on the rightfully vexed question of who can teach what, or the propriety and politics of non-minority faculty studying and teaching minority literature. This question involves important issues of appropriation, assimilation, and colonization, as it should. The question of which of these issues might apply—or, perhaps more accurately, the degrees to which they apply to my teaching of the Douglass text—can be addressed by asking the "rhetorical" questions of teaching: What? To whom? Where? For what purpose?

Sometimes teachers identified with or identifying themselves as "non-minority" will ask the question, "Can I teach Frederick Douglass?" in order, on some level at least, to receive blanket permission to do so. However, the most helpful answer to this question might be, "So who's stopping you." The problems with blanket permission are many, but perhaps the most relevant is that the desire for such permission can obviate the need for the ideological analysis of the particular rhetorical situation. Let me give you an example of such an analysis of my experience teaching "What to the Slave Is the Fourth of July?"

I might begin by describing my class to you, but such a description is already part of the process of analysis, not preliminary to it. I could also begin with historical context and argue that one reason for my teaching the Douglass text is that we have no African American faculty in our department—indeed, we have fewer than ten African American faculty at the entire university. In other words, if non-African American faculty don't teach African American literature, it might not get taught. An analysis of the cultural rhetorical situation, however, demands more than just a static explanation; indeed, the explanation itself is a rhetorical act. Am I telling you about the state of minority hiring at my school in order to excuse myself, for example, or perhaps to demonstrate my sensitive awareness of the poor progress of affirmative action in my department? The answers to these questions—or even the asking of them—are ultimately more useful to me than you, for they force me to consider my pedagogy as discursive action. Is my teaching African American literature compensating for and thus exacerbating our problems in hiring practice, or is it part of an effort to push those problems toward a critical mass? The attempts to answer these questions move me from seeking justification in some absolute, ahistorical sense to considering the relation of these particular pedagogical actions to larger scholarly and activist goals.

Above, I used the term "white-identifying" deliberately, because such a phrase focuses further attention on my description of the pedagogical situation in ways similar to Douglass's concerns above. Let's say I describe my classes as largely white, with one or two "non-white"—usually African American—students per class. Such a statement I would regard as true, but certainly not neutral. As the example of Douglass demonstrates, by describing the racial identity of my students I am in some crucial sense reifying discursively those identities. Consider the implications for the not uncommon pedagogical question a teacher like myself might ask in such a situation: How do I make sure that black students feel welcome in my class, or that they don't feel marginalized? But such questions of course already presuppose racial identities, and, what's more, some kind of racial solidarity between me and the "white" students in class from which other students might feel alienated. In short, by asking the question in the way I've asked it, I've already obviated the possibility of answering it.

This is not to suggest, however, some naive color-blind approach to the classroom, e.g., I'll just pretend there's no such thing as race.[1] After all, another, properly rhetorical answer to the question "How do I make sure that black students don't feel marginalized?" is to ask "What country are *you* living in to think that deeply ingrained social structures of racial marginalization can be left at the classroom door?" Regardless of how I may identify my students, as soon as I walk into the classroom the first day of class many if not all begin identifying me right away as "white," and it is this social dimension of racial identification that matters most, that is most the concern of a cultural rhetorical approach. As Douglass is pointing out—or at least, as he is pointing out in the rhetorical uses to which I am putting his text—race is rhetorical, not determined by logic, but precedent to and determinative of a certain kind of logic.

Racial identification is a discursive, rhetorical action that occurs over and over again every day in American society, in ways both repressive and resistant, reactionary and radical.

Thus, rhetoric can describe not only the act but also the goal of pedagogy, a pedagogy that through the awareness of its own use of cultural rhetoric encourages or even requires the same awareness in students, just as Douglass's speech can be read as demanding recognition not only of his own humanity but also of the provisional, politically dependent nature of his audience's humanity. If the only way to erase black marginality is by the total transformation of the racially-based social order, then a key element of that transformation is discursive. The development of cultural rhetorical awareness can be effected through the deconstruction of racial identity, through the defusion of marginality by destabilizing the discursive foundation of racial identity. But, as the vexed example of Douglass also shows, such a project also entails constructing an understanding of the forces motivating a desire to maintain reified social identities, to repress awareness of the way our own discursively-constructed identities are "shot through with intentions and accents."

I've begun American literature classes, for example, by problematizing my own racial identity in rhetorical terms as a way of introducing the larger question of how we in fact "know" our racial identities. In discussing both the instability and the power of categories of racial, gender, and class identities, I ask the class to think about what categories they placed me in as soon as I walked into the room. If they saw me, as many do, as a "white man" (the more popular media term is now "white male"), on what basis did they make that determination? My strategy, of course, is to ask what seems like a stupid question, exploiting my authority as professor to foster suspicion, skepticism, and perhaps a little bit of anxiety. In a series of deliberately rhetorical questions consciously patterned after Douglass, I problematize various ways one might answer my question through appeals to some objective or self-evident reality by pointing to the variability and therefore instability of the body itself (whether through the vagaries of genetic mutation; the violence of disease, accident, or surgery; or the evolution and revolution of the discursive systems that constitute our naming and thus understanding of the body).

Again, my purpose is not simply to deny my white or male identity, or even to take a vote on it, but to focus on the social, discursive, and rhetorical dimensions of that identity, and of *all* racial, gender, and class identity. My lecture (for that's what it is) is deliberately provocative, but its provocativeness is based on the rhetorical point made by Douglass: that no matter how much I protest against racial classification, such protest occurs in the rhetorical context of the viewers' gaze, a gaze I know already traps me into a racial identity. This gaze is a source of power for the audience, but it is a power that traps and inscribes them as well. If one of the purposes of Douglass's text was to open up for his audience the discursive practices that constitute the ideology of humanity for his audience, then one of my purposes is not so much to deny as to resist white identity, and in particular, to resist the building of community between me and my students on the basis of racial solidarity.

It's important to keep in mind that I offer this example not as a universally useful exercise or goal but as a highly contingent strategy. The building of community on the basis of racial solidarity can be, as we know, a powerful act of resistance; but not all acts of racial solidarity are equal, nor are all the contexts in which individual racial identity is constructed. Jay, for example, describes a very different rhetorical situation when he discusses his experiences at the University of Alabama in the early 1980s, teaching Douglass in classes more integrated than mine and finding himself in the absurd situation of being a "white" instructor teaching African American students about race in America in a school only recently desegregated ("The End" 16). Nor should my teaching strategies become compensatory in the sense of lessening the pressure to diversify our faculty; indeed, the cultural rhetorical approach emphasizes the rhetorical dimension of affirmative action: the powerful statement made not just by a stated commitment to affirmative action but also by the hiring of African American, women, and minority faculty.

It could still be objected, though, that my strategy of racial distancing, of seeking to subvert white racial solidarity between myself and the class, could work as a gesture of denial, a means of declaring myself "white, but not white like them," therefore abdicating my responsibility as role model for students who would potentially identify with me. For example, I've had a white female student ask me for my reaction "as a white male" to affirmative action. In this case it could be argued, and in fact I would agree, her racial and gender classification of me created a rhetorical space to make a reply against type, indicating support for rather than fear of racial and gender equality. And this is in fact what I did, but I was still troubled by the sense in which it is the very reification of racial and gender identity (and concomitant suppression of class identity) that exacerbates what is now tiresomely and obsessively referred to as "white male anger."

Clearly, the discursive creation of identity involves a process of identification, both the determination of who I am and who you are, and who is part of my group and who isn't. There's not enough space here to enter into a lengthy discussion of identity politics, except to stress that the cultural rhetoric approach suggests a strategic rather than absolute use of the politics of identity, a use based on the instability of the discourse of identity, an instability tied to variability of context. This strategic use of the instability of racial identity can be used to investigate the connections between knowledge and power, connections that inform the rhetoric of race by getting at the anxiety over social status described above by Wald. Such a discussion moves the question of slavery out of the category of historical curiosity, making it part of an ongoing socio-ideological discursive struggle over identity and power.

One component of this strategy in the context of Douglass is to examine student reactions to his texts in terms of the difference between identity and sympathy. Many white-identifying students in my classes will, in journal responses, express sympathy and often admiration for Douglass, but less often a sense of identity. Douglass refers to this distinction between sympathy and identity, or rather, we can use Douglass's works to explore this distinction through consideration of the title of the first version of his autobiography (or maybe the first of his autobiographies): *Narrative of the Life of Frederick Douglass, an American Slave.* We can construct easily enough an ideological contradiction operating in the epithet, "American Slave," but we can push this contradiction beyond the opposition between America as simultaneously land of the free and land of bondage to the term "slave" itself, and in particular the absent term of opposition that would define that term: slave as opposed to what? Many will suggest "free" in an abstract political sense, but how does that translate into the specific social and historical context of Douglass's rhetorical situation? According to Ann Kibbey and Michele Stepto, for example, "Precisely because Douglass always felt himself subject to the economic and social conditions in which he lived, he defines freedom . . . as something achieved at a particular place and time, within a particular economic and social structure, and not as a sheer act of personal will by an isolated individual in defiance of his circumstances" (168). Freedom, in other words, always operates in Douglass's text in a rhetorical sense; from the perspective of cultural rhetoric, such a reading does not so much designate a unique feature of Douglass's work as it does a recognition of the inevitable social history of the term, a history that suggests that any definition of freedom is "something achieved at a particular time and place, within a particular economic and social structure."

For pedagogical purposes, the rhetorical approach to the discussion of what freedom means in Frederick Douglass involves strategic questions concerning the socio-ideological context within which we choose to frame that discussion, a choice inextricably linked to the exigencies of the particular pedagogical context. In my own situation, again, as I construct the demographic context, I teach largely all white-identifying classes. Many of the students are working class to lower-middle class, most work full- or part-time to finance their educations, many are first-generation college students, and about forty percent are "nontraditional," that is, over the age of twenty-five. Given the critical emphasis many of the students (and the institution as well, in its official pronouncements) make between their education and their economic futures, I often take the cue presented by the term "American Slave" to discuss "freedom" in the economic context of slavery as a particular system of labor exploitation by asking what the difference is between a slave and a worker (or, as Herman Melville puts it in

Moby-Dick, "Who aint a slave?" [6]). Such a seemingly simple question can lead to a deeper consideration of the ideological arguments over this question that served as the discursive matrix within which the historical struggle against slavery took place, and which connect that struggle with larger arguments over the transformation of labor within the development of industrial capitalism. (We alter the context for class discussion in interesting ways, for example, by pointing out that while Douglass was a contemporary of Lincoln, both were contemporaries of Marx as well.)

In fact, many reactionary antebellum defenders of slavery tried to co-opt radical analyses about capitalist labor exploitation in order to construct an argument contrasting a supposedly paternalistic system of chattel slavery with a cold and heartless Northern system of "wage slavery." To co-opt is not to contain, however, and such arguments also inadvertently revealed the historical connections between the development of racist ideology in the South and the desire to obviate the formation of class solidarity among African and European laborers. (See especially Zinn and Morgan on the formation of systems of hereditary racial slavery in seventeenth-century Virginia.) More pointedly, such a rhetorical tack, focusing on the relative merits of chattel and wage slavery, threatens to unhinge that racist ideology, a point Wald argues that Douglass seizes on in his Fourth of July speech: "What, he asks implicitly, keeps the government from making white men slaves?" (89). In fact, one of the most notorious defenders of slavery, George Fitzhugh, made this implicit question explicit by arguing that slavery should not be solely based on race, but that the "benefits" of being slaves should be extended to poor whites as well. At this point, for the white-identifying student, Douglass in particular and slaves in general are not so comfortably "Other," and thus are not simply objects of sympathy and pity (as well as sources of hostility and defensiveness over imputations of guilt for supposedly "past" injustices).

Some instructors might worry that all this sounds like going far afield from the Douglass text, but such a worry stems from thinking of the text as an autonomous verbal icon and not, as I have been arguing, a rhetorical construct implicated and interwoven within larger socio-ideological discursive structures. These larger structures, however, are only manifested in particular texts. The relationship, in other words, is dialectic and not derivative. There is not a separate, static ideological world the texts draw on for material; ideologies are always constructed, reproduced, and transformed in particular, motivated rhetorical acts we call texts. As a result, such an approach never properly takes us "away" from or "outside" of the text. Douglass's story in the *Narrative*, for example, of the conflict he experienced as an African American slave working alongside immigrant Irish carpenters in Baltimore is not a tale of racist brutality "informed" by the kinds of rhetorical ideological maneuvers over the relations of slavery, labor, and race outlined above; rather, it is itself one such maneuver.

Similarly, as I have argued, our pedagogical practice is also implicated in the process of socio-ideological formation. I have argued here about the need to resist the formation of racial solidarity on the basis of whiteness in the classroom, but a rhetorical strategy aimed at resisting a certain kind of solidarity at the same time creates a kind of discursive pressure to construct solidarity differently, and again Douglass's Fourth of July speech serves as strategic evidence. The speech, both in its title and its initial delivery on the fifth of July, deliberately foregrounds the Fourth of July as the ideological enterprise in the formation of nationalist identity it was and is, an enterprise forming that identity along racial lines and a process that Douglass wishes to interrupt and to redefine, both by claiming for himself and other African Americans the right to participate in this enterprise and by laying out the conditions through which such an identity may—and may not—be constructed. Douglass's discursive deconstructions of the concepts of whiteness and of the Enlightenment concept of humanity rhetorically insert themselves between the desire of white-identifying listeners and readers to respond with a sympathy that maintains racial reification and the necessity to reconfigure personal and therefore social identity. Similarly, the teaching of Douglass's text in my classroom is part of a rhetorical strategy to problematize identity as a way of reconstructing identity, whether around constructions of social class or around our common situation and situatedness as rhetorical actors, both shaping and shaped by discursive ideological practices.

In *Playing in the Dark*, Toni Morrison's collection of essays based on another explicitly rhetorical performance, her delivery of the William E. Massey Sr. Lectures in the History of American Civilization at Harvard University in 1990, she addresses the necessity of confronting the rhetorical dimension of the construction of race:

> Race has become metaphorical—a way of referring to and disguising forces, events, classes, and expressions of social decay and economic division far more threatening to the body politic than biological "race" ever was. Expensively kept, economically unsound, a spurious and useless political asset in election campaigns, racism is as healthy today as it was during the Enlightenment. It seems that it has . . . assumed a metaphorical life so completely embedded in daily discourse that it is perhaps more necessary and more on display than ever before. (63)

My purpose in this paper has been to follow the leads of both Douglass and Morrison in considering what the rhetorical dimension of the construction of race has to offer to the construction of multicultural pedagogy, and to argue that one way to resist the dilution of multiculturalism into a harmless pluralism or worse, simply a marketing strategy, is to see the multicultural project itself as inherently rhetorical, as a discursive action aimed at the reconstruction of ideology. As both Bakhtin and Douglass teach us, neutrality is not an option.

Note

1. For a discussion of how supposedly "color blind" pedagogical practices can actually reinforce racism by refusing to address the connections between race and privilege, see Sleeter.

Works Cited

Bakhtin, M. M. *The Dialogic Imagination: Four Essays*. Trans. Caryl Emerson and Michael Holquist. Austin: U of Texas P, 1981.

Douglass, Frederick. *Narrative of the Life of Frederick Douglass, An American Slave*. Cambridge: Belknap P of Harvard UP, 1988.

———. "What to the Slave Is the Fourth of July?" *The Frederick Douglass Papers*. Series One. Volume Two. New Haven: Yale UP, 1982. 359–88.

Du Bois, W. E. B. *The Souls of Black Folk*. New York: Library of America, 1990.

Eagleton, Terry. *Against the Grain: Essays 1975–1985*. London: Verso, 1986.

Fitzhugh, George. "Southern Thought." *The Heath Anthology of American Literature*. Ed. Paul Lauter. 2nd Edition. Vol. 1. Boston: D. C. Heath, 1994. 1913–922.

Jay, Gregory S. "American Literature and the New Historicism: The Example of Frederick Douglass." *boundary* 2.17 (1990): 211–42.

———. "The End of 'American' Literature: Toward a Multicultural Practice." *The Canon in the Classroom: The Pedagogical Implications of Canon Revision in American Literature*. Ed. John Alberti. New York: Garland, 1995. 3–28.

Kibbey, Ann and Michele Stepto, "The Antilanguage of Slavery: Frederick Douglass's 1845 *Narrative*." *Critical Essays on Frederick Douglass*. Ed. William L. Andrews. Boston: G. K. Hall, 1991. 166–91.

Lauter, Paul. *Canons and Contexts*. New York: Oxford UP, 1991.

Melville, Herman. *Moby-Dick*. Evanston and Chicago: Northwestern UP and the Newberry Library, 1988.

Morgan, Edmund. *American Slavery, American Freedom: The Ordeal of Colonial Virginia*. New York: W. W. Norton, 1975.

Morrison, Toni. *Playing in the Dark: Whiteness and the Literary Imagination*. New York: Vintage Books, 1993.

Shumway, David R. *Creating American Civilization: A Genealogy of American Literature as an Academic Discipline*. Minneapolis: U of Minnesota P, 1994.

Sleeter, Christine E. "How White Teachers Construct Race." *Race, Identity, and Representation in Education*. Ed. Cameron McCarthy and Warren Crichlow. New York: Routledge, 1993. 157–171.

Smith, Valerie. *Self-Discovery and Authority in Afro-American Narrative*. Cambridge: Harvard UP, 1987.

Tompkins, Jane. *Sensational Designs: The Cultural Work of American Fiction*. New York: Oxford UP, 1985.

Wald, Priscilla. *Constituting Americans: Cultural Anxiety and Narrative Form*. Durham: Duke UP, 1995.

Zinn, Howard. *A People's History of the United States*. New York: HarperPerennial, 1980.

14 Homeless in the Golden Land: Joan Didion's Regionalism

Louise Z. Smith
University of Massachusetts–Boston

Not in the least an Americanist, I will prudently not rush into unfamiliar regions of this volume's conversation. Americanists may debate the definitions and the literary history of "realism," "regionalism," and "local color," but I will not. I will trust Judith Fetterley's "treasonous" assertions that "regionalism [is] a fiction characterized, indeed inspired, by empathy" but that realism, particularly "local color" writing, "ratifies the hegemony of the 'national' as a standard against which the local can be measured and found wanting[,]" found "quaint or queer" or freaky (889–890). "[E]mpathy primarily as a model of the relationships of 'persons' with differing amounts of cultural power" (890) lies near the heart of hermeneutics, a region where I feel more at home. Empathy is one element of the "understanding" that Hans Georg Gadamer calls the "fusion of horizons." Knowing that readers cannot transplant themselves from their present into someone else's present, let alone past, he urges

> *not covering up this tension* [between a text and each reader's present] by attempting a naive assimilation but *consciously bringing it out.* . . . Historical consciousness is aware of its own *otherness* and hence *distinguishes* the horizon of tradition from its own. (273, my italics)

In other words, through empathy one can recognize and to some extent understand the "other" without trying to erase, elevate, or subordinate it.

Empathy also undergirds the bridges of reception study, what Gadamer's student Hans Robert Jauss calls *Rezeptionsästhetik*, linking two "regions" of interpretation: literary and cultural. In both these regions, "rational certainty" is not a matter of mirror accuracy but of "conversation between persons" leading to "edification," that is, leading to "new, better, more interesting, more fruitful ways of speaking" about connections between our own culture and a distant ("exotic") culture or historical period and about connections between seemingly incommensurable disciplines and vocabularies (Rorty 156–57, 360). Even if some Americanists dispute Fetterley's use of "regionalism" to mean "empathy," they may accept the basic idea that rhetorical hermeneutics—the analysis of the tropes various communities of interpreters use and of how they use them, that is, of what "counts" as a significant and persuasive interpretation—links the interpretation of literature with the interpretation of cultural conventions (Mailloux 167–70). You can't have rhetoricity without empathy. A genre well suited to expressing empathy, says Fetterley, is the sketch, which makes it possible to tell stories about "elderly women with bristling chins," each of whom turns out to be not a "freak" but a "neighbor with a story and a secret and feelings," who lives "a ritualized and sacramental life" in a "world elsewhere" (884–87). So, I believe, does that other marginalized genre: the essay.

"Regionalism" and Reception Theory

Though Joan Didion's prose—flinty in detail, spare in commentary—may not spring to mind as a fount of empathy, I want to look at the "world elsewhere" in "On Going Home." Since the *Norton Reader*'s second edition (1969) included it, the essay has remained a staple of college composition anthologies (for example William Smart's *Eight Modern Essayists* [5th ed., 1990] and Janet Marting's *The Voice of Reflection* [1995]). "Home" in this essay is a region: geographically Sacramento rather than Los Angeles; psychologically a terrain for "guerrilla warfare" between generations who, nevertheless, join ranks as "we" against "Joan's husband"; historically a moment from which to see "other" Californias in 1954, 1910, 1900, and 1846. Didion was born in 1934 and published "On Going Home" in 1967. The essay is now older than many of its student readers, more and more of whom, as commuting students, have not yet left home. In 1997, they cannot live through their readings of this essay as their elders did back then nor as we may today, through memory. The "baby" to whom Didion couldn't give "*home* for her birthday" is now in her thirties, and late '60s apocalypse has given way to the *fin de siècle*. The essay's explicit literary allusions—"the question of whether or not you could go home again" echoing the title of Thomas Wolfe's 1940 novel, the question of what sense a young girl "in an 'amateur-topless' contest" could "possibly make of, say, *Long Day's Journey Into Night*" (1955)—are addressed to "those of us who are in our 30's now," in 1967. To "us" these titles had "the effect of 'romantic degradation' for which my generation strived so assiduously." But for younger readers, the *Norton Reader*'s seventh edition (1988) began to footnote the play as "a powerful domestic tragedy" (70); to young readers in 1997, the titles are obscure, their "romantic degradation" quaint. Today's textbooks seldom invoke the regional. Instead, psychologically oriented reader-response questions accompany this and other frequently anthologized essays by Didion (like "Dreamers of the Golden Dream" and "On Keeping a Notebook"). Such questions focus on intergenerational themes in one's own family, on one's own processes of leaving home or not, returning or not, on comparing one's own family rituals to those of Didion's family, on explaining why one sympathizes with Didion or her husband or her brother. Formal and psychological reader response seldom engages readers with regions beyond their own classrooms or with historical moments preceding their own in a work's reception.

Yet "America" changes. When Didion wrote "On Going Home," Paul Simon and Art Garfunkel sang of "Counting the cars / On the New Jersey turnpike, / They've all come to look for America" ("America"). But the nationally televised June 17, 1994, police pursuit of O. J. Simpson in his white Ford Bronco down the L. A. freeway strikes Sonia Maasik and Jack Solomon, editors of the textbook *California Dreams and Realities* (1995), as a "peculiarly Californian drama," what Fetterley (after Baym) terms a story of "beset manhood" (879). The editors ask,

> Which better reflects the truth behind the California dream: the self-invented celebrity who climbed from poverty to the summit of fame and fortune or the emerging image of a man driven by violence . . . . If the California dream totters, can the American dream be far behind? (1)

As one "myth" of California, they select Didion's "Notes from a Native Daughter" (1965), a more explicit account than "On Going Home" of why Sacramento, rather than L.A. and San Francisco, "*is* California" (19). Both essays (and others by Didion) recreate a "ritualized and sacramental life" in a "world elsewhere."

Worlds elsewhere always refer to worlds here. As "here" changes, so do they. Reception theory examines these contrasts in two ways: by describing "the historical moment of the work's appearance," and by reconstructing its original readers' "pre-understanding of its genre from the form and themes of already familiar works" (Jauss 23). By reconstructing "the horizons of expectations in the face of which a work was created and received in the past," scholars can both discover "how the contemporary reader *could* have viewed and understood the work" and examine the interaction of that reader's understanding with our own (Jauss 28–29, my italics). We need to examine several moments ("the synchronic cross-section of the literary production of a historical point in time necessarily implies further cross-sections before and after" [38]), but there are historical reasons why we should not take the scientific-sounding term "cross-section" too literally (Smith "Beyond"). Readers "here" can never know precisely, but can more or less understand empathically, what readers "elsewhere" expected or how they responded. Nor are historical "periods" completely distinct; indeed, anachronism is both inevitable and useful in teaching (McGillivray; Smith "In Search"). Using reception theory, we can ask about the regionalism in "On Going Home," about the kinds of empathy—of community and of genre— the essay embodies, about what kinds of cultural work the essay did for its original readers and for others since then, and about what inviting today's students to read it may mean.

Readers "from places like Toronto" and Other Regions

The New York Times Magazine, The American Scholar, Holiday, and *Vogue* had published Didion's earlier work, but none of them published "On Going Home." Nor did *The Nation* (to whose rejection letter the essay refers). With this essay, *The Saturday Evening Post* inaugurated

> a new feature, "Points West"—a column of commentary from the Los Angeles vantage point of John Gregory Dunne and his wife, Joan Didion. Dunne, 35, a former *Time* editor, has written for the *Post* on such diverse subjects as baseball, race riots, and the struggles of a labor organizer [Cesar Chavez]. Joan, a novelist (*Run River*) has reported from New York to Hawaii on murder, lost love, and Christmas puddings. (240 [June 3, 1967]:3)

How sweet. Notwithstanding Betty Friedan's *The Feminine Mystique* (1963), the *Post*'s editors still cheerfully inhabited a region where the serious male journalist of articles on manhood "beset" in sports, politics, and business had a surname but "his wife," who wrote of melodramatic and sentimental affairs (her novel *Run River* [1963] was about adultery and murder in a California family) could be called "Joan." Biographical commentaries relating the couple's collaboration on "Points West" to the shaky mental and physical condition in which Didion had recently moved with Dunne from New York to California (Henderson 1–16; Winchell) only return us to psychological regions. If instead we ask about readers' expectations, we find that Didion recognized at least two distinct audiences. As she reflected the year after "On Going Home" first appeared, some readers who knew her earlier work were shocked to find her publishing in the *Saturday Evening Post*:

> Quite often people write me from places like Toronto and want to know (demand to know) how I can reconcile my conscience with writing for *The Saturday Evening Post*; the answer is quite simple. The *Post* is extremely receptive to what the writer wants to do, pays enough for him [*sic*] to be able to do it right, and is meticulous about not changing copy. (*Slouching*, xii–xiii)

What was there about the *Post* that some readers expected to be at odds with Didion's "conscience"? Her phrase "places like Toronto" evokes what Fetterley would call a "nationalist" frame of mind, one in which urbane, high-brow readers see themselves as central and normative—"here." "Elsewhere," we might infer, there are "places like Sacramento" where small town, middle-browed readers (even Fetterley's "elderly women with bristling chins") see their reflections in Norman Rockwell's *Post* covers. Yet Didion publishes in the *Post* for squarely middle-class reasons: the pay is good, she picks her own subjects, and they leave her prose alone. Autonomy—financial and editorial—means more to her than political or class alliances do, and she expects readers of *Slouching*

Towards Bethlehem to understand that. But since "Toronto" readers in 1967
had no way of knowing the explanation Didion would give in 1968, reception
theory tells us simply to register their moral indignation both with authors who
publish in the *Post* and, implicitly, with its readers.

What of those "Sacramento" readers? Some of them undoubtedly read the
same things as "Toronto" readers. Didion's short story "Coming Home" began
with this epigraph:

> Folks just get a yearning sometimes to go back home again to the empty
> room, settle down with a bottle of Pernod and a few phenobarbs, and start
> a good quarrel. (*Saturday Evening Post* 237 [July 11, 1964]: 50)

That's not "Sacramento" but indeed New York, where in "Coming Home" two
ad writers who are married to each other bicker about how her work in California keeps them apart, who pays for her dress from Bendel, his apparent affair in
her absence, and his not wanting the baby they're expecting (whom she imagines will resemble not its parents but the Beech-Nut baby in the ad she tacks up
beside her bed). The story's romantic watercolor illustration shows a wistful
young woman brushing her long hair; vintage *Ladies' Home Journal*, it bears
little relation to the young wife's feeling of "pointlessness so keen that it verged
upon despair" (52). Psychological reader-response would note that this story's
conflict between career and domesticity reflects Didion's own at this period.
Reception theory, though, draws our attention to surprises ("negations") of readers' expectations: in 1963 *The Feminine Mystique* and in its wake "Coming
Home" in 1964, heralded radical feminism's attack on Rockwellian values in
the 1970s, and perhaps not incidentally, the *Post*'s demise in 1969. If Didion's
publishing in the *Post* surprised "Torontons," then "Pernod and phenobarbs"
surprised "Sacramentons."

What did "Torontons" and "Sacramentons" find in the *Post* alongside "On
Going Home"? This "cross-section" reveals one moment in the essay's reception: an antiphonal relation between Didion's "personal" essay and more "historical" pieces echoes a dialogue between biography and history within the
essay itself. Defying complaints in the May 20 Letters column that a bathing
suit feature (Sharon Tate in "Sexy Little Me") belongs in *Playboy,* not the
Rockwellian *Post*, the cover pictures a young woman in a "Nude Look" bathing
suit. This teasing mischief bizarrely sets off real malevolence: bold letters announce the final installment of Jean-Francois Steiner's *Treblinka*. Within the
essay, likewise, the persona finds in her dresser drawer "a bathing suit I wore
the summer I was 17" and an old letter, about which she muses "there is no final
solution for letters of rejection from *The Nation* . . . ." The euphemism for
Treblinka's function (a Nazi death camp's "final solution" to "the Jewish question") bathetically expresses adolescent disappointment. Yet the adult persona
can see her experience from two vantage points. From one, she re-experiences
her rejection as a nascent author (it felt like "romantic degradation") and for a

moment she becomes tone-deaf to the Holocaust's tragic vocabulary. From the other, she recalls having strived "assiduously" for that "degradation" and places her "rejection" within an historically longer and wider perspective. From this vantage point, she distinguishes those of her generation who can't go home again (those with "the sentimental and largely literary baggage with which we left home in the '50's") from the post-war baby boomers who don't need or want to ("the children born of the fragmentation after World War II" for whom that sentimental baggage is "irrelevant"). It would be easy for a reader to dismiss someone who seeks a "final solution for letters of rejection from *The Nation*" as hopelessly self-involved, but the dialogue of naivete with wisdom in "On Going Home"—reflecting the magazine cover's juxtaposition of sass and tragedy—is more empathic than dismissive: like Fetterley's "elderly women with bristling chins," this woman has "a story and a secret and feelings." Understanding supersedes judgment.

Right after Didion's essay comes V. S. Naipaul's article "What's wrong with being a snob?" He explains his preference for the honest snobbery of England's old regime over the Liberals' empty talk of "the romance of the 'classless' society," talk that is no "compensation" for England's contemporary social and economic decay (12, 18). "On Going Home" likewise opens by contrasting social regions—called "Sacramento" and "Los Angeles"—through the pronouns "we" and "he." Sacramento identifies the persona ("*We* live in dusty houses . . . filled with mementos quite without value to [her husband]") and restricts her talk to "people *we know* who have been committed to mental hospitals, and people *we know* who have been booked on drunk driving charges" and to other subjects colored by romantic degradation and obsolescence. These nobody bothers to explain to her husband, whose exclusion she reiterates: ". . . my husband's inability to perceive . . ."; ". . . my husband in turn does not understand . . ."; "Nor does he understand that . . . *we* are talking in code about the things *we* like best" (my emphases). Yet by the penultimate sentence she leaves behind the inverse snobbery of "the things *we* [her family] like best" and redefines "we" as herself with her husband and baby in Los Angeles: ". . . but *we* live differently now . . . ." She makes neither region the "norm" but quietly notes their differences, revealing what Fetterley calls a "ritualized and sacramental life" in a Sacramento that, at least for now, must be a "world elsewhere."

Differences between "elsewhere" and "here" in "On Going Home" are projected onto the national scene in Stewart Alsop's "Can Anyone Beat LBJ?" Two page-wide photographs show a housing tract (captioned "The average voter these days is middle class, lives in a suburban development, and worries about property values") and a 1930's breadline (captioned "Candidates today need the crabgrass vote, not the 'forgotten man' of the Depression") (28–29). Didion's family in Sacramento also "worries about property values" ("we talk about sale-leasebacks and right-of-way condemnations" which "my husband" does not understand). But their Sacramento, though as yet unmarked by "suburban development," is not safe from "crabgrass" concerns: as Alsop knows—even if "we" in Sacramento do not yet—property is the concern of the "average voter" in both old Sacramento and Los Angeles. The stable way of life Didion's family cherishes is already vanishing into the Vietnam era evoked throughout the magazine. Indeed, Robert F. Kennedy's stoic question, "Who knows where we'll all be six years from now?" (qtd. in Alsop 20)—in retrospect made poignant by his assassination in 1968 and by actress and cover-girl Sharon Tate's murder by Charles Manson in 1969—expresses the sense of disintegration implicit in Didion's tentative closing: "I promise to tell [the baby] a funny story." Promises kept belong to the "Sacramento" frame of mind; promises made, but subject to change, belong to "Los Angeles."

The preservation of "ritualized and sacramental life" enters this issue of the *Post* through an article on Bruton Shires (horses):

> Behind [the Shires] marched the ghosts of a million gallant war horses in full panoply of armor; horses of plow and wagon and dray; horses dragging gun carriages over field[s] . . . and into valleys. The Shires belonged to . . . a part of history that had to go on living. (44)

But "On Going Home" brims with images of history lost. The family's gravestones are "broken, overturned in the dry grass," and untended: "My mother shrugs." The "teacups hand-painted with cabbage roses and signed 'E.M.,' my grandmother's initials" are not passed on: "I return them to the drawer." The persona cannot give her baby "home," that is, a "sense of her cousins and of rivers and of her great-grandmother's teacups," so she substitutes "a xylophone and a sundress from Madeira," anonymous artifacts from regions "elsewhere" that have no particular meaning for anyone in "On Going Home." "Here" in L.A., the "ritualized and sacramental" has, as yet, no place.

Reception study helps us understand some of the "regions" within which readers in 1967 encountered "On Going Home." Didion's "Torontons," the "Sacramentons," and other groups of readers I have not identified could see the interplay between her essay and this issue of the *Post*—nudity and Treblinka, topless dancing and "final solution," property and crabgrass, FDR's and RFK's promises and family promises, preservation and entropy—from what Jauss calls differing "horizons of expectations." (If I had more space, I would offer you other "cross-sections," noting that earlier in the spring of 1967 the *Post* had offered readers excerpts from Dwight Eisenhower's autobiography, *Memories of My Boyhood* (April 8), articles on "Crime in Chicago" and on Lester Maddox (April 22), on the investigation in New Orleans of a plot to kill John F. Kennedy and on Sharon Tate's career (May 6), and on "The First Year of Medicare" (May 20); and I would explore what other "regions"—"Abilene," "Chicago," "Atlanta," "New Orleans," "Hollywood," and "Washington"—they might imply.) These earlier "horizons" enable "us" today—be "we" Peace Corps returnees, Vietnam vets, older and younger "Dead Heads," Granolas, Trekies,

Techies, Generation X, whoever—to know some of 1967's readers better, to move beyond reader-response's formalist and psychological interests and into a broader historical perspective, to realize (if some of "us" haven't already) that it wasn't Gen X's tragic hero, Kurt Cobain, who wrote "Things fall apart; the center cannot hold; / Mere anarchy is loosed upon the world" or who asked fearfully, "And what rough beast, its hour come round at last, / Slouches towards Bethlehem to be born?"

Sacramento and *Slouching Towards Bethlehem*

Yeats's "The Second Coming" (1920) is one of two epigraphs of *Slouching Towards Bethlehem* (1968), the essay collection that includes the revised version of "On Going Home" which textbooks reprint. The other is Miss Peggy Lee's: "I learned courage from Buddha, Jesus, Lincoln, Einstein, and Cary Grant." These stark contrasts—Yeats with Peggy Lee, Buddha with Cary Grant, religion with performance, high culture with jazz and film—might recall the *Post*'s cover contrasting Treblinka with the "Nude Look." What might Peggy Lee's statement mean? That in a Yeatsian apocalypse, the slight in stature devote daily acts of courage to accomplishing tasks of dubious importance—including, presumably, the writing of essays? That in an apocalypse the courage of historical acts becomes indistinguishable from that of theatrical acts? Is Yeats's title turned into a joke about Didion's essays making their second appearance? Does Didion's implied audience relish an intellectual tease? Or are they the obtuse readers who failed to grasp that in describing life in the Haight-Ashbury district of San Francisco (first in "Hippie Generation" in the *Saturday Evening Post* 240 [September 23, 1967]: 25–31, and later as the essay "Slouching Towards Bethlehem") she was "talking about something more general than a handful of children wearing mandalas on their foreheads," readers whose "feedback" was "so universally beside the point" that she became convinced that "nobody out there is listening" and that, therefore, "writing is an irrelevant act" (xi–xii). These readers, in other words, lacked empathy. What these obtuse readers did not grasp was that 1967's "Haight-Ashbury" is a "region" in Fetterley's sense, quite different from the regions of "On Going Home," yet all the same a "ritualized and sacramental life" that Didion wanted readers to see from the inside and to understand.

One way to explore the "ritualized and sacramental life" in "On Going Home" is through another "cross-section" in the essay's reception: Didion's own reception of the 1967 original as implied by her 1968 revision. Like other "cross-sections," this one can give only partial information; we cannot see the revisions she erased. Strikingly, Didion deletes the name "Sacramento" and substitutes more general phrases ("in the central valley of California," "their house," and "my father's house" in the opening paragraph, "home" in the third, and an exchange of "the indirect Sacramento way" for "the oblique way my family talks" in the fourth). Rhetorically, these substitutions shift attention away from the literal place and towards relationships (what Fetterley calls regionalism's "model of relationships of 'persons' with differing amounts of cultural power" [890]). These revisions may be a remedy for readers' failure to see a region— "Sacramento," "Haight-Ashbury," or some other "elsewhere"—as "something more general" (xii), as a model of relationships for "us" to understand (in Gadamer's sense of reaching out towards "fusion of horizons") rather than just a locally colorful neighborhood of freaks for "us" normal people to point at, scorn, or scold as "other."

The other revisions are all additions, most intensifying ideas already there. Just before the end of the first paragraph, she emphasizes her husband's exclusion from conversation. ("My brother refers to my husband in his presence, as 'Joan's husband.'") In the second paragraph, the added third through sixth sentences dramatize family tensions (she weeps after phoning home); near the end, the added phrase "of 'dark journey'" intensifies "of 'romantic degradation.'" In the third paragraph, a list of places where the past lurks ("engendered by meeting the past at every turn, around every corner, inside every cupboard") and the phrase "meet it head-on" augment the tension of confrontation. In the fourth, another dramatization ("not only because he is full of news of what by now seems to me our remote life in Los Angeles, people he has seen, letters which require attention") forms a transition from "we" identifying her with the Sacramento family to "we" identifying her with the L.A. family ("we live differently now"). In the last paragraph, a phrase ("would like to give her a picnic on a river with fried chicken and her hair uncombed") amplifies the persona's experience of "home," that which she cannot give to the baby. These amplifications enable readers to see more deeply into the "world elsewhere."

There is only one explicitly historical revision, and to understand it we need to combine the "cross-section" of Didion's revision with another "cross-section": "On Going Home" in relation to some of the other essays reprinted in the 1968 collection. Didion adds this sentence to the third paragraph:

> Nor is there any answer to the snapshots of one's grandfather as a young man on skis, surveying around Donner Pass in the year 1910. I smooth out the snapshot and look into his face, and do and do not see my own.

Many readers in 1968 and many more today might overlook this allusion. But "we" who read California history or who grew up in old California families like Didion's know that in 1846 members of the Donner-Reed party were caught in deep snow, starved, and survived by eating their own dead (Whitman). In "On Morality" (1965), Didion describes growing up with "wagon-train morality":

> my own childhood was illuminated by graphic litanies of the grief awaiting those who failed in their loyalties to each other. The Donner-Reed Party,

starving in the Sierra snows, all the ephemera of civilization gone save that one vestigial taboo, the provision that no one should eat his own blood kin. . . . We were taught . . . that they had somewhere abdicated their responsibilities, somehow breached their primary loyalties, or they would not have found themselves helpless in the mountain winter . . . , would not have failed. (*Slouching* 158-159)

In other words, "wagon-train morality" belongs to the frame of mind Fetterley calls "realism," one in which "normal" people—who shoulder our "responsibilities" and sustain our "primary loyalties" and therefore "would not have failed"—can safely condemn them: the "abnormal" and "freakish" cannibals, the "others." Yet, gazing into her father's snapshot, she must confront the possibility of being a descendent of the survivors, who *in extremis* did and did not see their own faces in those objects of "primary loyalties," the friends whom they consumed. In "Notes from a Native Daughter" (1965), she states this possibility explicitly: "Did not the Donner-Reed Party, after all, eat its own dead to reach Sacramento?" (*Slouching* 176). To see and not see her face in her father's snapshot is simultaneously to acknowledge *and* to deny this possibility, neither only to deplore nor only to defend cannibalism but to empathize with those who made agonizing choices. With empathy comes humility ("some hint of the monstrous perversion to which any human idea can come") but also a paradoxical insistence that except for "our loyalties to those we love —what could be more arrogant than to claim the primacy of personal conscience?" (161). Today readers can learn that even these loyalties, enacted in places like Auschwitz as "self-ishness extended to the person closest to you . . . appropriately called 'us-ism'" (Levi 80), can also become monstrous. In the "fusion of horizons" I am sketching, "worlds elsewhere"—two Sacramentos (the 1910 snapshot, the daughter's view of it), Treblinka, Auschwitz—are joined ethically and hermeneutically through empathy.

Homelessness can be hermeneutically good. If Didion actually could "go home again" in solidarity with "wagon-train morality" and with manifest destiny pointing towards Sacramento, she would be a realist glorifying the "development" of California as novelists have done. If she were completely estranged from "home," she would adopt a naturalist realism like that of Frank Norris (Didion "The Golden Land"). As a realist, she would want to see her face in her father's (embodying a heritage of toughness and responsibility); as a naturalist she would not (her father's face would reflect his ancestors' ruthlessness). Either way, she would understand less because—either in defending or in deploring—she would sacrifice understanding that "our town" isn't always the norm and a "world elsewhere" isn't just locally colorful, quaint and queer. By both "seeing and not seeing" her face in the Donner Pass snapshot, by inhabiting and not inhabiting Sacramento and Toronto and L. A. and Treblinka and other "worlds elsewhere," Didion becomes a regionalist both ethically and hermeneutically. Without setting up hierarchies and declaring norms, she respects differences.

That is what reception theory—with its historically grounded, imaginative "fusion of horizons" that still preserves the sense of "difference"—fosters. As Yeats wrote, "The best lack all conviction, while the worst / Are full of passionate intensity." To "lack all conviction" does not lead necessarily to quietism. One chooses and acts as best one can with empathy, trying to curb the "passionate intensity" of reductive "us-ness." The best are regionalists.

Regionalism, the Prose Sketch and the Essay

There are many other ways to make connections between the revision of "On Going Home" and other essays in *Slouching Towards Bethlehem*, and that kind of cross-section, like the one we made between the original essay and the issue of the *Post* in which it appeared, would further define a significant moment in the essay's reception. But instead, I'd like to turn to genre, that is, to reception theory's reconstruction of readers' "pre-understanding of [a work's] genre from the form and themes of already familiar works" (Jauss 23). From readers in "Toronto" and "Sacramento," we can turn now to those in "New York": the professional reviewers. They reveal a three-stranded "cross-section" of expectations *vis-à-vis* journalism, New Journalism, and the essay.

Journalism shaped some readers' "pre-understanding of the genre" of Didion's essay:

> Journalism by women is the price the man's world pays for having disappointed them. Here at their best are the unforgiving eye, the unforgetting ear, the concealed hat-pin style. But behind this poses the Joan Didion we might have had if we deserved her: the quiet, round-eyed child . . . [who] could still respond—if only she ever ran across it—to old-fashioned wagon-train idealism . . . . Instead, grimacing over old dreams and lost innocence, she rummages through her bureau drawers, coming up with the bathing suit she wore at 17 and her grandmother's hand-painted tea cup. The musk of lost values and a faint essence of self-pity hover in the air. (Maddocks 11)

Realists in the "man's world" of journalism have no truck with "wagon-train idealism" (note the substitution of "idealism" for Didion's word, "morality"). This reviewer expects a more robust sensibility and firmer convictions; he associates Didion's "faint essence of self-pity" with women's more general disappointment in men. If "journalism by women" differs from his "man's world" journalism, his must be the norm: a "concealed hat-pin" (like a "bristling chin") must be quaint, queer, freakish.

The "man's world" of New Journalism (a mixture of reportage with personal viewpoint) met Didion's work with mixed "pre-understandings." In 1965, she had written that fiction—by Pynchon, Friedman, Vonnegut, and Heller—lacks the "skill at contrivance [which] is the excitement" of both excellent novels and excellent films. Their fiction, she says, portrays "this outrageous world we live in" by employing a style of "outrageous improvisation." But to her this style is a "stunt," an "erosion of technique" that does not necessarily produce "authentic" writing ("Questions"). Now, printed on the very same page with Maddocks's scathing dismissal of "journalism by women," appeared an opposing view of New Journalistic fiction. A reviewer of Norman Mailer's *Armies of the Night* praises its "pugilistic prose," its "authenticity" of reconstruction of the march on the Pentagon, its "headlong, self-indulgent monologue," and "the arrogance, outrageousness, extravagance, irony, and sometimes underlying likableness of the writing"(Nordell). In other words, a personal point of view brought to bear on the "eventful" in the "man's world" of realism is praiseworthily "authentic," but not when brought to bear on worlds with whom Maddocks and Nordell feel no empathy. Even though Didion does not want to be a New Journalist, they're not going to let her! Other reviewers, however, saw her as one of the New Journalists. One reviewer saw in *Slouching Towards Bethlehem*'s theme of atomization an historical dimension ("The past, for most of us, is a special self-deception") (Simonds). Another praised her sensibility; for him, her "personality does not self-indulgently intrude itself on her subjects, [but] it informs and illuminates them," and her style offers "some of the best prose written today in this country" (Wakefield). Like other New Journalists, Didion is concerned with the historian's position both outside and inside the "eventful"; unlike them, her prose style is quietly precise. Scholars' analyses also emphasize these two features (Mallon 43; Strandberg; Coale 162; Chabot; Muggli; Anderson 133–73).

Still other readers' "pre-understandings of genre" are shaped by the essay in *belles lettres*. In 1981 Jerzy Kosinski characterized her work in terms distinct from those of New Journalism: "She is always at the center, our quintessential essayist," and a later commentator remarks that her "essays are shaped by her perception of the fictionality of our governing models of national and personal identity and by her inability to abandon or reformulate them" (Carton 35, 50). The essay and the prose sketch are similar genres. Recall that Fetterley distinguishes two genres in nineteenth-century American fiction. The major genre is the realist novel, wherein the "eventful" for women is marriage, for men the triumph (sometimes hollow) over whatever forces "beset" them. The marginalized genre is the prose sketch, wherein the conventionally "eventful" gives way to other relations and actions (885). A neighboring genre, marginalized in scholarship until being recently revived by the daily fare of writing courses (Rygiel, McCord, Atkins 3–17), is the essay. Theodor Adorno's contrast of the article and the essay (in "The Essay as Form") has become well known, and it seems to me parallel to Fetterley's contrasts between realism and regionalism, between novel and sketch. In a nutshell, what Adorno says is an article has conviction galore, proves its case with passionate intensity disguised as objectivity, seems "airtight" and complete but actually ignores inconsistencies and counter-evidence. But an essay "speculates," zig-zags along trusting to "luck and play" as it follows first one and then another and another line of thought to where each breaks down, "stops when it feels finished rather than when there is nothing more to say" (3–4). Like "On Going Home," an essay and a prose sketch "promise" another view, another story: you could see "elderly women with bristling chins" this way, and these other ways.

Regionalism and Meaning

Journalists, old and New, are in business to persuade an audience that, as Walter Cronkite always said, "That's the way it is." So are realist novelists. But regionalists have a different agenda. Didion seems to me to be a "resisting reader" of her experience, perhaps less resisting it from the outside in ways Fetterley demonstrates in *The Resisting Reader* (1977) than investigating its self-contradictions (or "self-transgressions") in ways Shoshana Felman undertakes in *What Does a Woman Want?* (1993). These self-contradictions in experience produce homelessness. In *Slouching Towards Bethlehem*, going home is a dream and California is a "golden land . . . because no one remembers the past" (4) because "every day the world is born anew" (28), perpetually a "promised land" (31). In a John Wayne movie, what seizes her imagination is the "bend in the river" where she locates "the shimmering border between the town's constraints and freedom" (31), between a world "here" and a "world elsewhere." That "shimmer" and a kind of "white writing" ("Why I Write") cleansed of asserted meanings are what her conscience demands (as in Mailer's novel *The Deer Park*, "*when the world stands clear in the dead white dawn*") because in her world meanings jostle and collapse like figures in "a painting by Hieronymous Bosch" (161 italics original). Essays collected in *The White Album* (1979) disclaim meaning: "I am telling you only how it was" (207).

In whiteness and shimmer, the essays resemble Mark Rothko's paintings. From 1940 until his death in 1970, Rothko painted rectangles. As Leo Bersani and Ulysse Dutoit describe them, these are universally "rectangles of different colors and of roughly similar size, painted over a third color that may have originally covered the entire canvas" (98). Paint fills the canvas except for a very narrow, shimmering edge, sometimes the white canvas and sometimes the background color, as if this edge is "perhaps a way of announcing a belief in the possibility of a subject," but the critique of clear boundaries subverts this belief (104–105). Rothko's use of very narrow ("vibratory") chromatic intervals focuses perception on nonnarrative elements:

> There *is* a relation here, but because its terms are almost identical it would be difficult to give a narrative account of that relation. The lighter and the darker yellows relate by *nearly reflecting each other*; they have no story to tell other than that of an inaccurate replication. (118 italics original)

No writer can be as laconic as a painter, but Rothko's work seems to me virtually an illustration of Didion's regionalism of homelessness. She sees and does not see her father's face; Rothko sees and does not see rectangles. If Rockwell painted an identifiable region, Rothko paints the idea of "regions"; he seems uncertain about their borders while nevertheless believing in their existence. Local color realism, as Fetterley explains it, clearly defines borders between nation and "other," normal and quaint; regionalism sees the nuances of color, the shimmer of boundaries. In lacking "all conviction," it reaches out hermeneutically towards others seeking a "fusion of horizons."

Works Cited

Adorno, Theodor W. "The Essay as Form." *Notes to Literature I.* Trans. Sherry Weber Nicholsen. (New York: Columbia, 1991): 3–23. Trans. of "Der Essay Als Form." *Noten zur Literatur I.* (Frankfurt am Main: Suhrkamp, 1958): 5–49.

Alsop, Stewart. "Can Anyone Beat LBJ?" *Saturday Evening Post* 3 June 1967: 20.

Anderson, Chris. *Style as Argument: Contemporary American Nonfiction.* Carbondale: Southern Illinois UP, 1988.

Atkins, G. Douglas. *Estranging the Familiar: Toward a Revitalized Critical Writing.* Athens: U Georgia P, 1992.

Bersani, Leo, and Ulysse Dutoit. *Arts of Impoverishment: Beckett, Rothko, Resnais.* Cambridge: Harvard UP, 1993.

Carton, Evan. "Joan Didion's Dreampolitics of the Self." *Western Humanities Review* 40.4 (1986): 307–328. In *The Critical Response to Joan Didion.* Ed. Sharon Felton. Westport, CT: Greenwood, 1994. 35–51.

Chabot, C. Barry. "Understanding Interpretive Situations." *Researching Response to Literature and the Teaching of Literature: Points of Departure.* Ed. Charles R. Cooper. Norwood, NJ: Ablex, 1985. 22–32.

Coale, Samuel. "Didion's Disorder: An American Romancer's Art." *Critique: Studies in Modern Fiction* 25 (1983–84): 160–70.

Didion, Joan. "Coming Home." *Saturday Evening Post.* 11 July 1964: 50–55.

———. "The Golden Land." *New York Review of Books.* 21 October 1993: 85–94.

———. "On Going Home." *Saturday Evening Post.* 3 June 1967: 8–9.

———. "Questions About the New Fiction." *National Review* 30 November 1965: 1100–1102.

———. *Slouching Towards Bethlehem.* New York: Farrar, Straus, & Giroux, 1968.

———. *The White Album.* New York: Simon and Schuster, 1979.

Felman, Shoshana. *What Does a Woman Want? Reading and Sexual Difference.* Baltimore: Johns Hopkins UP, 1993.

Fetterley, Judith. "Not in the Least American: Nineteenth-Century American Regionalism." *College English* 56 (1994): 877–95.

———. *The Resisting Reader: A Feminist Approach to American Fiction.* Bloomington: Indiana UP, 1977.

Gadamer, Hans Georg. *Truth and Method.* Garret Barden and John Cumming, eds. New York: Crossroad, 1986.

Henderson, Katherine Usher. *Joan Didion.* New York: Ungar, 1981.

Jauss, Hans Robert. *Towards an Aesthetic of Reception.* Ed. Robert Holub. Minneapolis: U of Minnesota P, 1982.

Levi, Primo. *The Drowned and the Saved.* Trans. Raymond Rosenthal. New York: Vintage, 1988.

Maasik, Sonia and Jack Solomon, eds. *California Dreams and Realities: Readings for Critical Thinkers and Writers.* Boston: Bedford, 1995.

McCord, Phyllis Frus. "Reading Nonfiction in Composition Courses: From Theory to Practice." *College English* 47.7 (1985): 747–62.

McGillivray, Murray. "Creative Anachronism: Marx's Problem with Homer, Gadamer's Discussion of 'The Classical,' and Our Understanding of Older Literatures," *New Literary History* 25 (1994): 399–413.

Maddocks, Melvin. Rev. of *Slouching Towards Bethlehem* by Joan Didion. *Christian Science Monitor* 16 May 1968: 11.

Mailloux, Steven. *Interpretive Conventions: The Reader in the Study of American Fiction.* Ithaca and London: Cornell UP, 1982.

Mallon, Thomas. "The Limits of History in the Novels of Joan Didion." *Critique: Studies in Modern Fiction* 21 (1979-80): 43–52.

Marting, Janet, ed. *The Voice of Reflection: A Writer's Reader.* New York: HarperCollins, 1995.

Muggli, Mark Z. "The Poetics of Joan Didion's Journalism." *American Literature* 59 (1987): 402–21.

Naipaul, V. S. "What's wrong with being a snob?" *Saturday Evening Post* 3 June 1967: 12, 18.

Nordell, Robert. Rev. of *Armies of the Night* by Norman Mailer. *Christian Science Monitor.* 16 May 1968: 11.

Rorty, Richard. *Philosophy and the Mirror of Nature.* Princeton: Princeton UP, 1979.

Rygiel, Dennis. "On the Neglect of Twentieth-Century Nonfiction: A Writing Teacher's View." *College English* 46 (1984): 392–400.

Simon, Paul, and Art Garfunkel. "America." *Bookends.* Columbia, KCS 9529, 1968.

Simonds, C. H. "Picking Up the Pieces." *National Review* 4 June 1968: 558–59.

Smart, William, ed. *Eight Modern Essayists.* 5th ed. New York: St. Martin's Press, 1990.

Smith, Louise Z. "Beyond the 'Imaginary Museum': Interested Readings, Interesting Tropes." *Rhetoric, Critical Theory, Cultural Studies.* Ed. William E. Cain. New York: Garland, 1996. 83–98.

———. "In Search of Our Sisters' Rhetoric: Teaching Through Reception Theory." *Practicing Theory in Introductory College Literature Courses.* Eds. James M. Cahalan and David B. Downing. Urbana: NCTE, 1991. 72–84.

Strandberg, Victor. "Passion and Delusion in *A Book of Common Prayer.*" *Modern Fiction Studies* 27 (1981): 225–42.

Wakefield, Dan. Review: *Slouching Towards Bethlehem* by Joan Didion. *New York Times Book Review* 21 July 1968: 8.

Whitman, Ruth. *Tamsen Donner: A Woman's Journal.* Cambridge: Alice James Books, 1977.

Winchell, Mark Royden. *Joan Didion.* Boston: G. K. Hall, 1980.

15 Beyond *Beyond the Culture Wars:* Students Teaching Themselves the Conflicts

James S. Laughlin
Virginia Polytechnic Institute and State University

While debates over the literary canon may seem like old news to academics, the culture wars seem to flare anew with each fresh round of funding in Washington and with each new publication by controversial spokespersons like William Bennett and Harold Bloom. Nor is it old news to our literature students, who, encountering the word "canon," wonder how it slipped by the writer's spell check. It may be "critical commonplace," as Charles Bazerman claims, "that disciplines are socially and rhetorically constructed and that academic knowledge is the product of sociolinguistic activities advancing individual and group interests" (61), but it's far from commonplace among my students. Informed of the meaning of canon and of the controversy which surrounds it, students' reactions are often of the "what's the big deal?" variety. After all, most can count on one hand the number of non-white or non-male writers they know, let alone have read in school. Their experience leaves them incapable of imagining what's at stake.

An Absence of Practical Applications

"A really clear vision," says Gerald Graff, "would see that when what educated persons should know is deeply disputed, the dispute itself becomes part of what educated persons should know" (44). Graff's solution to this difficulty in *Beyond the Culture Wars* has had a considerable influence in our profession over the last few years. Many have done their best to revise their syllabi and to reenvision the literature course as a place where they can "teach the conflicts" to their students. And many departments have tried to reconceive their enterprise, as my own department at Virginia Tech did in 1993 when, led by a teacher/administrator who was influenced by Graff's book, it revised "coverage" courses, such as its heavily enrolled American Literature sequence. Here's the strategy recommended for these new courses, taken from the department's revised *Faculty Handbook:*

> In suggesting that we organize our sophomore-level core courses as con-
> versations, then, we are attempting to hold before our students one aspect
> of the larger culture in which we find ourselves—setting it before them,
> letting them listen to voices quarrel and respond and backtrack, encourag-
> ing them to learn what's at stake and to have their own say. (33)

However, despite my department's week-long faculty development workshop designed to assist teachers in making these changes, I continue to see
colleagues struggling to imagine just how to flesh out this new model. The
courses many have created more closely resemble polite parlor conversations
than they do the heated and spirited debates Graff advocates as a way to engage
apathetic students. Nor do I believe my colleagues are alone. While many still
find in Graff's model a powerful impetus for reimagining literary education, its
translation into actual practice has stumped most teachers. Even Graff himself
has recently noted that "the question of practical application has persisted" among
teachers trying to imagine just how they might begin teaching the conflicts "on
an actual Monday morning in a roomful of actual undergraduates" (Foreword
v).

Rereading *Beyond the Culture Wars*, I find it no wonder that the question has
persisted, for in it Graff includes very little actual discussion of classroom practice or of the kind of writing that might help develop students' critical capacities. I see only two moments where he lets us inside his class. In the first, he
relates his revised approach to teaching *Heart of Darkness*. After a page of
explanation listing all of the essays and articles students read to familiarize
themselves with conflicting appraisals of the novella (critical articles about
Conrad, racism, colonialism, and the place of politics in the arts), and after
noting the debates he stages between himself and invited colleagues, Graff ends
with this statement: "To make sure my students enter the debate rather than
watch passively from the sidelines, I assign a paper on it or ask them to prepare
class presentations in which they give their views" (30).

Thus in one sentence, written almost as an afterthought it seems to me, we
get the only real mention of what students actually *do* in the classroom. The
model we have here seems like a pluralized version of the "standard story" that
Graff rejects later in the book, a story that "implies that the business of teaching
literature is basically simple: Just put the student in front of a good book, provide teachers who are encouraging and helpful, and the rest presumably will
take care of itself" (72). In the pluralized version, Graff's students are put in
front of many books. They get a wealth of conflicting interpretive essays and
other reading material thrown their way, with the result that they're somehow
educated on the conflict.

In the one other description of his students' work, Graff mentions distributing a *Harper's* article on opposing readings of "Dover Beach" and listening to
students take sides. Some of his students voluntarily followed up this exercise

by bringing in editorials on the culture wars, proof to Graff that "students' interest in the discussion was greatly heightened" (59). However, the fact that the editorial writers were attacking Graff, their teacher, goes a long way toward explaining their enthusiasm. He quips, "There is nothing like being bashed in the morning paper for your kind's crimes against the humanities for stimulating a provocative discussion in your afternoon class." (59).

For those of us not blessed with such fame (or infamy), the practical question of how to help our students actively enter into this debate goes unanswered. Certainly, bringing in for discussion hotly debated public issues related to the work of the class makes sense. No doubt all of us do this at times. Over the years my students have examined the controversy over the Mapplethorpe exhibit while wrestling with the related question of "what is literature," have seen the Senate debate over the Gulf War placed alongside Thoreau's "Civil Disobedience," and have read conflicting arguments about bilingual education to supplement their reading of Richard Rodriguez's *Hunger of Memory*, to name just a few examples. Sometimes students respond enthusiastically. But sometimes, as with the Mapplethorpe example, they are largely silent, uninterested—despite the loudness of the confrontational voices they are overhearing. My best students, and certainly upper-level English majors, can be motivated through my choice of intriguing supplementary material. But many of us are teaching lower-level non-majors in universities and community colleges who honestly don't see the point of listening to these intellectuals drone on about literary matters.

The Conditions of Engagement

If we analyze Graff's own epiphany with *Heart of Darkness* we can see what the problem is with a method that has the teacher bringing the conflict to the students. In *Beyond the Culture Wars*, the central moment Graff relates in his development from a traditional teacher of literature to a teacher of literary conflicts involves his radical reconsideration of Joseph Conrad's *Heart of Darkness*. Graff tells us that he has frequently assigned this novella since he began teaching in the mid-1960s and that he had always presented it "as a universal parable of the precarious status of civilized reason in a world overly confident of its having outgrown the primitive and the irrational" (25). But his reading of Chinua Achebe's essay on Conrad, "An Image of Africa: Racism in Conrad's *Heart of Darkness,*" changed all that. The evidence Achebe was able to amass and the logic of his argument charging Conrad with a deeply offensive "dehumanization of Africa and Africans," challenged Graff's conception of the work:

> In short, I was forced to rethink not just my interpretation of *Heart of Darkness* but my theoretical assumptions about literature. First, I was forced to recognize that I *had* theoretical assumptions. I had previously thought I

was simply teaching the truth about *Heart of Darkness,* "the text itself." I now had to recognize that I had been teaching an interpretation of the text, one that was shaped by a certain theory that told me what was and was not worth noticing and emphasizing in my classroom. I had been unable to see my theory *as* a theory because I was living so comfortably inside it. (29–30)

Graff's experience with *Heart of Darkness* is instructive in helping us answer the key question "How does one become engaged?" or put another way, "What conditions lead one to be receptive of new ideas and new ways of thinking?" In Graff's case, we can see that he was predisposed to care about what Achebe had to say regarding *Heart of Darkness* because he cared about the book. He'd read it and chosen it for his students for years, returning to it as a familiar favorite, as one sits down to view a favorite old film with a companion who has never seen it or directs a friend to listen with pleasure to a classic love song on the radio. Because he cared, he found that he had to respond to the challenge of Achebe's interpretation, just as we'd respond if our movie companion hated our favorite film or our friend found our chosen song demeaning toward the opposite sex. Note, for example, how twice in the passage quoted above Graff uses the verb "forced," emphasizing that he felt he had no choice but to respond.

These crucial conditions—of caring about something over time, of living comfortably with it, of experiencing a discomforting challenge that forces reconsideration, and of formulating a response to that challenge—are far from replicated when we bring the conflicts to our students in the form of literary disputes very few of them care about. Overhearing virtually any argument or heated exchange can perk up an audience a bit; no doubt we should expect more energy in a class where conflicts are aired versus a class where received wisdom is placidly transferred from teacher to students. But real change, real intellectual challenge that forces a reconsideration of assumptions and provides the opportunity to reconceive them along the lines of Graff's experience with *Heart of Darkness,* is unlikely to occur for most students in a classroom in which *we* teach *them* the conflicts.

Teaching the conflicts, then, while seeming to be an empowering pedagogy that involves students in their learning, can too easily be fitted into a traditional model of dissemination, of one-way knowledge-passing from the teacher to the learner. What we need to design instead is a way for students to experience a challenge in an area of interest and comfort for them, to come upon complexity and controversy themselves, and to work their way through the implications of the new knowledge they gain—in writing and in discussion—toward a revised relationship with their subject.

A tall order? Yes. But one approach suggests itself: reversing the agents of communication so that instead of teachers bringing their disciplinary conflicts to students, it is the students who bring their conflicts to the teachers. In other words, we can more fully activate our students by directing them to areas of disagreement in their own non-academic world that have parallels to the disputes in the academic world we would ultimately have them examine.

But where can we locate fields of interest for students which at the same time allow us to make complex connections to our discipline's culture battles? One answer is to turn to popular culture. Graff himself mounts a spirited and intelligent defense of the study of popular culture in English studies in *Beyond the Culture Wars*. (His discussion joins such a lengthy list of equally persuasive cases for the value of cultural studies that I believe it unnecessary to add my own here.) But he appears to have in mind solely the inclusion of popular works of literature alongside the more traditional works taught in the discipline. I believe there are other forms of popular culture that can work extremely well to engage students and raise issues that speak productively to conflicts in the humanities.

An Intelligent Investment

In my most recent literature class, it was a collaborative writing assignment on popular culture that provided my students the opportunity to teach themselves the conflicts firsthand in an area of personal significance and then apply their learning to a semester's worth of reading and writing in an *Introduction to American Literature* course. The assignment, completed largely out of class over the first three weeks of the course, required students to select up to 125 songs which would form the table of contents of an imaginary music anthology representing the best of rock and roll. In addition, each collaborative group had to explain and defend these choices, as most any anthology does, in a carefully crafted preface.

Many, I'm sure, would register objections to assigning such an unusual project. Let me respond to three familiar objections before turning to a full discussion of the assignment.

Why sacrifice valuable time in an already crowded course for this kind of a diversion? In fact, the kind of project I advocate here demands a relatively small investment when we consider the potentially large dividends. Completed within the first few weeks of the course, a time when many classes are still revving their engines, the project required that only two and a half classes be devoted to it (with one and a half classes given to the valuable discussion of the project's results described later in this article). During these weeks, class proceeded normally. Students read, completed journals, and discussed American literature. Or perhaps it did not proceed normally; I perceived an ease of communication and frequency of participation early on, attributing it to the fact that students had been formed into project teams immediately and then required to sit in these teams in class.

How much relevance does such an odd critical exercise really have to the multicultural debate? Quite a bit, actually. The resistance and opposition which have greeted various forms of popular culture over the years bear much resemblance to the outcry against the inclusion of new voices in the chorus of the Great Tradition. The rise of movies, television, and Pop Art, changes in fashion, the development of new popular musical forms like jazz, rock, and rap—all have in their turn reawakened the cultural debate that seems ever ready to stir in America, a debate aimed at defining and redefining the nation's collective past, present, and future. A look at the history of popular music reveals much that sounds familiar to veterans of academia's culture war, as the following two passages make clear:

> The history of popular music is littered with examples of opposition to and condemnation of new forms (new to the Anglo-American mainstream, that is) of Afro-American and Afro-American influenced music and culture—from ragtime in the 1890's to rap in the 1990's. In every case the dynamics of this opposition and condemnation have been similar. The music is 'inferior' (if it can be graced with the term music at all) and perceived as endangering preferred moral standards. (Bennett 1)

> The attitudes underlying such [gender] distinctions provide a partial explanation as to why women's roles in the music industry have frequently been overlooked and downplayed in many rock histories. If women performers (or songwriters, DJ's, managers, etc.) are only seen as exceptional because they are women, this justifies the relegation of women-in-rock to an obligatory chapter, where their contributions are acknowledged but are also portrayed as being a step removed from the history as a whole. (Gaar xii)

Interesting parallels also exist between debates over the canon in English departments and debates over the canon in music departments. Glenn Gass, composer and Assistant Professor of Music at Indiana University, notes that courses in rock are increasing and refueling the debate over what music is worthy of study:

> Seeing Rock and Roll next to Symphonic Literature and Music Appreciation in course listings must seem like a nightmare come true for more traditionally minded faculty members whose view of culture involves a refined sensibility that must be learned and earned. Rock courses are still waging the same struggle for acceptance that jazz studies faced on their way to becoming standard offerings, and facing the same prejudices that view "popular" as synonymous with cheap, crude, and unrefined. . . . Rock's assault on academia mirrors a heightened interest in world music and ethnomusicology and a general acknowledgment of the need to move beyond the near religious canonization of Western (white male) art music that has been the entire focus of musical higher education. (94)

The relevance, then, is clear and instructive, helping students to recognize cross-disciplinary developments in the advancement and contestation of knowledge.

But isn't this a rather roundabout way of engaging students with the litera-ture? Perhaps so, but then the roundabout way may be necessary. Returning to Graff, we can see that he believes it is, for the story of his own breakthrough as a reader is a roundabout experience. In *Culture Wars* he writes at length of his encounter with *Huckleberry Finn*, of how time spent researching the book paid off when he returned to reread it. "Getting into immediate contact with the text," he writes, "was for me a curiously triangular business; I could not do it directly but needed a conversation of other readers to give me the issues and terms that made it possible to respond" (70). As knowledge-making creatures, we proceed by making sense of the unknown in terms of the known. Thus the richer our base of comparable experience, the greater our success in critically examining a new encounter.

An Unusual Assignment

I wish I were able to say I knew all of the above about greater student involve-ment, about rock's history, and about the internal debates of music departments when I devised this project for my students. I didn't. (My students would help me to see these things, and one group's written preface supplied me with the Gaar passage quoted above.) What I did recognize was that I might be able to get at the canon controversy by giving them hands-on practice in canon-build-ing. Such a simulation would allow students to get behind the finished product of an anthology and experience a bit of the sticky process of selecting works and justifying their artistic merit. Why rock music? Most students, I guessed, would have a measure of expertise in the field of popular music of the past decade, an expertise that they were unlikely to have in any other artistic field. ("Expertise" seems the right word here, given my relative ignorance of the con-temporary music scene. Such a project guaranteed that they would be teaching me about present conflicts in this field.) And, at a time when "classic rock" and other "oldies" stations fill the airwaves, I assumed a number of students would even have a fair knowledge of music prior to the past decade ("Classic rock," notes Glenn Gass, "is history to [my students], their Great Tradition" [99]). Further, the pleasure of selecting and advocating for one's favorite bands and artists would, I hoped, energize the students beyond the traditional academic assignment (such as researching and reporting on the culture wars, or writing an agree/disagree response to the canon controversy). Finally, I had been seek-ing a collaborative project for the class, and this seemed an ideal situation, a clear instance of a group's work being able to go beyond the work of any indi-vidual, since inevitably different musical tastes and knowledges would be join-ing forces.

Worried as I get over the potential value and success of any new assign-ments, I make it a practice to attempt my own (at the least sketching an outlined approach, writing an introductory paragraph, or producing a very rough draft) before distributing them to students. In the case of this assignment, attempting a rough table of contents for such an anthology was a true enlightenment, making quickly apparent just how many and complex were the concerns that the editors of such a work would need to address. Among those concerns:

- How does one define rock and roll? Does rap fall under that term? Soul? Pop?

- At what historical point does one begin such an anthology?

- How does one group or order such a collection? Alphabetically? Chronologically? By sub-genre?

- What criteria ought to guide selection? Artistic merit? Record sales? Musical influence? Cultural impact?

These kinds of questions found their way into the final draft of the assignment (see Appendix). Students were requested to discuss them in a four- to six-page introduction addressed to a hypothetical editor at a major publishing company. Additionally, I was soon convinced that I'd need to confine students to *American* rock music—a daunting task in itself—rather than burden them with sifting through the history of British rock as well. What seemed like a high number of songs (I decided groups could include up to 125) quickly filled up.

It takes only a small leap for a teacher to recognize how the above questions might be translated and applied to an analysis of the canon controversy or to a critique of literary anthologies. It would take a larger leap for most students. In order to ensure that leap, I included a third requirement to follow the compilation of a table of contents and the drafting of an introduction or preface. In a final two- or three-page reflection, each group would link the work they did to issues of canon formation, discussing how their specific experiences in constructing a rock canon might enable them to comment on the formation of, and controversy over, the literary canon. All of these concerns were to find their way into the collaborative project I assigned. But, as always, I could not foresee all of the intriguing possibilities the assignment raised. Students' final projects and whole class discussions would go beyond what I could imagine.

From "It's So Easy" to "All Shook Up"

"It was a fun first session," one student reflected in her journal on her group's brief first meeting. Her group of four noted how the assignment went beyond the "normal boring type we usually get," then proceeded to quickly brainstorm a lengthy list of individual artists and bands. She records that they soon recognized their list was thin on 1950s artists and bands from the "psychedelic sixties." The group decided to assign two members the task of library research on 1950s rock and roll, while two others would try to fill in the gap on psychedelic music. Further, they decided to work independently for now, reconvening in five days' time to share research and their individual compilations of the top one hundred songs of American rock.

In that follow-up meeting, the group learned not only the range of their musical tastes (something they no doubt got an inkling of in their first session brainstorm), but how different were their organizational schemes and their rationales for inclusion. One member, for instance, grouped songs by theme, another by decade. A third member relied heavily on a book listing the *Billboard* charts' top hits. The fourth argued for the influence of a group's sound on future music or the number of times a song had been remade as a measure of its importance. A blues enthusiast, this fourth member also argued for the inclusion of blues songs as a crucial influence in the development of rock. Writing after this second meeting, the same student lamented "basically, we know we've got a lot of work left to do."

From the record of journals, final projects, and class discussions, it appears each group experienced the increasing complexities of the task. Significant differences in song selection and organization mark the final group projects I received. In comparing tables of contents, for instance, a reader first notices their differing starting points. While three groups begin with the expected icons of 1950s rock (Elvis, Chuck Berry, Bill Haley), another group starts earlier with Nat King Cole, and one group, claiming blues, white folk music, and jazz as the three sources of rock music, reaches all the way back to 1927 for two influential songs: Jimmie Rodgers's "Blue Yodel No. 1," and Blind Lemon Jefferson's "Matchbox Blues." Organizational schemes run from simple chronological grouping ("Rock: 1975–1979"), to musical category ("Bubble Gum," Classic Rock, Heavy Metal), to thematic clustering ("Party Hop Songs," "She's the Most," "Cool, Daddy, Cool"). Most groups included rap, but one group found it necessary to "tighten our definition of rock music and eliminate certain styles such as rap music and faddish or Top 40 music." One group found it essential to include a section called "British & Foreign Rock in American Culture: 60s/ 70s;" another included the song "Lucy in the Sky with Diamonds," arguing that "the history of Rock and Roll, American or otherwise, would be drastically different without the Beatles."

Criteria for selection also varied widely, prompting discussion and debate in the groups. One group used a book of *Billboard*'s top hits to help them decide which songs to put in the collection, but went further by including the music of such artists as The Grateful Dead and Jimmy Buffet who they felt, despite not making the charts, had a significant "cult" following that justified inclusion. Another group decided against including record sales in their decisions "because often times they can be misleading. Trends and teen fads can often throw off record sales" and lead to the kind of overnight hits the group felt offered no lasting contribution to rock's history. One group avoided "the biggest songs of a decade," focusing upon "influential and radical music that continued to expand and revolutionize American rock-n-roll." Cultural and historical illumination was the objective of at least two groups. "Our goal in making this anthology was to achieve the diversity upon which America has made its name," wrote one group. Another group stressed that their aim was "not only to give the listener an appreciation of the music, but also to give him or her an understanding of society at the time each work was made," a textual orientation akin to Jane Tompkins' suggestion that we replace an "is it any good?" judgment with "the notion of literary texts as doing work, expressing and shaping the social context that produced them" (200).

As if the assignment were not difficult enough, one group created their own challenges. A group of five young women decided to compile a history of women in rock and roll. It was a challenge that demanded considerable research to move beyond such figures as Diana Ross, Janis Joplin, Tina Turner, and Madonna and to uncover lesser-known women like Big Mama Thornton, LaVern Baker, Ruth Brown, and Joan Armatrading. Their work would lead to significant insights into the gendered nature of rock and roll and the male-dominated view of rock's history.

Making the Text Visible

Intending to explore the canon wars during the semester, I had deliberately chosen an anthology as our primary text. It is our anthologists and their publishers, after all, who are in the business of what John Rodden has called "selective enshrinement" (504)—selecting and promoting particular versions of the "best and most representative work" of certain literary periods. And it is largely through anthologies that our students become familiar with (at least excerpts of) canonical works. The course, then, would not only be about interpreting individual works, but about interpreting the text itself and the version of American literature it transmitted to this generation of readers. I chose the second volume of *The Heath Anthology of American Literature* (1990) because, like many recent collections, it promoted itself as a "'reconstructed' American literature text" (Lauter xxxiv), announcing its desire to include a mix of canonical and non-canonical writings and to "represent as fully as possible the varied cultures of the United States" (xxxii–xxxiv). My hunch was that its inclusions and distinct organizational units might appear sufficiently strange to students to prompt questions about the apparatus itself as well as its individual works.

Thus, when we were able to discuss the submitted rock anthologies as a whole group (I cut-and-pasted, distributing provocative and representative passages along with several quite different tables of contents), much of our discussion aimed at crossing the bridge between the work they'd done and the work the editors of our literary anthology appeared to have done. Their common experience led to surprising agreement on a number of important points. Among the most salient insights we arrived at after one and a half periods of discussion, written reflection, and argument (heated at times, as when two students accused me of "worshipping" 1950s rock and of insisting that they do the same):

- Categorization is necessary but limiting. As one group phrased it in the reflective third section of their project, "In anthologies of music and literature, the only way to take an enormous field and put it into a coherent form is to break it down into smaller pieces. The problem is that some excellent works are so unique that they do not really fit into any category." The placement of a song would likely affect how one listened to that song, the class concluded.

- The point marking the beginning or ending of any period of study is controversial, even arbitrary. Some would choose 1927 as the entry point to rock and roll, others, 1956. Similarly, our second semester of American Literature commenced in the year 1865, the Civil War conveniently dividing the two-semester sequence. Did the war in fact radically change the direction of American literature, one student asked?

- Several students noted the presence of more minority artists in rock's more recent years. And the inclusion of more women, my experts on women rockers noted, pointing out the great difficulty early seventies hard rock performers like Fanny (the first-ever all-female rock band to sign with a major label), Deadly Nightshade, and Suzie Quatro had in achieving success in what was still considered a "male arena." We pointed to parallels in recent multicultural textbooks and discussed cultural assumptions about which gender would be most likely to produce rebellious rock anthems in the field of music, or works of "serious intellectual merit" and "universal appeal" in the field of literature.

- The "best" or most representative works in any field are not self-evident, but are produced through a complex, highly subjective process of selection involving such factors as individual tastes and preferences as they have been molded by a compiler's membership in a particular race, class, age, gender, nation, and field of study, among other affiliations. "Different tastes were rampant throughout our project," one group stated. They found it necessary to assign each member a piece of the puzzle. "One imagines that [an editorial board] is run the same way," they concluded.

- The absence of British rock falsifies the story of American rock, said a member of the group that included British rockers in its anthology. The

class came to recognize that crucial developments, styles, and influences
crossed the ocean and redefined rock's possibilities for many American
artists.

- Access to resources is a factor affecting which voices are heard and promoted to prominence in the industry. To be heard a song must be recorded,
promoted, and played (on both the radio and television, these days); to be
read, a book must be published, promoted, and reviewed. One group reflected that while "rock music did spread over a wide array of cultural and
ethnic backgrounds . . . we found that it paralleled the typical literary
canon in that there are small bands and hidden talents that do not have the
means, power, or money to make it into mainstream rock-n-roll." The group
noted that they'd need greater access to lesser-known labels to truly define
American rock.

The above insights informed much of our work throughout the semester as
we read, discussed, and wrote about a mix of traditionally anthologized and
non-traditional works, ranging from Stephen Crane, William Faulkner, T.S. Eliot,
and Marianne Moore, to Abraham Cahan, Sterling Brown, Meridel LeSueur,
and Tom Whitecloud. What our rock project had helped us gain was a shared
vocabulary and experience through which to consider the cultural, historical,
political, economic, and aesthetic dimensions of canon formation. Such a basis
was especially important, I would argue, for a critical analysis of a revisionist
text like *The Heath Anthology of American Literature*, since the tendency in an
age of political correctness is for most college students to uncritically applaud a
text that so clearly announces its inclusive nature. (One student I had, a senior,
told me that this was the third English course she'd taken which included a
variety of traditionally marginalized voices, but the first where she was not
expected to cheer those voices.) Like James C. Raymond, I want students to
question the notion that the selections of these latest anthologies "are less reprehensible than those in earlier anthologies because they, the new ones, result
from a catholic and inclusive motive rather than an ideology of exclusion" (83).
"There is always and necessarily," Raymond reminds us, "an element of cultural and political aggression in every anthology" (83).

Since students had grappled with complex matters and had completed this
critical work early in the semester, I was able to engage them in a range of
significant questions which may have led nowhere prior to the project. Why, for
example, did the editors of our anthology begin this second volume with a grouping of eight women writers under a section entitled "The Development of
Women's Narratives"? Is their inclusion justified by the fact that women wrote
most of the popular best-sellers in the middle of the nineteenth century? How is
this different from choosing songs based on *Billboard*'s charts? We also considered how the long relegation of these eight women, along with most minority

authors, to marginal or "regional writer" status in the study of literature might have parallels in the music business, where women rockers and minority artists were for a time excluded from what was understood to be a white male enterprise. Even inclusion, as Annette Kolodny argues, may still lead to marginalization, if writers are treated as "anomalous" cases for editors to "bracket off" in new categories (297). Similarly Michael Omi argues that in the field of popular music, "race and race consciousness has defined, and continues to define, formats, musical communities, and tastes" (458). Omi notes that popular music genres act as "thinly veiled racial categories" and that "black performers who want to break out of this artistic ghettoization must "cross over," a contemporary form of "passing" in which their music is seen as acceptable to white audiences (459). Access to resources and promotional power are at stake, Omi stresses, since categorization and segregated airwaves affect play lists, listening market shares, and advertising contracts. A similar ghettoization may be discerned in the field of literature. Pound and Eliot speak for "modern man"; Langston Hughes and Gwendolyn Bennett speak for Harlem.

A host of fresh questions—some teacher-posed, some student-generated—continued to surface as we proceeded through our course text, each of them now visible as a direct result of our music project. Why choose Twain's "The War Prayer" and bypass his more famous humor pieces? How do we hear Gilman's "The Yellow Wallpaper" differently when grouped with W. E. B. Du Bois, Standing Bear, and Upton Sinclair in a section entitled "Issues and Visions in Post-Civil War America"? What arguments might be advanced for and against the inclusion of Native American ghost dance songs and Chinese immigrants' graffiti? What would those who argued for the inclusion of British rock in their anthology have to say about studying T.S. Eliot solely alongside American poets when he himself noted (in *The Criterion* of January, 1930) that no poet in America or England could serve as a model for him, and that happening upon the work of the French symbolist poets "affected the course of my life" (Ellmann 448)? Why was Meridel LeSueur's 1939 novel *The Girl,* which chronicles the lives of working-class women during the Depression, not published until 1978? How might students' difficulties in categorizing the explosion of musical styles in the 1990s illuminate the choice of the *Heath* editors to revert to a simple organization by genre of those works published after 1945?

As I expected, my own reading selections for the course came into question. Students wanted to know why I chose this work or author and not that one, what criteria I used, and how I organized the course. It was challenging but refreshing to be honest and open about the choices I made, and my attempt to articulate the reasons for those choices was self-enlightening. It was enlightening for students as well; devoting some class time to responding to student questions like these is not, as some might argue, self-indulgent. As Jacqueline Bacon reasons, "A pedagogical approach that highlights the contingency of decisions of text selection allows students to view course syllabi within the context of their wider reading" (505, see also Hogan 189).

Signs of Uncertainty and Success

And so all of our questions were answered and we went on to lead full, happy lives. In fact, of course, we raised more questions than we could answer, and we left untouched many dimensions of the canon debate and the larger culture wars. Nor did I expect profound enlightenment in my students in the three-week period they devoted to the rock project. But I did expect to help them develop a fuller awareness of the ways knowledge is organized in the academy and in the publishing industry. I did expect to foreground some complexities of a discipline that too often seems, for students, to have been shaped by the invisible hand of God, or, as David Richter phrases it, "sifted by time: only the greatest and the most universal had survived" (2). I did expect to shake things up a bit too, to cause the kind of disequilibrium which can lead to intellectual growth. The signs of that disequilibrium were inscribed in students' writing, as, for instance, in one group's schizophrenic reflections on the possibility of an objective standard of greatness. While one paragraph asserts that "given a greater distance to evaluate current works, it would be possible to realize what is truly American Rock Music," the very next maintains "it is true that anthologies are totally subjective."

How, or whether, each of this group's members has gone on to work out these conflicting positions is beyond me. But the persistence of students' references to their music project throughout the course, the heightened level of class discussions, and the sophistication of their written work—in, for example, questioning and disagreeing with literary critics and in pushing the analysis of individual works beyond explication to a range of cultural issues—all affirmed the value of involving students in this non-traditional assignment. It is my hope that they exported this learning and trained it critically upon other fields of study, where the play of competing ideologies similarly shapes disciplinary knowledge.

Final Observations and Possibilities

While I believe this particular assignment ought to prove successful in other classrooms, the basis for its success suggests alternatives. First, the assignment is a simulation, a kind of assignment that, along with the case study, is popular in such fields as business and marketing, but seldom seen in the literature class. Since the literature courses I teach are populated by non-majors, many of them business majors, such a simulation, conducted collaboratively, is likely to be more familiar and certainly more comfortable than the traditional essay assignment in literary criticism. By approximating actual, operational conditions, simulations work against a common student perception of assignments as intellectual exercises completed for the benefit of the teacher. (For the same reasons, case studies might also be promisingly pursued. For example, local controversies over the censorship of certain literary works in public schools might be introduced to students, who could read, interpret, and research the work in order to join the debate.)

Secondly, the success of the rock and roll project had, I've no doubt, much to do with students' enthusiasm for exploring popular culture. Rock, then, needn't be the only area toward which to send students. Other popular compilations might work nicely—the top fifty Hollywood films, television's finest shows, the greatest sports teams or individual athletes of an era. As noted earlier, disagreements over the cultural value of these popular forms parallel academia's battles over a multicultural curriculum. The crucial steps in any of these kinds of assignments, of course, are to require that students make explicit the intellectual assumptions that underlie their choices and method of structuring their collections, and that they reflect critically upon the relevance of the activity for an understanding of the current literary debate it foregrounds.

In his introduction to *Falling Into Theory*, David Richter illustrates the way students' everyday interests and concerns can open into surprising territory:

> Two teenagers arguing about whether one of their teachers is open-minded
> or wishy-washy, or about whether it is a band's material or performance
> technique that makes it so great, can get quickly to the edge of some region
> of theory, where fundamental questions about values and quality, means
> and ends, public and private experience are raised. (8)

I have argued that we need to see this capacity for interest and lively engagement as a resource in our literature classrooms, that while I continue to see the value of Gerald Graff's call to teach the conflicts, to begin by thrusting our disciplinary debates on students may not be the most effective method. Alternatively, we can build on students' interests in and familiarity with popular culture conflicts by devising inventive ways for them to teach themselves the conflicts in their own world before turning to consider the related conflicts in ours.

Appendix

Collaborative Essay: Anthology of American Rock Music

You have just been given the go-ahead by Random House to compile an anthology of American Rock Music. It will be an audio anthology of between 100 and 125 songs (presented on eight CDs) spanning the history of American rock and roll. Each of you will be part of a group of four to six people who will act as compilers and editors of the anthology. Your written work will be to provide James S. Laughlin, chief editor of the Music Division, with the following:

1. A **Table of Contents**;
2. A **four- to six-page introduction** to the anthology in which you discuss the following kinds of things:

- Your group's conception of the project. (How did you define your subject? What did you hope the anthology would accomplish, and for whom?)

- The nature of any concerns, issues, hesitations, problems, or difficulties you encountered along the way. What were they and what accounted for them?

- The basis for inclusion. This might include such things as what criteria guided selection. (Was it artistic merit, popularity by record sales, or what?)

- Your explanations/justifications/defenses of inclusions or omissions which may be questionable or controversial. By skillful argument you might justify highly unusual, radical, or unorthodox choices.

- Your rationale for grouping or ordering the collection as you did.

In addition to your work for Random House, your group will compose a **two- to three-page reflection** addressed to your English instructor, Jim Laughlin, on how this project speaks to the issue of canon formation in literature. What insights into the subject of the literary canon can you make as a result of completing this work? Why do you believe there has been such controversy and vehement argument in literary and political circles in recent years over the question of who is and who isn't taught and read? Are these arguments just a matter of different tastes, or different ideologies, or what? Should you even care? If so, why?

Purpose

What seems at first glance to be a strange and inappropriate assignment for a class in American Literature may in fact be usefully applied to the course. As the syllabus states, we'll be taking issue with canon formation in this class, a concern very much at the forefront of literary studies today. By involving you in the nitty gritty of selecting, organizing, and justifying an anthology, I believe you'll more fully understand the current debate over the canon and multicultural education. By choosing a subject in which most of you have considerable knowledge, even expertise, I hope to reproduce some of the same concerns that face experts seeking to make selective judgments in the literary field.

Procedure

As the syllabus indicates, *your group project will be handed in to me on Thursday, January 28.* We'll spend part of two periods in class working in groups on the project. Of course, you'll want to meet as a group outside of class to work some more. Individual groups will decide how best to proceed and how to coordinate the effort to involve all members. Certain people may be responsible for certain time periods or artists. One or more people may be responsible for library research. Some may be fact finders and organizers, others might handle the final writing. You decide. The group will receive one grade, no matter the differences in individual contributions. If you perceive that one or more of your group members are not pulling their weight, please let me know in writing *at least* one week prior to the due date. Please feel free to seek my help at any stage in the process.

Grading

As a music buff and child of the rock era, I will be very curious to see your song and artist choices. But as an evaluator I will pay closer attention to your four- to six-page introduction to the audio anthology. And I'll pay closest attention to the final two or three pages, in which you demonstrate how effectively you can transfer what you've learned into the sphere of literary studies. I'll be looking for your awareness of the complexities of the issues, concerns, and problems raised by such a project. As always, I'll privilege thoughtful content over form, but the two are never fully separable. Please turn in clean, professionally edited work that engages a reader through its effectively languaged ideas.

Works Cited

Bacon, Jacqueline. "Impasse or Tension: Pedagogy and the Canon Controversy." *College English* 55 (1993): 501–514.

Bazerman, Charles. "From Cultural Criticism to Disciplinary Participation: Living with Powerful Words." *Writing, Teaching, and Learning in the Disciplines*. Eds. Anne Herrington and Charles Moran. New York: MLA, 1992. 61–68.

Bennett, Tony, et al. *Rock and Popular Music: Politics, Policies, Institutions*. London: Routledge, 1993.

Department of English, Virginia Polytechnic Institute and State University. *Faculty Handbook 1994–1995*. Blacksburg: VPI&SU, 1994.

Ellmann, Richard, and Robert O'Clair, eds. *The Norton Anthology of Modern Poetry*. New York: Norton, 1973.

Gaar, Gillian. *She's a Rebel: The History of Women in Rock and Roll*. Seattle: Seals, 1992.

Gass, Glenn. "Why Don't We Do It in the Classroom?" *Present Tense: Rock and Roll and Culture*. Ed. Anthony DeCurtis. Durham: Duke UP, 1992. 93–100.

Graff, Gerald. *Beyond the Culture Wars*. New York: Norton, 1992.

———. Foreword. *Falling Into Theory*. Ed. David H. Richter. Boston: St. Martin's, 1994.

Hogan, Patrick Colm. "Mo' Better Canons: What's Wrong and What's Right About Mandatory Diversity." *College English* 54 (1992): 182–92.

Kolodny, Annette. "The Integrity of Memory: Creating a New Literary History of the United States." *American Literature* 57 (1985): 291–307.

Lauter, Paul, et al., eds. *The Heath Anthology of American Literature*. Vol. 2. Toronto: Heath, 1990.

Omi, Michael. "In Living Color: Race and American Culture." *Signs of Life in the U.S.A.: Readings on Popular Culture for Writers*. Eds. Sonia Maaskik and Jack Solomon. Boston: St. Martin's, 1994. 449–61.

Raymond, James C. "Authority, Desire, and Canons: Tendentious Meditations on Cultural Literacy." *Conversations: Contemporary Critical Theory and the Teaching of Literature*. Eds. Charles Moran and Elizabeth F. Penfield. Urbana: NCTE, 1990. 76–86.

Richter, David H. *Falling Into Theory*. Boston: St. Martin's, 1994.

Rodden, John. "Reputation, Canon-Formation, Pedagogy: George Orwell in the Classroom." *College English* 53 (1991): 503–30.

Tompkins, Jane. *Sensational Designs: The Cultural Work of American Fiction 1790–1860*. New York: Oxford UP, 1985.

16 Teaching Others: A Cautionary Tale

Joseph F. Trimmer
Ball State University

I slump in my swivel chair and stare out the window. My right hand rests on the grey forms I have stacked on my desk. Uneasily, I thumb their ragged edges. I know what they are:

COURSE AND INSTRUCTOR EVALUATIONS
Course English 389: Multicultural Literature
Instructor: Trimmer

I know (or suspect) what they will say, so I resist reading. Instead, I muse about my reading last semester. It had been glorious. From my little carrel in the basement of Bracken Library, I had mounted an expedition through the literature and history of other cultures. The stories were riveting. The histories unsettling. Like most travelers, I was enchanted by the exotic, baffled by the ordinary, but convinced I was learning. And when I returned from my journey, I had a tale to tell. I told it in English 389: Multicultural Literature.

At first my students seemed mesmerized as I mapped the new worlds I'd found. By midterm they seemed merely silent. Something was dreadfully wrong. I revised my tale, adding all sorts of glitter and spice from my incredible journey. A few students played along, smiling when they were supposed to. The rest preferred not to. They came to class, wrote the exams, but they had withdrawn. Each day I added more glitter and spice, hoping to lure them back. But they simply stared into their books, thumbed the pages and waited for the hour to end. I had lost them, but I didn't know why.

I look at my desk. The answer should be in the forms. I shuffle and stack them, take a deep breath, and start reading.

The first few are reassuring, even complimentary:

Dr. Trimmer seems to know a lot about literature.
He's very enthusiastic about different cultures.
He explained why we need to know about other cultures.

Toward the middle of the stack, they seem restive, confused.

> Professor Trimmer assumed we knew things about literature we didn't.
> He was interested in different cultures, but he didn't make them interesting
>   to me.
> He talked about different customs, but I just couldn't follow him.

Then, near the bottom, come the bad reviews—full of anger and disappointment:

> The instructor spent so much time covering the stories he didn't get to the
>   cultures.
> He went off on tangents talking about stuff that wasn't in the stories.
> He never accepted our opinions because we didn't have enough background.

The criticism cuts through the compliments confirming my worst suspicions. I stare out the window and slump deeper into despair. This was supposed to be my dream course. That was the point of last semester's seclusion. The search for compelling texts. The research on cultural contexts. The braiding of each into a coherent syllabus. I could barely contain my enthusiasm as I introduced the semester's reading. Even when the trouble started, I was inspired by the challenge. I was at the top of my form. Or so I thought. Now, as I sit staring out my window, I know my students are right. I failed. But like me, they don't seem to know why. I reshuffle the forms and read them again. I'm still confused. Their comments are incomplete and contradictory.

I swivel away from the window and stare up at my shelves. Row upon row of multicolored books. Perhaps the answer is up there. In those texts that taught me about literature and culture.

On the top shelf, stacked side by side, are the anthologies of W. W. Norton and Company. I pull down a tome and flip a few pages. The handwriting in the margins—malformed yet vaguely familiar—recalls the student who bought the book and tried to read it. I replay a few scenes from that old story:

The Bookstore. I stand in the middle aisle weighing the claims of the first volume of the *Norton Anthology of World Masterpieces:* "Enormous. Expensive. Do they charge by the pound? The paper is so thin. Like Mom's Bible. Two thousand pages. In one semester? And what about Volume Two?"

The Dorm. I sprawl on my bed sampling my purchase: "Everybody's from Greece, Italy, or England. So why do they call it *World Masterpieces?* Everybody's listed under some ISM. Is that what makes them *Masterpieces?* The intros cite headlines—wars, treaties, kings. Then switch to features—themes, fashions, trends. The bios read like obits. Born. Wrote such and such a story. Such and such a poem. Died. Is that all? The works remain. The short ones. Arranged by date. Explained by notes."

The Class. I listen to my teacher revise his syllabus, *again,* dropping and adding assignments in the second semester of what he calls lickety-split world lit: "I spent yesterday covering 'Grecian Urn,' so we're behind again. We've *got* to make it into the twentieth century. Go over the intro on *Romanticism.*" Skip

Goethe and Pushkin. Drop Shelley. Add the first Browning and the last Whitman. Read all of Dickinson. They're short." Like my classmates, I smile, make a few calculations, and convert the revisions into survival strategies. "The intro is a waste unless he writes *Romanticism* on the board. Browning and Whitman will probably be on tomorrow's quiz. Keats and Dickinson will definitely be on the midterm."

I close the tome and slide it back in its slot on the top shelf. The double volumes loom over my desk. I stare at their spines, remembering my quarrels with the lessons they taught me:

Literature is canonical. An official list of authors and titles has already been approved for study. This list may shift slightly, from time to time, as certain items gain or lose favor, but its essential pattern is fixed. It represents what generations of scholars consider the best that has been thought and said. "Should I read anything else?" Certainly! Especially the longer works by the approved authors. "What about the others—those not on the list?" That might be useful. Then you'd understand why they didn't make it. But the approved list is so long. Why waste your time on apocrypha? "What's that?" Minor stuff. Bad poems. Strange stories. Literature that doesn't fit.

Literature is universal. The intros teach you about the literary periods. The bios teach you about the author's life. They're helpful, but not crucial. Read the texts. The "masterpieces." They deal with universals—aspects of the human condition in every time and place. "What about writers from *different* cultures?" Exactly! They live in different cultures, but write about common themes—growing up, facing challenges, adjusting to defeat. "What happens when they write about those themes differently, or write about completely different themes?" Some writers do write about the unusual. Refer to local customs. That's covered in the footnotes. But if they focus too much on local issues they don't make it. They're not *world* masterpieces. They lose the general reader. "Who's that?" You, me, people like us.

Literature is sequential. The best way to cover literature is to follow the sequence. Start with the Classics. Work through the Renaissance, the Enlightenment, and the Romantics. Then on to the Moderns. "Why can't I start with the Moderns and go back?" You could, I suppose, but then you'd miss the sense of historical change. You know, cause and effect. "Did Chaucer *cause* Shakespeare?" Of course not! The evolution of literature has multiple causes and effects. "Does literature evolve? Does it get better?" Not necessarily. There are changes. Innovations. Stream of consciousness. Magical realism. "Where do innovations come from?" Different cultures. "Don't different cultures have their own historical sequences? Their own causes and effects?" Of course. But you can't cover everything. You have to pick the best. "Doesn't picking the best break up the sequence?" That's what anthologies are for. To make new sequences so local cultures don't get in the way.

I tilt back in my swivel and release a respectful whistle. The logic seems infallible. Anthologies plus surveys equals coverage. Ah! There was the sacred word. *Coverage.* What did it mean? When I *covered* something did I learn it, protect it, or conceal it? And what about the *uncovered*? My questions direct me to the bottom shelf and the book that reshaped my teaching and learning. I stretch past the forms to retrieve Ralph Ellison's *Invisible Man.* It rests comfortably in my hand, cracking open to a page covered by underlines and annotations. A map of the uncovered.

It was the 1960s. I had passed exams, finished the dissertation, and found a job only to be assigned a course on a subject I knew nothing about—Black American Literature. At first, I was disappointed. Why can't I teach the masterpieces I had been taught? Then I was angry. Why didn't they cover this stuff in graduate school? Finally I settled in and looked around. I came up with a few names—Wright, Baldwin, Ellison. I had read *Native Son* in a graduate seminar in "Literary Naturalism." It was mentioned as a minor example of the form. I had taught "Stranger in the Village" in Comp 101. All graduate TAs had to follow the departmental syllabus.

Invisible Man was a different story. I had picked it up at a used-book sale and started reading it on study breaks. After a few pages, I was mesmerized. In a secluded basement, illuminated by 1,369 lightbulbs illegally wired to Monopolated Light and Power, the invisible man told me what he had done to become so black and blue. This was the underground history of American culture. The unofficial version that never made it into the anthologies. I could recognize the broad outlines of the plot—growing up, facing challenges, adjusting to defeat—but I knew I was missing the heart of the story. The jive, the jokes, the inside stuff—the stuff I didn't even know was inside stuff.

What to do? I sat in my office trying to concoct a syllabus out of three texts. I arranged and rearranged them, hoping they would cohere but knowing they wouldn't. Especially Ellison. How could I teach a book filled with riddles I couldn't solve? Suddenly that seemed like a solution. I was young and desperate. So I took a chance.

I smiled nervously as I walked into class. Black students packed the front rows. A few white students had found seats in the back. "This is English 354. A Survey of Black American Literature. My name is Trimmer. . . . Let's begin with the obvious. I'm white. I don't know much about Black American Literature. But I have read one book that might help us. Ralph Ellison's *Invisible Man.* For now, it's our syllabus. We're going to read it together. Very slowly. There's a lot of stuff in this book I don't understand. There's probably a lot of stuff in this book you won't understand. Let's see if we can help each other. If you have a question, ask it. If you come across something you think we ought to know, tell us. We'll need to do a lot of research. But we can add what we find to our syllabus. We'll probably be all over the map. But I hope you'll stick it out.

By the end of the semester, we may know how to survey Black American Literature."

We did stick it out. Nervous at first. Testing each other. Asking questions about every page. None of us claimed to have *the* answers. Some suggested answers. Some suggested alternatives. Others tried to find common ground. Like Ellison's narrator, all of us—teacher and students, black and white—were naive, misguided, and misinformed. We bumped into assumptions or fell over expectations before we could identify the puzzle we were trying to solve. But together we crisscrossed the official and unofficial curriculum of Black America, introducing ourselves to the rich cultural contexts evoked by Ellison's novel.

> History—the causes of slavery, the effects of segregation.
> Sociology—the power of class, the promise of passing.
> Anthropology—the significance of masking, the sources of folktales.
> Religion—the rhetoric of sermons, the reasons for spirituals.
> Politics—the conscription by unions, the betrayal by communism.
> Art—the rhythms of jazz, the meaning of blues.
> Biography—the stories of those people whose lives punctuate Ellison's tale: Frederick Douglass, Booker T. Washington, Marcus Garvey, and W. E. B. Du Bois.

We also introduced ourselves to the history of African American literature. Ellison helped us piece together the complicated traditions of slave narrative, plantation verse, renaissance poetry, and protest fiction. In some cases, this sequence appeared separate but slightly unequal, offering subtle variations on traditional themes. In others, it appeared revolutionary, introducing dramatic innovations that challenged established patterns. In both cases, we were fascinated by this *other* literature and Ellison's place in its history. Students became specialists, exploring the dynamics of particular periods, recommending texts for our expanding syllabus, and teaching each other how their research could enrich our reading. Indeed *Invisible Man* created space for: *Up from Slavery, The Autobiography of an Ex-Colored Man, The New Negro, Cane, Their Eyes Were Watching God, Native Son, Notes of a Native Son,* and *Montage of a Dream Deferred.*

And, of course, we introduced ourselves to Ellison. In essays and interviews, he told us about his childhood in Oklahoma, his education at Tuskegee Institute, and his evolution as a writer amidst the intellectual crosscurrents of New York and Rome. In particular, he told us about how his understanding of cultural diversity encouraged him to read and respond to the multiple literatures of his heritage:

> The act of writing requires a constant plunging back into the shadow of the past where time hovers ghostlike. When I began writing in earnest I was forced . . . to relate myself consciously and imaginatively to my mixed background as American, as Negro American, and as a Negro from what in

its own belated way was a pioneer background. More important and inseparable from this particular effort was the necessity of determining my true relationship to that body of American literature to which I was most attracted and through which, aided by what I could learn from the literatures of Europe, I would find my own voice, and to which I was challenged, by way of achieving myself, to make some small contribution, and to whose composite picture of reality I was obligated to offer some necessary modifications. (*Shadow and Act.* New York: Random House, 1964. xvi–xvii).

Despite, or perhaps because of, our modifications to "English 354: A Survey of Black American Literature," the course was judged an enormous success. On their Course and Instructor Evaluation Forms, students joked about the teacher's inauspicious beginning and inexpensive book list, but switched quickly to bragging about what they had learned by reading new literary texts and researching different cultural contexts. I'm not sure we *covered* the history of Black American Literature. In fact, I'm pretty sure we didn't. We took too many wrong turns, spent too much time in back alleys, to stay on the main road. But according to Ellison, that's "how the world moves. Not like an arrow, but a boomerang" (*Invisible Man.* New York: Random House, 1952. 5). What we failed to cover, we tried to illuminate. And in the process, we discovered that culture was more complicated than wars, treaties, and kings; that literature was more innovative than themes, fashions, and trends; and that cross-cultural education worked best when students from different backgrounds taught one another.

Or at least that's what the students said they learned. I learned something else. I didn't like winging it across uncharted territory. I felt like a fool, incapable of responding to my students' questions. I felt like a fraud, manipulating them to search for their own answers. I felt like Rinehart, Ellison's rascal of illusion, exploiting the confusion and misperception of others. English 354 was a fluke. I had caught good students in a good semester and they had liked being in charge of their own learning. But such trickery was not teaching. Someone had to take charge. Someone had to know the answers.

During the next thirty years—as I aged gracefully into expertise, teaching the masterpieces of American lit—I took charge. It was easy. Because the books were written by and about people like me, I knew the answers. I didn't use an anthology. English 354 had taught me too much about the complexity of literature and culture to settle for that choice. But I used the *idea* of an anthology to demonstrate the limitations of conventional literary instruction. I selected individual texts to challenge the authority of the canon. I analyzed suppressed narratives to contradict the ubiquity of universals. And I introduced all sorts of glitter and spice to complicate the logic of sequence. It took a lot of work, but I did my job. The students did theirs. And everybody seemed happy. At least nobody said anything.

Which brings me to the '90s and my semester of seclusion in the basement of Bracken Library. Like that of the invisible man, my "hibernation [was] a covert preparation for a more overt action" (*Invisible Man* 11). Once again, I had been assigned a course in a subject I knew nothing about—multicultural literature. To be accurate, my quarrels with the *Norton Anthology of World Masterpieces* had taught me something about the "multiculturalism" of "world literature." My teaching of Black American Literature had also taught me something about the multicultural character of "minority literature." And during my years as an expert on the masterpieces of American Literature, I had read a few novels by some of America's most gifted minority writers. In sum, I had read enough to know that I didn't know very much.

The syllabus for English 389, Multicultural Literature, required me to cover Native American, African American, Asian American, and Chicano literature and culture. Given my expanded conception of literature and culture, and my exalted commitment to informed teaching, I was not about to take a chance with an old trick. So I prepared and prepared and prepared. And at the end of my hibernation, I was loaded for bear.

I made four trips from my carrel to my study, carefully unloading the books and books and books about books onto the lower shelves I had reserved for my new multicultural library. During Christmas vacation, I re-read the best of the lot as I drafted and revised my syllabus. Throughout the Spring Semester, particularly once the trouble started, I read them again—looking for information to inspire my silent students. I did what I thought every good teacher should do. I taught myself to be an expert on the subject I was supposed to teach. So why had I failed?

I push away from my desk to widen my perspective, scanning the shelves from top to bottom, from double-volume anthologies to multicultural library. I adjust and re-adjust my eyes, trying to focus on the big picture. Suddenly, that's all it is—a big picture. Splashes of color against a field of white. The stories of how I had been taught and what I had learned blur into an abstract painting, titled "My Education."

I look back at the forms on my desk. They were incomplete, contradictory, and confusing, but they were close. They didn't know how to say it *exactly*, but they said it. My education had interfered with their learning. They knew *I* knew something about literature: *Dr. Trimmer seems to know a lot about literature. Professor Trimmer assumed we knew things about literature we didn't. The instructor spent so much time covering the stories he didn't get to the cultures.* They knew *I* knew something about different cultures: *He's very enthusiastic about different cultures. He was interested in different cultures, but he didn't make them interesting to me. He went off on tangents talking about stuff that wasn't in the stories.* They simply wanted a chance to learn something about multicultural literature for themselves: *He explained why we needed to learn about other cultures. He talked about different customs, but I couldn't follow him. He never accepted our opinions because we didn't have enough background.*

I rub my eyes. Then look again at the forms on my desk and the books on my shelf. In between, in the shadows, an answer hovers, ghostlike, in my study. My seclusion made me an expert on literary and cultural difference. My expertise prevented my students from exploring literary and cultural difference. I was so inspired by my tale, I silenced my students. They wrote the exams, but had no tale to tell.

I stare out my window, again. I think about the invisible man: How many times will I have to learn the same lessons? How many times will I repeat the same mistakes? How much painful boomeranging of my expectations will I have to endure before teaching and learning make sense? I try to sort it all out, salvaging a few answers from my failure. The first two are commonplace, the result of old quarrels with anthologies and surveys:

1. Literature and culture are too complex to be collected in anthologies.
2. Literature and culture are too conflicted to be covered in a coherent master syllabus.

The third is controversial, the result of my inexperience with new material:

3. Literature and culture don't have to be covered. But they can be *illuminated* by examining the contexts evoked by individual texts.

The last two are conjectural, the result of my inability to teach what I had learned:

4. Multicultural literature *was not a product,* a new body of information to be packaged into double volumes and transmitted by super scholars.
5. Multicultural literature *was a process,* a new method of inquiry that encouraged students to mount their own expeditions through the history and literature of other cultures.

My sorting prompts a smile. My dream course had been spooked by a familiar demon. I had been tricked by that master magician—myself. The official explanation was "I was doing my job." The unofficial explanation was "I was showing off." The students had put up with me in class, but, given the opportunity, they had put me down in the forms. They were impressed with what I had learned. But in the worlds of multicultural literature there is too much to learn, too much to question, for one person to take charge of all the answers. Like me, they wanted to explore and map the history and literature of other cultures. Like me, they wanted to investigate and teach others what they had discovered.

I thumb the forms and think of Ellison: "'Ah,' I can hear you say, 'so it was all a build-up to bore us with his buggy jiving. He only wanted us to listen to him rave!' . . . But only partially true" (*Invisible Man* 439). I stack and reshuffle the forms. As I scan the comments, I get the message: "Stick it out. Give us a chance. Who knows but that, on the lower frequencies, we speak for you."

Index

Editors

Lil Brannon is professor of English and director of the Center for Excellence in Teaching and Learning at the University at Albany, SUNY. Her most recent book, *Critical Teaching and the Idea of Literacy* (with C.H. Knoblauch), was published in 1993.

Brenda M. Greene is professor of English and chair of the department of languages, literature, communications, and philosophy at Medgar Evers College, CUNY. She is currently conducting research on the literature of women of color. Her recent essays include "Addressing Race, Class, and Gender in *Their Eyes Were Watching God*" in *English Education* (December 1995) and "Reinventing the Literacy Text: Student Writers at Work" in *When Writing Teachers Teach Literature: Bringing Writing to Reading* (1995).

Contributors

John Alberti is assistant professor of English at Northern Kentucky University. He is editor of *The Canon in the Classroom: The Pedagogical Implications of Canon Revision in American Literature* (1995).

Patricia Bizzell is professor of English and director of the college honor program at the College of the Holy Cross. Her most recent book, *Negotiating Difference* (with Bruce Herzberg), was published in 1995.

Mary Louise Buley-Meissner is associate professor of English at the University of Wisconsin–Milwaukee; she has also taught and carried out cross-cultural research at several universities in the People's Republic of China. She is returning to China to complete research on a book about social and political changes in Chinese teachers' lives.

Judith Beth Cohen is associate professor in the Adult Baccalaureate College at Lesley College in Cambridge, Massachusetts, and an associate of the Bard College Institute on Writing and Thinking. She has published a novel, *Seasons* (1984), and numerous short stories.

Judith Fetterley is professor of English and women's studies at the University at Albany, SUNY. She is the author of *The Resisting Reader: A Feminist Approach to American Fiction* (1978) and of *Provisions: A Reader from 19th-Century American Women* (1985). With Joanne Dobson and Elaine Showalter, she founded the Rutgers University Press American Women Writers series. She is fiction editor of the feminist literary journal *Thirteenth Moon* and serves on the editorial boards of *American Literature* and *Legacy*.

Frances Smith Foster is professor of English and women's studies at Emory University. She has edited a number of works in African American and women's literature, including the *Oxford Companion to African American Literature* (1997), the *Norton Anthology of African American Literature* (1996), and *Minnie's Sacrifice, Sowing and Reaping, Trial and Triumph: Three Rediscovered Novels by Frances Ellen Watkins Harper* (1994). She is author of *Witnessing Slavery: The Development of Ante-Bellum Slave Narrative* (1994) and *Written by Herself: Literary Production by African American Women, 1746–1892* (1993).

Joyce C. Harte teaches at the Borough of Manhattan Community College, CUNY. Her most recent publication was "Caribbean Literature as Catalyst in the Composition Classroom" (with Keith Gilyard and June D. Bobb) in *Voices in English Classrooms* (1996).

Gregory S. Jay is professor of English at the University of Wisconsin–Milwaukee. His essay also appears in his most recent book, *American Literature and the Culture Wars*, published by Cornell University Press (1996).

AnaLouise Keating is associate professor of English at Eastern New Mexico University, where she teaches courses in multicultural U.S. literature and directs the composition program. Her book, *Women Reading Women Writing: Self-Invention in Paula Gunn Allen, Gloria Anzaldúa, and Audre Lorde,* was published in 1996.

James S. Laughlin, a former instructor in the English department and a writing consultant in the writing-across-the-curriculum program at Virginia Polytechnic Institute and State University, is now a management consultant in Massachusetts.

Elizabeth Nunez is professor of English at Medgar Evers College, CUNY, and director of the National Black Writers Conference and the college's honors program. A native of Trinidad, Nunez has published articles on Caribbean writers including Jean Rhys, Phyllis Shand Alfrey, Jamaica Kincaid, Merle Hodge, V.S. Naipaul, and George Lamming. She is author of the novel *When Rocks Dance* (1986).

Robert O'Brien Hokanson is assistant professor of English and writing coordinator for the communication competence department at Alverno College, Milwaukee, Wisconsin. He has published articles on American poetry and is currently developing curriculum and pedagogy for a first-year communication course.

Marjorie Pryse is professor of English and women's studies at the University at Albany, SUNY. She is co-editor (with Judith Fetterley) of *American Women Regionalists, 1850–1910* (1992).

Louise Z. Smith is professor of English at the University of Massachusetts–Boston. Since 1992 she has been editor of *College English*. Her most recent work, "Beyond the 'Imaginary Museum': Interested Readings, Interesting Tropes," appears in *Reconceptualizing American Literary/Cultural Studies: Rhetoric, History, and Politics in the Humanities,* edited by William E. Cain (1996).

Joseph F. Trimmer is professor of English at Ball State University, where he teaches courses in writing and cultural studies. His books include *The National Book Awards for Fiction: An Index to the First Twenty-Five Years* (1978), and (with Tilly Warnock) *Understanding Others: Cultural and Cross-Cultural Studies and the Teaching of Literature* (1992). In the summer, he teaches at the Martha's Vineyard Summer Institute on Teaching and Writing.

This book was typeset in Times Roman by Electronic Imaging.
Typefaces used on the cover were Caslon Antique and Caslon 540.
The book was printed on 50-lb. Lynx by Versa Press.